PRAISE FOR

THE IMMORTAL IRISHMAN

✳ ✳ ✳

"Without a shadow of doubt this is one of the finest Irish-American books ever written ... What Egan has done is restore the reputation and uncovered a host of details on a man I would venture to say had no peer in our history of Irish America ... Egan's take on Irish-American history gives this book a breadth and significance that would be very hard to match."
— Niall O'Dowd, *Irish America*

"Stirring and magnificent ... Egan combines deep reporting with masterful storytelling to chronicle this bigger-than-life figure."
— *Dallas Morning News*

"Exhilarating ... a rollicking, historical adventure story ... You may not have heard the name Meagher, but after reading Egan's excellent biography, you'll never forget it."
— *San Antonio Express News*

"Sensational."
— *AARP The Magazine*

"A fascinating, well-told story by an author fully committed to his subject. Egan's impeccable research, uncomplicated readability, and flowing narrative reflect his deep knowledge of a difficult and complex man."
— *Kirkus Reviews*, starred review

"As history, Egan's book is solid; as storytelling, it's captivating ... An impressive biography."
— *Publishers Weekly*

"Meagher lived life full-tilt, with old-fashioned honor as well as courage and dash, so inspiring Egan that the prose flashes and flares."
— *Booklist*, starred review

BOOKS BY TIMOTHY EGAN

THE

IMMORTAL
IRISHMAN

THE IRISH REVOLUTIONARY
WHO BECAME
AN AMERICAN HERO

✦ ✦ ✦

TIMOTHY EGAN

Mariner Books
Houghton Mifflin Harcourt
BOSTON   NEW YORK

First Mariner Books edition 2017
Copyright © 2016 by Timothy Egan

All rights reserved

For information about permission to reproduce selections from this book, write to
trade.permissions@hmhco.com or to Permissions, Houghton Mifflin Harcourt
Publishing Company, 3 Park Avenue, 19th Floor, New York, New York 10016.

www.hmhco.com

Library of Congress Cataloging-in-Publication Data
Names: Egan, Timothy.
Title: The immortal Irishman : the Irish revolutionary who became an American hero / Timothy Egan.
Description: Boston : Houghton Mifflin Harcourt, 2016. | Includes bib and index.
Identifiers: LCCN 2015037256| ISBN 9780544272880 (hardcover) |
ISBN 9780544944831 (pbk.)
ISBN 9780544272477 (ebook)
Subjects: LCSH: Meagher, Thomas Francis, 1823–1867. | Generals—United States—
Biography. | United States. Army—Officers—Biography. | United States. Army of the
Potomac. Irish Brigade | United States—History—Civil War, 1861–1865—Biography. |
Heroes—United States—Biography. | Irish Americans—Biography. | Revolutionaries—
Ireland—Biography. | Prisoners—Tasmania—Biography. | Governors—Montana—Biography. |
BISAC: HISTORY / United States / Civil War Period (1850–1877). | HISTORY / United States / 19th
Century. | HISTORY / Europe / Ireland. | HISTORY / United States / State & Local / West (AK, CA, CO,
HI, ID, MT, NV, UT, WY). | BIOGRAPHY &
AUTOBIOGRAPHY / Adventurers & Explorers. | HISTORY / Australia & New Zealand. |
BIOGRAPHY & AUTOBIOGRAPHY / Historical.
Classification: LCC E467.1.M4 E34 2016 | DDC 355.0092—dc23
LC record available at http://lccn.loc.gov/2015037256

Book design by Melissa Lotfy

Printed in the United States of America
DOC 10 9 8 7 6 5 4 3
4500649564

In memory of the family ancestors, Egans and Whites,
Lynches and Harrises.
Cast out of Ireland, they found homes in
Michigan, in Chicago, in Montana, in Seattle,
and never forgot where they came from.

We don't forget, we don't forget them things, Joxer.
If they've taken everything else from us, Joxer, they've
left us our memory.

— SEAN O'CASEY, *Juno and the Paycock*

CONTENTS

INTRODUCTION:
LAST DAY – JULY 1, 1867

Look to the edge of the swollen Missouri in Montana Territory, where the longest river on the continent holds a blush of twilight, to see what becomes of an Irishman just before he disappears. There he is, woozy and paper-legged on the upper deck of a steamboat at anchor. Not like himself. No great witticisms or Homeric allusions as the evening darkens. No stories ending in punch lines that prompt a toast. No snippets of mournful song. Not a jab of nationalistic indignity to rouse a heart. Though his face is bronzed by sun that squats on the high prairie for fifteen hours a day, his color is off: the blue of his eyes dimmed, the polish of his cheeks matted. He glances at the town, Fort Benton, scours the huddle of saloons, dancehalls, outfitters, cathouses and grub shacks known as the Bloodiest Block in the West. He can't be sure if that shadow, that clank of spurs on boardwalk, is harmless or the herald of an assassin. Saddle-blistered after a long ride through a territory nearly five times the size of Ireland, he should be falling into a deserved slumber. Instead he asks for a book and a gun from a new friend, John Doran.

"Johnny, they threaten my life in that town," he tells the pilot of the *G. A. Thompson*. The ship's guide, after a three-month journey upriver from St. Louis, is honored to host the greatest Irish American of his day. Eight hours earlier, when Doran heard that the Prince of Waterford had dismounted in a cloud of dust at Fort Benton, he immediately sought him out. Was this Thomas Francis Meagher, one and the same? The orator? Meagher of the Sword? The Civil War general? *Yes, yes indeed.* Meagher apologized for his illness, dysentery that's been with him for six days. They then spent the evening together, these two, swapping memories of their tortured island nation, sharing dinner, cigars and tea. Now Johnny has a pair of pistols to lend, he says. And just the book for him—a novel to take him back to Ireland. Yet Meagher is still troubled, not ready for bed.

"As I passed today," he tells Doran, "I heard them say, 'There he goes.'"

And why shouldn't the human flotsam of Fort Benton say such a thing? Until a few days ago, he was governor of Montana Territory, ruler of a Rocky Mountain kingdom stretching from the Badlands to the Bitterroots, a place of sudden riches and ever more sudden death. Check that—acting governor, a man in transition. He is still searching for permanence, somewhere to anchor himself. Though his words moved people to risk their lives on three continents, and he looked for a home on four, he never found *the place.* Always the exile. "I am here alone," he'd confessed in a love letter some time ago. He had no family in this vast continent, he'd lamented, no boyhood den to disappear into, no place he could find with his eyes closed. Most call him General Meagher, and some can even pronounce it—a single syllable, *Mar,* an honorable surname from County Tipperary, descendant of tribal chieftains at that. More than once, this General Meagher had stormed into a blizzard of musketry to slay the defenders of slavery. He led the Irish Brigade, the storied castoffs who fought for the Union under a green flag of a harp and a sunburst. Knocked senseless and left for dead in one battle, in another he was left holding a best friend while the soldier's heart gave out. This was the price to be accepted as an American.

"There he goes."

He can count the enemies: the Brits, certainly. Meagher is a fugitive, still, in the eyes of the mightiest empire on earth. No matter his U.S. citizenship, his officer's rank or his marriage to a well-known New Yorker with an impeccable colonial Protestant lineage. This governor is a convict. A wanted man. Another Paddy from the penal colony. Should he try to return to his father's home along the Suir, the authorities would shackle him to a moldy cell in the Kilmainham Gaol. Then, perhaps, back to Tasmania, where Great Britain had banished him among the brightest of Ireland's noncompliant political class.

The enduring struggle, dating to the twelfth century, could still cause a dustup in the nineteenth-century American West, 4,300 miles from the wellspring of all the ancient hatred. Meagher's very existence, defying England's repeated efforts to bury him, was a threat in the most troublesome part of the Empire. Meagher had shown the world that the Irish could fight, that immigrants and petty criminals from the hard filth of New York and the waterfront warrens of Boston would risk life in a civil war that was not theirs. And he made no secret of the bigger design: after they finished with the South, these same Irishmen, seasoned soldiers now, would steam across the Atlantic and liberate their homeland. Thomas Meagher, lover of verse, a man who got his start using speech as a weapon, leading the way. *Don't laugh.* The Wild Geese — triumphant at last.

More likely, the men who muttered "There he goes" on Fort Benton's sun-cracked, uneven walkways are enemies from within Montana. Vigilantes top the list. When Meagher arrived in Virginia City with his acting governor's title, the law belonged to a stiff-collared cabal who'd been there first. By the end of 1865, they had hanged forty citizens in barely two years' time, leaving the victims to sway from a favored tree for days in case somebody missed the point. Meagher believed that the hasty arrest and secretive sentencing of one poor soul was an outrage — an affront to the American sensibilities that he'd embraced with the guileless fervor of a new citizen. He issued a reprieve, which infuriated the vigilantes. Within a day, a posse grabbed the newly freed man and strung him from Helena's hanging tree — the governor's get-out-of-jail card still in his back pocket. Not long afterward, the executioners sent the governor a note, a crudely drawn hangman's knot, labeled "General Meagher."

On this lovely summer's eve, the moon nearly full, the river coursing down-continent at about eight miles an hour, a few kingfishers swooping for prey, Meagher could try to push his suspicions aside. The buoyancy of his heart has long sustained him. Fear, like self-pity, is a prison of its own making. So what if he's broke, his salary long overdue, his personal funds exhausted from trying to maintain the ragged appearance of government in a lawless land. He'd attempted to make a home from within the chilly claustrophobia of a log cabin in a mile-high shack town — Virginia City, the Montana capital. It was neither a city nor anything like Virginia. He couldn't pay the doctor who'd treated him for the turmoil in his gut. His credit, that of the U.S. government, would terminate with this last official act: getting a cache of arms from

Major General William Tecumseh Sherman, commander of the Army of the West, for use in a conflict with the natives.

Though Meagher was born into wealth, educated at the best schools and raised in baronial splendor, who dined at a table crowded with crystal from his native Waterford, he could count his net worth now, at the age of forty-three, in the hasty scribble of a few sentences. Two horses valued at $40. A stovepipe that might get $90. A note showing $500 owed him in back pay from the government. A few bottles of champagne, books of poetry, a half-dozen cigars. The laughable, leaky little log hut was not even his. The governor's mansion, hah! But—*damn it all*—why does money have to be the marker of a man? That was the thing about America he most despised, measuring existence by the size of one's pile.

Better to think of what could come next in a run of extraordinary luck, a commodity oversubscribed to the Irish. Was there a more tumultuous time to be alive in the two countries he called his own? Meagher didn't think so. His prayer to an oft-inattentive God—to be part of some Great Purpose and not just a bystander—had been answered. What more could a man want? Well, *more*. Meagher felt there had to be a coda of grand consequence. He had lived through the genocidal horror of the famine, said goodbye to friends swept out in the migration of two million Irish. He was bound to the penal colony of Australia, had become a free man in the most clamorous of free nations, fought and nearly died trying to hold this new nation together and now was looking for a home under the big sky of Montana. He had known the Liberator of the Old World, Daniel O'Connell, and the Great Emancipator of the New World, Abraham Lincoln. He had lived a dozen lives in his two score and three—lived an abundance of horror and no small number of triumphs. But more than that, he'd shaped his times. There were newly free men and women in the penal colony down under, in part because of him. There were free blacks in America, in part because of him. There would one day be a free Ireland, in part because of him. To escape England's gallows, Tasmania's sharks, the Confederacy's shells, even a train wreck that killed most of the people in his car—this was more than ordinary luck. Surely, something magnificent was still in store for him, something befitting this life.

He misses Libby. The New York beauty Elizabeth Townsend Meagher had walked away from her father's fortune, turned her back on his religion and his favor, to follow an Irish fugitive. They have become exiles together. "You know the worst," he had told Libby, in asking her to join him for the rest of his years, "and you know the best." She had nursed his wounds from Bull Run and Antietam, had protected his good name from the clucks of New York, had resisted her family's pleadings to give him up for someone more deserving of her status. Better to be an *old maid* than to marry this felon, she was told. Despite the constraints of the frontier, they were happier this last year in Montana than they had been in some time. After a dozen years of marriage, he was sure of it: he had found his life mate.

Steady, steady on the deck. A look again at the moon over the Missouri, enough light for him to spot an osprey riding an updraft. The river is unfathomably full for summer, carrying runoff, rain and spring water from an area twice the size of France. Meagher had lived by a river for much of his youth—the Liffey, all of seventy-eight miles long, rising in the Wicklow Mountains, flowing past his boarding school, emptying to the sea not far from a den in Dublin where he helped to plot a revolution. So many lives ago. This oversized Missouri, chocolate brown and bulked with reinforcement from the snow-shedding mountains, could make even the most convivial man lonely.

His stomach will not stop churning; it feels clunked. Perhaps a nightcap, then, to make sleep come easier. What would they say? That he was tanked, swaying on the upper deck, the poor son of a bitch. A man couldn't have a proper drink without someone bringing up the Curse of the Irish. Well, then, just one last look at the river and bid this summer eve good night, with that book awaiting him in bed.

At once a shout goes out, guttural and primal, followed by a splash and another cry. It's the general's voice. Doran can tell from the lower deck.

"Man overboard!"

Now the Missouri has Thomas Meagher in its grip; he's gasping and choking on sediment-thick water. A crewman throws out a line. In an instant, he's gone, disappeared, not a sound in the vacuum. Away he goes, down the big waterway, past snags and sandbars, to the undercurrents and waterfalls in the gravitational pull of the continent's eastern half, away to the Mississippi, to the Gulf, to the ages. His vanishing is one of the longest-lasting mysteries of the American West.

His life is the story of Ireland.

PART I

TO BE IRISH IN IRELAND

1

UNDER THE BOOTHEEL

For the better part of seven centuries, to be Irish in Ireland was to live in a land not your own. You called a lake next to your family home by one name, and the occupiers gave it another. You knew a town had been built by the hands of your ancestors, the quarry of origin for the stones pressed into those streets, and you were forbidden from inhabiting it. You could not enter a court of law as anything but a criminal or a snitch. You could not worship your God, in a church open to the public, without risking prison or public flogging. You could not attend school, at any level, even at home. And if your parents sent you out of the country to be educated, you could not return. You could not marry, conduct trade or go into business with a Christian Protestant. You could not have a foster child. If orphaned, you were forced into a home full of people who rejected your faith. You could not play your favorite sports — hurling was specifically prohibited. You could not own land in more than 80 percent of your country; the bogs, barrens and highlands were your haunts. You could not own a horse worth more than £5 sterling. If you married an Englishman, you would lose everything upon his death. You could not speak your language outside your home. You would not think in Irish, so the logic went, if you were not allowed to speak in Irish.

Your ancient verses were forbidden from being uttered in select company. Your songs could not be sung, your music not played, your Celtic crosses not displayed. You could be thrown in prison for expressions of your folklore or native art. One law made it a felony for "a piper, story-teller, babler, or rimer" to be in the company of an Englishman. Another six statutes banished bards and minstrels. You could not vote. You could not hold office. You were nothing. "The law does not suppose any such person to exist as an Irish Roman Catholic," said John Bowes, an eighteenth-century lord chancellor of the island. "Nor could any such person draw a breath without the Crown's permission."

The melodies of this nation and its favorite instrument were a particular target of English hatred. At one point, your fingernails could be removed if you were caught playing the harp. The Irish married to the sounds that came from that instrument, and they grieved in some of those same keys. But the indigenous music came to be seen as subversive—too nationalistic, too connected to the old stories. In 1603 it was proclaimed that "all manner of bards and harpers" were to be "exterminated by martial law." That same year, a few months before her death, it was said in Ireland that Queen Elizabeth had ordered her troops to "hang the harpers, wherever found, and destroy their instruments." The Virgin Queen allowed Shakespeare and Marlowe to reach great heights during her long reign, but Elizabeth had not a thimble of tolerance for a people she considered primitive. To encourage the elimination of one musical aspect of that culture, the government paid a bounty to anyone who turned in outlaws of the harp. The musicians were easy to round up; many of them were blind, music their only refuge and source of income.

What had the Irish done to deserve these cruelties? They had refused to become English.

Thomas Francis Meagher was born on August 3, 1823, in one of the largest houses of the oldest city in Ireland—Waterford. The workaday port on the River Suir was founded in 914 by Vikings with ambition and a talent for on-shore piracy. Thomas grew up just steps from where conquerors had tramped through and a tower that had withstood a siege by the hated Oliver Cromwell. As a boy, he climbed up the chapped hills across the river, looked down at the port and seethed at the sight of British warships in the harbor. He imagined the last gasping breaths taken by Francis Hearn, hanged from the Waterford Bridge until his neck snapped for his role in a failed 1798 uprising. He played inside the eleventh-century round tower of the Vikings, said to be the oldest surviving building in Ireland.

The town motto was *Urbs Intacta*—Unconquered City. But Waterford was the most conquered of cities, evident throughout the bundle of strong buildings, shoulder to shoulder along the quay. Every street and structure bore some scar of defeat. A cannonball was lodged inside that Viking tower, left over from Cromwell's rampage of 1650. King Richard II had landed there in 1394, leading the largest armada ever to sail into an Irish port—duly noted on a much-vandalized plaque. King Henry VIII had converted a monastery in the center of town into an almshouse. For 350 years, poor inmates were obliged to pray for the soul of the wife-killing king, as a condition of the charity. Thomas knew all of this, in great, gritty detail, not because of his schooling, which was formal and devoid of passionate obsessions, but because it was passed down—an inheritance of memory. The systematic savagery, the stripping of ethnic pride and religious freedom, the many executions of men of conscience: he carried these stories throughout his life, the weight increasing with the years.

The seven-plus centuries of organized torment originated in a letter from Pope Adrian IV in 1155, which empowered King Henry II to conquer Ireland and its "rude and savage people." It was decreed that the rogue Irish Catholic Church, a mutt's mash of Celtic, Druidic, Viking and Gaelic influences, had strayed too far from clerical authority, at a time when English monarchs still obeyed Rome. Legend alone was not enough to save it—that is, the legend of Patrick, a Roman citizen who came to Ireland in a fifth-century slave ship and then convinced many a Celt to worship a Jewish carpenter's son. Patrick traveled with his own brewer; the saint's ale may have been a more persuasive selling point for Christianity than the trinity symbol of the shamrock. There followed centuries of relative peace, the island a hive of learned monks, masterly stonemasons and tillers of the soil, while Europe fell to Teutonic plunder. The Vikings, after much pillaging, forced interbreeding, tower-toppling and occasional acts of civic improvement (they founded Dublin on the south bank of the Liffey), eventually succumbed to the island's religion as well. They produced children who were red-haired and freckled, the Norse-Celts. But by the twelfth century, Ireland was out of line. Does it matter that this Adrian IV, the former Nicholas Breakspear, was history's only English pope? Or that the language of the original papal bull, with all its authoritative aspersions on the character of the Irish, has never been authenticated? It did for 752 years.

So with the blessing of God, a Norman force landed not far from Wexford in 1169, followed by an invasion of Henry and his army two years later in Waterford. He was the first English king to leave a footprint on Irish soil, and would not be the last to pronounce the people ungovernable. He could have learned from the Romans, who called the island Hibernia and deemed it not worth the lost lives needed to force it into their empire. After Henry's march, the chieftains and family leaders who pledged fealty were allowed to hold on to their estates, and a degree of self-government was granted to those residents with Anglo-Norman lineage.

Still, the indigenous culture—lively, excitably clannish, infectious—would flourish, as the English print on the land faded. The horse racing, the storytelling, the epic versifying over strong drink and tables heavy with trout and partridge, became the way of the occupiers. English soldiers married Irish women and had big Irish families, and power grew ever more distant from the Crown. The sons of men named James and Edmund became Seamus and Eamann. The daughters of Mary and Evelyn became Maire and Eibhlin. To the horror of the royal court, these offspring of the invaders had become *ipsis Hibernicis Hiberniores*—more Irish than the Irish. They had gone native.

The remedy was one of the most exhaustive campaigns to strip a people of their pride of place that any government had ever devised—the Statutes of Kilkenny. Starting in 1367, assimilation was outlawed. Nearly three dozen laws criminalized Irish dress, Irish hairstyle, Irish sport, down to a detailed description of the lawful way to mount a horse. Punishment for riding without an English saddle was jail: the offender's "body shall be committed to prison, until he pay a fine according to the King's pleasure."

The statutes carried the death penalty for the worst offenses. Family mingling was at the top of the forbidden list, sanctions for "fostering of children" and "concubinage." Article VI went after a beloved Irish sport—"the plays which men call horlings, with great sticks and a ball upon the ground, from which great evils and maims have arisen." Henceforth, all men were to play English sports—archery, "throwing of lances and other gentlemanlike games." Though most people on the island, no matter their ancestry, were Roman Catholic, religion was strictly a nationalistic affair for one side. No Irish could enter a chapel, church, cathedral or any other house of prayer in his homeland if an

Englishman was present. Speaking Gaelic, or using Irish place names, could result in forfeiture of land and property to the king.

In love and play, music and worship, sport and dress, these laws were nearly impossible to enforce. The Irish language, scattered into corners and vales of the land, was banished but never killed. Stories still passed, secret societies developed, romances between English and Irish could not be prevented by whippings and threat of jail. The clans still reigned, enforcing their own laws, abiding by their customs. The English, badly outnumbered, retreated to a few towns along the eastern shore closest to their own nation. They built estates of thick limestone, peopled them with down-lineage barons and earls, ladies and lords. At Christmastime, the cream of the conquering class paraded in silk, fur and feather. English power was clustered around Dublin, an urban fortress, a nation within a nation. The siege mentality grew even stronger when a physical boundary went up—the Pale, from the Latin word *palus,* for stake. In places, it was an actual fence, marked by said stakes. By the late 1400s, the Pale covered four counties. Inside the Pale was an Anglo-Norman kingdom with armed security, a structured feudal system and a sense of settled superiority. Beyond the Pale—that was beyond all civilization, an unruly Ireland living on its own terms.

As the size of the Pale shrank, fear within it rose. By the early 1500s, the Irish inside the circumscribed area were acting freely Irish again. Power flowed back to families with ancient ties to the land. One of those clans produced a fine-robed young rebel by the name of Silken Thomas Fitzgerald, who raised a sizable force and launched a revolt in 1534. As Thomas marched on Dublin, the Pale panicked. He was within conquering distance of driving the English out when an invading army arrived to turn him back. It had superior new weapons—cannons. Whereas before it took waves of men on ladders to scale a compound, now a few well-placed iron balls could breach a fortress. Thomas was powerless in the face of English artillery. Captured, carted off to England, he was dragged through the streets and left to slow-starve in the Tower of London. As a rebel, he was supposed to have his genitals severed before execution. But as the son of the Earl of Kildare, Thomas had some special rights. He was hanged and then beheaded, his testicles intact. Thereafter, an English army garrison would remain in Dublin for nearly four centuries.

The Crown then launched a second big wave of suppression—

against the religion that had clung to the land since just before the time of Saint Patrick, more than a thousand years earlier. The change of faith came about because of a change of wives by the English king, Henry VIII. Yes, him. Athletic before an accident led to a life of sloth and overindulgence, the king grew fat, hateful and murderous in his middle age. At 400 pounds, he was a seasoned killer, having orchestrated the execution of wife number two, Anne Boleyn, and wife number five, Katherine Howard. After breaking with a corrupt Rome that would not grant him his first divorce, Henry declared himself leader of a new English church—from now on, the state religion of Ireland as well. The same year that Anne's head was severed from her body, Henry was declared the Supreme Head on Earth of the Church of England. Irish Catholics were ordered to become Anglicans or forfeit their land and all their holdings. Outside the Pale, this edict had the effect of a mortal ordering the sun to rise at midnight on a winter's eve.

Henry's legacy in Ireland was a religion planted by force but never to flourish in most of the country's soil. But not for lack of trying. Monasteries were seized. Priests were forced underground and into caves along the coast. The Latin Mass was outlawed. The remainder of the century was a bloody thrust and parry, the Irish attacking, the English countering. In the north, the Crown gave its combatants government backing to undertake widespread theft, the beginning of a process known as the Plantation of Ireland. Large estates, held by families for centuries, were confiscated. The owners and their servants and tenants were kicked off the land and left to starve. Villages were ransacked and burned, leaving hungry children to flee with their mothers. "Out of every corner of the woods and glens, they came creeping forth upon their hands, for their legs would not bear them," wrote Edmund Spenser, the English poet. "They looked like anatomies of death; they spake like ghosts crying out of their graves."

To populate these newly stolen lands, the English brought in Protestant settlers, many from Scotland, and were generous with their handouts. So was born another hyphenate from this soil: the Scotch-Irish. Those natives who trickled back, bereft and broke, were allowed in some cases to work their old property as serfs. Inevitably, the people rose up, first with guerrilla raids of pitchforks, pikes and arson strikes, and then with larger, organized rebellions. But by 1602, England controlled nearly all of Ireland. Foreign rule was buttressed by foreign religion. Both would be held in place by a foreign army.

The dispossessed took on their oppressor again in 1641. Sick with hatred for those who had cast them from their homes, they killed innocents and tyrants alike, rampaging through the north. Children and women—it didn't matter, if they were Protestants they were massacred. At least a hundred people were drowned in one town. The roads were choked with refugees. The Irish had been encouraged to strike by a burgeoning English civil war, and felt compelled to seize the moment and side with King Charles I.

Back in London, stories of atrocities stirred the English. Parliament called for Catholic Ireland to be destroyed once and for all. "No quarter shall be given to any Irishman, or Papist born in Ireland," a new law declared. Within weeks, the captain of the frigate *Swanly* seized a ship with seventy Irish. The sailors were tied, one to the other, and thrown into the sea. Extermination on a mass scale would be carried out over the next ten years. The most horrific slaughter arrived in the form of Oliver Cromwell, leading his New Model Army of 12,000 men, with another 7,000 in reserve. North of Dublin, he laid siege to the well-fortified town of Drogheda. For several days in late summer of 1649, his cannons fired away at the town walls. On September 11, troops stormed the broken city, using Irish children as human shields. By evening, the conquest well in hand, soldiers took swords to anyone still alive—no matter that they'd been offered safety if they surrendered. Children who had huddled with their mothers in St. Mary's Church were burned alive. Women who had escaped to a vault were butchered. By Cromwell's own account, only 30 people from a town of 4,000 survived. Those who lived were sold as slaves to Barbados.

Cromwell was in the country only nine months, but in that time he imprinted himself on every Irish parish and every Irish family. Only in the Burren, a moonscape of rock in County Clare, was he repelled. In that treeless plain, the land itself held him back—"for there is not enough water to drown a man, wood enough to hang one, or earth enough to bury him," said one of his officers. Throughout Ireland, Cromwell left behind "a name for cruelty such as the passage of three hundred years has scarcely erased from memory," wrote the historian Giovanni Costigan.

In his letters and official papers back to England, Cromwell gloated. He believed he had performed a righteous killing "upon these barbarous wretches." In describing his triumphs, he gloried in the intricacies of bloodlust by his fighting machine—death by sword to the heart and lungs, by fire to hair and face, by the crushing of skulls, the gouging of eyes, the strangling of throats, drowning and smothering, all for the greater good. "It hath pleased God to bless our endeavors at Drogheda," he wrote.

This latest failed Irish rebellion was capped by a disastrous epilogue: the systematic eviction of people from their homes and land, far more comprehensive than what had taken place earlier in the north. Under the Act of Settlement, Cromwell's soldiers and their supporters would seize more than half of all the good land in Ireland, about eight million acres. Any landowner who took part in the fight against Cromwell was arrested and sentenced to a life of bondage, his land confiscated. In this way, another 40,000 Irish were deported to the West Indies as slaves on sugar plantations. Nearly two centuries later, the French journalist Gustave de Beaumont toured Ireland with his lifelong friend Alexis de Tocqueville, fresh off a thorough exploration of the United States. "I passed through the country traversed by Cromwell and found it still full of the terror of his name," Beaumont wrote. The worst thing one Irish peasant could say to the other was "The curse of Cromwell be on you."

To ensure that the conquered people would never again rise above a degraded state, a series of Penal Laws were enacted at the end of the seventeenth century. These dictates, as with the Statutes of Kilkenny more than 300 years earlier, were a far-reaching attempt to tear apart what was left of the ties that held the Irish together as a people. With the plantations the English took land; with Kilkenny's statutes they took language, sports and culture; with the Penal Laws they took religion. Ever since Henry VIII tried to make the Irish bow to the king as the highest spiritual authority, persecution had been haphazard and poorly enforced. The Penal Laws would show the world how a well-armed minority could snuff out the native worshiping habits of a majority by criminalizing the faith of eight out of ten residents of Ireland. It was the Penal Laws that made it illegal for a Catholic to own a horse worth more than £5, to live in major cities, to pass property on to the eldest son. It was the Penal Laws that made education the monopoly of one religion, that led to the branding of priests with hot irons on their cheeks. And it was the Penal Laws that ensured that a Catholic would never sit on a grand jury, never vote, never raise a voice of protest or be granted the rights of citizenship, even as England expanded those rights to her own subjects. In Ireland, people were to be forever illiterate, forever poor, forever powerless.

The language of these laws could serve as a template for future despots trying to rid a land of its indigenous ways. "No person of the popish religion shall publicly teach school or instruct youth, or in private houses teach youth." Should a priest "celebrate marriage between two Protestants, or a Protestant and a Papist, he shall be guilty of a felony and suffer death." A Protestant landowner, subservient to the Crown, could vote for members of an Irish Parliament, though if that freeholder fell under suspicion, he was required to take this oath: "I am not a Papist, or married to a Papist." Catholic assembly in areas of "pretended sanctity" was outlawed as a form of insurrection—"all such meetings shall be adjudged riots and unlawful assemblies, and punishable as such." The long arm of London extended even to the Irish grave. "No person shall bury any dead in any suppressed monastery, abbey or convent." In all, the Penal Laws were a marvel of institutionalized racial and religious supremacy. The British had thought of everything.

"A machine of wise and elaborate contrivance," marveled Edmund Burke, the Irish-born statesman, "as well-fitted for the oppression, impoverishment and degradation of a people and the debasement in them of human nature itself, as ever proceeded from the perverted ingenuity of man."

The laws were enforced by an occupying army of at least 15,000 men and by schools of informants. The authorities had learned that a soldier was no match in efficiency for a well-paid spy. In some cases, the snitch could reap 50 percent of a guilty man's seized goods. "One half of all forfeitures shall go to his Majesty," a penal law of 1695 decreed, "and the other half to the informer." Some indignities were never codified, though the laws seemed to give blanket support to treat the Irish as subhuman. A poor man showing lack of respect to his Protestant superior could be whipped until he collapsed or beaten until his bones snapped. It was not uncommon, as on the cotton plantations of the American South, for a master of the estate to summon from his tenants an Irish girl to his bed.

And yet this well-constructed design, one of the most sophisticated attempts to deny a people of basic human dignity, failed miserably. The campaign to strip the Irish of their religion had the opposite effect, making them more loyal to their faith. Certainly, Rome was corrupt, deceitful, the Church ruled by a knot of conspirators whose pronouncements were delivered on a breeze of hypocrisy. The Church meddled in the affairs of every Catholic nation, blessing murder of their enemies and of nonbelievers. They persecuted men of science and voices of common sense. Even as the Renaissance brought fresh light, art and thought to Europe, as the Reformation prompted half of the continent to turn away from the medieval mandates of Rome, as the Age of Enlightenment spawned thousands of conversions from belief to reason, the Irish clung to their Roman Catholicism. For the same reason that hurling never died, that the harp became a national symbol, that epic poems were still recited in Gaelic, religion was a way for a conquered nation to remain defiantly Irish.

The English were much more successful at displacing people from the land. Sons and grandsons of Cromwell's soldiers passed on to their heirs the fields they had taken. Ireland became a nation of tenant farmers, of large families paying rent to live on ground once owned by their ancestors. From the Peruvian Andes, the potato found its way across the Atlantic in the 1500s. No one can say with certainty how it came to Ireland, though one consistent story has it that potatoes washed ashore after the wreck of the Spanish fleet in 1588. Scholars have disproven a long-held English version: that Sir Walter Raleigh first planted this miracle of starch and nutrition on his estate near Cork in 1589. And it likely didn't come from Scotland, where clerics banned the potato because it wasn't mentioned in the Bible. No matter. The potato did take to Ireland. It required little more than an acre of soil for a family of five to feed themselves with this one crop for a year, the diet supplemented by buttermilk and bacon and the greens of dandelion leaves, chives and cabbage.

By the late eighteenth century, the potato was the national food, with more than two million acres devoted to tillage of the tuber. The large estates were given over to grazing for cattle and sheep, and growing oats and barley. Those were the money crops for landlords who were gone much of the year. The small potato farms, worked by the peasant class, were not idyllic in any sense. In the rural areas, half the families of Ireland lived in single-room, windowless hovels. Huts were of thatched roofs over sod, the walls made of dried mud that liquefied in the rain, with beds of straw, floors of packed dirt, a table serving as the one piece of furniture, a hearth smoky from smoldering peat—and a pig in one corner, a family's prized possession.

"I have seen the Indian in the forest, and the negro in his chains and thought that I saw the very extreme of human wretchedness, but did not then know the condition of unfortunate Ireland," Beaumont wrote after two long reporting tours in 1835 and 1837. "An entire nation of paupers is what never was seen until it was shown in Ireland."

Thomas Meagher's family had money—*see here*, their very appearance proclaimed, *we're not all shoeless and hollow-eyed*—but only because they had fled. English rule had produced the poorest country in Europe, and also a nation whose most ambitious people left for better lives. From a tenant farm in County Tipperary, a young man in a family with 700-year-old ties to the land had picked up in the 1780s and sailed for Newfoundland. The big island of broken rock and blistering winds off the east coast of the North American mainland was England's oldest colony, but it offered the Irish a degree of respect unknown to them at home. They gave their adopted land a Gaelic name that meant "land of the fish." In 1788, Newfoundland was host to the first recorded game of hurling in the New World.

Thomas Meagher Sr., grandfather to the Waterford lad, started as a tailor in St. John's, where two thirds of the residents were Irish. He mended sails and suits, and jumped at the opportunity to move up in the merchant trade. The sea around him was a garden of cod, the fish that built empires and became almost its own currency. Meagher bought a sixty-ton brig in 1808, the first of his own fleet. He shipped salted cod to Waterford and returned with bacon, flour, oats and immigrants. He expanded the trade: sealskins, salmon and timber going one way; beer, linen and crystal coming back the other. He brought his son, Thomas Meagher Jr., into the business as a full partner in 1815. When he moved home to Ireland, he returned with an immense fortune of £20,000. By then, the Penal Laws had eroded: Catholics were now allowed to buy property in the cities and to attend their own schools, provided no Gaelic was taught. Still, they could not hold office.

In Waterford, shadowed by bareback hills of stone and grass, the elder Meagher moved into a Georgian villa once owned by descendants of Cromwell's army. It closed a loop, dating to when his people had been dispossessed in Tipperary by the Cursed One. His son joined the family three years later, and they all moved into an even larger house. The Meaghers took over much of the waterfront, their wealth further enhanced by marriage into another merchant family.

By 1825, when two-year-old Thomas Francis toddled around the mansion in Waterford, the high-ceilinged rooms draped in tapestries and furnished with oil portraits, the Meaghers were Irish aristocracy. They not only made more money than anyone in town, but they gave it away—to societies for the poor in Newfoundland and Ireland, to a refuge for orphans that offered trade skills for the boys and to a campaign to liberate Catholics at home. Had they discarded their religion, the family could have had full privileges of the estate-owning elite. At a time when life expectancy was not yet forty years, they could also expect additional decades, for the Meagher men were of a hardy stock, living into advanced old age. The women were not so fortunate. In 1827, Thomas lost his mother, Alicia, and ten years later his sister died. That left a girl and two boys—Thomas being the oldest—to be raised by grandparents, aunts and the stout, intelligent, lordly father. Thomas Francis was taught to love words and their power to change minds. But he must work within the system, his father told him. Respect the Crown. Honor the rule of law. Yes, he could sing the ballads of Hugh O'Neill or wear his Wolfe Tone cap around town, but he should not act on the ardor aroused by the summoning of those dead patriots.

Thomas challenged his father at every turn. He watched boats sail from Waterford, down the estuary of the Suir and out to sea, loaded with human cargo from the villages of Ireland. He caught glimpses of those faces turning for a last look. Why was there no future for them at home, he wondered in a later recollection, "compelled to surrender the land of their love and pride?"

At the Jesuit boarding school in Clongowes Wood, north of Waterford in County Kildare, young Thomas saw gray-staked evidence of the Pale's outer reach, not far from the fields where he kicked a soccer ball. Finding a ditch and the remnants of a wall, he could not fathom why people had been fenced out of their own country. Between clarinet recitals and lessons in Latin, Thomas pestered the Jesuits in the same way he had bothered his father. *Why are we not allowed to govern ourselves? Why can't we speak our language?* (Gaelic was still the primary tongue for one and a half million Irish.) *And what future is there for a nation whose landowners live in another country, collecting rents from the native inhabitants?* To these queries, the priests told the boy to mind his mouth. The Jesuits spoke a half-dozen languages, but Irish nationalism was not one of them.

"In that grand castle of theirs, they lived and taught rather as hostages and aliens than as freemen and citizens," Thomas recalled. He learned about the world's great powers and their wars, the clash of empires and the march of monarchs. But nothing of his own land. "As far as Ireland was concerned, they left us like blind and crippled children, in the dark," he said. "They never spoke of Ireland. Never gave us, even what is left of it, her history to read." He should consider himself fortunate to be among the lads at Clongowes, where it cost the equivalent of a full year's wages to attend. When he saw his father, the elder Thomas Francis reinforced the message of the educators: *Change will come to Ireland slowly, by peaceful means. Look what your family made of itself in Waterford. And consider the life that awaits you.*

But a day's sail away, those who held Ireland's future in their hands had another view. The stack of centuries since the Norman landing had taught the English there was only one way to rule these people. In Parliament, the question of the troublesome island came up once again. It was always on the agenda, one way or the other, like a roof with a perpetual leak. "How do you govern it?" asked Thomas Babington Macaulay, the historian and politician. "Not by love but by fear."

And yet something other than fear was in the air just then, the young sensing a hinge moment. The American Revolution had produced a raft of stirring thought—Jefferson and Paine, Franklin and Adams. They had whipped the British Empire! Expelled the occupiers! The words of these excitable New World rebels jumped off the page to someone reading them in a captive nation. The king has "plundered our seas, ravaged our coasts, burnt our houses, and destroyed the lives of our people," the Americans asserted in their Declaration of Independence. What Irishman was this Thomas Jefferson? *That's us!* Countries all over Europe were threatening to throw off their monarchies. Old ideas were buried. New ideas took wing.

To complete his schooling, it was decided that Thomas Meagher would be sent away to a prestigious school in the heart of England. His father hoped that this quarrelsome boy, too much the prankster, would return as a gentleman on a leash. In England, he could read Francis Bacon, John Locke and Voltaire. In England, he could memorize the Rights of Man from France and the Bill of Rights from the United States. On the eve of his departure, he vowed never to hold his tongue, and with the courage of someone yet to shave his first whisker, he laughed when warned that such a trait would buy him a death sentence in Ireland. He dashed off an ode to seizing life's moments, concluding that "no one should be secure of reaching a happy old age."

2

THE BECOMING

The boy sailed for England in October of 1839, his life compressed into a bundle of trunks, the wooden clarinet wrapped in layers. The Irish Sea coiled and cupped, passage seldom smooth. In Liverpool, the Empire's exotica spilled onto the docks, smells from the Caribbean, birds from the South Seas, dark-skinned, newly freed deckhands singing something that could not have come from Great Britain, and hundreds of Irish families looking to take the first steps toward a new life. He caught a coach to Manchester, changed for another to Whalley, and after a journey that had lasted five days in all he arrived in Lancashire, at Stonyhurst College. Home for the next four years was one of the largest buildings under a single roof in all of Europe. The pile impressed him — for its enormity, for its brooding setting in a valley of old sycamores and chestnuts, for the stone eagles perched atop twin cupolas towering over the rest of the manor. The tree branches were like wrinkled arms, he thought, holding the college in mystery. Years later, the deep-shadowed forests beyond the moats of Stonyhurst would make a similar impression on the imagination of another temporary resident, J.R.R. Tolkien. In its age and posture, its stained-glass windows and arched entrances, the shell of the college was a match for its mission: to educate the most influential Catholics of Europe.

He was taken to his room, cold and dimly lit, gas lamps in the hallways to find the way. Biting winds swept down from the Pendle Hills, a nag for all but the summer months. Heat came from the glow of burning coal behind grates in the common rooms. He traded his silks for a uniform of a blue swallowtail coat, gold buttons, a waistcoat and gray pants. He could wear only one pair of shoes from Sunday through Wednesday, and then change into a second pair for the remainder of the week. Two pairs, no more. Get rid of the accent, he was told immediately—*it won't do you any good here.* These were English Jesuits giving 200 boys an English education. Exploring the warrens of the old estate, he came to a high table, prominently displayed in the refectory: Cromwell's bed for one night. The hated Lord Protector had slept there during the English Civil War, placing the makeshift bed in the center of the room as a way to keep an eye out for assassins.

Thomas was sixteen, with sweet lips, an aquiline nose, eyes the color of the Lancashire sky when it cleared. His upper body was solid and sinewy, his dark hair curled just at the ears. The schedule at Stonyhurst was as follows: rise at 5:30 a.m., then off to the chapel for prayers and Mass. Breakfast in a drafty room. A full day of Latin, Greek, French, geography, history, literature, mathematics, algebra, science. Testosterone raged on the green lawn of the pitch, football year-round. Late afternoon was given over to study at long community desks under the gaze of a black-robed enforcer. Evening meal with his masters—"bug soup" and "dog stew," as the boys called the fare. In bed by 9 p.m. Students stayed at the college through Christmas and Easter, the only vacation being a month at the end of summer. *Don't even think of chasing girls in the village,* he was informed. At Stonyhurst, no women, not the mothers or sisters of students, were allowed. The one exception: the school allowed a few female cooks and cleaners inside, beauty being a disqualifier. The penalty for sneaking out, or any number of enumerated infractions, was painful: a thick leather strap-whacking to the open palm, nine lashes per hand. The beatings left blisters but seldom broke the skin.

For all of that, Thomas was lucky to be one of the young scholars of Stonyhurst. He'd been kicked out of Clongowes, a dark day for his long-suffering father, after running afoul of the priests. It began over a holiday goose, which Thomas had been called upon to carve for fellow seniors. He complained of the bird's size. The scrawny carcass was not fit for his tablemates, he protested—it would leave them all hungry. *Eat it,* he was told. In protest, the boys stormed out. They threw rocks at the main window of the frescoed dining hall. One of the stones broke the glass. Then they disappeared to Dublin for a night in the pubs. The students had learned to drink from the priests, who regularly served beer with lunch, champagne and port with dinner—alcohol considered a safe alternative to nonpotable water. Thomas had been punished many a time at Clongowes; "isolation," when he was required to sharpen the priests' razors against a granite wall, was the usual sentence. But this infraction was serious. For organizing the rebellion, he was expelled. He could save himself if he turned in the boy who broke the window at Clongowes. Thomas would not give up his mate.

His college choices were limited. Trinity, the Protestant hold founded by Queen Elizabeth in the days when her soldiers were hunting harpers, was the only university in Ireland. For just a few years now, the school had opened its doors to select Catholics, but families like the Meaghers distrusted the university. Using the pull of an uncle who was a Jesuit, the elder Thomas got his son into Stonyhurst, one of the best colleges in Europe. The school had wandered, an exile in Europe, before a wealthy alumnus offered his estate, Stonyhurst, beginning in 1794. The new home was made possible by a series of reform acts that allowed Catholics in England to acquire property, to practice their religion without fear of civil penalties and to attend their own schools.

From the start, one thing was clear about this Irish student Meagher: the lad could talk. He enrolled in the School of Rhetoric, and dominated the debate society. He studied the great orators, learning how to build his case without letting sarcasm sink it. His memory of epic poems was startling—he could spring through the marathon, not missing a stanza. When the words weren't coming out of his mouth, they poured forth on paper. He won a medal for a crisp essay on the evils of slavery in America. He compiled a history of the debate society at Clongowes Wood—later published by the school. His letters to girls were cheeky and flirty. "Next to seeing you is the pleasure of seeing your handwriting," he wrote to one. He signed his letters "Nimrod" in self-deprecation. He was popular, full of mischief, liked a joke and a prank, a smoke and a drink in one of many hidden pockets in the forty-four-acre expanse of Stonyhurst. Alas, at the largest regular gathering of the school day, his voice was rendered mute. Speaking at dinner was not allowed at Stonyhurst. The boys ate their unpalatable English suppers in silence, priests at their elbows.

On June 15, 1840, the college band assembled for a performance in commemoration of the Battle of Waterloo—the Duke of Wellington's triumph over Napoleon. When it came time to strike up the music, the first clarinet was a big hole in the presentation. Thomas sat with his instrument in his lap. The maestro was furious. Thomas refused to perform: no breath of his would sound a note for an English victory, he explained. Lashes followed.

In the years that Thomas was becoming a man, Great Britain was growing into the world's foremost power. Backed by the ferocious guns of the Royal Navy, the globe's biggest merchant marine fleet and deft diplomacy, a small island nation of eleven million people ruled a network of colonies, territories, protectorates and dominions that would eventually cover nearly one fourth of the world's land area. A third of all trade moved in and out of England. Getting a jump on the Industrial Revolution, with steam power and telegraph communication, Britain went on a tear of economic expansion; by the 1840s, per capita income was nearly twice that of Germany or France. The loss of the American colonies had been a blow, but the English never looked back. The continent of Australia was added to the Empire's fold in 1788, and the subcontinent of India had been tamed a few decades earlier. South Africa in 1815, Singapore in 1824, New Zealand in 1840, Hong Kong in 1841. The huge landmass of Canada was well ordered, filled with loyalists who had fled the United States after the Revolutionary War, while the French-speaking provinces were given a degree of home rule. Great Britain considered itself a benign imperial power—civilized men overseeing a mostly barbaric world. Legal human bondage was ended with the Slavery Abolition Act of 1833.

The greatest empire the world had yet seen got its start with the conquest of Ireland back in 1171. And tiny Ireland was still the most troublesome turf under the Union Jack. China, India, entire subcontinents, could be subdued with less firepower than it took to keep the Irish in place. While loosening the Penal Laws, one final attempt was made by the government to snuff out the last pulse of Gaelic nationalism. At the stroke of midnight, New Year's Day, 1801, the Irish Parliament was abolished and shuttered in Dublin. It had never been representative—the majority of the people had no voice. And any law passed by the body in Dublin could be overruled in London. The failed rebellion of 1798 was one of many violent expressions of frustration with a legislature that excluded at least 80 percent of the residents. But the

Thomas Francis Meagher at the age of seventeen, when he was a student at Stonyhurst College in England. Born into wealth, young Meagher chafed at British rule even as he was warned not to take on the most powerful empire on earth. COURTESY OF THE NATIONAL LIBRARY OF IRELAND

Irish Parliament gave the illusion of self-government for Anglo and Protestant gentry suffering through their tenancy as minority rulers of the island.

The Act of Union, as the breakup was called, was performed with a shopkeeper's precision: members were efficiently bribed to dissolve themselves. In return, Ireland was offered seats in the British Parliament. Good news: you could now vote to send a member to the House of Commons. Bad news: you could not vote unless you were wealthy. Property requirements mocked the pretense of democracy. The number of eligible voters in Waterford, with 28,000 people, fell to barely 700. Ireland had a population of about five million, nearly half that of England at the nineteenth century's dawn. But its caucus in the Commons would be 15 percent, ensuring that nothing which displeased the English majority would ever pass. And of course, you couldn't govern your own country if you were like more than three fourths of the people who lived there—Catholics who refused to take an oath to the Crown's religion. Oh, and there would still be an English viceroy, the Lord Lieutenant, who ruled Ireland from the Castle in Dublin. Taxes and tariffs rose. Once-vibrant cities fell into despair. The press was muzzled. Habeas corpus was suspended at whim. The Act of Union, in the words of the English Romantic poet Lord Byron, was "the union of a shark with its prey."

Surrounded by the trappings of an empire in full, Thomas Meagher chafed. But why resist it? A great life was ahead for a graduate bearing the stamp of Stonyhurst. All that a man might want came through England. Queen Victoria, just four years older than Meagher and crowned while still a teenager in 1837, was such a dear, as everyone attested. Meagher could serve Her Majesty abroad, gleaming in a crisp scarlet coat with a saber at his side, an officer, like any graduate of Eton and Oxford. Looking back across St. George's Channel was futile: the boy's homeland was no more. His passport carried the formal name of this entity: the United Kingdom of Great Britain and Ireland.

Resentment stirred with every display of England's might and pride. Not long before graduation, Tom was given a plum role in the school play, *King Lear.* He was the Earl of Kent, with ample lines for a voice already distinct within the ramparts of Stonyhurst. His master was a priest from Lancashire, Reverend William Johnson, an Anglophile to his bones. At dress rehearsal, a week before Christmas, the Jesuit came up behind Thomas and smacked him over the head with a wad of *King Lear.* You can't do Shakespeare that way, he told him. Why not? Thomas had the emotion, the lift of words, the rise and fall of the face at the right time. The priest slapped him again with the bard's leather-bound words.

"Meagher," said Father Johnson, "that's a horrible brogue you've got!" As the priest coughed up phlegm into a tattered handkerchief, Meagher launched into his lines:

> *Fare thee well, King; since thus though will appear.*
> *Freedom lives hence, and banishment is here—*

Thwop. Once again. The sting of the Jesuit.

" 'T'will never do, Meagher!"

But—

"That frightful brogue of yours will never do for Shakespeare."

He was stripped of his role. Earl of Kent no more, he was demoted to a lowly soldier, a bit part. On opening night, well into Act IV, Thomas jumped onto the stage. In the deepest invocation of his native Munster province, he bellowed his line: "The British powers were marching thitherward."

The audience roared, and Thomas repeated it, in a still more exaggerated Irish accent. For bringing the house down this way, the young scholar was flogged on both hands, and of course never returned to nobility in future performances. But one of England's finest schools had failed to squeeze the Irish from the man. "I had my revenge," Meagher noted later. His demotion "was not the first time the brogue entailed the forfeiture of title and estate."

Home, and free of school at last, 1843. He would be twenty in August. The steamer *William Penn* huffed up the Suir to Waterford, past the landmarks of his youth. Meagher was torn. He loved the old Viking port, but the tableau was stale. "Everything was the same as I left it." Along the quay strolled the clueless constable, chewing straw as always. The Protestant dean skipped past the Norse tower in his black knickers and ebony cane, little children laughing at him behind his back. Most everyone in town knew of Thomas Francis Meagher, the Prince of Waterford. *Here, this way for a pint, lad. Can you come by and visit the daughter? She's quite the pretty young lady now.* The road ahead could be without complication. Just say yes. Picnics in summer, lavish balls in winter, holiday excursions on the Continent. He could slide into the family business, live in the biggest house on the water, move money from one bucket to the other, never be cold, never break a sweat, never be hungry, never worry.

And, just now, the doors opened to the honeyed light of the family home: such a crowd. All the chums of the province out to greet him, gorgeous young women but also the first Catholic mayor of Waterford in nearly 200 years—his father, the elder Thomas Meagher. He controlled the city, its patronage, the courts. What a change! This political miracle had come about because of the Liberator, Daniel O'Connell, the most towering figure in Meagher's Ireland. He was Swaggering Dan to some, glib, his hand on a lady's rear. Tall, fleshy-faced. Though educated in Europe, a barrister and landowner who had amassed a fortune, he spoke Gaelic like a chieftain of old. Wherever O'Connell went, crowds followed. Many just wanted to kiss him, to say they had planted lips on the man who freed the Catholics.

Ireland's population boomed in the first four decades of the nineteenth century—from five million to eight million by the time Thomas returned to Waterford. As the great majority remained disenfranchised, even leading Protestants called for giving a voice to these powerless Irish citizens of the United Kingdom. O'Connell was elected to Parliament in 1828. But as a Catholic, like the vast majority of the population, he could not be seated unless he took the Oath of Supremacy to the Crown's religion. In Westminster, he forced the issue. Huge protests broke out at home, mobs of people on a scale never before seen, frightening the government. The British had 25,000 troops in Ireland now, which said plenty about the relationship between the government and the governed. No such force was garrisoned in Scotland or Wales. As the demonstrations swelled, Parliament caved in: it passed the Roman Catholic Relief Act of 1829, ending the last of the Penal Laws.

Standing up to the British Empire made the Liberator a national hero. His legacy in place, he moved on to a second monumental campaign: a repeal of the Act of Union. This was impossible, said even the most sympathetic of English liberal thinkers. Not so, O'Connell answered. Ireland would govern itself—soon, perhaps—if a political majority in England could be won over. His movement would be peaceful, lawful, civil. And he was joined in this cause by Thomas Meagher's father, who gave a considerable amount of money to the cause of Repeal, and who befriended the Liberator.

The elder Meagher, a man of few words, pressured the son of many words about his next step. The boy could speak, or at least understand, five languages now—Latin, Greek, French, Gaelic and English. But could he put any of them to good use? He would not be following the patriarch into the temperance movement, an attempt to right the character of the Irish by getting rid of drink. That was clearly not for bon vivant young Meagher. Well, then, maybe he could find a role in O'Connell's organization. Start small, learn from the master, try to persuade the persuadable in power. The elder Meagher informed his son that the Liberator knew something of the young man. What flattery was this? O'Connell had been visiting Clongowes, the school of his own family, when he was shown Thomas's history of the debate society. He was impressed. "The author of such a work," he said, "was not destined to remain long in obscurity." Indeed, Meagher was in a hurry to make his mark. He did not share his father's satisfaction at the pace of reform. Emancipation through the Catholic Relief Act was a sop. The

Irish still had no real power. To keep the Catholic vote to a minimum, property requirements were raised fivefold. It was thrilling to see the mayor of his hometown—his own beloved father—going to Mass, and the streets, courts and hospitals in the people's hands, but consider the larger picture, he argued.

"It looked well," said Thomas. "But it was a fair skin with cancer below it." Real power still belonged to England. Armed soldiers, as always, were never far. The sheriff was an appointee of the British ruler, the Lord Lieutenant. "Catholic emancipation has enabled a few Catholic gentlemen to sit in Parliament and there concur in the degradation of their country," said young Meagher, having done little to curb the impertinent bite of his opinions. "It has brought a handful of slaves from the field, and gives them appointments in the master's house." His father, by implication, was one of the bound.

Thomas appreciated all that his family had done to educate him, to build a sumptuous life in occupied Ireland, but the merchant business was not for him, nor was his hometown—its entitled class "stiff with illiterate conceit." In September, a month after his twentieth birthday, Thomas gave his first political speech. He'd been attending Repeal meetings, in awe of the Liberator. Abolishing the Act of Union, the cause of Repeal, made the boy's pulse jump. Looking very much like the well-dressed schoolboy, Meagher gave the dinner speech of one such gathering. Afterward, the mighty O'Connell clapped the kid on the shoulder. "Well done, young Ireland." Did he have plans? In fact, Thomas had been thinking of moving to Dublin to study law. O'Connell thought this a fine idea. He had a big Georgian home there, in Merrion Square. The Liberator offered to write a letter of recommendation.

At age sixty-eight, O'Connell was living off past glory. He had gained a great amount of weight, and preferred evenings of praise from adoring fellow countrymen to effective provocations. But here, fourteen years after emancipation, he roused himself for the last big battle in the campaign he'd waged his entire adult life, declaring 1843 the Year of Repeal. His gatherings ballooned—vast protests, dubbed "monster meetings" by the London press. In Sligo, in Cork, in Limerick, in Wexford, the Irish were rising in a single voice to break from England. O'Connell never issued a call to arms, never cast an aspersion on "the darling little queen" he professed to adore. But he had crossed a line with the English overseers. Around 300,000 turned out in Waterford, the largest crowd in the country's history. The next protest, planned at the sacred site of Clontarf, north of Dublin, where the high king Brian Boru had driven the Vikings from the land 800 years earlier, would be even bigger—a million Irish, possibly. The diaspora in Scotland and Wales, in Liverpool and on the Continent, made quick plans to mass at Clontarf.

The Empire struck back. Warships crowded into Dublin's harbor, a blustery reminder that the Royal Navy could level the city in an afternoon. The British prime minister, the Right Honourable Sir Robert Peel, 2nd Baronet, despised the Irish. They were mongrels, incapable of caring for themselves, a nation of drunks. As home secretary, Peel had signed on to Catholic emancipation in 1829 while holding his nose; it was the only way to avert a full-fledged revolution. He hated O'Connell in particular, had challenged the Liberator to a duel some time ago. Now he was in a position to shut the great man down at the height of his influence. Just days before what would have been the largest single protest in Ireland, Peel declared the Clontarf meeting a criminal assembly. Anyone who attended would be arrested.

Meagher watched his hero. The old boy had moves in him yet, yes? The nation would stand with O'Connell—just say the word! "Hope, delight, ecstasy, defiance—a tumultuous life leaped to the summons," Meagher said. But O'Connell surrendered. He lost his nerve and called off the protest. Everyone should go home peacefully. Those boats that had been chartered to cross the Irish Sea turned around. Shortly thereafter, O'Connell himself was arrested on a trumped-up charge. Prime Minister Peel won this duel.

Dublin, winter of 1844. Black rain on black cobbled streets, carriages splashing through puddles, the bruised-looking Liffey lumbering to sea. Thomas moved in with Patrick J. Smyth, a schoolmate from Clongowes, in a comfortable home in the city. Studying and sputtering with mentors at the dining halls of the Queen's Inns, he couldn't keep his mind on the law; it grew less interesting by the day. At night, Meagher and Smyth attended soirees with other educated strivers. Thomas was often mistaken for an Englishman. Something about the accent, proper and upper class. If only Father Johnson could hear this. Dinner parties and dances grew stale. The life felt fake, treading in mediocrity while his country fell into a torpor. He was not proud of himself. "Flaunting and fashionable," he said, by way of self-description. What rubbish. Irish high society was a fraud, "the pretentious aping of English taste, ideas and fashions," he called it. His worst fear was that he would become "a silken and scented slave of England." The city itself had long been cleansed of indigenous taint, its streets named for the conqueror's kings and queens, for earls of this and dukes of that.

Outside the warmly lit interiors of the salons, the Crown kept guard over it all from the immense stone fortress of the thirteenth-century Dublin Castle, just blocks from the river. The garrison in Ireland was larger than the Empire's troop placement in India. In Dublin alone were 10,000 men, with hussars bunked at the Royal Barracks, the light cavalry unit ready to strike—where? Why, here at home! Meagher sleepwalked his way through the shortest days of the year. The colossus O'Connell was tried in January 1844. He had been mayor of Dublin two years earlier, in the promising period that followed emancipation, but now he was just another educated prisoner of English rule. No Catholic would ever convict O'Connell, and so, as was common in political trials in Ireland, the jury was packed with Protestants under orders of the prosecution. The Liberator was found guilty and sentenced to a year in jail. Off to prison he went—a heavy-lidded, wheezing old man, his spirit broken, a warning to anyone who would think of defying the British Empire in its backyard.

3

POETRY IN ACTION

It was poetry, the bend of words to frame a cause, that lifted Ireland from its gloom in the last good months before catastrophe. Thomas Davis, educated at Trinity, the Protestant son of a British army surgeon, came forth with a burst of verse that roused a generation. He was trained as a lawyer, but wrote as if he'd never put his nose inside a book of law. He was romantic, able to call upon the nation's gauzy clutter of mythic figures without having his head in a cloud. And he possessed a clear vision for his native land. It was not Catholics versus Protestants, not the north against the south, Orangemen against Friends of St. Patrick. With a pair of journalists, Davis founded the most influential journal of nineteenth-century Ireland, the *Nation*. Though only 10,000 copies were printed each week, the paper was passed around, twenty-five readers to an issue, and became the island's first national publication. In a country where most peasants were illiterate, the poetry of Tom Davis spread by word of mouth—stanzas repeated on a sheep path or a loading dock. On publication day, long queues formed on the streets for fresh issues. The paper's essays were muscular, unblinking, original. The writers were young, educated, not afraid to poke at the old order, to mock English rule with unflinching satire, to recast tired stories into allegories of modern struggle. Davis himself was an elegant agitator with a fine face, though prone to wheezing and a cough, which made him seem vulnerable.

In the lengthening light of spring, 1845, Meagher grew infatuated with this rarest kind of subversive: a poet with power. He memorized Davis's best lines, and repeated them in argument. He waited outside the paper's office to try to meet him. He dropped his law studies, to the disappointment of his father. He scribbled verse in his room, sent poems to the *Nation*. He imagined himself *one of them*. Everything Davis wrote, Meagher consumed.

"This country of ours is no sand bank, thrown by some recent caprice of earth," said Davis in one essay. "It is an ancient land, honoured in the archives of civilization, traceable into antiquity by its piety, its valour and its sufferings." For people accustomed to looking down as they walked, to being told they were apes in waistcoats, beggars fit for Calcutta's Black Hole, this jolt of strong prose and rhyming journalism was spine-stiffening. The Davis lament for Owen Roe O'Neill, who died young while trying to ease Irish pain during the Cromwell conquest, was a favorite:

> *We thought you would not die—we were sure you would not go,*
> *And leave us in our utmost need to Cromwell's cruel blow—*
> *Sheep without a shepherd, when the snow shuts out the sky—*
> *Oh! why did you leave us, Owen? Why did you die?*

The guiding words of the new journal were a call to action, but a clever call, saying much without saying anything that could get a poet strung from the gallows:

> *As your fears are false and hollow*
> *Slaves and dastards stand aside—*
> *Knaves and traitors, Faugh-a-Ballagh.*

That was it. *Faugh-a-Ballagh:* Clear the way! Meagher heard the ring of a bell. At night, he parked himself in the rear of Conciliation Hall, a chamber of Irish discontent under high ceilings along the quay. This was home to the oratorical music of Gaelic nationalism. Here Meagher saw the poet Davis speak, his words no less lofty in person than they were on paper. Here he heard people question the Liberator, or at least the timidity of his followers. O'Connell had been released after less than a year of incarceration. The great man returned home to Merrion Square, his health ruined by the cold months in a cell. He was nearing seventy and out of ideas. Yet he insisted on controlling the forces calling for freedom, with his sons doing much of the speaking for him, while insulting the new voices—heralded now as the Young Ireland movement.

And here in Conciliation Hall, Meagher was witness to the jaw-dropping transformation of William Smith O'Brien at a midnight gathering. This well-manicured, flawlessly tailored man on the cusp of middle age was the unlikeliest of rebels: born into a baronial estate in Limerick, a Protestant who claimed direct lineage to the tenth-century high king Brian Boru. He looked every bit the part of the castle-owning gentleman, Church of England parishioner and member of Parliament that he was—a Tory as well, with a brother who'd been knighted. Tall, his voice bearing the accent of privilege, he rose now to stand with Young Ireland—a stunning betrayal.

"I have come here to tell the attorney general that, though I am not ambitious of martyrdom, if he wants another victim, I present myself to him." Meagher leapt to his feet. *Hear, hear, Smith O'Brien!* "Why are we forbidden the name and rights of a nation? The Englishman is proud of his country. The Scotchman is proud of his country. The Frenchman thinks there is no country in the world like his own . . . Shall Ireland be the only country in which nationality is forbidden?"

After the speech, Meagher introduced himself to Smith O'Brien, offering his services. *Anything, sir.* Smith O'Brien put him to work. Over the months, Meagher labored daily on repeal language for a parliamentary committee. Nights were spent back in Conciliation Hall. And in the margins, he wrote poetry and sent it off to Charles Gavan Duffy, a cofounder and the editor of the *Nation,* a man more level-headed than his writers, perfect ballast for unrefined voices such as Meagher's.

"He was at that time a youth of two-and-twenty, who had scarcely heard his own voice except in a college debating society," Duffy recalled of Meagher. "But there was a mesmerism in his language which touched me. I speedily made his acquaintance, and soon had the happiness of counting him among my friends." What he liked in young Meagher was what others found appealing: his humor, his loyalty, the blaze of passion in his eyes, his unparalleled gift of gab.

Among those who were also stirred by the fresh winds of the *Nation* was a mystery poet whose cover letters were signed in the name of a gentleman of Dublin. Duffy set out to meet this man of great promise, showing up one day in the parlor of the verse maker. To the editor's shock, there was no man but a tall young woman with dark hair, "flashing brown eyes and features cast in an heroic mold." Duffy had never seen a more beautiful face of sedition. She introduced herself as

Miss Jane Francesca Elgee, as much an establishment pillar as Smith O'Brien. Daughter of a Protestant, from a family of starchy loyalists, Jane had cast off her past and reinvented herself as a distant descendant of Dante. A silly conceit to some; a conscience in full flower to others. She was now an aspiring rebel, signing her poetry as Speranza, an Italian name for hope. "All the literature of Irish wrongs and sufferings had an enthralling interest for me," she said. "Then it was I discovered I could write poetry."

Jane was drawn to Dublin's sexually liberated crowd, those who rejected the teachings of the Catholic Church and the manners of the Victorian state, and took their opinions from the *Nation*. The talk was wild and promiscuous. Drink flowed, but a stronger intoxicant was a shared sense of invulnerability. Jane boasted that the best political voices of her land were rhymers, a trade-in-words that would have meant banishment centuries earlier. "They are all poets," she said of Young Ireland, "and I know of no genius outside their circle in Ireland." Her family was appalled that she would write for "a seditious paper fit only for the fire," as an uncle of hers had put it. She wore their disapproval like a black corsage at a ball. In her hands, rebellion was ambrosial. Personal notes were scented and sealed with bright red wax, to keep the allure alive when she was not present. Soon, Speranza was one of the *Nation*'s stars — "a substantial force in Irish politics," as the editor Duffy called her, "the vehement will of a woman of genius."

When the poetess saw Thomas Meagher for the first time, she swooned. His voice, his wit, the way he carried himself for one so young. Thomas was Jane's age, and shared with her an eloquent rage. "He was handsome, daring, reckless of consequences," she wrote a friend, "with wild, bright, flashing eyes, glowing colour and the most beautiful mouth, teeth and smile I ever beheld."

Summers were the "meal months" in Ireland, more than sixteen hours of daylight, when the nation grew enough to feed itself but also had to purchase food while awaiting the harvest. The potato was the easiest crop to cultivate. The New World import required so little care that merchant seamen put seed tubers in the ground in the spring and came back after months of absence to reap their bounty. But more than two million people — about a fourth of the population — did not earn regular wages, getting by on what they could scrounge from their patch of dirt, with a little bartering and piecework on the side. It was subsistence life, not unlike an Alaska native who feeds his family with what comes from the sea. And the rural Irish more than got by: a family derived most of its nutrition from potatoes. Many varieties were tried—*rocks, cups, codders, thistlewhippers, skerry blues*. The most popular were *lumpers*, large and knobby, with pale brown skin and yellow flesh, not particularly tasty; they looked like unevenly shaped stones. Living in tiny huts on rented acreage, a family could get ten months of food out of their potato patch, with some left for the pig. Meat and bread were rare. Meals were simple: a pot of boiled spuds, lathered in butter if lucky, a little bacon fat, with mustard at the center of the table, cabbage as well, pickled for preservation or fresh. At this setting, an adult could consume more than a day's worth of carbohydrates, potassium, Vitamin C and fiber.

June of 1845 broke hot and dry, the most incongruous kind of Irish weather. In peasant plots, even in bogs and on mountain slopes, green shoots sprouted quickly and flowered—the gorgeous lilac-and-gold heralding of a healthy potato crop, beauty and food. July turned gray, the woolen coat of a heavy fog lying over the land. August was unusually rainy, as it was throughout much of Europe, and cold as well. Not ideal potato weather, but nothing people hadn't seen before. Lumpers didn't need much, even in weak soil. But in September, taking a carriage ride through the wet country on the way home to Waterford, Meagher saw something quite frightening in the land that rolled away to the horizon: potato fields, black-topped and broken. He was startled. It was not just a patch of coal-dark foliage here and there, but ruin and spoilage everywhere, as if someone had come through and sprayed acid over the green of Ireland's living pantry. And the stench—it was foul and stomach-turning.

This blight had first appeared on the Isle of Wight; the news was then forwarded to Prime Minister Peel. Spores from diseased potatoes had come across the Atlantic from the United States, most likely in the holds of trading ships. A fungus later diagnosed as *Phytophthora infestans*, it spread quickly, needing only water to thrive. The tragic turnover of millions of acres, from life-supporting earth to a garden cemetery, happened without warning, a swift pox on the land. Some blamed static electricity from trains, newly introduced to the countryside, though the blight spread far beyond the rail tracks. One day fields were upright and promising; a week or so later the crop collapsed in a fetid heap. A single plant could release millions of deathly spores. Below ground held the true horror: dark, moldy, stinky masses of inedible tubers. Even potatoes that looked healthy at harvest turned to gray mush that fall, touched by the hand of the blight.

In short order, Ireland was the focus of one of the world's great agricultural mysteries: what was this crop-killing fungus, and why had it spread so quickly? And then, more urgently: what could be done to keep the population from starving? The *Gardeners' Chronicle* was one of the first publications to raise an alarm. "The crops about Dublin are suddenly perishing," a government botanist announced in London, holding up the journal. He then asked a question of fatal consequences: "Where will Ireland be in the event of a universal potato rot?" Two months later, a delegation of government experts who had toured the fields came back with an answer. "We can come to no other conclusion than that one half of the actual potato crop of Ireland is either destroyed or . . . unfit for the food of man." One half. Which meant, by a rough calculation, at least 500,000 Irish could starve.

Stories came in from Munster and Moneygall, from Cork and Connaught. All anecdotal, but all with the same grim conclusion: the sole source of food for thousands of Her Majesty's Irish subjects had collapsed. "I cannot recollect any former example of a calamitous failure being anything near so great and alarming as the present," wrote an Anglo-Irish landlord, Lord Mounteagle. "I know not how the peasantry will get through the winter."

An American visitor, the former slave Frederick Douglass, toured Ireland in the fall on a speaking tour, just as people were beginning to starve. Elegant in his tailored suits, quoting Dickens and Shakespeare, Douglass drew enormous crowds. "I find myself not treated as a color, but as a man—not as a thing, but as a child of the common Father of us all," he wrote. But he was not prepared for the misery of hungry Irish peasants, living "in much the same degradation as the American slave." He saw families in windowless mud hovels, ragged-dressed, listless on straw beds, gaunt from malnutrition. It was shocking.

Prime Minister Peel dismissed the early reports from Ireland. In his younger days, he'd been one of the Crown's overlords in the country, and liked to think he knew the people all too well—"cordially detested" them, he once said. The Irish: *good God*, everyone knows they're prone to high drama. "There is such a tendency to exaggeration and inaccuracy in Irish reports that delay in acting on them is always desirable," he wrote in October of 1845. Still, the English government took some precautions against a revolt of the hungry: boats laden with grain grown on Irish soil now left port under armed escort. When Thomas Meagher saw this curious sight in Waterford, he knew the struggle ahead was about much more than the science of potato blight.

At the very time the spores of starvation were blowing over a year's worth of Ireland's food, dark news hit Dublin. In a stroll through town, Meagher came upon a mournful crowd outside the offices of the *Nation*. People were howling, teary, others walking around dumbstruck. "Thomas Davis is dead!" The bard of Young Ireland was thirty years old, preparing to be married. The poet took ill one day after guiding the latest issue of his paper to bed, and retired to his mother's house. His temperature shot up. He shivered and sweated. His throat turned red and sore, and a hideous rash appeared over his back. It was nothing, he told the editor Charles Duffy, a minor bit of cholera. He was gone within a week, a victim of scarlet fever. His last day was September 16, 1845.

The brow of Ireland turned gray overnight, it was said. Mourners packed into Conciliation Hall. Irish soil, wrote the *Nation*, would hold no more precious dust than his. Meagher was beside himself. Davis had written more than eighty ballads, poems and songs. His essays numbered in the hundreds. Meagher called him "my prophet and guide." Without Davis, he was lost. Sharing his thoughts at a memorial, Meagher touched others who felt as he did. They urged him to take the stage. Without introduction, Meagher walked solemnly from his usual back bench to the front of the hall and gave his first speech in the most prominent venue for Irish ideas. His words were not polished or planned.

"He is no more. He is not here. His meteoric genius has ceased to be, his noble heart to beat. But there are thoughts of his, generous sentiments, liberal views, enlightened principles of his, which death could not strike down. These shall dwell among us."

Over the next year, the death of one voice gave way to the other. Through the spring and into the summer of 1846, Meagher crafted a rallying cry, picking up where the poet had left off. He could sound naïve or too indignant. He still had that trace of Stonyhurst when he spoke formally. But he was devoid of cynicism. "Let earnest truth, stern fidelity to principle, love for all who bear the name of an Irishman sustain, ennoble and immortalize this cause," he said. "Thus shall we reverse the dark fortunes of the Irish race and call forth here a new nation from the ruins of the old." Quickly, Meagher picked up a following. "As handsome and chivalrous as he was eloquent, he became something of a popular idol," wrote Arthur Griffith, a later fan. When word of a coming oration was announced, Conciliation Hall was packed. And his speeches were printed, sometimes word for word, in the *Nation*.

"It was like listening to mystical, sonorous music to hear Meagher pour out passion and pathos and humour," wrote Duffy, whose red pen had snuffed many a fulsome line. This man of "rare and splendid gifts" did not look the part of voice of a nation. He couldn't shake his youth, the dew still on the boy; but he spoke like someone who had seen much more than his actual years. "To the common eye, indeed, the new recruit was a dandified youngster, with a languid air and mincing accent obviously derived from an English education; but it was a vulgar error," said Duffy. "Nature had made him a great orator, and training had made him an accomplished gentleman."

A gentleman, also, who kept his barbs within the constricted bounds of allowed public discourse. "I am not one who wantonly would run down the English name," Meagher said in 1846. "I have learned to respect that country for many fine virtues, for many great deeds. With just a few exceptions, her conduct toward other countries has always been just, generous and magnanimous." But why, he wondered aloud, did those virtues stop at the Irish Sea? "Toward Ireland, her conduct has been mean, unjust, contemptuous."

The Young Tribune, the Dublin crowd started calling him—and not always in praise. O'Connell's men laughed at Meagher for his age, his face unlined and unlived in. Who was this beardless lad from Waterford? And by what authority did he challenge the Liberator's gradual progress toward repeal of the act that bound Ireland to England? On what authority did this upstart speak for anyone? No authority. Meagher had been elected to nothing. Only one of his poems had been printed in the *Nation*. All his power came from the spoken word. In Conciliation Hall, Meagher asked for some reprieve for his age. "Youth is a season of promise more than retrospect."

O'Connell took him aside, urging him to come over to the house for a private talk. In his library at the Merrion Square home, he slapped a big arm around Meagher.

"Surely, your father is not a Young Irelander?"

"No, he is not," Meagher answered. "But at least he is for repeal."

"Why not walk in his footsteps?"

"For the plain reason that I have a head and legs of my own."

Abruptly showing Meagher the door, the Liberator said, "Beware the danger that Young Irelandism will lead you to."

"It may lead me to danger. But it will guard me from dishonor."

What motivated Meagher, the fount of his fury, was the fast-developing famine; it epitomized all the wrongs of Ireland. Through the winter of 1846 and into the spring, hundreds, then thousands of people dropped dead of starvation. Bellies of little children swelled, their faces went powdery, their hair fell by the handful, and they sniffled away to a corner of a hut or a roadside ditch, their parents soon to follow. Others were sickened by scurvy, their gums swollen and bleeding, skin blue-splotched. They had subsisted, for a time, on nettles, blackberries and raw cabbage, none of which could be foraged during the cold months. A doctor in Skibbereen found seven people under a single blanket, unable to move; one had been dead for hours. Coffins were reused after hasty ceremonies, the bottoms cut out, the deceased dropped into the ground.

"I saw wretched people seated on the fences of their decaying gardens, wringing their hands and wailing bitterly at the destruction that had left them foodless," wrote Father Theobald Mathew in a letter to British high authorities. Mathew was no mere observer; he was the "temperance priest," the best-known cleric in Ireland, who had prompted more than a million people to pledge to abstain from alcohol. But for all that drink had done to his countrymen, he said, it was no match for the indiscriminate sweep of hunger. An English traveler, James H. Juke, was aghast that a day's sail could take him from a well-fed nation to an island of the wretched and dying. He saw Irish trying to exist on sand eels, turnip tops and seaweed—"a diet which no one in England would consider fit for the meanest animal which he kept."

The potato blight had not spared England, nor Holland, parts of France and Germany. Their crops also failed. But only in Ireland were people dying en masse. The cause had been planted in the land—not the potato, but English rule that had driven a majority of Irish from ground their ancestors had owned. "The terrifying exactitude of memory," in Tocqueville's phrase. Famines had come before, epochs of hunger that killed upwards of 70,000 in the worst case. But this starvation reached across the island—it was now the Great Hunger, *an Gorta Mór*, with a fatal toll ten times that of the Great Plague of London in 1665.

And here was the tragedy: there was plenty of food in Ireland while the people starved. Irish rains produced a prodigious amount of Irish grains. Almost three fourths of the country's cultivable land was in corn, wheat, oats and barley. The food came from Irish land and Irish labor. But it didn't go into Irish mouths. About 1.5 billion pounds of grain and other foodstuffs were exported. The natives were hired hands and witnesses to these money crops, grown by Anglo landlords. Same with cattle, sheep and hogs raised within eyesight of the hollow-bellied. Famine-ravaged Ireland exported more beef than any other part of the British Empire.

Meagher and his allies tried to comprehend this incongruity while moving to the larger questions. If English rule was to blame for death by hunger—a preposterous idea in Westminster—could English rule now keep people alive? What responsibility did one of the most advanced nations on earth have for a sibling ravaged by a primitive scourge?

The new growing season, spring of 1846, was a chance to start clean with a crop that had not been contaminated. Potato shoots came up strong, unblemished, and with that, an indulgence of hope: perhaps the killer had run its course. But by midsummer the blight reappeared, arriving without portent as it had the year before. Hungry people clawed at the ground, digging for small, half-formed, blackish tubers—an effort to salvage something. In 1845, the blight had destroyed nearly half of all the potatoes grown in Ireland, just as the government panel had predicted. But 1846 was worse: nearly all of Ireland's potatoes were ruined. And yet, in that year the nation grew more food than all the people of Ireland could have consumed, most of it bound for export. The harvest in corn, wheat and barley was said to be the biggest ever.

To the leaders of Young Ireland, the solution was obvious: shut down the ports and feed Irish-grown food to the dying. In speeches, Meagher read a list of the tonnage of cereals and grains, beef and pork

sailing out of Ireland daily—one column of export numbers, followed
by a column of death tallies taken from those same harbors. "Close the
ports!" he cried. Verse in the *Nation* demanded the same thing:

> *Not a grain should leave our shore, not for England's*
> *golden store;*
> *They who hunger where it grew, they whom Heaven*
> *has sent it to,*
> *They who reared with sweat of brow—they, or none, should*
> *have it now.*

Without slop to feed the pigs, which meant money to pay the landlord, the rural Irish had nothing at summer's end, when the rent was
due. Now they were thrown off the land—mass evictions to go with
mass hunger. Potato patches were never worth much to landlords as
it was; here was a chance to clear the estate of tired tenants and crops
that didn't pay. "What the devil do we care about your black potatoes,"
a landlord shouted to one family, as reported in a Dublin paper. "It was
not us that made them black. You will get two days to pay the rent, and
if you don't, you know the consequences."

If a family refused to leave, as many thousands did, their home was
torn down by the authorities. The battering ram in full swing—a thick
piece of timber thrust back and forth from a tri-pole frame—was the
last image that many poor Irish saw of their cottages. British troops assisted British-trained police in home-dismantling missions, and their
work was swift: a single crew sometimes destroying twenty or more
thatch-roofed huts in a half day's time. In the villages that Meagher
visited that year, he followed the sound of commotion and crying, witness to the same scene numerous times: soldiers with loaded muskets
enforcing an eviction, the roof yanked or torched, walls pulled to the
ground with a horse-drawn heave.

"A savagery unmatched by Cromwell," he called it. Then, out, out,
out—to the elements. "They sleep in their rags and have pawned their
bedding," a police inspector wrote.

A poem in the *Nation*, by Speranza, spoke of increased desperation:

> *There is woe, there is clamour, in our desolated land,*
> *And wailing lamentation from a famine-stricken band;*

"The Ejectment," from the Illustrated London News, *shows a family being evicted from their home in 1848, at the height of the famine. As with thousands of similar evictions, the roof was torn down and the dwelling destroyed. More than a million Irish died during the Great Hunger.* COURTESY OF IRELAND'S GREAT HUNGER MUSEUM, QUINNIPIAC UNIVERSITY, HAMDEN, CT

> *And weeping are the multitudes in sorrow and despair,*
> *For the green fields of Munster are lying desolate and bare.*

Europe had not seen a famine on this scale since the Dark Ages. William Smith O'Brien, the Irish aristocrat who had joined with the younger voices, took up the call in Parliament, where he had a seat in the Commons. Furious, he ripped into the Empire, jabbing at the complacency of fellow members. This was a moral crisis, not a food crisis. One half of the United Kingdom of England and Ireland was falling apart, and what did the other half do but sit and watch—bystanders to a mortal disaster. If a foreign army had landed on shores under the Union Jack and moved to wipe out entire cities, would not the British throw off the invader? As a country, Ireland could not do anything about the famine, for it had no government of its own. The Irish were dependent on the will and whim of England. The Crown had to do *something*. In protest, Smith O'Brien refused to attend any official business until Parliament acted. For his defiance, he was arrested and confined to a cell for three weeks. Meagher visited him in London. He was moved by the sight of the older, gentleman rebel giving up his freedom to jab the conscience of England. Meagher and Smith O'Brien, joined by the *Nation,* spoke as one: Shut the ports. Pay the exporters to redirect their goods to the people, if you must, but keep the food in Ireland. At the least, send relief, immediately.

There was the rub—interference. The British ruling class was in thrall to the idea of unfettered free markets. The term *laissez faire* was not just a fancy import but a governing principle. To interfere would be to upset the natural economic order. The market, in time, would make all things well. The Americans sent corn, flour, clothing, from Jewish synagogues, from Quaker churches, from Catholic parishes in Boston, New York and Philadelphia. The Choctaw Nation was particularly generous. The Indians were sympathetic, they said, because of the hunger they had endured during their Trail of Tears march out of their homeland nearly twenty years earlier. In England there was considerable debate over whether to even allow these food ships into Irish ports. What would that mean to the free market? To the price of grain grown by English farmers?

The task of doing something about Irish starvation fell to Charles Trevelyan, an inflexible nobleman from one of England's oldest families. He was thirty-eight when given the job. Facing a torrent of criticism from the United States and Europe, the English agreed to let the relief ships dock in Ireland, and to supplement them with Indian corn purchased by the government. But this food would not simply be handed out. You couldn't just give it away. No, no, no—the Irish must pay for it, so as not to upset the hand of private enterprise. Much of it would be stored, under guard, at major cities and distributed only after it had been purchased. Some would be distributed at segregated workhouses, where a man had to move stones all day, and a woman knit till her fingers bled, in order to get a portion of stirabout, a poor substitute for oatmeal. Of course, if the Irish wanted to raise money through local taxation and buy the relief food for themselves—splendid! The magic of the market would remain undisturbed.

"It forms no part of the functions of government to provide supplies of food," Trevelyan said in 1846. And to his subordinates in Ireland he delivered a stern message: "Do not encourage the idea of prohibiting exports ... Perfect free trade is the right course." His biggest fear was not that a quarter million of Her Majesty's subjects would die on his watch, but social change: "Dependence on charity is not to be made an agreeable mode of life."

Not to worry. The donor corn was too hard for the stomachs of the hungry. It was indigestible, causing cramps and violent diarrhea. And, little surprise, those at death's door had no money. Relief was a failure, just as Trevelyan predicted. The starving wanted to be fed without paying for it, which he would never allow. Trevelyan shut down the food depots. "The only way to prevent the people from becoming habitually dependent is to bring the relief operations to a close," he said. He was cheered by many in the English press. The Irish were cunning dogs who would no doubt have traded donor bread for pistols. And, surely, famine reports were exaggerated. "Is it possible," wrote the *Times* of London, "to have heard the tale of sorrow too often?" Indeed, the men who herded contemporary thought for the most influential British minds believed so.

In Cork, a riot broke out at a food warehouse. Troops fired into the crowd of emaciated Irish. Nearby, when the hungry tried to prevent a boat laden with oats from sailing out of the port of Youghal, soldiers crushed them at the dock. Shots were sprayed into protesters in Waterford who had begged and then threatened merchants who exported grain. Two people were left for dead, twenty-seven wounded. Refugees poured into the cities, quivering beggars carrying all their possessions in a bundle, into more workhouses thrown together by the Crown. The young, their teeth stained green from chewing weeds, their skin dripping from bones, their feet hardened and bare and black, presented the most tragic sight. "No words can describe this peculiar appearance of the famished children," wrote Elihu Burritt in a letter to America in 1846. "Never have I seen such bright, blue clear eyes looking so steadfastly at nothing."

As the Great Hunger escalated, some of England's most educated thinkers provided an explanation that allowed them to sleep better at night. Perhaps the Irish deserved their fate, what with their large families and foolish farming of a single crop. Monoculture, the oafs—don't they know any better? What's more, the Irish national character was "defective," as Trevelyan himself confided to a fellow aristocrat. The Irish are a "selfish, perverse and turbulent people," said the man in charge of relieving their plight. Also, there was something to be said for this business of Malthusian thinning. It was nasty, the famine—no doubt. But all for the better in the long run: "an effective mechanism for reducing surplus population," said Trevelyan. Ireland had grown by 70 percent in a few decades. This excessive breeding was *unsustainable,* the girls *too bloody fertile.* The famine was a culling, nature at work. Through the summer of 1846, death tallies bore this out. Entire villages were disappearing. In Skibbereen, the most southerly town in Ireland, more than 50 percent of the children enrolled in a workhouse died within a few weeks of admission. At the edge of town, soil that once held potatoes was turned for mass graves.

Certainly, not all of Britain displayed a cold heart to the Irish. Quakers from London offered their services, and sent back withering critiques of their government. Residents of County Donegal "were scarcely able to crawl," wrote a Quaker minister, William Forster. Starvation, he noted, had disfigured the children, leaving them with faces of old people. In Galway these British clerics found "walking skeletons, the men stamped with the livid mark of hunger, the children crying with pain, the women too weak to stand." And at higher levels, Sir Randolph Routh, chairman of the Relief Commission, repeatedly took issue with Trevelyan. He blamed English landlords, not the character flaws of Irish peasants.

In public, Trevelyan was sympathetic to the most awful sorrow ever to sweep over Ireland. In private, as the famine dragged on, he saw something larger at work—divine design. The Great Hunger, he wrote to a concerned landlord, could very well be "the judgement of God," the Almighty's answer to overpopulation. How so? And what kind of God was this? "Being altogether beyond the power of man, the cure has been applied by the direct stroke of an all-wise Providence."

The cure.

In Conciliation Hall, hatred of the English hardened. And no one in Dublin nurtured this loathing more than John Mitchel. The son of a minister from the north, Mitchel married his girlfriend Jenny when she was sixteen, then moved to Dublin to practice law. The life of a barrister bored him. He craved conflict, and the best way to get it was to spit in the eye of the British lion. Mitchel was an unabashed nationalist; he couldn't give a damn for religion, holy poetry or mythic Celts. Nor did his sympathies for the downtrodden extend beyond Irish shores. His every breath was suffused with hatred of England. The *Nation* had published a string of Mitchel's strongest rants. So when Thomas Davis died, Duffy approached the fire-breathing lawyer about becoming an editor. Mitchel agreed. Writing from the influential perch of his new forum, his pen was unbound, laced with bite and sarcasm. "My dear surplus brethren," he began one open letter to his fellow Irish. "The Almighty, indeed, sent the potato blight, but the English created the famine," he wrote in another essay. He called England "a ferocious monster" and "the most base and hostile tyranny that has ever scandalized the face of the earth."

When the new editor met Thomas Meagher, he wasn't impressed. Meagher was just a boy in nobleman's clothes, and "rather foppish" at that. Mitchel had soon gained stature for his essays, and had about him the air of a man who knew he was good. He had no time for taking on someone who might need training wheels, despite his following. Meagher showed up at the *Nation*'s office in Dublin, blabbering a blue streak to Mitchel, a blunt assault of his personality. *The famine! And this bastard Trevelyan!* Tangled up in talk, the pair walked out of the building on D'Olier Street, away from the river, through College Green, Grafton Street, beyond the city, toward Donnybrook, to the country, drawing out most of a day. As it turned out, Meagher and Mitchel shared a similar metabolism and a passion for political vandalism. One could speak, the other could write. A cynic with a dour view

Thomas Meagher, in a sketch done when he was a leader of the Young Ireland uprising. Barely out of school, Meagher found his voice and helped stir a starving nation. He was known as the Young Tribune. COURTESY OF THE ALLPORT LIBRARY AND MUSEUM OF FINE ARTS, TASMANIAN ARCHIVE AND HERITAGE OFFICE

of humanity, Mitchel was yet moved by Meagher's high-flown spirit. Perhaps he was the only man in Dublin who could draw out something other than Mitchel's dark side.

"What talk!" Mitchel recalled. "What eloquence of talk was his! How fresh and clear and strong! What wealth of imagination and princely generosity of feeling! To me it was the revelation of a new and great nature, and I reveled in it." Over several months, the friendship deepened. When Meagher staked out a risky position at Conciliation Hall, the editor had his back.

And the Young Tribune certainly needed it. Into the summer, with the death of a nation under way for all to see, Meagher sharpened his attacks on the inaction of O'Connell's organization. This was no time for taking time. That year, 1846, the Tory government of Robert Peel fell in England, giving way to a possible Whig coalition led by the diminutive Lord John Russell. The Liberator wanted to align his members with a new Russell coalition — they'd surely be more likely to help the starving, open to some sort of Irish independence, he reasoned. O'Connell was delusional, but no one in power would say so. He went so far as to back a Whig candidate in Ireland over his own party built around repeal of the Act of Union. This infuriated Meagher. An alliance with the Whigs would only swap one form of "vassalage" for another, he said. It was a sellout.

Sketched from life and drawn on stone by John Joseph Egan.

Thomas F. Meagher

"Abhor the sword and stigmatize the sword?
No, my Lord, for at its blow a giant nation
Sprang up from the waters of the far
Atlantic, and by its redeeming magic the
Tattered colony became a shining free republic."—

*The Meagher speech in condemnation
of the use of the sword in July 1846*

Another sketch, drawn about the same time by John Joseph Egan. Lines from Meagher's famous Conciliation Hall speech were printed below. COURTESY OF THE LIBRARY OF CONGRESS, LC-USZ62-97750

"Go into the churchyard," Meagher thundered, "write *Fool* upon every tombstone that commemorates a Volunteer, and thank your God that you live in an age of common sense, with philosophy and starvation."

Meagher's instincts were correct. Not long after Russell became prime minister with O'Connell's help, he arranged to have the editor Duffy arrested. And he made it clear the Irish would get no further food relief unless they paid for it. Change of government, but no change of heart. Trevelyan's philosophy still ruled. If anything, the new British authorities made life even more painful, passing a law that forbade a head of household from getting food relief if he held a quarter acre or more and had refused to give it up to the landlord. This swelled the ranks of the dispossessed, the homeless, the hungry. Duffy's troublesome journal, the *Nation*, was preaching social disorder, stirring the starving, in the new prime minister's view. At the same time, Russell also fortified the Irish garrisons. This, then, was the latest British response to Ireland's national tragedy: let food flow freely out of the country, arrest and jail those who spoke for the famished, make it more difficult for peasants to stay on the land, and restock the army barricades—bullets over bread. Smith O'Brien, the statesman and member of Parliament, was no more a criminal than the erudite editor Charles Duffy. They were both manacled for free speech. O'Connell made excuses for the Whigs. Meagher, alone among the leaders not yet thrown in jail, seemed capable of stating the case clearly. His was "the language of popular passion," said Duffy.

Young Ireland was with the boy from Waterford. His cause, he said, was carried by a fierce urgency. No person of conscience could sit by, could wait out another election hoping for good will from London, as people fell to their deaths by the thousands. To counter Meagher's insurgency within, O'Connell set a trap. At the next formal meeting of his Repeal association, he would propose a vote. Either you sided with the Liberator or followed the "clap traps of juvenile orators." His loyalty test came in the form of a resolution: whether to denounce any use of force against England. The stage was set. A vote was called: everyone on record.

On July 28, 1846, Conciliation Hall was packed, almost as many women as men. Lines formed outside the doors. The poet known as Speranza, Jane Francesca Elgee, took a seat up front and met Meagher's eyes—prompting a whippet of whispered gossip. O'Connell stayed away, sending his two sons, and some muscle as well. Gathered in this assembly were the lucky few of Ireland. They had food, money, an education, while their starving fellow citizens scavenged the streets, looking for scraps. The winds of summer carried the deadly potato spores to all parts of the island, even the prosperous north. There, loyalty to the Crown could not buy immunity from the blight. Meagher, just a few years out of college, was preparing to take on the titan of nineteenth-century Ireland, a man he'd been "trained to love," as Duffy said, for his entire life. Indeed, Meagher had worshiped the Liberator.

The O'Connell proposal, called a peace resolution, was put to the floor. Meagher had thought about his heroes in the United States, a nation barely fifty years old, thought about the philosopher Thomas Jefferson but also the warrior George Washington. That new country was not formed by words alone. Much blood had been shed. When Meagher rose to state the case for struggle with arms, he was met with catcalls and hisses from the old guard.

"Let him speak!"

Meagher turned to face the O'Connell family, with praise for the Liberator.

"I am not ungrateful to the man who struck the fetters from my arms, whilst I was yet a child; and by whose influence my father—the first Catholic who did so for two hundred years—sat for the last two years in the civic chair of an ancient city."

With warm words for the old patriarch of Ireland, Meagher softened some of those with knives in the crowd. It was temporary, a rhetorical tactic.

"But the same God who gave to that great man the power to strike down an odious ascendancy in this country, and enabled him to institute in this land the glorious law of religious equality—that same God gave to me a mind that is my own—"

Here the crowd seemed to come Meagher's way, ripples of approval and support.

"—a mind that has not been mortgaged to the opinions of any man or any set of men. A mind that I was to use and not surrender."

Applause, much more than a smattering, followed. Meagher reminded everyone of his movement's motto: Ireland for the Irish. Now to the big question: would the people in this room remain passive, or stand and fight for their starving brothers and sisters?

"The man who will listen to reason, let him be reasoned with. But it is the weaponed arm of the patriot that can alone prevail against battalioned despotism. Then, my lord, I do not condemn the use of arms as immoral." He went through countless examples of history, the pivot points where mortal risks had to be taken. He reached now for his best example of this, the American Revolution.

"Abhor the sword? Stigmatize the sword? No, my lord, for at its blow a giant nation started from the waters of the Atlantic, and by its redeeming magic, and in the quivering of its crimson light, the crippled colony sprang into the attitude of a proud republic—prosperous, limitless and invincible!"

The crowd was on its feet. Meagher had clearly won the day—"it was thrilling music," in Duffy's words, for someone to finally shake the Irish from a national coma. Jane was mesmerized; writing as Speranza she penned the rough outline of a poem: "In his beauty and his youth, the Apostle of the truth ..." Another witness called it "perhaps the greatest speech" ever delivered in Conciliation Hall.

O'Connell's men moved to cut the boy off. Meagher, in his defiance, had just divorced himself from the Repeal organization. He would not be allowed to continue. Tempers flared, punches flew. Meagher walked out, joined by the member of Parliament Smith O'Brien, by the writer Mitchel, the editor Duffy, the poet Speranza and many others. They would never return. O'Connell's day was done, his organization broken. The zest to fight followed Meagher out the door. Everything still inside the hall was yesterday. To save Ireland in its darkest hour would now fall to a handful of young men and women who knew more about sonnets than sidearms, who thought a few well-chosen words and a charge of peasants with farm tools could blunt an empire.

4

PITCHFORK PADDIES

Winter was severe. Between slashing rains, snow swiped at the bare side of Ireland, five months of ashen chill. Peat smoke drifted from thatched hovels holding families bundled in nothing but the vaporous heat of their bodies. Big white whooper swans pecked for grass in the Shannon River marshlands, the flash of their yellow beaks one of the few signs of normalcy in a year of the walking dead. Nature was not out of whack: there was no drought, nor shortage of fish and birds. The human ecology was sick, a still life of starvation. In damp corners of workhouses, bony clumps shivered—the Scarecrow Irish, they were called. These dormitories for hunger exiles were supposed to be places of relief and rebound. But they charged for bread, charged for tea, charged for a bunk. All to be paid for by digging roads that no one would travel on and ditches that would never drain a field. In 1847, the workhouse was home to almost three quarters of a million people. Families were separated, children from parents, wives from husbands. The poor were required to wear a uniform, not unlike the clothes of a convict. Those who left without paying for their government outfits could be jailed for stealing. Those who couldn't keep up the staged labor were listed as debtors. Thus the workhouse produced a reliable result: you went in a man, it was said, and came out a pauper. The British relief system was tidy, the simple life summaries of the starving noted on handwritten single lines that filled pages bound in leather and constantly updated. Name. Age. Address. Condition. The latter had three general categories: helpless poor, able-bodied poor, dead.

In the spring of 1847, the English opted for a new approach: soup kitchens. These had been tried, in a different form, by Protestant Bible societies. They were schools for famished Irish children, who were fed on the condition that they accept the proselytizing of a hated religion—forcing parents to choose between starvation and giving up their faith. People who consented were derided as "soupers," or those who "took the soup." The Crown now offered a secular alternative. To supplement the workhouses, they would open communal food stations, clean and modern. A prominent French chef, Alexis Soyer, was named Head Cook to the people of Ireland. He devised a formula to feed a hundred people a day for less than a pound sterling. And no, it wouldn't be gruel for the dying, but a fine soup, very tasty, one that he'd served to noblemen and members of Parliament. Each person would be allowed up to a quart of the Frenchman's broth a day. For that portion, the recipe called for one half ounce of meat, a quarter ounce of dripping fat, one ounce of flour, a snippet of brown sugar, and turnip shavings, onions and celery tops.

To great fanfare, the first of Monsieur Soyer's kitchens opened in Dublin on April 5, under a portrait of Queen Victoria, the Union Jack flying next to a chimney. The well dressed and well fed paid a few shillings in donations to watch the poor sip their soup, as a sketch in the *Illustrated London News* showed. A line formed outside. Inside was a 300-gallon boiler, with ladles attached to a chain. At the ring of a bell, the starving shuffled to group tables, there to consume their ration with their own bowls brought to the soup kitchen. The bell rang again after six minutes, time up. The press was encouraged to report on this development—dispensaries of flavored hot water, presented to the world as evidence of England's benevolence. But within weeks it was clear that an all-liquid diet, while keeping some people alive, made matters worse for many others. When experts at the *Lancet,* the British medical journal, examined the contents of Soyer's broth, they were appalled. They found a typical portion to be far below minimum daily requirements for calories and nutrition, a thin substitute for genuine relief. They called it "soup quackery."

Just as Meagher feared, the new government was a disaster for Ireland. The Whigs that O'Connell had joined forces with did less for the people than the Tory administration had done. Prime Minister Russell, mocked as a midget in physical stature—he stood five foot four by the most charitable sizing—was no giant in the political realm either. To cover his right flank, he pushed ever harsher against the Irish, sending extra troops to assist in the increasingly hostile evictions of peasants from their ramshackle homes. He announced that food would continue to flow freely out of Irish ports—hands off, no interference with free trade. *Laissez faire,* following Trevelyan's advice, would continue to guide British policy. For those still with illusions, Russell made it clear several months into his leadership what to expect. "It must be thoroughly understood," he said, "that we cannot feed the people." And by summer's end of 1847, he made good on that declarative: the soup kitchens were closed, a failure even at saving face for England. What's more, the government felt the Irish had been ungrateful through two years of the famine. "They have hardly been decent while they have had their bellies full of our corn and their pockets of our money," said Charles Wood, the chancellor of the exchequer.

The public voice of the opposition now fell to young Meagher. His writer friend John Mitchel matched him, with less eloquence and more bitterness, in the *Nation*. Duffy was out of a prison. He'd soon be back in, held for publishing Mitchel's prose. And the middle-aged gentleman Smith O'Brien took the cause anew to the heart of Parliament. Meagher's "Sword" speech was a turning point. It made him famous; copies were printed and consumed in the cities, passed on and memorized in the country, studied for clues inside Dublin Castle. The political lethargy of Ireland was gone, replaced by a desperate urgency. Meagher had not called for armed uprising, nor violence in blocking the food ships from leaving Irish ports. His message was in the abstract—a philosophical *what if?* Those who were not hungry, who had standing and the promise of a good life like Meagher, were now bound by conscience to take a great risk. Otherwise they should be counted among "the genteel nobodies, nervous aristocrats, friends of order and starvation, of speedy hangings," as Meagher framed the choice. The hard shove of his words worked. By year's end, it was clear, in meetings where the new Irish Confederation was formed to organize clubs against England, that the young, the connected, those who might otherwise govern an independent nation, were with Meagher's forces. Speranza wrote "The Young Patriot Leader," a poetic tribute that had been started earlier in Conciliation Hall. It was also a public love letter to the voice of the fledgling rebels. In part, it read:

Oh! He stands beneath the sun, that glorious Fated One . . .

In his beauty and his youth, the Apostle of the Truth,
  Goes he forth with the words of Salvation,
And a noble madness falls on each spirit he enthralls,
  As he chants his wild paeans to the nation . . .

See our pale cheeks how they flush, as the noble visions rush,
  On our soul's most dark desolation—
And the glorious lyric words, Right, Freedom, and our Swords!
  Wake the strong chords of life to vibration.

Ireland's lowest ebb brought the poets of protest closer to each other, even as Britain moved to scatter and isolate them. Under new Coercion Acts passed in Parliament, the authorities could declare early curfews and restrictions on movement. It was a crime on many a night for the Irish to be outside their homes between dusk and dawn. "Has it come to this, that a citizen of Dublin can't walk the streets of his native city?" asked a doctor who was stopped by police during an evening stroll. For others, defying the nighttime shackling made the heart skip. Young Ireland's leaders held secret dinners, breaking the law while breaking bread. They sang songs that had been outlawed during the Penal Era, kissed and drank and made eyes at each other—"much wooing and some marrying," in Duffy's recollection. Planning more than a few months ahead seemed an impossible eternity. The flushing of pale cheeks, the "noble madness" that Meagher had fired in Speranza, was expressed away from the pages of the *Nation* as well. Jane Elgee made clear in her letters that she was a woman who acted on her passions, while not naming her lovers. Her red-sealed and scented notes landed with regularity. "I don't care for a friendship unless it's fringed with— not quite love, perhaps—but something that is always on the point of becoming so," she said.

At home in Waterford, father and son fought. The elder Meagher was running for a seat in the House of Commons on O'Connell's ticket, allied with the British prime minister. Thomas loved his father, he told him, but he had to be true to his conscience: he could not vote for him, not as a partner of the English government. The patriarch warned his son that he was traveling with a dangerous crowd in Dublin, perilously close to becoming an outlaw. And to what end? Did he have any career ambitions? There was time, still, for a gentleman's life, the Waterford Club, formal dinners, family wealth, a proper young lady not given over to seditious verse, working steadily, evenly, lawfully, respectfully for change. This held no appeal for Tom. He could not look at a table set with the world's finest crystal without thinking of all the images he'd seen of the Scarecrow Irish. He felt a sense of duty that made for sleepless nights.

"The people will not consent to live another year in a graveyard!" he proclaimed upon returning to the public forum in Dublin. "Ireland will be burnt into one black, unpeopled field of ashes rather than this should last."

And, a few days later, he posed two questions: "Do you prefer a soup kitchen to a customs house? Do you prefer cemeteries to cornfields?" As a student of rhetoric in college, Meagher had learned a thing or two about poetic license. But if anything, he understated the calamity facing Ireland. William Bennett, a Quaker on one of the surveys of the sick and dying, sent this report back from County Mayo in 1847:

> My hand trembles while I write. The scenes of human misery and degradation we witnessed still haunt my imagination, with the vividness and power of some horrid and tyrannous delusion, rather than the feature of sober reality. We entered a cabin. Stretched in one dark corner, scarcely visible from the smoke and rags that covered them, were three children huddled together, lying there because they were too weak to rise, pale and ghastly; their little limbs, on removing a portion of the filthy covering, perfectly emaciated, eyes sunk, voice gone, and evidently in the last stage of actual starvation. Crouched over the turf embers was another form, wild and all but naked, scarcely human in appearance ... We entered upwards of fifty of these tenements. The scene was invariably the same.

Meagher played the prosecutor. To the charge that the famine was the fault of a "defective part of the national character," as Trevelyan and the British press had insisted in year two of the Great Hunger, Meagher again drew attention to how much food was still leaving a land of the starving. "England has bound this island hand and foot. The island is her slave. She robs the island of its food, for it has not the power to guard it. If the island does not break its fetters, England will write its epitaph. Listen to a few facts ..." He then cited an astonishing tonnage of beef, butter, pork, bacon and flour that had sailed out of Ireland. "Tell the minister, sir, that a new race of men now act in Ireland—men who will be neither starved as the victims nor serve as the vassals of the British Empire."

That minister, Lord Russell, was hearing the same thing from his chief overseer in Ireland, the Earl of Clarendon. "Distress, discontent and hatred of English rule are increasing everywhere," Clarendon wrote to London. Reports came in daily of people dying on city streets and country lanes, dropping at the doorsteps of workhouses. And now was news of another, more efficient killer of the Irish—typhus, the disease that found its home in filthy, crowded spaces. The hard winter drove more people to cluster for shelter and warmth; even jail was better than freezing to death. But the public places, holding people in dirty rags, were perfect incubators for a mortal disease conveyed by lice. The more the starving huddled for warmth, the likelier they would bring themselves to quick death. Typhus was a corporal torture of a week to ten days, disfiguring and befouling victims before it killed them. Cheeks swelled. Rashes and sores appeared all over the body. Limbs shook and twitched. Fingers and toes went black and gangrenous. The faces of handsome Irish children became heavy with age and ugliness, their eyes colorless. And just before dying, the sick emitted a distinct odor—the grim stench of typhus. As press accounts of this latest scourge spread, even residents of Calcutta now sent relief.

In the countryside, peasants shot their landlords with the weapons of their masters. Stolen guns were stockpiled, pikes sharpened and stashed. As defeated and weak as the people were, the Irish were showing signs of an uprising. Confederation clubs based on the principles of Young Ireland were formed around the country. For now, their meetings consisted of passing on stories of atrocities and singing underground songs, including one that alluded to a ban on wearing shamrocks by Irish soldiers in Great Britain's army—"They're hanging men and women for the wearin' of the green." They awaited further word on how to act.

From Dublin Castle, Clarendon recruited fresh informants. He needed to know all the plans of Young Ireland and would pay handsomely for inside information. At the same time, Clarendon fired off a series of remarkably candid assessments to Prime Minister Russell. "A great social revolution is now going on in Ireland, the accumulated evils

of misgovernment and mismanagement are now coming to a crisis."
As to the cause: "No one could venture to dispute the fact that Ireland
has been sacrificed" to British economic policy, he wrote. "No distress
would have occurred if the exportation of Irish grain had been prohibited." And there it was, official acknowledgment of the deep complicity
by England in one of the world's worst human atrocities.

So it was simple after all, just as Meagher had stated: the Great
Hunger was unfolding in the midst of great plenty. There would have
been no famine — "no distress," in Clarendon's words — if food produced
in Ireland had been kept in Ireland. This startling admission was contained in a private correspondence, not made public at the time. Out-
wardly, Clarendon stiffened his resolve. He warned the Dublin leaders
that they would face arrest if they continued with their provocations on
paper and from podiums. After closing the soup kitchens, the government announced that no further relief would be forthcoming that year
unless the Irish paid for it. In place of food, Russell sent another 16,000
troops to Ireland.

In the spring, Daniel O'Connell left for a pilgrimage to Rome. The end
was near, he told his family, and he wanted to see the Vatican before he
died. Enfeebled, sick and slow-footed, he'd given one last speech in Parliament, a pathetic plea to help the hungry across the water. "Ireland is
in your hands, and in your power," he whispered, a sliver of his old self.
"If you do not save her, she cannot save herself." He made it to Paris,
on to Lyon, Marseille. After sailing to Genoa, he was bedridden, his
breath labored. He would not take another step, dying on May 16, 1847.
In accordance with his wishes, his heart was carved from his chest, put
in a silver cask and forwarded to Rome. His body was to be entombed
in Ireland. In the United States he was hailed by Frederick Douglass
as a friend of the slaves, throughout Europe as a friend of the Jews. At
home he would always be the Liberator, the man who freed the Catholics. In mourning, in anger, his supporters did not follow his lifelong
philosophy of nonviolence, but turned on those who had challenged
him in old age. Meagher was assaulted, as was Mitchel; the office of the
Nation was vandalized. The Music Hall, on Lower Abbey Street, where
Young Ireland held rallies after breaking with O'Connell, was attacked
by a mob. Leaping from the crowd, a man lunged for Meagher with a
knife, just missing him.

After the scare, an excitable, opinionated young man named John Donnellan Balfe offered his services to Meagher. He was also a graduate of Clongowes Wood, though six years older than the Young Tribune. Balfe was hard-drinking and voluble, a towering six foot four inches, with a whisk broom of a red beard and a nose showing an early-middle-age blush. He had once been a guard in Windsor Castle, on duty at the coronation of Queen Victoria, as he told it. But he had since soured on the British Empire, he explained—aghast that the richest nation on earth could let its partner under the Crown go to an early grave. He offered to protect Meagher. And he could write, with a pen almost as toxic as Mitchel's. Young Ireland's leaders liked Balfe's energy. In no time, he had worked his way into the inner circle, doing political jobs for Smith O'Brien, writing with Duffy, socializing with Meagher. They dispatched Balfe to London, where he had many connections, to make common cause with a movement of young reformists, the English Chartists.

Meagher toured the countryside to the west and north, recruiting for the Irish Confederation movement. "Every eye is fixed as he depicts the wrongs of England, and every hand is clenched," wrote George Pepper, a witness to one speech in Ulster. "The next day, 5000 people joined the Young Ireland party and prepared to raise the standard of revolt." The goal was to build a community of the defiant in every town. One trick of the charismatic Meagher was to set up hurling clubs, that infectious sport of rebels past, as a gateway to politics. The shop clerks, the small-town editors, the barristers, the nonstarving young—they were quick to join the cause. Catholic clerics remained on the fence, fearing that an uprising would get out of hand. Meagher didn't hide his whereabouts. He publicized his appearances, laughed openly at the Crown's informants in his audiences. Away from the stiff formality of Dublin's podiums, he was playful, closer to the people, and working to rid himself of his upper-class accent. At last, he felt, the Irish were rousing themselves—for what, he did not know. He attracted enormous crowds, the women in particular drawn to the radiant eyes and silken voice of the young man now called Meagher of the Sword. "A glorious canvass today," he wrote Duffy. "All the people—emphatically, the *people*—and the girls, and women. My God! I can hardly believe my senses!"

That he could find any reason for lightness of soul in that year was a triumph of hope over the grim spectacle of a collapsing nation. Ireland was starting to empty out. Emigration was already woven into the national experience. But nothing like the famine years. Clothes in a bundle, families fled their villages on foot, trudged to cities like Limerick and Cork, Newery and Waterford, from there to the transatlantic departure point of Liverpool. Passage to Canada cost about £6 for a family of five, more than triple that to get to the United States on one of the better ships. It took five to eight weeks to sail to the American mainland, four months or more to Australia. The English wanted them gone, particularly to Canada and Australia, two of the Empire's big empties in need of field hands and laborers.

What started as a trickle became a river of out-migrating people: almost a quarter million in 1847. Those who had some money would host a wake—a departure ritual, not unlike one held for the dead. By law, each passenger on an emigrant ship was entitled to ten cubic feet in steerage. But once at sea, captains did what they pleased. In crammed and filthy spaces over a great ocean under sail, typhus followed the poor out of Ireland. The disease and all its grotesque humiliations were more feared than a storm. In the cheap ships, where humans were cargo on the way to North America, just as timber was on the return, nearly one in five emigrants died that year. Thus a new term was added to the pile of Irish miseries: the coffin ships. Speranza's poem "The Exodus" was full of rage at the hemorrhaging of the island.

> *"A million a decade!"—of human wrecks,*
> *Corpses lying in fever sheds—*
> *Corpses huddled on foundering decks,*
> *And shroudless dead to their rocky beds;*
> *Nerve and muscle, and heart and brain,*
> *Lost to Ireland—lost in vain.*

Her voice matched the mood of 1847. In County Tipperary, corn stores were pillaged, the grain spilling onto wet streets, onto the sticky bare feet of the hungry. In Donegal, a mob stormed a flour mill. Just outside Limerick, 5,000 people crawled and stumbled up a hill to declare to the skies, to the English, to God, a single vow: *We will not starve.* The cry went unanswered: by year's end, about 400,000 people had perished. English authorities started shipping Irish orphan girls to

Australia, there to labor as domestic servants. Trevelyan approved, noting that Australians were less likely to object, because they were "not quite so fond of grievances as the excitable and imaginative Irish."

A warm summer in Ireland had produced a huge harvest in grain, bound once more for stomachs in foreign lands. To those holding dead children in their arms, the polemicist John Mitchel had a response: drive the English to the sea. He baited the Castle, calling the Lord Lieutenant "Butcher Clarendon," betting that an overreaction on England's part would prompt the masses to rise. Duffy was not yet there with him, and when he tried to moderate Mitchel's tone at the *Nation,* his best-known voice quit. Mitchel soon started his own paper, for those who no longer saw a lawful way to right the wrongs in Ireland.

Meagher struggled with his feelings. His heart was with Mitchel, but his head was full of his father's caution. Who would fight? What would they fight with? The country people had no shoes, let alone guns. Against upwards of 50,000 troops and assorted mercenaries and police backups, how could a ragged formation of Irish with pitchforks possibly prevail? "Without discipline, without arms, without food, beggared by the law, starved by the law, demoralized by the law, opposed to the might of England they would have the weakness of a vapor," he said in a speech in Dublin in early 1848. "Be bold, but wise. Be brave, but sober . . . watch, wait and leave the rest to God."

But just a few days later, his caution was gone. The curfews, emptying Irish neighborhoods of their own people at night, infuriated him. British artillery pieces rolled down city streets, and dragoons of snarling men passed by, leering at the women, insulting the men. "When I see all this my heart sinks under a weight of bitter thoughts," Meagher wrote Smith O'Brien in January of 1848. "I am almost driven to the conclusion that it would be better to risk all, to make a desperate effort, and fix at once the fate of Ireland."

A few weeks later, deep into the Irish winter, the tug of insurrection pulled him further. A revolt in Sicily, an uprising against Bourbon royal rule, boosted the hopes of Young Ireland. A handful of pamphleteers had inspired Sicilians of all ranks to take over the streets of Palermo. The news from France was even more breathtaking: firing nary a shot, citizens forced King Louis Philippe to abdicate and flee in disguise. From the Hôtel de Ville in Paris, the birth of a new French republic was announced—with a poet, Alphonse de Lamartine, among

the leaders. *A poet!* In Vienna, a populist blow at the heart of the Aus-
trian Empire drove a despotic leader out of the country. In a flash, the
impossible seemed within reach.

In Dublin, an immense crowd squeezed into the Music Hall on
March 15, 1848, ready to accept a baton of revolution from the Continent to Ireland. Smith O'Brien gave a speech of pragmatism: all of the
island must be engaged in the struggle, starving and well fed, Catholic and Protestant, landowner and tenant. They would attempt to unite
with the O'Connell faction, and across the water, with like-minded
friends in England. Meagher followed with his usual flair, and an unusual dose of militancy. "If the government of Ireland insists upon being a government of dragoons and bombardiers, of detectives and light
infantry—then up with the barricades, and invoke the God of battles!"
he said, to a roar of applause. "Should we fail, the country should be no
worse than it is now. The sword of famine is less sparing than the bayonet of the soldier."

The Castle feared that an uprising in Dublin could happen any day—
"a rebellion of slaves," in Clarendon's words, that might wash over the
island. He kept abreast of the strategy, the specific plans, the strengths
and weaknesses of the leaders. What he knew came from a talented
"Mr. B." This was John Donnellan Balfe, Meagher's fellow Clongowes
graduate. Not long after Balfe had dedicated himself to Young Ireland
and the personal protection of Thomas Meagher, he offered his services to the Castle—a well-placed informant. "I am now at the disposal of Your Excellency, should it be deemed serviceable to the causes
of peace and order to obtain exact information on the procedures of the
War Bodies," he wrote the Lord Lieutenant in March of 1848. When
his movements attracted the suspicion of those he would betray, he was
grilled by Mitchel and Duffy. Balfe explained it all away to their satisfaction. As proof, he continued to write incendiary articles of his own.
Once hired by the Castle, Balfe delivered—times, places, names, dates,
conversations—and was well paid for it. The English were building a
case from the inside. "Balfe is a treasure," Clarendon wrote his superiors
in London, "and through him I hope to defeat much that is intended."

Clarendon dispatched troops to the hospitals, to the General Post
Office, to the Bank of Ireland, to Trinity College, to line the Liffey's
docks, to squat in Merrion Square and St. Stephen's Green. Dublin was
fully occupied and under heavy guard. The Royal Navy redirected ves-

sels from the Portuguese coast to Ireland. The big gunships steamed north, toward the ports. The armored brawn of the British Empire was brought to bear against a few unarmed essayists, orators and poets, not a seasoned soldier among them.

"Ireland is a starved rat that crosses the path of an elephant," wrote Thomas Carlyle, the Scottish philosopher. "What is the elephant to do? Squelch it, by Heaven! Squelch it!"

Less than a week after the Music Hall event, the squelching began. Meagher and Smith O'Brien were arrested and jailed for their speeches. Mitchel was locked up at the same time. His offense was the prose he'd been rushing into his new journal. All three were soon out on bail. Meagher never felt more alive.

"The language of sedition," he told a cheering crowd, "is the language of freedom."

Just days after his release, Meagher was off to Paris with a small delegation, including Smith O'Brien. He stopped briefly in London for dinner with his father, a member of the House of Commons. Once again the elder Meagher tried to persuade his son to give it up. "He warned me," Meagher recalled, "about trusting the fortunes of our cause" to luck and desperation. It was too late. Meagher's ideas had taken flight, and he was aloft with them. He had to see this through.

In Paris, strolling along the Seine, seeing the great public spaces of the City of Light bedecked in a tricolor of inspiration, Meagher's step was quick. At night, the Young Irelanders walked the gaslit length of the Champs-Élysées, ducked into clubs, into theaters, pressed influential Parisians about the logistics of throwing off an oppressor. One night Meagher tried to strike up a conversation with a beggar who'd been foraging for fish bones in the garbage outside a restaurant. The man growled at them with a profane slap at the English.

"We are not *Anglais*. We are *Irelandais*."

"*Irelandais?*" the pauper said. "*Tous ivrognes.*" All drunks.

The delegation from Dublin aimed high: a recognition by the new French government of the legitimate grievances of Ireland—and, in the event of armed revolt, support. They poured their hope into Lamartine, for surely a man who roused his countrymen in verse was a kindred soul. They waited in bistros and cafés, day after day, for an appointment. At last: an audience with Lamartine, the acting foreign minister. But the Paris poet was dismissive and noncommittal. Good luck, gentlemen. What he didn't say was that England had warned the fragile new French government not to interfere with the affairs of Great Britain.

Back home, the Confederation clubs marched in formation into the Music Hall, looking for the first time like an organized force, one that might be converted into a corps of fighters. As the restless settled into their seats, a woman dressed in white walked slowly down the aisle. All eyes turned to the poet Jane Elgee, towering over Duffy, her editor and escort. In a nest of Ireland's budding rebels now stood "a tall, stately and most beautiful lady with exquisitely chiseled features, dark eyes and hair," wrote one witness, Michael Cavanagh. Her poetry, signed as always in the hand of Speranza, had shown a rough edge of late, born of the great loss afflicting Ireland. Lines from "The Famine Year" called out English genocide:

> But our whitening bones against ye will rise as witnesses,
> From the cabins and the ditches, in their charred, uncoffin'd masses,
> For the Angel of the Trumpet will know them as he passes.
> A ghastly, spectral army, before the great God we'll stand,
> And arraign ye as our murderers, the spoilers of our land.

When she sat, a chant rattled the walls of the great hall.
"Speranza! Speranza!"
She rose and acknowledged the crowd, tried to sit, but again they took it up.
"Speranza! Speranza! Speranza!"
On it went, "a soul-thrilling scene," Cavanagh recalled, that was quieted only when Duffy forced the meeting to business. At the end of the session, Young Ireland was ready to take on the Empire. The time had arrived, Jane sensed—there was no turning back. "I believe insurrection is certain," she wrote a friend in Scotland. "Truly, death is certain, either by the bayonet or on the scaffold."

Despite the rejection by the French, the lift of a Paris spring proved lasting in one respect. Meagher conceived an idea for a flag: one third green, one third orange, as a nod to the Protestant north, and a unifying white in the center. He presented it at a gathering in Dublin. On stage was a harpist—the oldest of political prisoners in Ireland—dressed in the musician's costume that had been outlawed by the Penal

Laws. The silken flag of three colors was unveiled. "I present it to my native land," said Meagher. "And I trust that the old country will not refuse this symbol of new life from one of her youngest children." A few days later, the banner flew over Waterford, and in time became the national flag of Ireland. The internal dithering was over; he felt invincible now. "He would have gone to battle for Ireland more joyfully than to a feast," Duffy noted with some amusement. In perpetual motion, Meagher was at his best.

The Crown forced a quick trial on the Young Ireland leaders. Ten thousand people lined the streets leading up to the law courts. Meagher was thrilled. He poked his head from a carriage taking him to an uncertain fate in a hissing rain, waved and exulted with the men and women of Dublin. The jury was packed, as usual, with Protestants and loyalists, but a lone dissident had made it onto Meagher's panel; it was enough to prevent a verdict. "We are eleven to one, my lord, and that one is a Roman Catholic!" a juror shouted out to the court as Meagher was released. A Quaker and a Catholic provided the margin of liberty for Smith O'Brien.

Now the Castle's plan to sweep away Young Ireland by trial would have to change. At the prime minister's urging, Parliament rushed through a much harsher, much broader law: the Treason Felony Act, essentially making it a crime to be an Irish nationalist. Any slight against the Crown or Her Majesty's government in Ireland would be considered grounds for a hard felony. This offense carried the penalty of "transportation"—the inventive British term for shipping someone out of the country to one of the Empire's distant colonies, for labor or imprisonment. In fact, it was a vanishing.

The first victim of the new law was John Mitchel. He was arrested on May 13, 1848, dressed in criminal gray and locked deep in Dublin's Newgate Prison. The dungeon was filled with emaciated Irish who had stolen a loaf of bread or a meat pie—crimes that now warranted transportation. Mitchel was tried a week after he was plucked from his home. This time the Castle took no chances. Of 3,000 Catholics eligible for his jury, not a single one was chosen. It took less than two hours to reach a verdict, followed immediately by the sentence:

"Jailer, put forward John Mitchel." He moved toward a bewigged and petticoated judge, his stare as level as a plumb line, the heavy clank of metal shackles on the floor.

"The sentence of the court is that you be transported beyond the seas for the term of fourteen years."

Meagher was dazed by the suddenness of it all. Ten days earlier, Mitchel had been a journalist with a cause; now he was headed for banishment in the West Indies. Throughout his life—at home with his father, at Stonyhurst, in courts where he studied when he first moved to Dublin—Meagher had been taught that the English, for all their faults, revered the rule of law. What he witnessed in 1848 was a farce, a system of "subsidized perjurers and armed butchers," as he called it. He rushed to the front of the gallery, shouting while reaching to grasp the hand of his departing friend. Police officers seized him. Blows were exchanged. Meagher was dragged outside, blood on his waistcoat.

Later than night, plotting with Smith O'Brien and Duffy, Meagher was beside himself, the eloquence replaced by a sputtering rage. They had to rescue Mitchel, he insisted. A call to the people was needed. Storm the prison.

Duffy feared the cost. "There was not a week's supply of food in Dublin," he said, "and all the food in the island, except what was growing in the soil, was in warehouses where the English army could reduce it to ashes in four hours." Would Britain starve a nation to death as a punitive move? It already had, Duffy argued.

Thanks to the industrious spy Balfe, the Castle was one step ahead of the Young Irelanders. Just hours after being sentenced, Mitchel was frog-marched away under heavy guard, through a long tunnel from the prison to a dock and a warship waiting in the harbor. Before dusk, a mere two weeks after his arrest, he was on his way across the Atlantic. From his cell in steerage, he started "Jail Journal," a diary:

"May 27, 1848—On this day, about four o'clock in the afternoon, I, John Mitchel was kidnapped and carried off from Dublin, in chains, as a convicted 'Felon.'"

At home in Waterford, on Tuesday, July 11, Meagher walked the length of the main room in the big family house. His father sat in a stuffed chair, trying to reason with him. Deep, wheezing sighs. A furrowed brow. Fear, and a hint of disgust. One year into his term as a member of Parliament, the elder Meagher was serving a government that was at war with his son. Out the window, the Suir in its summer sloth glided by, blue water to the sea. Smith O'Brien was in Limerick, trying to time an uprising by the Confederation clubs. Assorted members scrambled around the island on the same mission. One was sent to America, for guns and money. Another was assigned the task of winning over the Catholic Church; no revolution could succeed without parish priests blessing the barricades. Mitchel was in his prison cot on a ship anchored off Bermuda, struggling with the heat and his asthma. An antique clock ticked in the Meagher home. His father started in again, very deliberate, the words slow. *You know the consequences will be dire, son.* The boy's fate was not, as Mitchel had said just before his goodbye, in the hands of Ireland. He could call it off. Britain did not need another Irish martyr. *Stop this madness now.* The patriarch was a man of sizable influence, a loyal subject of the queen. And certainly, the good life was tempting. A few days earlier, friends had asked Thomas to dinner on St. John's Hill in Waterford, in a home as anchored and ivy-covered as he was unmoored and peripatetic. A pleading followed.

"There's no use. You'll fail. You'll lose everything."

"I must stand my ground," said Meagher.

"Oh, nonsense. Quit it and come with us."

"Where to?"

"To Italy, to Greece, to Egypt."

Meagher thought about Rome in the fall, as Ireland turned sodden and cold. He thought of the Nile, the pyramids, carefree days with "a party of honest, cheerful, spirited fellows, full of life, intelligence and the best good nature, to ramble from the Suir to the Mediterranean." He was still a member in good standing at the Waterford Club. He liked the whiskey and wit, a welcome place for him by the fire at night, even after a speech in which he'd excoriated the Tories who held sway in that den. There, he was a Meagher from Waterford, all politics checked at the umbrella stand. But enough daydreaming. Ireland was in ruins. And now, a bang at the door.

"Police!"

At the porch stood Captain Gunn and Constable Hughes, both acquaintances of the family.

"Sir. We have a warrant for the arrest of your son."

"On what charge?"

"Seditious language. A speech at Rathkeale."

A neighbor spotted the authorities and dashed down the street, pounding on doors, sounding the alarm. Church bells rang, alerting the rebels of Waterford in the clubs Meagher had helped organize. A crowd quickly formed, blocking the streets. Meagher went to the window and pleaded with the mob to disperse, else one of his friends could be shot. He would work it out with the police in private. He made his case for ten minutes, to no avail. In his parlor, he was soon joined by the leading citizens of Waterford. Outside, the crowd filled the mall that met the quay, 20,000 or more people—most of the town. For a second time he went to the window, begged people to peacefully retire. Now soldiers appeared, an entire unit of the 4th Light Dragoons and three companies of the 7th Fusiliers, with loaded muskets and fixed bayonets, all advancing on the Meagher household.

Word came of Irish clubs in neighboring communities rushing with knives and pikes to his defense. At 6:15 p.m., young Meagher stepped outside, accompanied by the chief of police and two constables. With a nod of his head, he could spark a war. But he feared the streets of his hometown would be a river a blood, his father's house burned to the ground. Do nothing rash, he pleaded with the crowd. They pressed in as the guards escorted him to a carriage. They pumped his hand, tousled his hair, patted his back, kissed him. The soldiers drew their swords as Meagher was pushed into the transport. Two lines of troops on either side. Slowly the carriage moved toward the bridge over the Suir, and with it moved the crowd. Women leaned from open windows in second stories along the quay, waving handkerchiefs. Young men pushed past the troops, pressed up against the carriage windows.

"For God's sake, sir—give us the word. Give us the word!"

Here was the revolution, if only he would say yes. His supporters cut the reins from the horses, leaving the carriage dead on the road. A priest jumped up on the driver's seat, pleading for calm. By 7 p.m., animals and buggy were reunited and started to move again. A volley of stones came from the crowd. One hit Captain Gunn in the eye. He raised his pistol, held it above the swarm of Waterford citizens. At the bridge, the crowd had formed a human barrier. Thomas Meagher would not be taken from Waterford. Fretting, looking for a peaceful way out, the prisoner saw no choice. His allies were just townspeople with stones. The British forces could mow them down in a minute's time. Three of the Empire's warships lurked in the river, the *Dragon*, the *Merlin* and the *Medusa*. Waterford might be blown to rubble before midnight. The faces of the mob—tight, clenched—were familiar, his neighbors, his family, his lifelong friends. Meagher poked his head out of the carriage to speak again. He vowed to return, soon, when the time was right. After this pleading, the crowd moved aside to allow the carriage to cross the river. On the other side was an obstruction of heavy timbers. As the soldiers removed this latest obstacle, they were pelted with rocks. Then, free of Waterford at last, the police escort made a gallop to a terminal for the mail train, seventeen miles away. Meagher was conveyed under guard on the overnight transport. He arrived in Dublin at 3:15 a.m. He had not slept. In his jail cell, replaying the past twelve hours, he was troubled by a persistent thought: had Ireland missed its moment?

As promised, Meagher returned. He paid an outrageous sum for bail and was released. His restraint and good conduct in Waterford had persuaded a judge to unshackle him, pending a hasty trial. Then the Crown could put him away for good. At once, he rushed south, to match strides with the other Young Ireland leaders. They called for a mass meeting at a sacred site—the sentinel of Slievenamon, known in Gaelic mythology as the Mountain of the Women. But only men were summoned to this summit; on Sunday, July 16, 50,000 answered the call. Wearing a green cap with a gold band, Meagher trudged up the mountain under a blistering summer sun. Near the top, at 2,300 feet above sea level, he looked out at the rumpled, rock-fenced spread of three counties, Tipperary, Waterford and Kilkenny, staring down at slight, gaunt-faced men ready for battle, squinting in the bright light. Just after 2 p.m., Meagher turned to address his countrymen, to speak and commit an act of legal treason before 50,000 witnesses. He was an accidental rebel, Meagher explained. But with the Great Hunger, he saw with perfect clarity the worst of all English crimes. That tragedy had left him with no choice. As a final incentive, two months earlier, Charles Trevelyan had declared the famine over, despite all evidence to the contrary. He'd seen early reports of peasant fields growing free of blight, and took the opportunity to proclaim victory and bring what passed for British relief efforts to a close once and for all. For his work during the famine, Sir Charles Trevelyan had been knighted.

"The potato was smitten, but your fields waved with golden grain," Meagher shouted down from Mount Slievenamon. "It was not for you. To your lips it was forbidden fruit. The ships came and bore it away, and when the price rose it came back, but not for the victim whose lips grew pale, and quivered and opened no more." Many in the crowd bowed their heads, a tribute to the lost, and murmured a prayer. "The fact is plain that this land, which is yours by nature, and by God's gift, is not yours by the law of the land. There are bayonets between the people and their rightful food." He brought up John Mitchel, more than 3,000 miles away in the hold of a ship. He named others who were in jail, awaiting Mitchel's fate.

"Will you permit the country to be deprived of these men?"

"Never!"

"I stand here on the lofty summit of a country which, if we do not win for ourselves, we must win for those who come after us." The hungry masses were primed to fight. They awaited a signal from the young leaders.

By sunset, Meagher was back at his father's house in Waterford. He stayed for four days, barely sleeping, couriers bringing him news of the others. Any knock on the door could be a soldier with orders to whisk him away. Father and son knew an end was approaching; the reasoned pleas from the elder Meagher were over. The plan now was to start the revolution in Kilkenny, the lovely medieval town built along a kink in the River Nore. It was chosen for its strategic position—inland, safe from the Royal Navy's gunships. And think of the symbolic importance: a free Ireland rising from the very place where an enslaved Ireland had been designed with the Statutes of Kilkenny. A carriage arrived for Thomas. He bounded up to the drawing room, where his father sat with his aunt. He put on his tricolor sash, buckled on a sword belt to hold a saber that had been in his family for a hundred years. He was free of worry, free of misery, imagining himself leading an army of Irish into Dublin to take the Castle, to sweep the English away forever. "I was full of liveliness and hope at that moment, and welcomed the struggle with a laughing heart," he wrote. "That evening, July the 20th, 1848, I saw my home for the last time."

THE MEANEST BEGGAR
IN THE WORLD

Underground now, traveling in the shadows beneath the murk of Munster skies, at night moving from cairn to cairn in countryside lit by spotty moonlight. When the rains came that week and the temperature dropped, he shivered and took shelter below rock overhangs. The fields were littered with abandoned scraps of the island's struggles. Here a broken-topped round tower from the tenth century, there a moss-covered altar from the fourteenth, where a priest once celebrated an illegal outdoor Mass, with a tiny window through the rock pile as a lookout for authorities. It was refuge then for a spiritual outlaw, now for a political one. Meagher had no sooner left for Kilkenny than the British government dropped a legal bomb on the Irish: habeas corpus was suspended immediately, the country placed under martial law. Anyone could be arrested and held without cause, without hearing, without bail, even without being told what they were held for—indefinitely. As of July 22, 1848, the leading journalists, poets, barristers and orators of Young Ireland were criminals in the eyes of the Empire. Arrest warrants were issued for all. A price was put on Meagher's head, a bigger one on Smith O'Brien's.

"Death itself could not have struck me more suddenly than this news," said Meagher. He blamed himself for not seeing it coming. Of course England would suspend the rule of law. What in Ireland's history made him believe otherwise? Optimism, as always, was the blind spot of youth. Still, he had to try to ignite something in Kilkenny. He reminded himself of the line of the late poet Thomas Davis: "We promised loud, and boasted high, / To break our country's chains, or die." The last word seemed the more likely outcome.

"We are driven to it," he said to Patrick J. Smyth, his friend since they were choirboys at Clongowes. "There is nothing for us now but to go out. We have not gone far enough to success, and yet, too far to retreat."

In Dublin, on his way home for dinner, Duffy was arrested yet again. The police put him in a carriage and rushed him off to prison. With the editor of the *Nation* in jail, Jane Elgee helped to put out the paper with two other women. In a fit of high outrage, she dashed off a piece calling for all of Ireland to take on the government without hesitation. "*Jacta Alea Est,*" she titled her charge, The Die Is Cast, though she had slightly mangled her Latin. It was unsigned, as protection—no Speranza this time.

"England has done us one good service at least," she wrote. "Her recent acts have taken away the last miserable pretext for passive submission ... We appeal to the whole Irish Nation—is there any man amongst us who wishes to take one step further on the base path of suffering and slavery? Is there one man that thinks that Ireland has not been sufficiently insulted, that Ireland has not been sufficiently degraded in her honour and her rights, to justify her now in fiercely turning upon her oppressor?"

To the Castle, this was the final slight they would take from these rhymesters and revolutionaries. A spy had alerted the authorities of the coming issue. Before it could be distributed, British troops stormed into the offices of the paper, seized all copies, grabbed the press, type and manuscripts, and carted it all off to the fortressed walls of official England in Dublin—the Castle. Jane Elgee was not apprehended; her role was unknown. But Duffy would soon be charged with treason felony for her essay "*Jacta Alea Est.*"

Meagher and a friend, the *Nation* journalist John Blake Dillon, boarded a train in Dublin. Two women recognized them, giggling as they looked their way. At the next stop, the rebels got off at a small village. Meagher pulled his cap over his face, head down. The men passed police officers on the way to an old tree, where they took shelter from a summer squall. Still, the rain filtered through the canopy, soaking Meagher's clothes and shoes. The great "liveliness" he'd felt barely a week before was gone. "I entertained no hope of success." But his words of the past two years carried a responsibility; there was no escaping what he had helped to start. "Our entire career, short as it was, seemed to require from us a step no less daring and defiant than that which the government had taken."

They hired a coach, rode all night. At 5 a.m. they arrived at the Georgian mansion of Ballinkeele for a rendezvous with Smith O'Brien, protected there by a friend in the titled class. A light frost covered the large grounds. Meagher's wet clothes were now stiff. They found Smith O'Brien in bed, the aristocratic sheen gone. Over coffee, the rebels considered three choices: to turn themselves in, to flee Ireland or to fight. With little discussion, they chose insurrection, hoping that outrage over the suspension of habeas corpus would fan a broad uprising.

Off to Kilkenny. In town, some black humor: the Royal Agricultural Society was holding its annual cattle show. Amid the starving, several hundred of the fattest, healthiest beeves on the island were paraded down High Street by a cluster of pipe-smoking, plaid-vested noblemen. Perfect, Meagher remarked: they could start the revolution with enough meat to feed those manning the barricades, while holding hostage a half-dozen baronets, a couple of dukes and a marquis or two.

At noon on Sunday, just outside of town, Meagher and Dillon went to Mass, greeted by an affable priest with unwelcome news: don't look for many clerics on the front lines of a revolt. The killing of an archbishop in France a month earlier, during a violent outburst by the still-untamed remnants of that country's revolution, had chilled the ardor for fighting the state. Nor was the condition of the congregants encouraging—they were weak, thin-limbed, dazed. "The truth," said Meagher, was "cold and nakedness, hunger and disease, to the last extremity." He saw no future Irish warriors in this chapel; they were the kneeling dead. It should have been obvious that a people mortally weakened by hunger could not be moved to anything but a prayer and an extended hand begging for crumbs. Famine was supposed to be the motivation for revolt. Instead, it was the undoing of it.

A meeting with the mayor, a sympathizer and a confederate, brought more bad news. Of 1,700 club members in town, only one in four had weapons, such as they were—sharpened farm tools, scythes, pikes and pitchforks. The rebels decided to spread out to the nearby towns of Carrick, Callan and Cashel, where the men were said to be better prepared to fight, and then return to Kilkenny.

In Callan, a market town 600 years old on a fertile plain, a reception awaited: a band, a bonfire on the main street, the houses bedecked in laurel boughs, green flags draped from windows. The pending arrival had been announced earlier. Hundreds of skinny young men rushed to greet Meagher and Dillon. Black-eyed girls, as Meagher remembered them, "bounded through the crowd, threw their arms around our necks and kissed us." Cromwell had been through Callan in 1650, destroying much of the town and gutting its Norman castle. A force of hussars, having just marched into town that morning as news of Meagher's pending arrival spread, stood by, carbines and swords at the ready. They were Irish hussars, to Meagher's delight. He might have remembered Duffy's line about similar soldiers in Dublin: "Their Irish hearts were not dead under the scarlet jacket." Ever the fatalist, Meagher climbed up a step above the crowd and called for three cheers for the boys of the 8th Royal Irish Hussars. He was careful with his words to the people of Callan, nothing too specific, just keep up the spirit, lads, word will come, and again, *how about another hand for those hussars.*

On to Carrick, a change of horses along the way, a full gallop. "What a hurry we were in to be shot," said Meagher. A guesthouse took them in, with a dinner of hard-boiled eggs, salted butter, a cup of milk. When Meagher went outside in the dark, three policemen were lounging by a carriage. They'd been spotted. One of the officers approached him, tipping his hat.

"Here's hoping that Mr. Meagher is in good health, and won't come to any trouble, for I know your family."

"How's that? Were you ever in Waterford?"

"Yes, sir ... I seen your father and the rest of the family, at your grandfather's funeral, and a splendid funeral it was. It covered the length of the quay."

They waited out the daylight inside the house, getting back on the road at night. Exhausted. A gray dawn. Midmorning, into Carrick, and *sweet mother of Jesus, what's this?* "A torrent of human beings, rushing through lanes and narrow streets, surging and boiling ... with sounds of wrath, vengeance and defiance." Again, women with hugs and kisses, and men with slaps on the back, here to hail the liberators. Banners and music, but mostly huzzahs, cheers for the boys of Young Ireland. The bony hands, waves of voices, hair tousled and disordered. The crowd's purpose was inchoate, like the revolution itself—a mist of hope here and there, with no real foundation. For country towns like Carrick, the uprising was all of the stomach; maybe some morsels of food would come from these witty lads. For the leadership, the uprising was all of the heart: language and history against muskets, cannons and warships. An iron will, no matter how lyrically shaped, they had to know, never beats an iron fist.

Smith O'Brien had made his way to Ballingarry, County Tipperary, where he took up with a small force, some of them armed. He was no soldier. He was trained in philosophy and speech, politics and law. But the oldest, most experienced member of the rebel leadership forced himself to be a general on this first and last day of the Young Ireland revolution, July 29. His band spotted a hostile group of police and followed them to a house with a large cabbage patch out back, home of the Widow McCormack and her five children. The police took the family hostage and went inside, barricading the windows with furniture and mattresses. Smith O'Brien ordered them to throw down their arms, release the widow and her children, and come out.

"We shall not hurt a man of you," said Smith O'Brien. "You are Irishmen." In response, the police opened fire. One of Smith O'Brien's men, Thomas Walsh, was shot dead, dropping at Smith O'Brien's feet. Another, Patrick Kavanagh, was gravely wounded. He fell to the ground, blood spurting from his thigh over the cabbages. The children shrieked. Police reinforcements, more than a hundred, soon arrived. Smith O'Brien and his men scattered. He was ushered out of Ballingarry at night.

A few days later, though dressed in a hooded cloak, he was recognized at the railway station in Thurles. Arrested without a scuffle, he was turned over to a British general in charge of the occupying force of southern Ireland. The officer wanted to make sure he had his man. The informant John Balfe was brought just outside the cell, shielded from view. Balfe pointed to Smith O'Brien and identified him as the leader of the Young Ireland rebellion. The prisoner had no idea he was being betrayed.

"Ballingarry killed us all," said Jane Elgee after the debacle of

Widow McCormack's cabbage patch. "I have never laughed joyously since."

For more than a week, Meagher slept in haylofts and roadside ditches, an invisible man by day, a phantom on the run at night. The time he spent in midsummer fields gave him a close view of yet another collapse of Ireland's food, for the blight had reappeared. The year before, potatoes had come up clean and remained so to the harvest. But the planting had been small, producing not nearly enough food to curb the Great Hunger. This year, more seed potatoes were put in the ground, and with every spade of earth turned to cover a future meal went a dollop of hope. But here it was again, acres rolling away beyond rock fence lines to other acres, in shades of hideous black—"from sea to sea one mass of unvaried rottenness and decay," said a man who was on the run with Meagher.

A fellow rebel, Terence MacManus, went looking for Meagher, searching throughout the south for him. A prosperous Irish wool broker from Liverpool, MacManus was drawn to the spirit of 1848, giving up his business for revolution. He had been with Smith O'Brien at Widow McCormack's. But with a bounty on his own head, and unable to find Meagher, he decided to make a run for America. He was able to board a ship lying at anchor in Cork. Just before it sailed, the police found him. They dragged him off to jail, a state prisoner.

In a hideout provided by a priest, Meagher was told to try the MacManus option, to leave the shores of his homeland. The cleric had it all arranged—ship, travel logistics, connections in New York. Meagher never gave it a thought. It would be unfair, he explained, to run away while his brother rebels faced a vengeful Crown. The priest tried another route, negotiating with the Lord Lieutenant. What came back from Clarendon was an offer: Meagher's life would be spared if he pled guilty to crimes against England. He rejected it immediately. But the British press, which had already made a laughingstock of Smith O'Brien's stand at the cabbage patch, printed a lie floated by the Castle—that Meagher had cut a deal to leave the country. Meagher was infuriated by this slap at his honor. He sent a letter to the *Evening Mail* in Dublin, demanding a correction. "My character is now more dear to me than my life," he wrote. It is "all that now remains to me."

In hiding, in desperation, the outlaw and his confederates hatched one final plan. They schemed of taking over the Rock of Cashel, the great, chiseled stone stronghold that rises out of the Tipperary Plain. The kings of Munster had been seated there starting in the fifth century. One of the exalted shrines of Ireland, the rock was a religious center until a siege by English forces resulted in a massacre of nearly 1,000 in 1647. The bodies were stacked five deep in the churchyard. Try to imagine, Meagher said, the new Irish tricolor flying over the highest turret of that ancient and nearly abandoned castle. They took off at once, three men on foot at night. Passing the police barracks outside the village of Holycross on August 12, a sergeant thought he recognized Meagher in the darkness.

"Fine night, gentlemen," said the officer. It was *them*. He made a signal, and six officers grabbed the rebels. Meagher's pants were ripped and filthy. He was wearing a straw hat, like that of a peasant. For the arrest, the sergeant was rewarded with £100 — almost a year's pay. Bound in chains, Meagher was taken by train to Dublin, thrown into a cell in darkest Kilmainham. A few days later came the indictment: the charge for a quartet of Young Ireland leaders was high treason — "to have levied war on our Sovereign Lady the Queen in her realm." It carried a penalty of death. When news of the arrests arrived with the mail in the West Indies, John Mitchel predicted a grim outcome. "It is possible these four worthy men will be hanged."

When it opened in 1796, Kilmainham Gaol was supposed to be a model prison — airy, perched atop a hill, large enough that prisoners were not just tossed into a heap, but given separate quarters. It soon became a byword for hell. Debtors were locked away and forgotten. In the famine years, the jail was a warehouse of the hungry, their crimes dominating the ledgers — "attacking a bread cart," "stealing a goose," "being in possession of stolen butter." And the design was significantly flawed in one respect: the impenetrable fortress was made of limestone blocks, which not only held the moisture from Dublin's porous skies, but emitted it as well. The walls of Kilmainham wept.

This concentration of petty criminals, not far from the Castle, was also a favorite lockup for prisoners of conscience. Robert Emmet had been chained inside the jail before being hanged and beheaded, his body torn into four parts and dumped in the streets. Emmet's back-

ground—a Protestant from a wealthy family, a student at Trinity—
could not spare his life for leading an uprising in 1803. Like Thomas
Meagher, Emmet had been the darling of Dublin, an orator with flair
and flash. Emmet's fate now looked to be Meagher's—his crime called
for the guilty to endure the ritualized barbarism that had been the
English penalty for high treason since 1351. Whether it had a deterrent
effect was beside the point. It killed traitors. The guards at Kilmainham
may have reminded Meagher that, following the butchery of the beloved Emmet, no one would claim his body parts.

For a month, the Young Ireland Four—Meagher, Smith O'Brien,
MacManus and a heavy-drinking law clerk named Patrick O'Donoghue—marked the days in Kilmainham. O'Donoghue, with his rough-
whiskered face and mournful eyes, had been thrown in with the leaders
of the uprising because he'd been a close associate of Smith O'Brien's in
the days leading up to the cabbage patch debacle. At summer's end, the
prison filled with people who preferred the loss of freedom over death
by starvation. Each cell had a tiny barred window that had been cut
into the thick flank of the limestone walls. Over the course of a day, you
could follow the sun's direction by how a square of light moved across
the cold floor and walls.

Meagher the elder came to commiserate with his son. He was working his connections, scheming of some way for the boy to plead guilty
to a lesser charge. Thomas would have no part of it. He welcomed the
clothes his father brought him, the blankets and good food. (A typical
day's ration at Kilmainham called for milk and stirabout in the morning, bread in the evening.) He had plenty of regret—over the timing of
the revolt, the failure to secure support from Catholic priests, the poor
organization of the clubs, the foolish belief that starving people might
put up a fight against the British Empire. Worst of all: two years of ag-
itation never came to a climax—there was no showdown, nothing to
rouse the Irish on three continents. "We were routed without a struggle," Meagher said. "A humiliating fiasco." But he had no remorse for
his actions.

In mid-September, the prisoners were taken by train from Dublin to
Thurles, and then by coach to the town of Clonmel, in south Tipperary.
The authorities wanted the trial to be held somewhere out of the way,
far from the crowded discontent of Dublin. Smith O'Brien went first,

facing a jury of select Protestant loyalists. The trial lasted nine days. It took barely nine minutes to reach a verdict. A member of Parliament for seventeen years, a father of six, heir to a castle and descendant of a family of Irish kings, William Smith O'Brien was found guilty and faced the death penalty. "I have done only that which, in my opinion, it was the duty of every Irishman to have done," he said. MacManus the wool broker and O'Donoghue the disheveled law clerk followed with the same result.

Meagher, the youngest of the four, was the last to be tried; the case against him was the weakest. He had thrown not a stone, pulled not a trigger, ignited not a fire. He had not been at Ballingarry, had never erected a barricade. Meagher wore a black frock, black silk stockings and a light-colored waistcoat to the proceedings. He had many admirers in the gallery, women in the majority, slipping him papers to autograph and a stream of notes. Among them was Jane Elgee, having retired her nom de guerre, Speranza, for now. The long-limbed poetess dressed in her usual low-cut dress and short sleeves of lace, a ribbon in her hair.

At night, the prisoners played backgammon, drank whiskey that had been smuggled in, and recited poems about patriots and love of the land. Most evenings, they would assemble in a common room on the second floor of the jail before retiring to individual cells. They were all doomed; all but one of them knew it formally, and yet the mood was light, following Meagher's cue. He was the prankster, as he'd been at Stonyhurst. Smith O'Brien credited Meagher with keeping his spirits up, telling racy stories into the late hours. And he led them in song with his clarinet, the one he'd used in his first insubordinate act at school in Lancashire. The guards couldn't help but like him, and looked the other way when favors came to the cell. One of those favors, as insinuated by a cryptic aside, was Jane, who apparently contributed more than her poetry to the cause of Young Ireland. "He was brought to see me at his particular desire," she wrote to a friend, without elaboration.

On Saturday evening, eight days into his trial, Meagher was alone in a cell, awaiting a verdict. In case anyone doubted the outcome, a scaffold was under construction outside; guards could be seen checking the "drop." Meagher was prepared to die. He saw a priest. He wrote a storm of letters, telling friends old and new that he loved them. Late that Saturday, a message arrived. "The jury has disagreed!" A cheer rattled the stone walls of the jail. But then, ten minutes later, a second message: "The report was false. He is convicted." The prisoner was led back to join the others. He would be sentenced the following Monday. Instead of a mournful face, Meagher greeted his fellow traitors with a flash of a smile, eyes lit, a clap of his hands.

"Here I am, boys! Here I am and found guilty! And glad, too, that they did convict me, for if I had been acquitted, the people might say I had not done my duty. I am guilty and condemned for the old country ... Come in, come in! I'm starved. Let us have one hour's fun." One of the men could not stop crying. Another held Meagher in a tight hug, refusing to let him go.

On Monday, October 23, 1848, Meagher dressed again in his black suit and walked under armed escort into court. Just before sentence was passed, he was given a chance to offer a few words why he should not be executed. He rose from the dock, silent for a long moment, taking in the packed courtroom, making eye contact with all.

"My lords, you may deem this language unbecoming in me, and perhaps it may seal my fate. But I am here to speak the truth whatever it may cost. I am here to regret nothing I have ever done, to retract nothing I have already said. I am here to crave with no lying lip the life I consecrate to the liberty of my country ... No, I do not despair of my poor old country, her peace, her liberty, her glory. For that country I can do no more than bid her hope. To lift this island up, to make her a benefactor to humanity instead of being the meanest beggar in the world, to restore her to her native powers and her ancient constitution—this has been my ambition, and this ambition has been my crime. Judged by the law of England, I know this crime entails the penalty of death, but the history of Ireland explains this crime, and justifies it. Judged by that history, I am no criminal."

If the presiding judges were moved, they showed no indication of it. The applause from everyone else was deafening, as at the close of a great play, Meagher in the starring role of the drama he'd always dreamed of. The judges banged their gavels and ordered bailiffs to bring the room to order. A lone member of the bewigged panel then pronounced his sentence. Mercy was expected, per the jury's recommendation for a man so young.

"You, Thomas Francis Meagher, are to be taken hence to the place from whence you came, and be thence drawn on a hurdle to the place of execution, and there hanged by the neck until you are dead and that afterwards your head shall be severed from your body and your body divided into four quarters, to be disposed of as Her Majesty sees fit."

In Dublin, Charles Duffy was the last of the Young Ireland leaders whom the authorities tried to put away. He had faced several earlier trials, but managed to elude a Crown-ordered outcome. They had him dead to rights this time. Even though he wasn't physically present, he was editor of the *Nation* when the journal printed "*Jacta Alea Est.*" He had languished in jail for months without trial, the blunt effect of the suspension of habeas corpus. Maybe he would sit an entire year. There was no hurry on the part of England. Jane Elgee was torn: she knew her close friend might be banished from Ireland, forced to sweat away the days in the penal colony of Australia for something *she* had written. Overwhelmed by guilt, she went to the prosecutor's office and confessed. The piece in the *Nation*, from the title to the overt call for insurrection, was hers.

This put the Crown in a difficult position. Beautiful, famous, well-spoken Speranza, daughter of a fine Protestant and monarch-loving family, was the kind of martyr that might prompt the Irish to take a second look at rebellion. A deal was cut: no prosecution if Jane Elgee promised to give up writing political poetry. She agreed. "I shall never write sedition again," she told a friend in a letter. "The responsibility is more awful than I imagined or thought of." With "*Jacta Alea Est*" removed from Duffy's indictment, no verdict could be reached. But he was not given his freedom. A retrial was ordered—the fifth.

At the same time, the global Irish community, its ranks swelled by famine exiles, called on England to spare the lives of the political prisoners in Clonmel. From the U.S. Congress, from newspapers in New York, Sydney, Toronto and even London, the Crown was castigated for sentencing these young men to death. How dare England condemn the savagery of other nations when it was throwing body parts of its brightest Irish subjects into the streets. Meagher seemed resigned to death, but he would not go quietly. He had a string of visitors, friends, members of the press. He dashed off more letters, decorated his cell

and wrote poetry standing up. One, titled "Prison Thoughts," was composed just days after his death sentence had been pronounced.

> *I love, I love these grey old walls!*
> *Although a chilling shadow falls*
> *Along the iron-gated halls*
> *And in the silent, narrow cells,*
> *Brooding darkly, ever dwells.*

His celebrity grew with every day that brought him closer to the
knotted end of a rope. Words from his speech in the courtroom at
Clonmel were framed and hung in Boston slums and Liverpool docks
and Australian farm huts. His boyhood friend Patrick Smyth, soon to
depart for America, was surprised to find Meagher so upbeat. "He was
never more exuberant than when he lay hopeless of life, awaiting the
final strokes of destiny and death," he wrote. When a reporter from a
Dublin newspaper arrived to do a profile of the Young Tribune in his
last days, he discovered a witty jailhouse host. "Imagine a little room,
about the size of an ordinary pantry, lighted from the top by a large
skylight, with bare whitewashed walls, neither fireplace nor stove, and a
cold stone floor," the journalist wrote. "These were the materials Meagher had to work on, and this dreary spot, which would have struck a
less brave heart with helpless despair, he had with his own hands converted into a genuine expression of the poetry which formed the ba-
sis of his character and genius." The writer noted piles of letters, book-
shelves stocked with all manner of tracts, bright rugs, paintings on the
wall, scraps of half-written verse on a small desk. Meagher left the visitor in stitches. The mirth, at times, may have been forced. Alone, in his
darker moments, Meagher gave away his earthly possessions and tidied
up his affairs.

Early one morning, a gust of jailers came through and rushed the
four prisoners out of their cells. They were shaken awake, chained, then
led to a coach, which conveyed them to Dublin under the escort of
British soldiers. After getting word of a plot to rescue the prisoners, the
Castle had decided to ferry them out of Clonmel. Distance from the
executioner's hurdle lightened the spirits of the state prisoners. Smith
O'Brien got to see his mother and his wife, Lucy, at Christmas. They
brought along a surprise—a newborn child, his seventh. As at Clonmel,

Meagher was the most upbeat. To his journalist friend Blake Dillon he wrote that England would never be able to kill the spirit of the people. "Beyond these shores, whenever two or more Irishmen are gathered together, everything almost can be done." The convicts' lives were on hold while a legal review worked its way through Westminster.

In the late spring of 1849 came word that the judicial process had gone full circle: their appeal was denied. But in a concession to world pressure, the Crown decided to show some mercy. It was announced that Her Majesty Queen Victoria had been advised by the government to commute the sentence of death, and the gracious sovereign had consented. The decision, as it was widely interpreted at the time, had everything do with a plan by the queen to visit Ireland later that year.

The young rebels would live another day. But they would live as prisoners in Australia, specifically the island of Tasmania, Britain's most distant penal colony—then called Van Diemen's Land. The royal clemency was *transportation for life,* which meant that four men who had been willing to die for Ireland would never see it again. They were crushed by the new sentence: they had expected execution or a pardon, but not purgatory at the other end of the world. They would depart within days. What had been a leisurely nine months to say goodbye now became a hasty exit. Meagher stuffed his trunks with books and writing materials, the nutrients of his life. On July 9, he penned his last letter from Ireland, to a friend, John Leonard. It was a requiem for a battered country.

The next census would show that the nation's population had fallen by nearly two million—one in four people had died or emigrated. Even Lord Lieutenant Clarendon felt England had committed something close to mass murder in the Ireland he oversaw. No other nation in Europe, Clarendon wrote to Prime Minister Russell in 1849, would "coldly persist in a policy of extermination." The Irish left their homes unwillingly, as convicts or rejects to Australia, men to build roads in the Antipodes, orphan girls to become house servants. And they left willingly, forming the scattered parts of the global Irish diaspora—the Lennons from County Down to Liverpool, eventually to produce John of the Beatles; the Kennedys from County Wexford to Boston, eventually to produce another John, the first Irish Catholic president of the United States; and the Kearneys from County Offaly to New York, to produce a second American president, Barack Obama.

Nations do not die in a day [Meagher wrote his friend]. Their lives are reckoned by generations, and they encompass centuries. Their vitality is inextinguishable . . . Forget my privations, forget all the happiness I have sacrificed, and change what would otherwise be a weary bondage into a tranquil, happy dream. Besides, I feel I have simply done nothing else but my plain duty, and hence I cannot be otherwise proud and happy at this moment. My heart, indeed, was never so firm . . . Orders have come,

Yours devotedly,
Thomas Francis Meagher

That morning, Meagher, Smith O'Brien, MacManus and O'Donoghue were loaded into a carriage under escort of fifty mounted police armed with pistols and carbines. Weeping and farewells, as family pressed for a last touch. After saying goodbye to his wife and seven children, Smith O'Brien couldn't contain himself. He'd been unflinching for a year. As the finality of the sentence sank in—*banishment for life*—he broke down, tears smearing his face. Meagher tried to comfort him, but it wasn't easy. For men of their class, manners were a buffer.

The guards led them to the harbor, where a brig, the *Swift*, lay at anchor. Up to the deck, leg irons dragging. On board, the captain read them the rules. In bed by 9 p.m. No talking to any of the ship's officers or deck hands. Two meals a day. The ship eased its way out of Kingstown Harbor, turned south in the Irish Sea, west into St. George's Channel, down the coast, the outline of the Wicklow Mountains coming into view. At dusk, dinner of sea biscuits, a jug of colored water, dried beef. The next morning, with clear skies, the *Swift* sailed along the broken coastal edge of County Waterford. The last look tugged at Meagher's heart. "I pass by," he wrote, as mournful as he ever sounded, "and my own people know nothing of it." Ireland shrank on the horizon, smaller, smaller, smaller, and then disappeared altogether. The brig aimed for the open Atlantic, *upon the seas, beyond the seas,* as British courts intoned in the formal sentencing to the penal colony, from an island home to an island more strange than any in the Western imagination, where a man of twenty-five could not possibly picture himself growing old—a captive, a convict, an exile for the remainder of his days.

PART II

TO BE IRISH IN THE
PENAL COLONY

6

ISLAND OF THE DAMNED

So long as the ocean had no end, life had no starting point. For 112 days, Thomas Meagher's world was a brig barely thirty yards in length, stem to stern, floating from the Northern Hemisphere to the Southern, past two continents to get to a third—the world's largest prison. The convicts slept in bunks belowdecks, their door locked and lanterns extinguished at night by a seaman they were prohibited from speaking to. The wooden belly of the *Swift*, in the last days before the Empire's fleet started its transition from timber and sail to iron and steam, groaned through a 14,000-mile course, a distance more than half the circumference of the earth at the equator. A cabin the size of a closet in the Meagher family home held some of the most loquacious, best-educated, daring young men in Great Britain, on their way to a dumping ground for robbers and pickpockets, forgers and whores. "Brave men," John Mitchel said of his coconspirators, "who fought for an honorable chance of throwing their lives away."

By 1849, the Crown had sent almost 40,000 Irish to the penal colony of Australia, a fourth of them women. Only about 1 percent were political prisoners. The rest were transported for stealing bread or shoes, dodging rent, cutting down a tree, housing a fugitive or other petty crimes. Given their status, and the attention of the press in the United States and Europe on these well-known and well-connected rebels, the Young Ireland leaders on the *Swift* were not mistreated. They were free of leg irons, had the liberty to stretch and walk on deck several times a day. At a regular evening meal of dried peas, salted beef and hardtack, they were allowed a bottle of porter. They bathed in seawater brought aboard or, when the brig squatted in a calm, were dipped into the ocean for a brisker full-body cleaning.

Their leader, the aristocrat, the member of Parliament, Smith O'Brien the stoic became the sad man of the sea. He wept, again, for the hole in his life without wife and children, for the birthdays he would never attend, weddings he would not see, the home fire that would not warm him. Meagher had no one. He'd left a lover in Ireland, he told those closest to him, keeping the details vague. Best not to look back at what could never be. To rebuff the grief of forced removal, the prisoners came up with all kinds of diversions. Backgammon, from a little box brought aboard by the merchant MacManus. Fishing, also with MacManus's string and hook. Rope-splicing, hammock-scrubbing, singing, dancing, debating the great issues. Reading the classics, contemporary tracts, books in Latin and Greek, much poetry, including the epics of Ossian in Gaelic. Next to Smith O'Brien, Meagher's library was his closest friend. The banished national orator read aloud to the law clerk, Patrick O'Donoghue, a poor man among Young Ireland's prisoners of means, often sick and ill-tempered, his eyes troubled. And not a day passed without writing, of verse that spoke of loss, and letters to people who might not open them for almost a year. One poem penned by Meagher found him still defiant, still upbeat.

> I would not die! I would not die!
> In Youth's bright hour of pleasure;
> I would not leave without a sigh,
> The dreams, the hopes, I treasure.

It was no good to be sentimental, but Meagher had his weak times. Sitting on the deck, "on my way to world's end," his mind replayed moments in Waterford, the capsules of happiness. "I travelled back through the waves and seabirds and the clouds, through boisterous and dismal scenes of all sorts to that big weather-slated house," he wrote Duffy, in a long letter that was published in the *Nation*, reborn after a jury failed yet again to convict its editor. Meagher came to admire the *Swift*, taking the trade winds in her sails, "a sprightly, handsome, little brig—as steady as a rock, but as graceful as a swan," he noted. "I wish you could have seen her in a storm: at no other time did she look to such advantage. With a broken, scowling sky above her, and a broken, scowling sea beneath, she gallantly dashed on."

Down the length of the Atlantic they sailed in the summer of 1849, past France, Spain and Portugal, south to the Canary Islands, the African west coast, through the Cape Verdes archipelago, crossing the equator with a ceremony that included an extra ration of grog. On July 20, a year to the day of the failed uprising at Ballingarry, Meagher announced that he was adding a nationalistic flourish to his name—as long as he was a prisoner of the British Empire, he would go by O'Meagher.

After two months, the *Swift* arrived at Cape Town, the tip of Africa. A political storm rocked the harbor: the colonists were in open rebellion at British plans to build a penal colony there. The Irish prisoners were hailed as victims of a cruel system, and heroes in their own right. Plans to go ashore were quashed, as was a chance to stock up on fresh food. Quickly, the *Swift* scooted away. From September 12 until October 27, over the most empty part of the Indian Ocean, the prisoners saw no land in a final leg of nearly 6,000 miles. The earth was an infinity of water, the horizon broken only by the occasional iceberg carried by currents from Antarctica.

For all the Irish thrown to sea in that century, Meagher and his mates had to be counted among the more fortunate. The Great Hunger had forced a Great Exodus. About 1.8 million sailed across the Atlantic from 1845 to 1855. Just under 1.5 million of those emigrated to the United States; the rest went to Canada. "In a few years more, a Celtic Irishman will be as rare in Connemara as the red Indian on the shores of Manhattan," wrote the London *Times*. Peasants who had never been more than a few miles from their rural homes found themselves propelled through an ever larger, unfamiliar world: from the doorstep of a hut reclaimed by a landlord, to a fetid workhouse in the city, to the dank, crowded hold of a typhus-infected ship on the high seas. In 1847 alone, 17,000 Irish died in the Atlantic crossing, almost one in fifteen—most from the dreaded "fever" that spread through lice in the coffin ships. Only the slave trade, the Middle Passage shipment of 12.5 million blacks from Africa to the New World, had a higher death rate on the Atlantic. The bodies of the dead were buried at sea. Thus a ship that had departed with intact families would arrive with orphans, widows and broken men. Typically, the vessels were cargo-carrying work ships, hastily outfitted to haul humans instead of goods, and they were filthy. Three hundred people shared two water closets. The ration, for those paying the base fare, was one pound of food a day per adult, and a gallon of water for drinking, washing and cooking. Home at sea for up to two months was an allowance of space, six feet by six feet for four people.

The Irish had no word in Gaelic for "emigrant"; the closest approximation was *deorai*—exile. The passage in the North Atlantic made many of those exiles feel that the greatest gamble of their young lives was a terrible mistake. Typhus, of course, was much feared. So was the outbreak of fire, from cooking in tight quarters. But what most terrified the uprooted, most of them dirt farmers and laborers unfamiliar with the ocean's tantrums, were storms. The worst kicked up in the early spring and late fall, when the journey was cheaper but more hazardous. A morning with a sea of glass might snarl into a sudden tempest, waves crashing over the deck, sails fluttering like ravens in a frenzy. During such storms, passengers were locked inside their steerage cloisters, the air thick from lack of ventilation, possessions flying across the cabin. "Every timber writhed," wrote one passenger. "The smallest nail had a cry of its own."

But at least the Irish leaving home for North America left of their own free will, and they had some basic rights. Their water ration was quadruple the two pints a day allowed convicts shipped to Australia. The Irish sent to the West Indies were simply human property. Barbados, Jamaica, Bermuda and other isles under a hot sun relied on slave labor, usually African, for the tobacco and sugar trades. These shackled ranks were increased by the conquered of Ireland. In a seven-year span after Cromwell crushed the Irish, more than 50,000 men, women and children were sold into slavery in Barbados and surrounding islands. That was followed by waves of indentured servants, working as field laborers for up to seven years to earn their freedom. Felons, from political prisoners like John Mitchel to poor Irish categorized as "vagabonds and rogues" by the British judicial system, continued to be sent to the Caribbean and to Australia until the 1860s, their conduct shaped by the lash. "On Britain's convict ships," Mitchel wrote, "the sun never sets."

The original design for Australia was not to be a continent for the condemned. Rumors of a large landmass in the Southern Hemisphere had passed among the world's sailing nations for years. France, Spain, Portugal and England had all sent explorers to the big blank spot on the world map, and their navigators had sighted shards of land without comprehending the size. More often, they missed it entirely. It was the peripatetic, globe-roaming mariner Captain James Cook who finally went ashore and planted a flag. Cook had left England in August of 1768 on the HMS *Endeavour*, a ship about the same size as the *Swift*. By April of 1770, after charting the Maori stronghold of New Zealand, he saw a "sandy, scrubby" coastline that "resembled the back of a lean cow," as one of his officers wrote. By August, two years after leaving Portsmouth, Captain Cook claimed the land for King George III, a monarch soon to wage war on his rebellious American subjects. With a round of musket fire, a newborn colony sixty times larger than England became part of the British Empire. The Crown's botanists would bring back 1,600 plant species new to science.

Now, to people it. The Aborigines, having lived there for about 30,000 years, were considered a minor nuisance, part of the exotic fauna of the land down under. They were hunters and gatherers, black and naked, dismissed by the English as Stone Age relics. Britain planned a series of settlements on the eastern shore of Australia, as a source of food, fiber and timber, and to ward off the French. But it proved nearly impossible to persuade enough free citizens of London or Manchester to sail more than halfway around the world to start life fresh in the eighteenth-century version of Mars.

The solution was to export the wretched masses of the British underclass. The slums of England had produced a surfeit of petty criminals, Dickens's characters scheming for shillings and begging for handouts—far too many for the limited jail space. Cheap gin, made of distilled corn, aggravated the problem. At one point, Royal Navy hulks were converted into makeshift prisons on the Thames. Forced exile—er, *transportation*—would provide a labor force in bondage, and get rid of both the prisoners and the prisons back home, at a fraction of the cost of warehousing the unfortunates in Britain. In London, a burglar was a net drain on the Crown. In Australia, he could be forced to work seven years for nothing. Plus, with the loss of the Empire's colonies after the American Revolutionary War, England needed a replacement destination for its official rejects. The new penal colony was a *splendid idea*, the governing elites agreed—"a remedy for the evils likely to result from the late alarming and numerous increase of felons in this country," as the establishing document for Australia explained. For almost a cen-

tury, this experiment would become the world's most far-reaching disposal system for the doomed.

At the same time, England would encourage free settlement, with
land grants and other incentives for those wishing to live without leg
irons. The creation of Australia was always an audacious construct:
could you produce a civilized society, a bit of Olde England trans-
planted to a brown and baked land, in the midst of what was an enormous police state? A class system refined to its smallest syllable and nu-
ance of accent, its soup-sipping to choices between bouillon and melon
spoon, its racial and ethnic categories delineated by crackpot theorists
down to cranial millimeters, would take on grotesque proportions in
the Antipodes.

The First Fleet sailed in May of 1787—eleven ships carrying 1,030
people, including 548 male and 188 female convicts. The prisoners were
carpenters, factory workers, weavers, field hands, sailors, shoemakers,
all gone bad in some trifling way—"a Noah's Ark of small-time crimi-
nality," as Robert Hughes wrote. Settling around Botany Bay, in what
would become Sydney, England's pioneer contingent nearly starved to
death in its first two years, saved only by ships' rations and the discovery that kangaroo meat was edible and abundant. Other villages and
prisons were planted along the eastern coast of Australia and down
into Tasmania. Over the next eighty years, Great Britain would force
164,000 people to cross the oceans for penance there. One in four were
Irish, the minority within a minority—colonized twice.

When the *Swift* sailed up the Tasman Sea and anchored at last in
Hobart Town on October 29, 1849, the prisoners from Ireland braced
themselves for home in a hellhole. This island off the southern shore of
the mainland, Van Diemen's Land, had been stocked with convicts—
more than 30,000 of the 65,000 inhabitants had the *stain*. At midcen-
tury, the rest of Australia was trying to phase out its prisons, its torture
dens, its manacled work crews, and to become a functioning civilization with a decent reputation. Not so with Tasmania, as the most far-
flung colony in the British Empire would soon be called. The worst of
the woebegone men and women in the system were now concentrated
in the very place where Thomas Meagher had been sentenced to spend
the rest of his life.

In 1849, the island held "a larger portion of the most depraved and

unprincipled people than anywhere in the Universe," in the estima-
tion of a former governor, William Sorell. Many had been "assigned"
to farmers. In a system where banishment was called transportation,
"assignment" was the Empire's euphemism for slave labor. These serfs
moved about among the free settlers, those who had come to Van Diemen's Land to make a go of it—living in a half-dozen or more small
towns, tending sheep, working as merchants, traders or government officials. Other convicts were latched together on labor crews, working
twelve-hour days on a diet of wretched gruel, building roads, bridges
and water systems, or planting crops, cutting trees.

The hardened and most hopeless among the criminals were housed
in caged compounds patrolled by guards, former convicts themselves.
In those cells, it was rare to find a prisoner whose back was not a map
of lacerations from cat-o'-nine-tails. One Irish felon had endured 2,000
lashes from the flesh-ripping *cat*, some inflicted for singing "treasonous songs," others for "being cheeky," as his record indicated. Another
Irish prisoner, Francis MacNamara, took 650 hits from the whip; sentenced to seven years for stealing a piece of cloth, Frankie-the-Poet was
famously flogged for his verse, which made fun of his jailors. Still another class in the penal colony, white bushrangers were runaway convicts who robbed, raided and plundered while living off the land, in
caves and makeshift shelters. They were much feared. The lowest Tasmanian caste was the natives, reduced by 1849 from a population of perhaps 4,000 people on the island to a spectral few. The Aborigines were
almost completely wiped out—by Old World diseases, hunger and settlers who killed them for sport. After a half century or so under the flag
of Great Britain, the colony in the way down under, as one early historian summarized it, was now known as "that den of thieves, that cave
of robbers, that cage of unclean birds, that isthmus between earth and
hell."

Just before nightfall, the *Swift* dropped anchor. October was springtime, the air fresh, the land sprightly and green with follicles of new
growth. What greeted the prisoners was stunning: cliffs that seemed
sculpted by artists rising on one side of the Derwent River, the oth-
erworldly carvings on the flanks of the Tasman Peninsula in a different direction. In broad view from the ship's deck, rising from Hobart's
harbor, was the snowy-headed eminence of Mount Wellington, 4,170
feet. Perhaps hell would not be so bad after all. "Nothing I have seen in

other countries—not even my own—equals the beauty, the glory of the scenery through which we glided up from Tasman's Head to Hobart Town," Meagher wrote of his first impressions. "The fresh, rich fragrance of flowers" and orchards temporarily lifted his spirits. "Gazing at them, we lost sight of our misfortunes, and the dull, cold destiny which at that moment, like the deepening twilight, fell upon our path."

More surprises were in store. The secretary of state for the colonies, Earl Grey, had decided in London that the Young Ireland felons would not be locked away in a cell or assigned to a work crew but given a fair degree of freedom. The island's governor, the dyspeptic Sir William Denison, disagreed. Why should these poets, journalists, orators and barristers be treated any different from the shoeless, illiterate scum held in the confined holds of Van Diemen's Land? They were *traitors!* But Lord Grey, under pressure from progressives at home and influential Irish abroad, wanted to show the world how benevolent Her Majesty could be with the cream of Ireland's political crop. Better not to make martyrs of these men a second time over. Ireland, still ravaged by the Great Hunger, might have another uprising in it.

A second ship arrived a day after the *Swift,* carrying a few more of Erin's illustrious class of convicts. The most notable was Kevin O'Doherty, a bright medical student and close friend of Meagher's. O'Doherty had been moved to action after treating famine victims in Dublin, appalled by the Empire's indifference to the starving. He saw the dead "piled in on one another," he wrote. "The cold and hungry in every tenement with nothing to cover them." He could never look at England in the same way, feeling conscience-bound to do something— in his case, lending his voice and pen to Young Ireland. He had been a few examinations short of full certification to practice medicine when he was transported to the penal colony for a term of fourteen years.

Governor Denison was instructed to offer O'Doherty and the other prominent prisoners a choice: they could be held under guard, or they could be free to build a life on the island so long as they gave their word as gentlemen never to escape. The latter was known as a ticket-of-leave, and usually reserved for a prisoner who had served most of his time honorably. To Meagher, the limited freedom seemed a sensible choice. An escape, he reasoned, "was out of the question," not because it would be difficult to slip away, but because the odds of surviving as a fugitive in the wilds of the island were considerable. It was snake-infested, cold at night, without obvious food sources. Escapees had starved and drowned, died of exposure, poisoning and accidents, been killed by unmoored bushrangers, been forced to eat each other. The island itself was a bit larger than Ireland. If one could make it to water's edge, then what? How to get 14,000 miles back home, where, of course, you would be jailed as a fugitive? The west coast of North America was 7,500 miles away. In "a choice between two evils," as Meagher called it, everyone but Smith O'Brien took the ticket-of-leave. It came with some conditions: each man would be confined to a district and could not visit any of the others. They must report regularly to the authorities and never be outdoors past sunset. Smith O'Brien thought it dishonorable to make such a deal. As the only member of Parliament ever to be transported, it was beneath him, he said, to give his word that he would never attempt an escape. He was promptly shipped away to a smudge of rock in the Tasman Sea—Maria Island, where he was held in solitary confinement in a cabin.

Meagher set off to explore his prison without walls. On land, wobbly-legged after nearly four months aboard the *Swift*, he was put in a carriage at 3 a.m. for a ride of almost a hundred miles, to the uplands. In the first blush of light, he saw rows of corn and blue smoke rising from clusters of homes along the Derwent River. He passed blackened tree stumps and land carved fresh for roads and footings for houses— the birthing of a society. The morning unspooled slowly, in Meagher's glimpses, with scenes of horse carts and cows, shepherds with kangaroo-skin knapsacks tending thickets of sheep, green parrots in the trees. "I almost forgot that I was hurrying away still further from my own poor country, and journeying amid the scenes of a land which I could take no interest in."

When he arrived at Campbell Town, the largest hamlet in his assigned district in the middle north of the island, his heart sank. "A glance," he noted, "was sufficient to inform me that this celebrated town consisted of one main street, with two or three dusty branches." As he walked past a handful of shops to a lodging house, people stared at him—*Meagher of the Sword, is it!* "To bed, then, I went and dreamed all night of Eden." But it was the Eden of the Charles Dickens novel of shysters and malaria, *Martin Chuzzlewit,* he said. After three days, Meagher decided to move on. The next settlement in his district was Ross, "a little apology of a town." Still, it was preferable to the first place—"a vulgar, upstart village with too much glare, dust and gossip, where it would be hard to do anything else than yawn, catch flies and star-gaze."

The way to get by in this Tasmanian limbo was to keep an active imagination. Meagher was twenty-six years old, still in "the morning of my life," as he observed. He had money from his tolerant father; he could afford to start something as an exile in his assigned rectangle of Tasmania. But what? A soft-handed man who spoke five languages, who lived for the thrust and parry of ideas, who had studied law but was never more at ease than when reaching for oratorical high notes in a packed hall or bringing home the punch line of a ribald tale, found himself completely alone and adrift. There was no one to speak with aside from a few settlers who exchanged perfunctory words with him, no epic struggles aside from his own fight with a Goliath of boredom. His life had no purpose.

"Existence, thus harassed, deadened, drained, ceases to be a blessing—it becomes a penalty," he wrote Smith O'Brien. When darkness came at day's end, it was the slam of a heavy door closing. Women were scarce, the young even more so, though he was tempted by the married ones. Nearby was a prison stocked with impoverished single mothers and pregnant girls from Britain's back alleys, called "the female factory," another tier of hell for those rotting in the Southern Hemisphere. *Good God.*

Sustained by a residual fume of optimism that his adult life had thus far failed to validate, Meagher took up residence in Ross, in the district he was forbidden from leaving, two rooms in a four-room cottage, seventy-five miles from Hobart. Out back, the landlady—"an amiable female of stupendous proportions"—had planted cabbage, parsley, onions and potatoes. So, he could garden. He could write. He could go for long strolls. And what mysteries appeared in the bush: hundreds of creatures never seen in Ireland. Gum trees were thick with cockatoos, the showy-crested parrots. Dangling from limbs was the occasional koala bear. On the ground appeared freaks of evolution, stuck in transition—graphic fodder for the theory that Charles Darwin was already developing when he visited the island in 1840. Here was the platypus, with the bill of a duck, the tail of a beaver, one of the few mammals to lay eggs. The echidna, a spiny anteater, with a pencil-thin beak and a coat of cream-colored quills, ambled like a pensioner out of a pub after last call. Kangaroos and wallabies were somewhat scarce. Prized for their meat and hide, the great bounding, pocket-pouched marsupials, long of tail and short of upper paws, had been overhunted on the island. The Tasmanian devil, carnivorous with an iron-forced clamp of a jaw, had a reputation that belied its habits. The devil was no bigger than a dog, and did indeed cast a hungry eye on fellow mammals, but mostly small livestock. All of this was dawn-of-Creation new to the son of Waterford.

But no amount of stimulation from nature, no mental calisthenics, could ease the torture of being alone in this closet of the world. Meagher was not suited to the life of a hermit. One solitary day passed after another, the summer sun pressing down through December and into January of the new year, 1850. "I am as companionless and desolate here as Stylites on the top of his pillar," he wrote Duffy in February, referring to the Byzantine-era ascetic. "Only one human being, for instance, has passed by my window today; he was a peddler, with fish and vegetables." He lamented his exile — "so many thousands of miles away from our homes and friends, to this cheerless penal settlement."

As a gentleman under the sentence of oblivion, he belonged to the smallest and most select niche in this controlled netherworld — neither hard-core criminal nor free settler. And yet he held no deeper grudge against England than that of a typical Irishman. By the Crown's laws, he was a traitor. And for all the emotional pain of banishment, he felt he had been treated fairly in Van Diemen's Land; he'd heard what cruelties were being inflicted on common criminals trapped throughout the penal colony. He did not live in fear of the lash, or starvation. As for his life cause, he would never give up. The failed uprising was just an episode; it did not have to be the end. As long as he drew breath, the fight for a free Ireland would be the animating force of his days, he vowed — even from this far corner of the earth. "I am with her still," he wrote. "Her memories, her sorrows, her hopes mingle with my own." But this round was over. "We played for a high stake, the highest that could be played for. We lost the game by a wretched throw, and with a willing heart and ready hand, we ought, like honourable men, to pay the forfeit and say no more about it."

He worried about John Mitchel, confined to an offshore ship somewhere on the other side of the world. Ever since being sent out of Ireland in the days before the failed uprising, Mitchel had struggled for breath—gasping in the hold of his vessel or moaning in a hospital in Bermuda. "Asthma! Asthma!" Mitchel wrote in a typical diary entry. "The enemy is upon me." It got worse with colder weather. "To tell the plain truth, I am very ill," he said on December 1, 1848. "I am grown ghastly thin and my voice weak. I am like a sparrow alone upon the house-tops." He wondered if his last days were upon him. "Am I to die groaning in a wooden gaol here in the Atlantic?"

By the spring, the Crown had decided to remove Mitchel from his confinement in Bermuda's waters and transport him elsewhere. He sailed on the *Neptune,* leaving on April 23. To where he did not know. After a slow trip along the South American coast, the ship crossed the Atlantic and arrived at Cape Town on September 19. There, settlers continued to stiffly resist British attempts to plant another penal colony. "No man can guess what our ultimate destination may be, probably Australia," Mitchel wrote, "and of Australia I have felt the utmost abhorrence." For the time being, he was stuck, back in the familiar "wooden gaol" at anchor. Through the southern spring and early summer of 1850, the *Neptune* did not leave the African port, nor did Mitchel come ashore. The last thing Meagher heard of his friend, through the months-old mails, was that Mitchel was adrift at sea.

Meagher also fretted about Smith O'Brien, whose defiance on Maria Island was slowly breaking his will and his body. He suffered frequent chest pains, grew thin and weak. This son of Irish kings, this master of Dromoland Castle, was crushed upon first seeing the two-room cabin on the wind-raked island where he was ordered to spend the remainder of his days. O'Brien had a quartet of guards watching him at all hours. He was allowed to speak to only one other human, a Protestant chaplain. "No person, not even a child, is allowed to approach me except the officer who brings me my meal." He could not receive simple treats, sugar or raisins, from the outside. Meagher was aghast. He wrote to Governor Denison in his most formal and solicitous tone, his rebel pen fully holstered. "May it please Your Excellency," he began, and then detailed the contents of recent letters he'd received from Smith O'Brien. "His strength has been greatly weakened, and his health in general very seriously impaired." Could the gracious, kindhearted, most excellent sir, "influenced by a sense of common justice and humanity," find it in his knighted heart to look into Smith O'Brien's condition? A few days later, Meagher opened a short note from the Convict Department acknowledging receipt of the letter, but nothing more. Yet Meagher's note worked after all. O'Brien was soon in the care of a Maria Island gentleman, a doctor with a passel of pretty daughters.

In the Australian fall of March and April, the vines of gloom found Meagher. The ragged, gossip-snarled island still held nothing for him — it was "a raw, ill-formed colony . . . teeming with all the vulgarities of English life," he wrote Duffy. The natural world was inside out. The swans were black with red beaks — the reverse of the white, yellow-beaked whoopers that crowded the Shannon. At dusk, the casuarina trees looked to be bleeding olive green through long droopy needles. The night sky held the Southern Cross, a complete stranger of stars to Meagher. At midday, the sun felt oddly bright and close to the skin. And how absurd was it to apply the societal frosting of Britain — a regatta on the river, Royal Botanical Society meetings over tea — to an island penitentiary. His walks were longer, deeper into the woods, hiking to exhaustion. He bought a horse, got a dog, went for bouncy rides till dusk, chatted endlessly with his mount, a four-legged recipient of the most refined language spoken under the Tasmanian sun. Exercise was his only escape, "dashing through the woods, clambering up hills, clearing fences." Deeply tanned, in robust good health, his body was lean and muscled, in contrast to his sagging soul.

He was becoming a different man — someone he did not recognize and did not like. "I felt, day by day, the impulses which prompted me to act a generous part at home withering and dying fast," he confided in a letter to a fellow exile. "I felt, with equal pain, despondency and remorse, a spirit of indifference, inertness, and self-abandonment seizing my heart." Days passed with just "my books, my pen and my horse." The emptiness, from lack of company, was a sickness in itself, dragging a bright man to his depths. He was sinking with every passing day, he admitted, his innate high spirits drained away, under "the thought that our lives as far as we can see are purposeless." At times, he convinced himself that he was in Ireland again, and tried to people the penal colony with apparitions. The large body of water in his district became one of the lakes of Killarney, mist shrouding the stone-stacked and chiseled castles of Celtic royalty. The island in its center was not an unpopulated tract of gum trees but the Abbey of Innisfallen, where Brian Boru was said to have received his education. All around him were round towers, cloistered with ale-brewing, manuscript-translating monks. And here—close and real enough to touch—was Ross Castle, once more the ancestral home of perhaps the last fortress to fall to Cromwell. A willful delusion, all of it. But it was a form of madness to keep from going mad.

It was during one of his endless walks in the highlands that Meagher hit on an idea to relieve his loneliness. His district was thirty miles long by ten miles wide. The neighboring confinement belonged to Kevin O'Doherty, the aspiring doctor who'd arrived on a separate ship. Meagher discovered that a little murmur of a creek touched both of their districts. *Mmmm* . . . And there was a bridge just across this water. Neither of the convicts, standing on that span, would be in violation of the terms of their ticket-of-leave. But why stand? Meagher arranged for a table, chairs, a linen cloth and a multicourse luncheon, a pub owner bringing plates of mutton, steaming potatoes, gravy, cheese and grog. They sang and laughed and almost fell into the water. After "very copious libation," they named the bridge the Irish Pier. The felons agreed to meet again. Same time next week, 11 a.m.

O'Doherty missed his lover, Eva Anne Kelly, a black-haired poet in the cause of free Ireland and the other voice in the one-two female punch at the *Nation*. The couple had planned to marry before the Crown's prosecution broke it off. Still, he was faithful to her—one of the reasons why he was nicknamed Saint Kevin. Not so some of the other Young Irelanders. They were men of deep-felt political convictions, but men all the same. Meagher's sickly shipmate on the *Swift*, the excitable Patrick O'Donoghue, had written his wife about the "vice of all kinds, in its most hideous and exaggerated form, openly practiced by all sexes and classes" on the island. He then practiced some of it himself, though he did not share this with his wife. At a picnic he "got lost in the bush," as the story was relayed in a letter between Irish prisoners, "and by remarkable coincidence, the hostess of the party got lost too." On the island, O'Donoghue didn't try to keep this tryst a secret— the woman was very pretty, he bragged. Smith O'Brien, father of seven, his features as chiseled as those of a statesman posing for currency, soon had a young companion for his walks on Maria Island—one of the teenage daughters of the doctor who'd been treating him. On a seat in the garden, the girl was seen reaching into the open fly of Ireland's forty-seven-year-old political exile—giving him an "old fashioned," as the Victorians called the stroke of a hand. Two of the constables who

kept an eye on Smith O'Brien had witnessed the act through a tele-
scope and reported it to their superiors. When confronted, the convict
was noncommittal, but he made a reference to "a kindly desire to miti-
gate the loneliness of my solitude."

For his part, Meagher put his energies into his new home, a cottage on Dog's Head Peninsula at Lake Sorell. He'd been given land
by a sympathetic settler in the higher reaches of the island. A large
skiff was hauled up by oxen, outfitted with sails, topped with an American flag and tied to a primitive pier in front of his cabin. Meagher
had told his friends he was done with romance. He intended to live
solo and celibate. But in naming his boat, he showed that he had not
completely forgotten about a woman who had been dazzled by him in
Ireland. This *Speranza* gave Thomas Meagher days of lonely pleasure
on the open water of the lake, gliding from imaginary Ross Castle to
the island holding Innisfallen. Back in Dublin, the inspiration for the
boat's name, the poet Jane Elgee, had married Sir William Wilde, onetime oculist to Queen Victoria. They kept a strain of Irish nationalism alive, though contained within the parlor of their sumptuous home.
Jane also gave birth to a boy who would become a brilliant dramatist,
and be jailed for another Victorian crime: the love of another man. He
was Oscar Wilde, but was better known to the Irish worldwide as the
son of Speranza.

Through the Tasmanian winter, word passed of plans for an escape.
What was once considered impossible had grown in schemes hatched
on three continents. Several of the leaders of the failed uprising of 1848
had made it to America, and there they joined the extensive network
of powerful Irish New Yorkers. A thousand people met in Manhattan's
Tammany Hall, protesting the treatment of the exiles, cheered on by
Horace Greeley, the influential editor of the *New York Tribune*. Money
that had been raised for guns in Ireland now went to springing political prisoners from the penal colony. The cause was not dead yet. If one
could be liberated, he might start something fresh. Meagher's boyhood
chum Patrick Smyth plotted from New York to get his friend off the island. It was more important, Meagher insisted through letters to third
parties, to free Smith O'Brien. Meagher was also concerned that the
older man would not live long in solitary confinement. But also, given
his status, a liberated Smith O'Brien would be a greater coup.

At the same time, Irish in the United States, England and Canada, and settlers in Australia, pressured the Crown to pardon the prisoners. American officials, meeting the prime minister in London, repeatedly brought up names that the British thought had disappeared from their shores, never to be heard from again. A measure was introduced in the U.S. Senate calling for their immediate release. Even the new president, Millard Fillmore, who took office in the summer of 1850 after the death of Zachary Taylor, appealed to England to release the Irish political prisoners. Should they escape, he assured the fastest-growing voter bloc in America, they would find "safe asylum and full protection" in the U.S.A. And every time a letter made it out from one of the Tasmanian exiles, it found its way into publication in a prominent newspaper. In London, public opinion was turning against transporting convicts altogether. The time was right to bring Smith O'Brien out from confinement on Maria Island. Meagher pledged to pay for most of it, using a loan from his father. A ship was selected, the *Victoria*, piloted by a paroled pirate from Hobart, Captain Ellis.

For two days in August 1850, Smith O'Brien walked the cliffs of Maria Island, scanning the sea. He had never been so low. "I suffer from depression," he wrote his brother Robert. "I find the long evenings desolate. It is dark at four o'clock and I do not go to bed until ten." It would have been far better, he said, to be executed in Ireland. His guards had agreed to give him leisure every now and then to walk alone. Just now, he saw something on the horizon, and waved a white cloth. It was a small boat, with two men paddling and one steering — a craft to take him away to the *Victoria* and then to the French territory of Tahiti. That was the plan, everything in place. When the little craft stopped moving, Smith O'Brien dove into cold winter water and swam furiously toward it, a sick man, frail and desperate. But as he neared the skiff, it remained stalled in place. At the boat's edge, he cried out, extending a hand; no one attempted to reach back. He splashed around, spitting water, before turning back toward the beach. On shore, a dripping, gasping, freezing Smith O'Brien made a dash for the bush, but was picked up by constables who had been watching the entire time.

As it turned out, the bid for freedom was doomed from the start: the Irishman had been betrayed. British authorities knew everything. Within days, Smith O'Brien was removed from Maria Island and hauled off to the convict station at Port Arthur, on Van Diemen's

Land—"as near a realization of a Hell upon earth as can be found in any part of the British dominions," he wrote. Finally, he was a broken man, he admitted, his will to resist gone—"thoroughly beaten by English power." Governor Denison used the episode to argue for harsher treatment of the other Irish political prisoners. He suggested to his superiors in London that these men belonged in chains breaking rocks, or maybe in long-term residency inside the blood-stained cells at notorious Port Arthur, the last home for many a convict who died young of abuse. Smith O'Brien's ordeal was a warning of things to come. Let this be an example, the overlord of the Tasmanian penal colony proclaimed, for anyone else considering a similar move. Escape was futile. The Irish were stuck on this island of the damned for life.

7

THE TRAITOR OF TASMANIA

A most curious man arrived at the southern end of Van Diemen's Land in the fall of 1850 and began hacking a settlement out of the woods near a small stream, with forty or more convicts at his service. Bewhiskered, red-nosed and belligerent, the tall stranger had money and a cache of letters of introduction bearing all the seals of authority the Empire could bestow on a civilian traveler. One note was from the highest colonial official, Earl Grey himself. Another was from the Crown's ruler in Ireland, Lord Clarendon, who had called him "a treasure." These documents were his secrets—he would not show the letters unless his hand was forced. The well-connected pioneer was an Irishman, but what Irishman came to the penal colony with such authoritative backing? None other than John Donnellan Balfe, known to Thomas Meagher as a fast friend and fellow graduate of Clongowes, last seen cheering on the rebels of 1848. Amid all the chaos of the uprising's collapse, during the state trials, the convictions, the rot in jail, Balfe had disappeared. Of course, if you knew where to look, you could find him in Dublin Castle, where he'd fed the English a steady diet of insider information on his countrymen. Three years after Balfe had started down the road as a traitor, two years after he'd fingered Smith O'Brien to a dragoon sergeant and recounted the whispered words of Meagher, Mitchel and Duffy in their secretive moments of plotting, his treachery had yet to catch up with him. For his service to the queen, Balfe had been well paid. Now he wanted to get rich, starting with an exceptional land grant. The informant had followed the men he'd betrayed across the globe to the island in the Southern Ocean, a free man among convicts, a spy among patriots. Young Ireland knew nothing of his arrival, nothing of his past.

Up in the hills, in the center of the island, Meagher continued to craft his own small world in the wild, trying to make a life at Lake Sorell. His cottage had a room for his books and a writing desk, a room for his bed, a small kitchen, a porch on which he could sit and watch *Speranza* bob in the lake and muse on what could have been. He bought another horse and some sheep, and hired an ex-convict, Tom Egan, to help him become a farmer. He fished for black trout and silver eels, hunted duck, snipe and quail. Four hours a day were devoted to reading or writing, but "without purpose," he confided in one letter, "for the future is an utter blank to me — it's a dull, dead sky without one faint streak of light."

He was sustained, still, by family money, though his father had reprimanded him for spending a small fortune on the failed escape attempt of Smith O'Brien. "The adventure in which you risked so much had been excessively improvident and fruitless," the elder Meagher wrote.

The mountain lake was big, seven miles by eight, and empty; the only person Thomas spied was the occasional shepherd, mumbling to himself along a rock path. Meagher and Egan sailed to an island midlake, where they cleared the land and planted oats, turnips, carrots, onions, cabbage and other crops. Egan was a paroled criminal from County Kildare, transported for theft in the famine years. He was a faithful companion to the Young Tribune, but no match in intellect, wit or conversation. Meagher resumed his long hikes with his dog, alone with his troubled thoughts about an Ireland still bleeding people, still in triage.

Walking along a muddy and pockmarked road one day, Meagher came upon a disabled carriage stuck in a ditch. He removed his coat, rolled up his sleeves and went to work righting the wheels. The owner, Dr. Edward Hall, was with two of his six children and their governess, an eighteen-year-old beauty named Catherine Bennett. They lived in Ross — the "little apology of a town" dismissed earlier by Meagher. Desperate for fresh company, Meagher opened the faucet of his charm. The doctor was impressed when he realized the identity of the well-spoken Samaritan.

"The celebrated Thomas Francis Meagher? The Exile of Erin?"

"Indeed." He corrected him — it was *O'Meagher* for now.

Meagher's cottage at Lake Sorell in the penal colony of Van Diemen's Land, drawn by fellow exile John Mitchel. Lonely, adrift, feeling that life had passed him by, Meagher spent long hours in solitude in the upper reaches of Tasmania. COURTESY OF THE TASMANIAN ARCHIVE AND HERITAGE OFFICE

Catherine had large dark eyes, skin without blemish, long black hair tied up in the back. She was somewhat tall. Surely the prettiest girl Meagher had seen in the penal colony, "rounded and elegantly formed," as one acquaintance described her. Meagher detected Ireland in her voice. She was, in fact, the daughter of a felon from County Cavan in Ulster Province, Bryan Bennett. Convicted of robbing a mail coach on the open road—a highwayman, in British criminal parlance—Bennett had been transported to Tasmania more than twenty years earlier. After serving his time, he was given a small plot of land to start fresh. But the *stain*, the first thing to be detected in the identity-sniff of the Australian class system, remained on the Bennett clan. Meagher rode with the family back to their home in Ross. He stayed a few hours till his curfew at dark, finding much to like in the governess and drawing a few disapproving glances from the doctor and his wife. Was he flirting with the fine-featured help? Well, yes. And who could blame him? Nearly all his friends would, as it turned out. He was a prince of Waterford. She was the daughter of a man who held up the mail coach. As Meagher bid the Halls good night, he promised to call again. By then, his charm had worn off the doctor.

When last heard from, John Mitchel was somewhere in the watery emptiness of the Southern Hemisphere. It had been almost a year since his ship left Bermuda. If not dead, he could be alive in some distant port, or adrift—his journey proof of his adage about the sun never setting on England's convict ships. As always, Mitchel spoke for himself, to his diary, in educated prose that was never without bile. He noted in early 1850 that a dispatch from Lord Grey had arrived at Cape Town with Mitchel's fate: he would join the other Young Irelanders in Van Diemen's Land. There was no other choice; England was down to a single overseas penal colony. "So it runs," he wrote. "I am to spend certain years, then, among the gum trees in grim solitude." When he arrived in Hobart, following more than ten months on the *Neptune,* he had none of Meagher's enthusiasm for the beauty of the place. He saw only the cesspool of the British Empire. It was "an island of the unblessed," he wrote, holding "assortments of the choicest and rarest scoundrelism in all creation." His mood was influenced by his health, for Mitchel's asthma had left him weak and unable to sleep a long night.

When the authorities examined this pale, wheezing prisoner, they were concerned enough to let him live with a close friend and fellow political exile, John Martin, in the hamlet of Bothwell. Martin was serving a ten-year sentence for writing a single editorial encouraging Irish home rule. A Presbyterian and a scholar, he had joined the rebels after losing his mother, in 1847, to a disease she contracted while helping famine victims at a workhouse. With Mitchel now joining Martin, there were seven well-known Young Ireland convicts on the island.

After a few weeks at his new home, Mitchel's health improved. His Tasmanian misanthropy did not. "All the shepherds and stock-keepers, without exception, are convicts—many of them thrice-convicted convicts! There is no peasantry. Very few of them have wives; still fewer family: and the fewer, the better. Their wives are always transported women, too: shop-lifters, prostitutes, pickpockets, and other such sweepings of the London pavements. Yet, after all, what a strange animal is man! The best shepherds in Van Diemen's Land are London thieves."

After Martin informed him that their district touched that of Meagher and O'Doherty, Mitchel made plans for a reunion. Mitchel was already referring to his friend as the Hermit on the Lake. They had last seen each other two years earlier, when Mitchel was dragged from a Dublin courthouse in leg irons and Meagher had to be subdued while rushing the prisoner's dock. Mitchel was disgusted with how the 1848 rebellion had turned out, an object of ridicule and scorn, and a further indictment of the Irish character. A spring of so much promise had fizzled into a summer of disaster, "a poor extemporized abortion of a rising," Mitchel called it in a diary entry.

Riding more than twenty miles to the highlands that held Lake Sorell in a stony embrace, the convicts reached a plateau, with mountains in the distance, on the lakeshore shy of Meagher's cottage. It rained, lightly at first, then in bullets, followed by snow flurries. The meeting point was the hut of a shepherd named Cooper which touched each of the districts. When Mitchel and Martin arrived, Cooper told them Meagher was not there—he'd gone looking for them. Soaked and shivering, the two visitors went inside to warm themselves by a fire. Cooper made tea. Near dusk, after four hours of waiting, Mitchel heard the clip-clop of approaching horses and then the boisterous laugh of Thomas Meagher, joined by O'Doherty, the medical student. Meagher leapt from his mount, rushed to the hut and fell into the arms of his fellow exile, the man who had been his political and literary soul mate in Dublin.

Lean, his face burnished by sun and wind, Meagher never looked better, Mitchel recalled—"fresh and vigorous." As for Mitchel, at age thirty-six he was no longer handsome, but frail, with sunken cheeks, bloodshot eyes and a hesitant step. The years in confinement at sea had further squeezed out whatever optimism and openheartedness he had left in him. Still, any animus that remained over the botched revolution disappeared at Lake Sorell. The four exiles—Kevin O'Doherty, John Martin, John Mitchel, Thomas Meagher—names that had been bundled in indictments for crimes that called for hanging or banishment, tumbled into a ball of backslapping and guffawing and cheek-kissing. They were schoolboys after a soccer goal, soldiers surviving a lethal attack. They were an Irish generation's best hope, thrown to the other side of the earth, *beyond the sea*, clustered in a shack of rough-cut logs barely a hundred feet square. "We all laughed till the woods rang around," Mitchel wrote, "laughed loud and long, and uproariously."

Cooper cooked lamb chops and damper, a kind of flatbread, over the open fire, and they drank tea late into the night. It was hard to hold the food down for the merriment. "I suspect there was something hollow in that laughter, though at the time it was hearty, vociferous and spontaneous," said Mitchel. "But even in laughter the heart is sad." They talked of Ireland, mostly—"the golden hopes of our sad, old country," as Meagher said. They summoned the memory of friends and lovers, martyrs and poets, those taken by starvation, those taken by fever, those who fled to America, those who stayed and mourned, and of course the plume-capped villains who ruled their homeland. On this evening, the future was not dead. They were too young to rot, or settle into domestic peace on an island prison. The slide into gentleman's oblivion must be resisted.

All plans were tentative, but Mitchel, because of his sickly condition, had been informed that he could bring his wife and three boys out to live with him. The prospect of living *here*, even with his loved ones, did not warm him; he detested the place more with each passing day. "The birds have a foreign tongue," he said. "The very trees whispering to the wind whisper in accents unknown to me." O'Doherty was not offered a similar conjugal privilege for his beloved Eva, but he asked every month. To improve his chances, he dispensed free medical care at a clinic in town.

The exiles tossed log after log onto the fire, no one sleepy, laughter chasing away the chill, Meagher in his deep singing voice leading them in rounds of "The Bells of Shandon." To a man, they never had a happier night in the penal colony. "So ends my first visit to Lake Sorell, and it has pleased me well at any rate to find that my friends are all unsubdued," Mitchel wrote. "The game, I think, is not over yet."

When the island's governor got wind of the convicts' reunion, he was furious. Denison wanted the Irish to suffer—alone—in emotional pain, if not physical torment. His most effective weapon was depriving the exiles of each other's company. Van Diemen's Land was not supposed to be a holiday, never. Technically, he could do nothing to break up dinner at a common point in three districts; it was still within the bounds of the parole terms, so long as no one stepped over the line into another's space. *A silly game*—it must be reported up the lines of colonial authority and amended by the Empire. But he did go after other Young Irelanders who'd been spotted out of their districts trying to visit Smith O'Brien. In swift punishment, Denison took away the limited freedom of three prisoners: the merchant MacManus, the hard-drinking and hard-on-his-luck clerk O'Donoghue and the medical student O'Doherty. As an extra measure of petty tyranny, he meted out his sentence on Christmas Eve: three months of strenuous labor during the peak of the Australian summer. O'Donoghue was in no shape to be cracking stones in hundred-degree heat. He had broken two ribs in a drunken brawl and could not inhale without wincing in pain.

Meagher was shocked. He too had dashed out of his district on horseback in an attempt to visit Smith O'Brien, but had managed to slip back to Lake Sorell without being seen. Meagher considered giving up his parole, he told Smith O'Brien by letter, to join the others in chains rather than live by an agreement with "a government capable of acting in so coarse, so imperious and brutal a manner." The Young Ireland leader advised Meagher to stay put; they needed people on the outside. A note from O'Doherty on the chain gang reinforced that view. He labored in a gray uniform, harassed by sexual predators, and was hungry all day from a diet of nothing but mutton broth. "I am treated as a common convict, obliged to sleep with every species of scoundrel, to work in a gang from six o'clock in the morning to six o'clock in the evening—being all the while next to starved," he wrote. He advised Meagher to do everything he could "to keep out of the hands of these men, as you would the devil himself."

The brutal sentence was all the more cutting for its timing. A few months earlier, Queen Victoria had granted the island province a degree of self-government. Property-owning male settlers in the penal colony would now be free to elect representatives to their own regional parliament. *Imagine.* On Van Diemen's Land, a legislative council of twenty-four members could write their own laws, appoint their own judges, levy some taxes for roads and schools. Certainly, the political prisoners of Ireland were happy that the chokehold of England had been loosened in one of its territories. But they could not shake the magnitude of this irony. Here they were, sentenced to life under house arrest. For what? Fighting to gain in Ireland the very freedom that had now been granted on their island penitentiary. A paroled rapist, trailing sheep on a Tasmanian bluff, had more political rights than a law-abiding citizen of Erin. Once again the British Empire had demonstrated that there was no greater blind spot on its map of benevolence than the conquered land closest to home.

Exercising the new liberty, several newspapers went on an aggressive campaign against Governor Denison for his retrograde attitude toward convicts and for defending the very concept of a penal colony. Why not end transportation altogether? On the Australian mainland, that idea was ascendant, with majority backing. Well, then, was Van Diemen's Land forever doomed to hold the Empire's human castoffs? This question would be at the heart of the upcoming elections. To counter the growing abolitionist sentiment, the governor hired a crafty polemicist to make his case — Balfe. The informant had done a considerable amount of ghostwriting in the months leading up to the uprising of 1848, sowing discord among the rebels under one pen name, trying to push Young Ireland's leaders to violence under another. Now a ventriloquist for the Crown, Balfe had many voices. As "Dion," his assumed name for the system, the spy wrote essays in support of Denison's restrictive policies. His main argument was profit: the island needed the slave labor of convicts in order to prosper. Free men would mean costly wages for a land that relied on cheap exports of wool, mutton, timber and other goods. The principle of an unfettered free market, so revered in British policy that a million Irish were allowed to die of starvation, had no place in this colony.

With his closeness to the governor, Balfe became more visible, moving about socially, throwing around the names of his connections in Westminster. But one day in Hobart his past caught up with him. Not long after Patrick O'Donoghue had finished his punitive stint on a work crew, he bumped into Balfe on the street. He was flabbergasted. What was Balfe, a free Irishman among his old condemned colleagues, doing in Van Diemen's Land? The informant tried to explain and dissemble, but none of it added up.

"Would you believe it? Balfe! John Donnellan Balfe, who represented himself as a Club member, as a Confederate," O'Donoghue wrote. This jolt of news was contained in a letter to Meagher and later forwarded to Duffy in Dublin, who would help to untangle all the threads of his treachery. "Would you believe it—this devilish rascal—this big, bloated and besotted scoundrel." O'Donoghue was beside himself, spittle in his words. "And make no mistake . . . he had taken a grant of land. And day after day in the company of government officials . . . A huge rogue and renegade—there he is! With his dingy spectacles, one of which is cracked. There he is!" Young Ireland had finally found its traitor. Balfe now had little choice but to cling to the Crown's skirt. He needed the protection and the money. And for his latest service to England, he was given a plum government job to go with his sawmill business— he was named deputy comptroller of convicts, overseeing the men he'd betrayed.

In the last months of 1850, the Hermit on the Lake was a clatter of joy. Yes, Meagher agonized over the troubles that had befallen his mates, and he eagerly awaited news of his tortured homeland—a distant signal to telegraph a way for his tomorrows. But now he was preoccupied: he couldn't get enough of Catherine Bennett. For the first time since he'd been shipped to the penal colony, he seemed to be lifting the blanket of despair over his fate. The courtship was no casual affair. Meagher threw himself all in, writing notes in his best hand, singing to the governess in his most beatific tones, tossing off bits of verse as if the words were gold dust. The dazzle of the blue eyes, the turn of phrase, the dimpled smile—the full force of his physical charisma was unleashed on his *Bennie.* Meagher designed his days around her. He still went through the motions of farming, but his heart was not into turnips and carrots. By the late Tasmanian spring, his deadened soul and the somnambulism of the long walks in the woods were a thing of the past. Catherine had renewed "the proud and generous nature that was sinking, coldly and dismally, into a stupid and sensual stagnation," he told one exile. "Glory! Glory! be to Heaven, I am myself again."

But his friends saw only disaster. For one, something more than his heart was throbbing. Meagher was full of lust in a land with very few acceptable single women. To his mates, it was understandable that a man in his prime could not bear "sensual stagnation." Still, couldn't he find someone more fitting of his class? Mitchel, Smith O'Brien, Martin—all may have hated Britain for its persecution of Ireland, but they adopted an English view of one's proper place. A man of wealth, a *gen-*

tleman, a graduate of Stonyhurst, did not take up with a felon's daughter. Meagher had arranged a few surreptitious introductions of the beauty of Ross to his fellow exiles. Smith O'Brien was impressed by her looks, and little else. "She is in person and manner very pleasing," he wrote in his journal, "but in a worldly point of view the connection cannot be seen as advantageous to him." Martin was more blunt. "God help the poor fellow!" he wrote a friend. "I fear—I fear!—one of the finest fellows that ever lived is in great danger of rushing headfirst and with eyes open to the very pit of destruction." What did this country governess, *this girl,* know of history and literature, of politics and art? How could she ever hold up her end of a conversation with the man described as the greatest orator of his generation? As for Mitchel, he was "astonished," he said, that his friend would try to live the rest of his days with someone lacking a hint of sophistication.

But Meagher could not be stopped. Around Christmas, he proposed. He was deeply hurt that his friends thought he was marrying beneath his standing; he couldn't convince them otherwise. "I know full well," he wrote O'Doherty in the neighboring prison district, that "I shall not elevate myself by the connection on which I have passionately and proudly set my heart." Still, for him, love trumped class. Couldn't they see that? The trappings of position, material goods, family name—*damn it all,* he was a felon serving a life sentence in a faraway penal colony. "Let the world pursue its own course and seek enjoyment, wealth, grandeur through the glare of gold, and old family plate amid the emblazonery [*sic*] of crests and shields." A date was set for Sunday, February 22, 1851. He circulated a note. "No gloves, no cards, no cake. Everything very quiet."

The simple ceremony took place at the home of Dr. Hall. Looking out at the guests, Meagher spotted someone with familiar eyes, much of his face covered in a ragged beard, barely recognizable—Terence MacManus. The wool broker from Liverpool, late to Young Ireland's cause, was the only man from their circle to attend the wedding. His very appearance was a crime. He had been doing hard labor in a prison camp when word came that he was to be released from the chain gang—a reprieve made possible by a legal technicality. MacManus promptly announced that he would no longer abide by the overall terms of his sentence, and went into hiding. Police throughout Van Diemen's Land were searching for him. MacManus wished the groom well. He said the island was no longer for him. He intended to escape, and had one small request of his friend: to take care of his dog, a greyhound named Brian. *Yes, yes, of course*—the dog would join Bennie and Thomas in exile at Lake Sorell. Meagher embraced him. They held a look, each wanting some of what the other had—a look that also meant farewell, *see you in another world.*

New life. 1851. A farmer. A husband. Maybe soon, a father. The cottage at the lakeshore took on Bennie's touches, warmer, softer. He sang for his wife instead of the habitués of the island's gum trees. He skipped like a four-year-old, one visitor remarked. He worked his land with the convict Tom Egan, took *Speranza* out for long sails. No wind scared him. He tried to establish new records for the trip from the lake island to his cottage—getting down to thirteen minutes, and that through a nasty squall. The home of Mr. and Mrs. Thomas Francis O'Meagher would never be a cell. He built shelves, added a second writing desk. Despite "the remoteness of my friends," as Meagher told his unbending mate O'Doherty, he was happy. "With regards to Bennie—there she is, sitting up in an armchair, looking fresher and more beautiful than ever, in sparkling good spirits." Meagher was dutiful, riding into Ross to get things for his bride, tending to her when she fell ill. She was sickly for a girl of nineteen, suffering from rheumatism, her joints swollen and painful, and often confined to bed.

To outsiders, Meagher seemed the portrait of a contented country squire. In that sense, he was exactly what the Crown wanted—both gentleman and oblivion, without a hint of fight left in him. They'd neutered him. One of the greatest public speakers of his era now rarely even granted his dog an audience. "A sunburnt man in a sailor's jacket stands in the stern, holding the tiller," Mitchel said of one visit with his newly arrived wife, Jenny. "By his side, on a crimson cushion, sits a fair and graceful girl. That sunburnt fellow is Meagher—and the girl? Why, it's Mrs. Meagher."

It had been three years since Jenny Mitchel had seen Meagher, and the antipodean air had done something for him—he "is looking handsomer than he ever did in Ireland." Jenny found the young wife to be "one of the beauties of this country," but like her husband, she didn't approve. In background, in mind, in spirit, Catherine was ordinary. "It's a pity on the whole, (between ourselves)," Jenny clucked in one letter back to Ireland. "I fear his father will be very wroth with him." Her husband, brutal in his sarcasm, was prescient about the fate of the couple. "Why, it's almost like living."

As it turned out, he knew Meagher all too well. The spell of newly-wed rapture could not last. The man was born for struggle on a grand stage, Mitchel believed. Just as Meagher could never be content sipping spirits in the old boys' club in Waterford, could never be a dandy of Dublin, he could not live a life of passive domesticity at Lake Sorell. Certainly, Meagher was *trying* to give up the Big Fight, to turn a page, even as he acknowledged how difficult it was. "I am compelled to a life of uselessness and can do little or nothing to realize the dream that gave light and music to my early years," Meagher wrote a friend on the island. Without meaning or purpose, the days started to move slowly. Though he was master of a small house, it was a forced charade, mostly cosmetic. He was still in prison, his every move monitored, his every plan subject to second-guessing and approval by the island's governor. He kept thinking about what the census of Ireland had revealed: the shredding of a nation, one in four gone by emigration or starvation. The former would never forget; the latter would never be forgotten. That burden of memory was never heavier.

As the bliss dissipated, Meagher grew tired of his leash, tired of his routine, tired of reporting himself every week to the authorities in Ross, "there to take my bow before the magistrate of the police district," tired of being on the wrong side of the small town's gossip, tired of the laughable imitations of Britain latched to this far domain. "Van Diemen's Land could never be my home—not so long as the English flag flies here," Meagher wrote to Duffy. After barely half a year of married life, Meagher was ready to chuck his domestic existence and take some risks again. "How my heart beats and pants for a quick deliverance from this abominable captivity."

When he got word of Balfe's treachery, he jumped at the chance for retaliation. The blather he had heard back in Dublin about their shared Clongowes connection, school and tradition, bound by Jesuit loyalty and all that. To *think* of the midnight meetings where Balfe had been shoulder to shoulder with the young men sketching a free Ireland. Meagher plotted his revenge. But the pen would have to come before the sword.

Writing under the name of Virginius, from the poems of Thomas

Macaulay, Meagher produced a series of missives in a local paper about Balfe's betrayal of Ireland. He found a wide audience in the political ferment of the island's first election. *This man Balfe*, this snitch for hire, had once stood with the rebels on Tara Hill—"when he was loudest in denouncing the government of which is he now the tool," Meagher wrote. In town, the revelations prompted protests and calls for Balfe's head. One man paraded around Hobart with a placard bearing Balfe's name and the image of a dog. "If found," it read, return "to his master, Sir William Denison." Balfe denied the accusations and threatened to strike back. When asked by a newspaper about Balfe's claim of innocence, Meagher sent a cryptic quote from a Virginius poem:

> *Wherever you shed the honey, the buzzing flies will crowd.*
> *Wherever you fling the carrion, the raven's croak is loud.*

As Virginius, Meagher also set his pen to flight on behalf of a self-governing Tasmania. It was high time, he argued, to put an end to the humiliation of this land stocked with condemned human beings. How could people expect to live as a civilized community when the broken souls of Britain were regularly offloaded in its harbors? As he had written while a schoolboy at Stonyhurst against slavery in the United States, he now mounted a vigorous takedown of state-sanctioned human bondage in Van Diemen's Land. Coming from a convict, these words carried more than a hint of self-interest. But Meagher was on the side of inevitability. Of late, the Young Ireland felons had been welcomed into the homes of solid, landowning citizens of impeccable English lineage. In just a few years' time, Her Majesty's proper subjects in the penal colony had been won over by the Irish poets, orators, statesmen and wits exiled in their midst. They wrote letters and columns, and strategized with these progressive Tasmanians on how to win the right to rule themselves.

All of this activity enraged the head jailor, Denison. With great alarm, he reported to colonial authorities that people of standing had opened their doors to these . . . *traitors.* At the same time, his mouthpiece Balfe continued to argue the governor's line: a colony built on the backs of convicts had no future without them. They needed slave labor to survive, and it was their sovereign right. But his arguments smelled, it was said around Hobart and Launceston—the stench of yesterday.

On election day, in a political triumph unmatched in Ireland, the

ideas helped along by Meagher carried the day in the most distant outpost of the British Empire. The results sent a resounding message: those
who wanted to put an end to the penal colony routed Denison's loyalists and took control of the new legislative council. In short order, that
council called for transportation's demise. The governor was appalled
at the rise of "the democratic spirit" and said it "needs to be checked"
immediately. "The elements of which society here is composed" could
never rule themselves, he warned London. They were fatally flawed humans, with a "low estimate placed on everything which can distinguish
a man from his fellows." Most galling to Denison was that the political
pot was being stirred by the Irish rebels—his prisoners—"attempting
to sow dissension among the people of this Colony." They had helped
to accomplish something in the penal colony that they were never able
to pull off in their native land. Meagher was behind the high prose of
democracy, and Smith O'Brien was drawing up a constitution for the
newly democratic state. A constitution from a convict. They were *incor-
rigible!*

Shortly after the election, MacManus put into play the plan for freedom he had mentioned to Meagher at his wedding. He had gone on
the lam, sheltered by sympathetic free settlers. He emerged as a sick
man in a hospital, bedridden, unable to move. Denison sent a doctor
and police to check up on him, with orders for an arrest to follow. But
the sick man was an imposter, with a remarkable likeness to the Irish
broker from Liverpool. As Denison's doctor was fussing over the pre-
sumed felon, the real MacManus was making his way at night to a little port on the north shore. He was taken from there to a trading ship,
the *Elizabeth Thompson*. He sailed to Hawaii and then to San Francisco, arriving on June 5, 1851. In the gold rush boomtown, chock-full
of Irish miners, MacManus was greeted like a hero. At a reception that
included judges, a senator, and members of Congress, San Francisco
Mayor Charles Brenham offered this toast to the fugitive: "Ireland gave
him birth, England a dungeon; America a home, with a thousand wel-
comes."

The escape was thrilling news to Meagher, and infectious, when
word finally arrived more than six months later. His itch to flee, to get
on with a life where he could have some impact, had to be scratched.
He didn't hide his feelings from his wife. They could never have a

proper family, he argued, living under sentence, their children doomed by the *stain*. He was offended to see the cold stares directed at his lover, wife of a convict. "I had not been four months married, when I saw that she had to share the privations and indignities to which her husband himself was subject," he wrote. "A prisoner myself, I had led another from the altar to share with me an odious captivity . . . this I could not bear. Hence I came to the determination of breaking loose from the trammels which bound me to that hateful soil."

Catherine O'Meagher was a free citizen. She could come and go as she pleased, anywhere in the British Empire. But there was a problem: Bennie was pregnant. This only hardened Meagher's resolve. No child of an Irish patriot would reside in the oppressor nation's confinement. Because of her fragility, Meagher was convinced that Bennie should not travel until the baby was born. He would get out first; the family would follow, traveling in style with Meagher money. When they next saw each other, God willing, they would be new parents to a freeborn Irish child.

Coordinating an escape from a base in New York, and with the elder Meagher in Waterford, was no easy thing. A letter sent at Christmas would not arrive in Ireland until April. A ship had to be in place at the right time, the captain paid off and sworn to secrecy. It could all go wrong so quickly; witness the betrayal of a hired mariner in the Smith O'Brien debacle. Following the MacManus breakout, the governor had tightened his control of the state's prisoners. Although it was clear, with the election results in Van Diemen's Land and a change in the political winds in England, that transportation of convicts was headed for history's attic, Denison made life worse for those still tied to life sentences. Anyone trying to escape would be shot.

Meagher took up the challenge with relish. "Could you bring a gun?" he wrote O'Doherty in one of his last notes to a fellow exile. "I intend to go armed to the short collar—a brace of pistols, the rifle . . ." And there was the odd code to which Meagher adhered: he had given his word of honor, after all, that he would not flee, a word that meant something to Victorians of standing.

A few days before the new year, he took Bennie down to her family home and said goodbye. The plan: when she got word of his whereabouts, she would travel first to Ireland, to be with the elder Meagher in Waterford. Then they would reunite in America. She should prepare to be separated from her husband for up to two years. Back at Lake Sorell, Meagher stocked up on provisions: dried food, hardtack, extra clothing. After spotting the fire lit by a supporting family—the signal that all parts of the escape plan were in place—he said goodbye to Egan; enjoy the fruits of their labor. On the morning of January 3, 1852, Meagher sent a note to the magistrate of his district, for same-day delivery—the strange formal act of transition from gentleman's oblivion to gentleman's escape.

> Sir:
>
> Circumstances of recent occurrence urge upon me the necessity of resigning my ticket of leave, and consequently withdrawing my parole.
>
> I write this letter, therefore, respectfully to apprise you, that after 12 o'clock tomorrow noon, I shall no longer consider myself bound by the obligation which that parole imposes.
>
> In the meantime, however, should you conceive it your duty to take me into custody, I shall, as a matter of course, regard myself as wholly absolved from the restraint which my word of honour to your Government at present inflicts.
>
> I have the honour to be, Sir, with sincere respect, Your obedient servant,
>
> > Thomas Francis Meagher

With those words, the exile hoped never to encounter the British Empire again as anything but an equal. Within minutes of receiving the note, the magistrate dispatched a heavily armed patrol up to Lake Sorell. One of the constables, an Irishman, refused to go, and was replaced. The order to police was explicit: if the convict resisted, they should kill him.

8

FLIGHT

One last look, and quickly: the books, companions through the loneliest months, would have to stay, same with the gifts of fellow convicts, the walking stick from O'Doherty, the letters of support, scented and unscented. He needed his cache of food, a hat to shield his face, clothes, clothes, clothes, stuffed into a bag. He shut the cottage door and took the first step outward—his feet, his horse and the wind to carry him with luck more than halfway around the world, to freedom. It was seven o'clock on Saturday evening when friends on horseback arrived with news that constables were on their way to seize Meagher. The Irishman and his coconspirators, neighbors who had agreed to help, crept 300 yards away to a wooded hideout. He heard the approach of the police and waited, voice muffled, in a crouch. Word came from one of his supporters: *they are in your house.* He sprang up and mounted his horse, moving into the dying light of a Tasmanian summer day, January 3, 1852. Now he revealed himself, rising in his stirrups, hat in hand, face visible. He gave the British Empire one shot at him. Now he would perform his gentleman's duty and be done with his captors.

"I am O'Meagher!" he shouted. "Catch me if you can."

The police had only that glance of a defiant equestrian, for he was off with his posse as soon as the last words left his mouth—*done a bolt*, as the locals called it. They went into the bush with a shout, "Hoooooeeeeeeeee," followed by cheers. At a full gallop, they dashed along a path around the rim of Lake Sorell. He knew this part of the island better than his pursuers, could ride it in the haze of dusk, knew the dips and turns, following a barely visible trail. They stopped at Cooper's hut; Meagher's friend was asleep. Startled, he came out with just a nightshirt on, asked who was calling and if there were women present. Meagher identified himself. He paid the old shepherd for past kindnesses, all the times he'd opened his shack for a gathering of exiles.

"Goodbye, Cooper. I'm off."

They raced upward, through the Western Tiers Mountains, toward the coast, in darkness, pushing the pace. At the hut of a shepherd named Job Sims, Meagher dismounted and went inside. There he shaved off his mustache. He could count on support from many of the Irish, Welsh and English convicts living in the wild north of the island, and could have hid out there for weeks. But Meagher was eager for open water and beyond, to get to the shore and a rendezvous, 140 or so miles away, as quickly as he could, even if it meant exhausting his mounts or risking accident. All night they moved across the island, cresting the Tiers, downslope to the northeast coast.

Sunday was hot, buggy, exhausting. Meagher wrote a short summary of his escape for publication in a local newspaper, and included the names of witnesses who could verify his account should someone challenge his word—to prove he had acted honorably. After a change of horses, he pushed on in great haste, refusing to rest, not with guards in pursuit. The chill, the fright, the uncertainty of moving through Ireland four years earlier in the last days of the uprising, came back to him— daylight hours in Munster haylofts, nights moving in the shadows.

That Sunday morning, Governor Denison got word of Meagher's escape. He cursed his name and accused him publicly of breaking his word. It was one way to hurt him, should he get away—sully the reputation of the great orator. The other way was to catch him. And if so, Denison had already planned a punishment. He announced that he would ship Meagher to the hardest of the hard labor camps still in operation on the island, Port Arthur—its walls spattered with blood from the backs of men shredded with cat-o'-nine-tails, its timber crews chained while felling trees, its isolation a punishment in itself. "I will send him to Port Arthur," the governor announced, "and make him a bottom sawyer under a very good top one." The implication, of rape and work that would break or kill him, was lost on no one.

By Sunday evening, the escapee was in Westbury, north of Lake Sorell. There were not many people in the region, but enough Irish settlers and paroled convicts that Meagher did not have to hide. He found shelter for the night, a meal and hearty encouragement to make it off the island. The next day, new volunteers offered to ride with him, following the Tamar River as it widened and spilled into the sea in a northern heave. His destination was Waterhouse Island in Bass Strait, the big sea-lane separating mainland Australia from Van Diemen's Land. It was a shipping channel linking the Indian Ocean to the Pacific through the Tasman Sea, a useful shortcut for traders and raiders, pirates and ferrymen, the currents swift. Two fishermen had been paid in advance to take Meagher to the island. From there, he would catch a ship—the *Elizabeth Thompson*, the very vessel that delivered MacManus to freedom a year earlier. Everything had to line up with precision. Communication was by signal flares, handkerchiefs and shouts. If the timing was off, it would doom the escape; Meagher had just one chance to catch the ship. The details had been worked out over months, which meant much could have been lost as the plan passed from hand to hand. Was the vessel to meet him Tuesday or Wednesday? Was it the south side of Waterhouse Island or the north? Would the captain wait if Meagher didn't see him at first? And what about betrayal, as happened to Smith O'Brien on Maria Island? A setup?

Late Monday afternoon, Meagher reached Bass Strait, at the mouth of the river that drained the northeast corner of Van Diemen's Land. He said farewell to his companions on land, thanked them for aiding his liberation attempt and took up with two brothers for hire, the Barretts, fishermen with a small open boat they had built themselves. The craft did not look seaworthy. Waterhouse Island was about two miles offshore, flat-topped and cliffy, a barren, treeless squat of sand. To get there, the convict and the fishermen had to row along the coast for almost forty miles and then cross the two miles through open water, with the hard currents and chop of the strait, surf breaking over the bow. They paddled under the summer sun, fighting strong northwesterly winds, and had trouble staying on course; the strait ran almost like a river between the ebb and flood stages of the tide. When the winds calmed, the water was clear enough to see dark images lurking just below the surface: the shadowing of sharks. Makos were the most common species, up to ten feet in length, the fastest of all sharks—flashes of gray in the shallow waters of the strait. Those fish the Barrett brothers could club away. What they feared were the great whites prowling these waters, twenty feet long or more, with a slashing maw of razor teeth.

The wind galloped, the sea rose. Meagher was ordered to lie at the bottom of the boat, as ballast. Waves of two feet, four feet, six feet, fifteen feet. Head down, Meagher faced the faded canvas of the boat bottom, full of patches; it had ripped before, clearly, and the passenger wondered whether the pull of the sea would tear it wide open. Meagher popped his head up to get a look.

"Any danger?"

"Too late for that."

The fishermen wrestled with the surf, leading their craft up to the crests of waves, then plummeting down, the stern buried in water before it reappeared. As the boat rode the bucking sea, the oars flailed in the air. When Meagher popped up for another look, all he could see was foam and froth. The wind screamed for two hours. Meagher was terrified. Finally, in late afternoon, the speck of Waterhouse Island came into view. It was not even a square mile in size, barely a bump of land sheared off at the top of ragged cliffs. They found a cove and beach and went ashore, dragging the scuffed-up skiff to above the tide line. Meagher saw no trace of human activity save the shell of a shipwreck decomposed by sun and surf. Exhausted, the men fell to the ground and rested till dark. A meal of smoked herring and biscuits, washed down with sherry, served as dinner revival. With pieces of the wreck they made a fire. The carrion of the ship was also scavenged for shelter: scraps of sail were wrapped around the broken mast, making a tent of sorts.

On Tuesday morning, day four of the escape, Meagher scanned the strait for his rescue ship. The news of his flight was out, and two Tasmanian newspapers were openly rooting for Meagher against the Crown—"here's to every success and a continuation of freedom," wrote the editors of the *Hobart Town Guardian*. On this day, a feral dog, a black and tan Newfoundland, had found the sun-blasted crew on the beach. Don't say anything to it, the fishermen warned; it was a ghost on four feet, an evil spirit haunting the island. But Meagher took to the stray, soon to be his only mate. The day passed without anything to give him hope. The strait kicked up with the afternoon winds. Nothing appeared on the water.

Wednesday, same thing—all day squinting into the sun, looking for large sails, the white clouds of rescue, chatting with the fishermen brothers. On Thursday, they ran out of food. The Barretts had anticipated a trip of no more than two days, and had taken just enough rations for that spell. They had no choice but to return to Van Diemen's Land and leave Meagher alone on his pancake of sand. He understood: they had done all they could for him. And in case anyone doubted their duty to the escape, or if he were to die and they would be accused of foul play, he would vouch for them. Here ... he'd put it in writing. Meagher crushed a tin drinking cup, flattening it completely, then blackened it over a fire. On this dark surface, he used the tip of a knife to write a primitive letter telling of his position, requesting provisions, and an explanation: the Barrett brothers had done their service for Ireland in the strait separating the Australian mainland from Van Diemen's Land. The fishermen rowed away. "I was alone on that morose island," Meagher wrote.

He was hungry, unable to forage much from the tiny wasteland of Waterhouse Island. Any food would have to come from the sea, at low tide—what could be chipped from rocks and cracked open. It was hard work, his hands bloodied, and for little protein. He followed the patterns of birds, their feeding habits, where they ended their days, where they delivered food. He found nests in the cliffs, climbed up, and there reached for eggs. It was not enough, and meant a dangerous struggle with protective avian parents. He would starve to death if he couldn't find other sources of food. Or he would die of thirst. He had enough water, if rationed wisely, for another week or so, but that was it. The island had no fresh water of its own. Meagher would need to capture rainfall. But in summer it could be a long time before anything fell from the sky. At night, the biggest fear was what slithered along the ground—big, fully-fanged black tiger snakes. Of all the Tasmanian exotics that frightened exiles in the penal colony, tiger snakes were the worst, at least by reputation. They crawled in the darkness, impossible to see, leaving a signature in the sand. Their venomous bite killed more humans than any other creature on land. Carnivores without discriminating taste, they attacked by flattening the body, lifting a swollen head up and then springing on prey with a quick stab through the air. Venom from the bite caused instant numbness, followed by shortness of breath, gasping and death. If Meagher kept a large enough fire going, perhaps the heat would keep the tiger snakes away. But it would also attract the police, on patrol offshore.

On day seven of the escape, Friday, Meagher took up position under the unreliable shade of his ripped sail. He saw one passing ship, far out in the strait. Joy! Could this be the *Elizabeth Thompson*? He threw timbers of the shipwreck onto his smoldering blaze, stoking it to bonfire size as a signal. He jumped up and down, waving his coat, shouting, screaming into the strait, the wind grabbing his voice and tossing it away, up toward the Tasman Sea. This went on for some time, but the ship did not appear any larger on the horizon. It shrank and then slipped away entirely. The next morning, a week and a day into his penal colony break, Meagher spied a second ship. Again he built his fire to a height that rose above the flat of the island; again he jumped and shouted and waved his coat like a flag.

"Here! Here! Over here!"

But this ship disappeared like the other one, northeast with the winds, in the direction of New Zealand, more than 1,200 miles away. Meagher was left with his feral dog and the longing—what it might be like to snuggle in bed with his bride tonight, to be cooking lamb chops with Egan, watching the last light on Lake Sorell, a book to read, poems to write, songs to sing. Better to keep the mind on Bass Strait, on transport. It had all been arranged, after all, half of it paid for in advance. And this captain was reliable, yes? MacManus had been delivered to a joyous throng in San Francisco. Imagine, then, what reception awaited Thomas Francis Meagher on the other side of the Pacific— that ocean of no end, that leviathan of water.

Another day broke with a heavy mist, visibility limited. Meagher saw something emerge on the strait and built his signal fire. But it was not a full-sailed ship that took shape, not a mighty trading vessel. It was an eight-oared boat, low to the water, moving at a strong clip from the mainland to Meagher's island hideaway. This could not be good. Meagher entertained a dread thought: "The police must have seen the fire."

For all the talk about the code of honor among prisoners in Australia, the Irish convicts always felt they had a higher obligation: to escape. The British Empire showed no honor in the forced removal of families from their homes—children taken for stealing bread, noblemen banished for speaking out, mothers plucked from their hearths after stealing some cloth to weave into a quilt. From the arrival of the first political prisoners, transported following the failed rebellion of 1798, to the present year of 1852, when nearly a thousand Irish were freshly deposited in Van Diemen's Land, the true badge of distinction belonged to the person who could break from Britain's hold. Only a few ever made it. And fewer still among Meagher's class, for the political prisoners were the rarest of escapees.

Early on, all getaway attempts were futile; the bush was too harsh, the sea too forbidding, the distance from safety too far. But the land down under bred ingenuity in many ways, especially among the convict class. One man disguised himself as a kangaroo—hopping about in skins—to get away from awful Port Arthur. He looked so convincing that a guard mistook him for the real thing and shot him for sport. Mary Bryant, sentenced to seven years for stealing a silk bonnet, escaped from the mainland in the six-oared cutter of the provincial governor, with her children and roustabout husband aboard. She knew nothing of the sea. But after packing rice, dried meat, charts and a compass, and returning to shore several times for fish, turtles and crab, the family navigated through the Great Barrier Reef and made it, over 3,000 miles, to Dutch Timor. Upon landing, they announced themselves as castaways, a ruse that lasted until the husband, on a drunken binge, spilled the true tale of their identity and spectacular escape. The family was promptly shipped back to England and a new prison. Alexander Pearce, banished for stealing six pairs of shoes, also made his getaway by stolen boat. But he and four companions were not mariners. They washed ashore back on Tasmania and were soon starving. After drawing lots, they cannibalized the loser. Pearce, the lone survivor, was caught and hanged.

By the time Meagher found himself a wanted man, the penal system, driven by newfound political freedom in the colony, was nearing its final days. But what truly hastened the closure of the Empire's largest gulag was gold. In April of 1851 came news of an enormous find of the world's most valuable commodity beneath the hard-crusted wasteland of New South Wales. As with all such mother lodes that drive people to a frenzy, the stories spread with their stock of superlatives, many of them exaggerated. The goldfield was said to be much larger than what drew the forty-niners to the Sacramento River in California—more than 300 miles long. A single lump of gold weighed seventy-five pounds. With sudden wealth, newly rich men lit their pipes with pound notes. In a half year's time, horse thieves moved from tented shacks to brick estates. Five months after the discovery in New South Wales, another big strike occurred in the state of Victoria. Now, it was all the colony could do to keep its officers and bureaucrats, its guards and farmers, from dropping everything and rushing off to "the diggings." In 1852, the year of Meagher's attempted escape, 100 million tons of gold were exported from Victoria, enough to sink a fleet of the queen's ships. And in that same year, 300,000 immigrants came to the penal colony—by choice.

Gold made Australia more profitable as a free man's destination than a prisoner's hold. The next year, the last convicts arrived in Van Diemen's Land, including another thousand Irish. Three years after that, in an effort to shake a half century of notoriety, the island changed its name to Tasmania. Transportation was over for all but the far western coast of Australia, north of Perth. And while the end of the convict ships did not mean that those who were under sentence were paroled or given more liberties, it took away whatever justification remained for the British Empire to discard its undesirables 14,000 miles from home.

In the cove where Meagher had made his camp, the swift-moving rowboat came ashore. Several men charged from the vessel and came face-to-face with the sun-ravaged Irishman. One man had lost half his nose. Another had lost an ear. A third looked at Meagher through a single eye, the other closed and scarred. A fourth man was missing half his fingers. And the fifth man had but a single front tooth; he smiled at Meagher. They did not look like representatives of the long arm of the Crown: they were scruffy, unshaven, their clothes soiled, foulmouthed and foul-smelling. But then, Meagher didn't look like a Waterford gentleman. He too was scruffy, unshaven, his clothes soiled. And hungry— he'd been kept alive by a diet of fern roots, small fish and eggs from the cliff nests. The escapee explained that he was a gold prospector. A prospector? *Well, who wasn't?* All of Australia was fortune ground, after all, needing only to be scratched. Meagher's cover story defied credulity; it was preposterous to think that gold could come out of the wind-tousled sand-cake of Waterhouse Island. He said no more.

The strangers set up a large tent of their own, picked away at the shipwreck and by nightfall had a roaring fire. They hauled out food, enough provisions to tide them over for weeks—crab, onions, dried lamb meat, biscuits—as well as alcohol and tobacco. A seafood stew was concocted over the fire in a large pot. The exile was invited to join them. Ravenous, he fell on the feast. The men told their story: they were convicts, just escaped from Hobart, stealing a boat and racing up the eastern shore of the island to get to Bass Strait—a trip of nearly 500 miles. *Hurrah!* And they too were prospectors of a sort, crossing Bass Strait on the way to Port Phillip in Victoria, on the southern coast of Australia, where another big gold strike had just been announced. In the ground-scraping rush for nuggets, no man had a past; all were equal in the chase.

Meagher considered these escapees "pirates," as he called them, and found their company delightful—not only for the food and conversation, but for the sprightly optimism of the newly sprung. In his first days of freedom, Meagher had felt the same way. The pirates stayed on the island for several days. Meagher promised to repay them for all they had given him. "I had the best and most of everything," Meagher wrote, "the snuggest corner of the tent, the rarest morsels of the daily stew, the choicest pipe full of tobacco." What he couldn't hide were his true intentions, for no prospector spent the day staring at the sea. Meagher told the truth: yes, he was looking for something other than gold—a way out of England's human dump. It solidified their bond. All had *done a bolt*.

After ten days on Waterhouse Island, Meagher spied yet another object floating on the blue horizon, though it was somewhat difficult to make it out in the usual morning mist. This one did get closer and bigger, and assumed the shape he'd been longing for: a large sailing ship. It got near enough to shore that Meagher could discern a flag fluttering from the mizzen: the stars of the Australian League. From the deck, a signal gun was fired, startling Meagher, followed by a second blast, then a third. A man could be seen waving a white flag on board. The *Elizabeth Thompson* had arrived. Meagher jumped up and down, yelled with joy, rolled up his bundle of filthy possessions and waited for his deliverance. But with the wind and current, the seas were unstable and white-capped; the ship, even after shortening her sails, could come no closer. Meagher would swim if he had to. The pirates offered to row him out to his liberators through the high, rough chop. They rode the waves, rolling and dipping, out to greet the big vessel, swamped several times, sharks starting to circle. As they tied up to the *Thompson*, Meagher turned to his fellow escapees. "I emptied my pocket of all the money in it and handing it down to the leader of the gang, bade them farewell forever."

On the quarterdeck, Meagher met Captain Betts, a short, well-fed, convivial man with enough wit and a stockpile of stories to match Meagher's tales. They were carrying wool from down under to England by way of South America. The crew seemed more than happy to have a lively new passenger. Meagher kept his identity secret. To everyone but the captain, he was not a political prisoner on the run but a paying traveler with an unusual way of embarking. He could not risk a leak. The *Thompson* may have been sailing under the Australian League flag, but she had to follow the Empire's rules. To his delight, he found that Captain Betts could quote poetry at length—Byron in particular. The ship sailed northeast, through Bass Strait into the Tasman Sea, out to the open Pacific to cross the earth in the Southern Hemisphere.

In the days that followed, Governor Denison was removed by his English superiors and sent to a new post. He was bitter to the end at the collapse and liberation of his kingdom of felons. Another 10,000 convicts would be sent to the western shore of Australia—but that was it for the experiment of trying to make a cage of a continent. The last ship of captives from Great Britain arrived in Australia in 1868, just a few years after Abraham Lincoln freed four million slaves in the United States.

Breezing through the warm waters of the South Pacific, looking back in the direction of Young Ireland's banishment, Meagher was a prisoner no more. Now he was a fugitive, soon one of the world's best known. His calling would be to translate a history of famine and oppression, exile and humiliation, into a life of possibility in a country founded on the opposite principles of the penal colony.

PART III

TO BE IRISH IN
AMERICA

HOME AND AWAY

He had seen half the world from a ship's deck, and yet nothing prepared him for how many of the earth's uprooted strivers had stuffed themselves into New York City in 1852. Carriages dashed and shifted, horses clopped and whinnied, stevedores grunted and cursed, all in waves—not the music of commerce, but the off-key chorus of chaos. Boatmen, ferrymen, porters, carters, stage drivers, washerwomen, predators of immigrants, domestics walking other people's children, and teenage girls in face paint handing out fliers for the afternoon melodrama on the Bowery. Was that the Teutonic tongue coming from Kleindeutschland, the third-largest German-speaking community in the world? And Yiddish rising from the cluster of rag merchants a few blocks in the other direction? What hybrid of the Queen's English was this dialect of free blacks working dockside? Surely, a hint of County Kildare clattered from that street-cleaning crew, and his own Munster brogue rolled out of a basement shebeen. All of this in the kinetic claustrophobia of the Lower East Side, nursery of a nation whose people were looking less like those of the mother country by the day. Around one turn, the smells were unpleasant in the late-spring humidity, sweat twined with horseshit, dogshit and pigshit, the piles to be swept into the river by day's end—6,000 cartloads a night. A few blocks on, he was hit with a waft from the fresh-cooked offerings of barefoot girls, who enticed customers with this chant: "Hot corn! Here's your nice hot corn! Smoking hot, smoking hot, just from the pot!"

The island of Manhattan was smaller than the prison district where Thomas Meagher had been condemned to spend the rest of his life.

But it held a world of fellow exiles—from Russia's pogrom-swept villages, from the Rhine's ruined farms, from Africa's plundered hamlets and from ashen-blighted fields abandoned by those strong enough to walk away from the Great Hunger. On May 27, the day Meagher stepped ashore, this New York was home to just under 20,000 Jews, 12,000 African Americans, 60,000 Germans, at least 160,000 Irish. It was the densest concentration of Irish anywhere: more than one in four New Yorkers in a city of nearly 600,000 had been born in Meagher's homeland.

He walked by City Hall, where men not long from Limerick or Kilkenny held actual power, up Broadway past the booksellers and portrait studios. Onward, toward Canal Street, then right in the direction of the Bowery. On alternate days, bare-knuckle boxing shared space with Shakespeare plays. A scattering of Irish soon became a thicket. They looked worn down and dirty-faced. Their tenements were awful—wooden gaols that could combust in a poof from an untended cigar. Here, flop joints, groggeries and a row of slouch-roofed boardinghouses anchored a city block. The Bowery itself, once a footpath for the native Lenape, had the distinction of being the only major thoroughfare in New York City never to have a single church built on it. Nearby, a former brewery, converted from making beer to warehousing immigrants, was home to a thousand people, some living in stairwells and doorways. For 37 cents a week, you could sleep in a windowless room on a floor with straw; for 18 cents, just the bare floor, with a bucket for the latrine.

Then, south to the center of this stew of start-over people—Five Points. He knew this neighborhood, five blocks in the heart of the Sixth Ward, by reputation. Charles Dickens had come through a few years earlier, notebook in hand, two cops by his side. The novelist was stunned to see the mix of races, Irish and blacks drinking together, dancing in the saloons, a born-in-America toe-and-heel tap that was a blend of Gaelic jig and West African step dance. In darkened corners, mixed-race couples kissed and groped. Where Anthony, Orange and Cross Streets came together, Dickens saw a place "loathsome, drooping and decayed." No part of London could match the wretchedness of the neighborhood. It was without grass or trees, without a sliver of green. Thereafter, tourists paid armed men to guide them through an evening of slumming among the poor Irish—for a chance to be appalled at "shanties in which the pigs and the Patricks lie down together," as the *New York Times* informed a readership accustomed to bedding in clean linen.

The curious didn't come to see the shoemakers and tailors, the fruit sellers and bricklayers. They came for what the great writer called "a world of vice and misery." And though Dickens made Five Points famous, the gangs made it notorious. The Plug Uglies fought the Roach Guards; the Bowery Boys warred with the Dead Rabbits. More political than territorial, the Irish gangs were trying to get a piece of New York action before Tammany Hall refined municipal mayhem into a smooth-running graft machine.

Organized crime, an oxymoron in Five Points, was often overshadowed by those babbling to themselves in the neighborhood's midst; for the change in worlds broke minds as well as souls. Two thirds of the inmates at the New York City Lunatic Asylum, a gray granite fortress on Blackwell Island in the East River, were Irish. As well, Erin's castoffs were at the top of all the social pathologies in the city but one—suicide. The Irish killed themselves with liquor, with accidents prompted by drink, with neglect, with disease, with violence, but would never end their lives by their own hands, for that would ensure that misery followed them to eternity.

For these cobblestone streets of squalor, had families traded clan gatherings in emerald valleys? For the piss-and-brew stench of a tenement, had they swapped sea-scrubbed air? Did a million people flee starvation for a slum with the highest death rate in the new nation? "The first thing a visitor notices is a lamentable want of ventilation," wrote the *New York Tribune* in an exposé of the "Dens of Death" in Five Points. "Swarms of children whose appearance is the best argument that can be found in favor of public wash houses," noted the *Tribune*, the city's most influential paper. "Covered in rags, encased in a coat of dirt, their hair matted into one mass with grease and dust, their limbs distorted by disease or bruised and disfigured by accident . . . utterly ignorant of such a place as school." Not true! There on Mott Street, around the corner from St. Patrick's Cathedral, were clean-faced urchins attending Public School 5. But that was the exception. The most powerful Catholic in New York, the iron-fisted Archbishop John Hughes, had called the inhabitants "the poorest and most wretched population that can be found in the world." If it wasn't obvious to Thomas Meagher in his introductory stroll, the bishop made the point: here was "the scattered debris of the Irish nation." Little wonder the newspapers drew cartoons of them as filthy apes lacking only a tail, whiskers coated in suds, the women more debauched than the men.

Never had so many Irish come ashore than the year leading up to Meagher's first day in America's biggest city. They were rural peasants, mostly, without skills or trades, illiterate, swept across an ocean by catastrophe, the first big wave of the largest transfer of people the world had yet experienced in so short a time. They left more than 20,000 tiny villages to press into one large village of wretchedness in lower Manhattan. Between 1847 and 1851, about 1.8 million immigrants landed in New York City, of which 848,000 were Irish. Some dispersed to Boston, Albany, Philadelphia or Baltimore. Some found their way to the Midwest, to farms and fresh air; to the South; or farther west, to new land taken from the Indians or to the gold-littered streams of California. But most settled among the clot of fellow Irish, barely a mile from where their ships had landed, rarely wandering north of 14th Street. A handful tended pigs and lived out of shanties beyond 59th Street, where the city had plans to build a greensward called Central Park.

The Irish did not know it yet, on this last Thursday in May, that one of the most prominent of their political refugees walked among them — an escapee from Tasmania by way of South America. But he was expected. The *Boston Pilot* had reported in its May 15 edition that the Young Tribune was free. After changing ships in Brazil, from the *Elizabeth Thompson* to the American-flagged *Acorn*, he was due to arrive in the city any day, having been at sea for five months. The paper put the stamp of destiny on Meagher before he even saw New York Harbor. "In him, the Irish will find a chief to unite and guide them."

Ignorant of his future burden, Meagher thumbed through *Doggett's Directory* in search of familiar names. For one day more, he was a stranger in a new land. Dublin's loss, following the uprising of 1848, was New York's gain. Young Ireland's prominent plotters did not dwell in Five Points. They lived well, as barristers, publishers, journalists and politicians — power brokers many of them, still in their twenties. They joined the company of other Irish who had prospered in the city. That

archbishop, John Hughes, was the son of poor farmers in County Tyrone. Now he was the most influential cleric in the country, signing his
letters to the editor, his church edicts and personal notes with his signature cross, which looked like a dagger. And so he was known as Dagger
John. Another Tyrone man, Charles P. Daly, would soon be chief justice of the city's common courts. The district attorney—the law in New
York City—was John McKeon. "What he is," a profile in the weekly
Irish American exulted, "any of us might be." In the Old World, the
police were enforcers of a brutal system that kept the natives in their
place. In the New World, they were heroic, and many spoke Gaelic.
Half the cops in the Sixth Ward were Irish.

Meagher's destination on this day was 39 William Street, in a hive
of silk-vested prosperity a few steps from Wall Street. Here were the
law offices of Richard O'Gorman and John Blake Dillon—two great
friends of Meagher's, and two men who might have been hanged,
drawn and quartered had they not fled. Dillon, a cofounder of the *Nation,* had been with Meagher in the shadows during the last days of
the uprising. After the Empire put a bounty on his head, he escaped to
France and New York. A family friend and schoolboy chum from Clongowes Wood, O'Gorman had joined Meagher in Paris in 1848 for the
ill-fated mission to enlist the help of a new French government. After the failure of the revolt, O'Gorman hid out in the wilds of County
Clare for a month, the subject of a manhunt aided by a huge reward for
his capture. Four years after the debacle in a Tipperary cabbage patch,
both rebels were well-compensated, well-connected elites in the fastest-growing city in the world.

When the partners greeted the man who walked into their office,
they did a double take. The guest was stout, no longer boyish, his face
the color of stained walnut. But when Meagher opened his mouth, all
doubt dissipated—he was the same sparkler of a man they had known
in Dublin, his declarative sentences delivered with customary snap and
punch. They embraced and pinched each other's cheeks as if they were
ghosts brought to full-fleshed form.

Many other Young Ireland coconspirators were building new lives
in New York, Meagher's mates informed him. Michael Corcoran was
living above a tavern at 42 Prince Street. Corcoran had Ireland's struggles in his blood: his great-great-great-great-grandfather was Patrick

Sarsfield, defender of Galway and Limerick against William of Orange in the late seventeenth century. Born to a modest family in County Sligo, Corcoran joined the Royal Irish Constabulary at nineteen, but didn't last long as an enforcer of the Empire. The famine radicalized him. He became a double agent, working for the Crown by day, undermining it by night. At last he took off his badge and took up with Young Ireland. Corcoran, O'Gorman, Dillon and Meagher—all outlaws in Ireland. Here, free men. And get this—*we have the run of the city!* This could happen, one day soon perhaps, in Waterford or Cork. British troops, don't forget, had taken over New York for seven years of the American Revolution. They torched buildings, forced people out of their homes, harassed Catholics—so true to form, the Empire. Under occupation, the city dwindled to 12,000 people. General Howe had landed on Staten Island with the largest expeditionary force that England had yet raised. And now look at this town: New York's population had quadrupled in the last thirty years, with nary a bewigged old Tory in sight. The Irish in America could write anything they wanted, mount a stage and vent without restraint against Britain, ridicule the queen, condemn the prime minister, slam Parliament, defy the Anglican Church, call out the men who let their ragged nation starve—and the Crown couldn't touch them.

America was a fascinating mess, O'Gorman told Meagher: wild, profane, dangerous, but it worked. At least *he* thought it worked. The fastest-growing political party in the United States at the time—the Know-Nothings—did not. To them, the former colonies were losing their Englishness, too fast, to the Irish, to the Germans, to the Jews, to all the foreigners clamoring for rights. The Know-Nothings vowed to close the gates and keep the newly arrived from becoming citizens. Still, there wasn't quite the passion for politics on this side of the Atlantic. More than anything, Americans were "a money-making people," O'Gorman said. Get rich, no matter how, and you could walk anywhere and prompt a tip of the hat.

Word galloped around the city that the daring escapee was on American soil. It spread from the law office on William Street to Five Points, to the saloons, to the armory. A young acolyte, Michael Cavanagh, who had seen dozens of Meagher speeches in Dublin, tracked him down in the city of Brooklyn. "When I knew him in Ireland, he was a handsome, well-built young fellow," Cavanagh recalled. "Now his form was much more robust in appearance and his features bronzed by exposure to the southern sun and the sea breeze during his circumnavigation of the globe ... His youthful lightheartedness and tone of voice had undergone no perceptible changes with the vicissitudes of his fortunes. Frank and free, he was Tom Meagher—the best beloved of his race and generation ... On him were centered the hopes of his exiled countrymen on this continent, to unite them in one solid organized body for the attainment of Ireland's freedom."

Expectations, expectations. Meagher couldn't slip into everyday anonymity, couldn't keep leisurely hours in the office of Dillon & O'Gorman. During his second night in America, soldiers from the 69th New York State Militia showed up outside O'Gorman's home in lower Manhattan, where Meagher had gone for dinner. The regiment was Irish, with a tougher edge and less blarney than any of the dozen or so formal organizations of expatriate Hibernians. On this occasion, they brought the Brooklyn Coronet Band with them. The crowd swelled to more than 7,000 people. They serenaded the fugitive, cheered and fired guns into the air. Irishmen with guns — *what fantasy was this?* They demanded he speak: a few words, please, from the greatest orator of his generation. He was flabbergasted. He had done little of merit, he protested. The uprising of 1848 was a bust. He had escaped the Crown's noose, yes, and its pitiful island prison in the Antipodes, but had nothing to show for his time on earth. A million people had died of starvation in his homeland, and yet England never displayed a hint of remorse for its role. And it was not right to exult in his freedom while his friends—five of the seven Young Ireland leaders, Smith O'Brien, Mitchel, Martin, O'Donoghue, O'Doherty—remained bound to Van Diemen's Land. These few words did not still the crowd. People demanded more. A parade. A feast. A citywide celebration.

ESCAPE OF THOS. F. MEAGHER
HIS ARRIVAL IN THIS CITY

The *New York Times* greeted the escape as a great feat. "His arrival has created universal satisfaction here." The *Irish American* splashed a drawing of his handsome visage across the top of its front page, recounting his life and the details of his getaway. The story quoted from a dozen papers across the United States, after the news had gone out by telegraph.

POWERFUL ENTHUSIASM

THE WHOLE COUNTRY RISING

Here was the man the Irish had been waiting for. They hailed him for resisting family wealth and comfort, for his call to arms when his country had been "turned into a huge cemetery." This "apostle of freedom," as the paper labeled him, had "looked danger and death in the face like a man." A hero, without doubt, perhaps a savior. "All honor to Thomas Francis Meagher." The press in Ireland was equally effusive, a few weeks later. "Meagher in America!" wrote the *Nation*. "What a triumph, what happiness in the words!" They had high hopes for the next act of a man who had yet to reach his twenty-ninth birthday. "We conceive a great career for him under the flag of Washington. He does not go there as a political speculator ... He goes there to lead and amalgamate the Irish race in America."

More expectations. Within weeks, Meagher clubs sprang up in Manhattan, Brooklyn, Jersey City, up and down the Eastern Seaboard from Boston to Baltimore, west in Ohio, south in Charleston. Soon the clubmen were singing a song, "The Escape of Meagher." In Philadelphia, a militia calling itself the Meagher Guard was formed, setting a pattern for other cities. Speaking invitations poured in. The governor of Maryland asked for a visit. The governor of Indiana opened his mansion—*at your service*. Colleges, state legislatures, mayors, parish priests. In the nation's capital, senators, congressmen and judges insisted they be allowed to pay tribute to him. Even the president asked for Meagher. But Millard Fillmore would have to wait.

He needed a drink, to collect his thoughts, some time alone, rest. This welcome had gotten out of hand. It was too much, too fast, a dizzying clamor for a man just days removed from nearly a half year on a small ship on the open seas. He couldn't walk outside without being recognized, slapped on the back, sloppy-kissed on the cheek. Thousands of people wanted a chance to "grasp you by the hand, to testify to you their adoration," as a resolution from Brooklyn's governing council had it. This was read to his face, in the street, after dignitaries waited for him outside his temporary residence. Meagher spent most of a week responding to the glut of correspondence and a stack of invitations. They could not be stopped. The Common Council of New York honored Meagher at the Astor House, a hotel whose master suites were larger than the Lake Sorell cottage. It would be an *insult*, they let him know, not to show up. Here they outlined plans for a citywide public reception, and offered to put all the services of New York at his disposal. Again Meagher deferred with just a few words.

"Whilst my country remains in sorrow and subjection, it would be indelicate of me to participate in the festivities you propose," he said at the Astor House. Even so short a response produced a call for more. *Nonsense. Speak!* As was said at Clongowes, at Stonyhurst, in Conciliation Hall, from the stumps of eucalyptus trees in Tasmania: *the boy could talk.* He brought up "the companions of my exile," saying, "my heart is with them at this hour." He said he had lost none of the vigor to fight for a free Ireland. He longed to see his country, to see his wife, to see his father, to see soggy old Waterford and the River Suir, to walk the Burren up north, to toss a twig into the Shannon. He wanted the English boot off Ireland's throat. But he could not return—he was forbidden—so long as a life sentence hung over him. He was a fugitive, albeit a suddenly famous one; as such, he would always have to look over his shoulder. Mostly, he wanted New Yorkers to know how grateful he was to them. "To this land I came, as an outcast to seek an honorable home, as an outlaw to claim the protection of a flag that is inviolable . . . a quiet sanctuary in the home of Washington." Quiet it would never be.

He lost a son before he ever saw him. Catherine gave birth while Meagher was in the middle of the South Pacific. A boy. But sickly, just like his mother. They had planned in advance to name the child, if a lad, Henry Emmet Fitzgerald Meagher. Smith O'Brien comforted Catherine, as did her highwayman father. The dead infant was carried down to a cemetery in a small cedar coffin and buried behind St. John's Church in Richmond, Van Diemen's Land. The baby had lived only a few months, his remains now forever a part of penal colony soil. When he died, on June 8, 1852, Meagher had no idea even of his birth. The mails were four to six months behind the news. He had expected his Tasmanian wife to start making her way to Ireland, to be with the Meagher family, and then to join him in America. In the days of his expansive reception, he looked forward to a reunion of a young family of three.

The accolades continued to pour in. St. John's College—later Fordham—situated on an old farm off the Bronx River, gave him an honorary degree. This from the Jesuits, who used to torture him at Stonyhurst. And speaking of school days, here was Patrick Smyth, *the devil*—his favorite mate. They'd known each other since their parents had dressed them in short pants. Smyth was full of international mischief, working with the Irish Directory to get political prisoners out of Tasmania using funds from wealthy New York donors. He had plans to spring John Mitchel. Smyth joined Meagher for a morning neither man could resist: a review of the New York state militias on the Fourth of July. Hundreds of soldiers on horse and on foot passed by, bayonets gleaming in the sun, swords at their sides, hurrahs with every step. The exile was delighted. "Would to God that we had these men upon the old sod," he said to his friend. At the end of the review, the major general proposed a cheer: "To Thomas Francis Meagher—a traitor to England!"

Three weeks later, another review, this one much larger, at Castle Garden, the old fort at the tip of Manhattan, designed to repel the British in the War of 1812, soon to be an immigrant landing depot. This was the parade he had tried to resist, but after two months of pressure, he gave in. Soldiers again, from militias all around the Northeast, "a great muster of the exiled children of the Gael," as one witness remembered it. This time, the orator orated—for almost an hour, his first speech before an American audience. What some listeners remembered were two passages, one an ode to a people whose past was soaked in sorrow, the other a celebration of the new nation that gave them refuge. "The history of Ireland suggests despondency, and reconciles us, by anticipation, to the worst. Yet, as her sufferings have been long, her happiness shall be great." And then, to the United States: "Here, the poorest trader that drives an honest bargain in the meanest quarter of the city—the poorest merchant who sheds his sweat upon the garret for his bread—is cheered by the proud thought that he, as well as the wealthiest, is an active and essential component of the State."

As atop the mountain of Slievenamon, the July sun did not make the words spoil or the crowds wither. The Famine Irish in America wanted him to lead. Meagher was reluctant to get involved in national affairs; he was in a no man's land, as strange in its way as his Australian prison. He was not a citizen, had no rights of the republic. His passport was English and convict. The Empire wanted him for high crimes against the Crown. He was living day to day, at the mercy of his host nation. He quickly tried to change that. On August 9, Meagher appeared in Superior Court and announced his plan to become an American, taking an oath of intent. With relish, he unshackled himself from his jailer. "I, Thomas Francis Meagher, do declare on oath this is my intention to become a citizen of the United States and to renounce forever all allegiance and fidelity to any foreign Prince, Potentate, State or Sovereignty whatever, and particularly the Queen of the United Kingdom of Great Britain and Ireland." Damn, that felt good, Meagher confided.

It wasn't long before the attacks began. The ranks of the Know-Nothings swelled. What was happening to the United States was a conquest, they claimed, indirect and unplanned, by foreign hordes, unknowing of *our ways,* with foreign values. No country on earth had tried to form a common bond without common ancestry—it could not be done. And America was not by design a haven for the world's rejects. It was a Protestant nation, Anglo-Saxon, and would descend into Babylon if it allowed itself to be mixed with "mongrel races" and "Papists," the Know-Nothings charged. There was yet no statue welcoming the tired, the poor, the huddled masses. The young country had thrown off a monarch, yes, and the superficial trappings of class, rank and title, but it was full of Anglophiles still.

The Know-Nothings had grown out of the American Nativist Party, which was violently anti-Catholic. In 1844, they unleashed a terror campaign against the Irish in Philadelphia. The party called for American-born citizens to arm themselves against the "bloody hand of the Pope," and formed a paramilitary arm—the Wide Awakes. At a huge rally in Kensington, Pennsylvania, where immigrant textile mill workers and factory hands lived, one speaker said the Irish were "scum unloaded on American wharves." The nativists stormed through Irish neighborhoods, burning St. Michael's Church, St. Charles Seminary and St. Augustine's Church. The mobs moved on to Philadelphia proper, forcing the mayor to declare martial law. When a nun stood in the door of the Convent of the Sacred Heart, defying the rioters, she was hit in the head by a shower of rocks and fell, unconscious. The nativists overran the Hibernian Hose Company, a station for Irish firemen, and burned it to the ground. They took 5,000 books from the library of an Augustinian priest and used them for fuel in a giant bonfire in the streets. Throughout the summer, rioting flared, with homes gutted, shop windows smashed, gunfire going both ways. More than thirty people were killed. As the authorities tried to quell the violence, nativist leaders urged their followers to respond to questions from police with a single answer: "I know nothing"—giving rise to the party's new name. That fall, they elected mayors in Philadelphia and New York.

Refining their tactics in the 1850s, the Know-Nothings joined forces with the temperance movement and pushed for prohibition of alcohol, restricted immigration and no citizenship for the masses filling the tenements. They counted a million members nationwide. "Every day the papers tell of attacks on Catholics, especially the Irish," Father Pierre-Jean De Smet, an influential French-born Jesuit, wrote a friend in the summer of 1854. "Several churches have already been set on fire, and there is open talk of murder and pillage." By the end of the year, De Smet feared for his life in a dangerous and hate-filled land. "I cannot say much about the United States," he said. "American liberty and tolerance, so highly boasted, exists less in this Great Republic than in the most oppressed country of Europe."

The Know-Nothings went directly after Meagher, trying to scuff the hero with planted newspaper stories about his bad character, and with a song to counter the one celebrating his escape. In the nativist version, he was a coward, a wife abandoner, a whoremonger. "This reptile snake," the song's lyrics proclaimed. "This wordy-warrior knave!" He was shamed for the way he fled Tasmania, a disreputable act for a man living by a gentleman's code. Further, his freedom would never have been possible without "Papist aid"—that global Catholic conspiracy, a centerpiece of Know-Nothing obsessions. Of course, the nativists didn't particularly care about the British Empire's code of honor for transported prisoners. But they did care about preventing a leader rising from the Hibernians of New York. "As there is no word in the Irish language synonymous with Scoundrel," went one takedown, anonymously written and widely reprinted, "henceforth let us use the name of Meagher."

To the Irish, the attacks on them went to the heart of their ambitions and character. They had left genocidal starvation in a conquered land to thrive in a free one. Without citizenship, stepping up would be difficult. As for the campaign to ban liquor, whiskey was *uisge baugh*—the water of life. The pubs and basement bars, more than 500 of them on the Lower East Side alone, served as communal dens and political wards. Church and saloon were the two main institutions. The Irish became Democrats almost to a man, because they were the enemies of the Know-Nothings. And in New York they became Tammany Hall Democrats, whose first order of business before every meeting was to read aloud parts of the Declaration of Independence, that robust denunciation of all the British wrongs against a subject people. New York needed muscle to build a vast sewage system, to pave the streets, to install the web of tracks for streetcars that would carry thirty-five million passengers a year by decade's end. Tammany would provide the labor, and get a piece of every dime to the public works.

Meagher followed a hurried route to citizenship before the Know-Nothings could close the way. But he also had to make a living. He could study for the New York bar and join Dillon & O'Gorman. Writing was a brighter prospect. Yet a prose-cloistered Hermit of New York City would fare no better than the Hermit on the Lake. What could he do? For a man with a restless tongue, the solution was obvious: speak. In the fall of 1852, he was booked into New York's Metropolitan Hall for his first lecture, on the penal colony of Australia. A crush of people showed up, including many non-Irish, waiting in line for hours before the doors opened, paying 50 cents to hear the Young Tribune. He did not disappoint. The *New York Times* reported that 6,000 people packed the hall. The *New York Herald* wrote, "Never has that building so filled with human beings before." Afterward, Meagher was given a check for $1,650—more money than he had ever earned for anything. What a country: they would pay him to talk.

He toured for a year. Albany and Utica, Buffalo and St. Louis. He was greeted with a thirty-two-gun salute in Massachusetts, and feted by the Meagher Guard in the Know-Nothing war zones around Philadelphia. In an age when well-crafted, finely delivered speech was king, in parlor or theater, Meagher was soon a sought-after celebrity. Along the way, in the fall, he put in many good words on behalf of the Democratic candidate for the highest office in the land. And that candidate repaid the favor. President-elect Franklin Pierce invited Meagher to his inauguration. Pierce huddled in private with the exile at the Willard Hotel, the city's finest, where incoming power resided before moving a few blocks over to the White House. In less than a year, the convict Tom

Meagher had gone from muttering dirty jokes around a smoky fire in a Tasmanian shepherd's hut to gold-rimmed tea service with the most powerful man in America. "I am rejoiced to see that the brilliance of his oratory has been in no respect diminished by the long eclipse which he has endured in Irish prisons and the forests of Van Diemen's Land," Smith O'Brien wrote a friend upon hearing of Meagher's reception.

Meagher's wife got a similar welcome in Ireland. When Catherine arrived in Waterford in June of 1853, upwards of 20,000 people turned out to greet her. The mayor spoke of her as a patriot's angel, leading the town's favorite son out of the despair of his banishment. "You found him a lonely exile, separated from all that could comfort and console him, and you renounced home and friends to cheer and soothe his sorrows . . . You crossed twelve thousand miles of ocean in search of him." Considerable searching remained. She was not a public person; she recoiled at the crowds and the rapturous treatment from the Irish press. She preferred not to speak. The elder Meagher welcomed Bennie as a lost daughter. And in the sixty-four-year-old patriarch she found a comforting hand and a steady soul. Together, they sailed for America.

Meagher had moved into the Metropolitan Hotel, at Broadway and Prince Street, living off the earnings of his lecture circuit. His father and Bennie arrived in late July, peak cruelty of the city's humid summers. It had been four years since Thomas had seen his father, and nineteen months since he had kissed his wife. Thomas Senior was ageless in his energy, a family trait, but dour as before about the adventures of his globe-roaming criminal son. He was a member of the British Parliament still, reelected the year before, serving the government that had jailed, banished and continued to pursue his namesake son. While the younger Meagher seldom held a thought that went unspoken, his father had opened his mouth a mere half-dozen times during a decade in Parliament—and those were mostly formal utterances. His wealth was fabulous, said by the *New York Times* to be in excess of $700,000— an exaggeration, but not by much. The famine had subsided at last, after the nation had been emptied of its people. The country was exhausted and hollowed out. As to the exile: what ungodly thing was he up to in this loud, steaming city? Young Meagher shared his enthusiasm for the big land—full of Irish, full of young people, full of opportunity. A convict anywhere in the British Empire, here he counted a president and senators among his friends. And down the street, at Niblo's Theater, the "T. F. Meagher Polka" was performed nightly, rousing the sweaty masses to the dance floor.

All of this meant little to Bennie. She had been happiest in the Lake Sorell cottage. The heat, the noise, the filth, the crowds of New York made her ill. Husband and wife shared grief at the loss of an infant son, and their lovemaking held the promise of another. He took her to Niagara Falls, to the Catskills, to the lake country of upstate New York, in search of air that was closer to the cool breezes of Ireland. The more he showed her of his new life, the less connected she felt to him. He had a destiny, he insisted, still vague, but some great purpose for living. He would love to return to Ireland, but it was impossible. The only hope was a blanket pardon for the seven leaders who'd been banished to Tasmania, currently the subject of considerable international lobbying. Friends who saw the couple commented on how oddly matched they were: he the extrovert, she the shrinking violet; he the sponge of others' passions for causes and ideas, she the lover of solitude; he the verse-quoting, music-loving performer, she the early-to-bed keeper of her thoughts. "It is said they do not suit," Smith O'Brien's wife Lucy had noted in a letter, sharing the consensus view of the gossips. "His fault, I am told."

Thomas had a big birthday coming up on August 3—his thirtieth—just a few days away. The Meagher Club of Boston wanted to honor him at a banquet with all the cacophonous fixings of Irish sentimentality. His father and Bennie declined to join him, citing the weather: it was too unbearably sticky and hot to travel. At the same time, Meagher was weighing a fresh round of lecture invitations, out west in the fall. But Bennie was not inclined to sail down to Nicaragua, cross the isthmus of Central America, then journey up the coast to San Francisco. Instead, at summer's end she opted for first-class passage and a quick trip back to Ireland with her unexcitable father-in-law. The plan was to reunite with her husband next spring. She was pregnant again. Maybe things would change.

In Waterford, Catherine gave birth to a boy, aided by the best medical help in the province. It was not enough. The complications of the baby's entry killed her on May 9, 1854. She was twenty-two. Catherine was buried among Meagher family members at Faithlegg Cemetery. Meagher got the news a few weeks later. An Ireland he was prohibited from seeing now held the corpse of his young wife and the living presence of his son—Thomas Bennett Meagher. He had to find a way to get back to Waterford.

In Tasmania, Patrick O'Donoghue plotted his escape. He had no money, and was not on the list of exiles chosen for subsidized freedom by New York's Irish Directory. Between his binge drinking, incendiary essays and time in the Crown's hard labor camps, the former law clerk put together his plan. In December 1852, nearly a year after Meagher had left the island, O'Donoghue disappeared into the Tasmanian wild—gentleman's code be damned. He found his way to Melbourne, where he stowed away on a ship at anchor, at one point hiding in the idled stove of the engine room. After changing vessels in Tahiti, he arrived in San Francisco, a journey of 185 days. From there he went to Brooklyn, and summoned his wife and child from Ireland. No festivities, no press attention, no military parades awaited O'Donoghue. He was unknown, except as a steady friend to a well-spoken rebel. Meagher tried to renew ties with the man he once read to as the *Swift* sailed to banishment. He invited him to be his guest at the birthday party in Boston's Faneuil Hall. At the event, O'Donoghue couldn't control himself; a falling-down drunk, he became quarrelsome and incoherent. When he insisted on speaking before the assembly, a fight broke out with the organizers. O'Donoghue spent the night in jail, bloodied and dehydrated. In Brooklyn, in the week that his family was going through the quarantine process at Staten Island, O'Donoghue became violently ill with severe diarrhea. He sweated, stumbled and vomited, hugging the water closet. He died on January 22, 1854, without ever seeing the wife and child who were only a few miles across the water. The papers said he was estranged from his fellow escapees. In distance, that was true: Meagher was then in California, as was MacManus.

John Mitchel fared better. He had Patrick Smyth and the Directory working for his family. The scheme was to get Mitchel's clan and Smith O'Brien out, but the old man of Young Ireland refused. "This is your chance," he told Mitchel. On June 9, 1853, Mitchel resigned his ticket-of-leave and headed for the bush on horseback. For the next seven weeks he hid out, disguised at one point as a priest. The sympathies of the island, in its last days as a convict destination, were with the escapee. He had many new friends. He found his getaway ship in Melbourne. In Tahiti, he boarded an American vessel, the *Julia Ann*.

The asthmatic Mitchel, pinch-faced and thin, bowed to the flag of the country where he would next make his home.

His arrival in New York, on November 29, 1853, was second only to Meagher's. Four of Young Ireland's seven had now *done a bolt*. An immense crowd met him at the harbor. Meagher jumped aboard the ship to welcome his fellow exile to America. In characteristic form, Mitchel told the press he intended to stir up trouble, and soon. Barely a month passed before he was putting out a newspaper, the *Irish Citizen*, a forum for his fire-breathing pen. His intent was to "expose the odious designs of England." He soon turned to other targets: the Know-Nothings and, curiously, the Catholic Church, enemy of those same nativists. The clerics had betrayed Young Ireland, Mitchel felt, when they could have been at the front of the pitchfork brigade.

Meagher was nominally a partner in this journalistic arson, but he spent most of 1854 in California. While he was gone, Mitchel offended some of New York's most influential citizens and appalled his readers. He published letters that were sympathetic to slavery and its outspoken supporters. He attacked the book that had shaken the conscience of many Americans — *Uncle Tom's Cabin*, which had sold 300,000 copies in a year. The novel was a response to the Fugitive Slave Act of 1850, which made the free North an accomplice to the slaveholding South. All runaways were now property, to be returned by law to their masters. Posters in Boston warned blacks to avoid the police, for they had been empowered by the federal law to act as "kidnappers and slave catchers." Where did Mitchel's sympathy for slavery come from? The Irish, as Frederick Douglass had observed, were the blacks of Great Britain, barely a step above field hands in Alabama. Mitchel had written tough, passionate prose on behalf of starving peasants in bondage to absentee landlords. How could he view slavery as a benign institution? His friends were flummoxed. Charles Duffy, who once employed Mitchel as an editor at the *Nation*, was one of the few in his circle who had seen this side of him, while working with the writer in Dublin. He kept those views out of the *Nation*, a patron of free men everywhere. "Mitchel tried my patience sorely by defending Negro slavery and denouncing the emancipation of the Jews," Duffy wrote. "I could not permit the *Nation* to be carried over to the side of oppression."

At his new home in Brooklyn, with his mother, his wife Jenny and their teenage boys, the Mitchel household was a refuge of plantation sympathy in the Yankee North. "My objection to slavery is the injury it does to the white masters," Jenny wrote a friend in the spring of 1854. "You will find this hard to believe (as I did myself at first) but it is no less true that Negroes are happier in their state of slavery than when they get their freedom." She wrote just as the Kansas-Nebraska Act became law, allowing an expansion of slavery, by vote of the people, into the territories. With this, the human property market pushed north and west, to ground fast filling with people who had left countries where fate was determined at birth.

In New York, which had abolished slavery in 1827, Mitchel was in the wrong state with the wrong cause in the wrong year. The South was much more receptive. He gave the commencement speech at the University of Virginia. Traveling farther, he found Richmond a charming rascal of a town, Charleston most welcoming and the grassy hills of Tennessee to be heaven. In a letter to an abolitionist, he described how he wanted a plantation of his own—"well-stocked with healthy Negroes." Barely a year after arriving in New York, Mitchel closed his failing paper and moved to the South. There, nearly four million people— more than half the size of depleted Ireland—were property.

That year, the last three of Young Ireland's prominent convicts in Tasmania—William Smith O'Brien, John Martin, and Kevin O'Doherty— got the break they'd been waiting for. The British, at war with Russia in the Crimean Peninsula, were recruiting Irish to carry their fight. The penal colony's political prisoners were a sticking point. Why fight for a jailor nation? Smith O'Brien was beloved, with a global following. The other two had been model convicts. Under considerable pressure, the Crown pardoned all three. The reprieve was conditional at first— they could not return to Great Britain—then without restriction. As they left the island, one of the banished, Martin, lamented that the land he'd come to as a prisoner was now more liberated than the one he was returning to as a free man. "Would to God that there were in my unhappy country a government to which I might be a loyal subject." O'Doherty, who had kept Meagher company through lunches on that bridge in Tasmania, was reunited with his lover Eva, the poet, in Paris. They married, and he opened a practice in surgery, having completed all his medical requirements. Smith O'Brien decided to see the world before returning to his ancestral castle: India, the Middle East, Turkey,

Greece, finally back in the embrace of Lucy and their seven children. He thought about running for Parliament again or touring the United States.

But the pardon left the escapees in America in a purgatory between New World and Old. These men would remain fugitives, the Crown declared. They had refused to apologize for their crimes or even admit to the wrongdoing of vexing Britain. The new prime minister, Lord Palmerston, was initially thought to be open to giving a pass to the prominent Irishmen in America. He soon made his intentions clear: this would never happen, for they "had broken all ties of honour" by escaping. Meagher was crushed. Had he not fled Tasmania, he would be free to return home and pick up his life. Now he would never see Waterford, never sit beside the slow-moving Liffey on a spring afternoon, never reminisce inside the stone walls of his first school, never again see Dublin or the Dingle Peninsula, never take the stage at Conciliation Hall, never reunite with Speranza over dinner or share the verse of Thomas Davis with Duffy. Never see his father in the house that was meant to be his someday. Never walk hand in hand with his son on soil where Meaghers had walked for centuries. He called himself a "homeless exile"—out of opportunities to liberate his old country. There was an outside chance, though, to help liberate the enslaved millions of his new one.

10

IDENTITY

He started to drink. On one level, this was not new; alcohol was the mother's milk of Irish schoolboys, served by the Jesuits. He had quaffed ale at Stonyhurst, in tandem with blasts from his clarinet. In the heady days leading to the uprising, whiskey had united the rebels in Dublin and lubricated the first drafts of seditious speeches. The ration of English porter was a highlight of long days at sea aboard the *Swift*, sailing toward the bottom of the earth. Tasmanian grog had taken some of the sorrow off the fog of life in Van Diemen's Land. In New York, the saloon was a living room, because most Irish did not have a den to call their own, and because there was no warmer place on cold nights. Also, every respectable pub, including one that just opened in 1854, McSorley's, had a shank of the old country's turf in the window — the only grass in Five Points, it was said. When Meagher drank at banquets, at dinners after speeches, at parties, he was the life of the place, the hail-fellow-well-met. Now Meagher started to drink without purpose. His young wife was dead. His homeland was denied him forever. He wasn't sure how long the public speaking could continue before he became a minstrel act with a brogue. He knew what the drinking could do to him, for he had seen what it did to O'Donoghue. And he knew that nothing bothered his father more than a *fluthered* Irishman.

"I am a teetotaler myself," the elder Meagher had declared in 1847, "and I do not like to see any man drunk."

The attacks became more personal. The Know-Nothings continued to go after Meagher's character, heckling him on stage and in print.

They were emboldened and ascendant. In 1854, the Know-Nothings took all eleven congressional seats in Massachusetts, swept the Bay State legislature, captured nearly half of New York's delegation and won six governorships. In Boston, moving swiftly to blunt the power of the second-largest population of Irish in America, newly elected nativist Governor Henry Gardner tried to rush through laws making it harder for immigrants to become police officers or hold office. By the end of 1855, the Know-Nothings were the second-largest political party in the nation, and the only one ever founded in opposition to a specific ethnic group. Handbills in New Orleans shouted for action at election time. "Americans! Shall we be ruled by Irish?" Members promised to support only American-born Protestants, and pledged to never marry a Catholic. In Congress, they pushed legislation that required an immigrant to live in the United States for twenty-five years before becoming eligible for citizenship. This at a time when life expectancy at birth was thirty-eight years. Another bill would cut the allowable cubic footage for a ship arriving with castoffs from Ireland. Through legislation to shrink vessel size, the Know-Nothings would try to hold back the human tide.

To those who took the country's founding principles to heart, the rise of the nativists was dispiriting. "As a nation, we began by declaring that 'all men are created equal,'" Abraham Lincoln wrote a friend in 1855. "We now practically read it 'all men are created equal except Negroes.' When the Know-Nothings get control, it will read 'all men are created equal except Negroes, and foreigners, and Catholics.'"

Meagher had to contend not only with the Know-Nothings but with their enemy the Roman Catholic Church. He had criticized the clerics who interfered with European campaigns for democracy, and resented, still, the Church's stance in his own rebellion. Embracing women as political equals, as the Young Ireland rebels did, put further distance between Meagher and the Church. His faith had not lapsed. His doubt, bordering on scorn, was for the men who ran that faith. "For this I was denounced from pulpits and throughout the bigoted Catholic press," he told Smith O'Brien in a letter. One of the harshest assaults came from James McMaster, a New Yorker who ran *Freeman's Journal*, a billboard for the archdiocese. In the summer of 1854, the editor went after Meagher and Mitchel—"these very silly, bad and contemptible boys." He wrote that their failed rebellion had made Ireland "a laugh-ingstock to the world." He not only ridiculed the cause for which they had risked their lives, but mocked their escapes.

Meagher exploded. This man knew nothing of life in the penal colony, the perils of Bass Strait, the meaning of that overused word—honor. The more it gnawed at him, the angrier he became. If drink pushed him over the edge, so be it. On July 18, 1854, Meagher stormed down to McMaster's office, past the fresh-planted rows of telegraph poles on roads ripped open for streetcar lines. He called loudly on the editor to come out and confront him. Fists clenched, Meagher ordered the editor to print a retraction.

"Act like a man!"

McMaster refused. He locked the front door of his building, leaving Meagher to steam out on the street. Returning to his room at the Metropolitan Hotel, he could not sit still. He grabbed a small riding whip and went out again, in the insufferable afternoon humidity, to confront McMaster. He found the man walking near his home and called on him once more to print a retraction. When the editor scoffed at him, Meagher attacked. The two men tumbled to the ground, a whirl of bloodied fists and spit. McMaster pulled a gun from his vest pocket, aimed it at Meagher's head and fired. The bullet grazed his forehead, leaving a powder burn over one eyebrow. Failing to kill the Irishman, McMaster pointed the revolver square at Meagher's face. Before he could get off a second shot, Meagher lunged for the weapon. Police arrived; both men were arrested. Now Meagher was back in jail, this time on a third continent. He posted $500 bail, though no criminal charges were ever filed. But friends noticed: far from an Irish messiah, Meagher was a mess. And a humbled man.

"It is full time for me to be kindly let down from my 'distinguished stranger' position," he wrote a friend.

In November, traveling over the rails through Michigan, he could not sleep in the 3 a.m. murk of a fog-encased night, his car overheated by engine steam. The train was full of immigrants—mostly Germans, but a significant number of Irish—going west with their belongings. Meagher found an empty seat in the front row of a cooler car and fell into a slumber. A horrid sound jarred him awake. A jolt threw him forward. A piece of the ceiling fell off and hit him on the head, a gash that drew blood. From above, exposed timbers crunched and tumbled. Underfoot, metal buckled and folded. Meagher would have been tossed from the car, but his foot was trapped by the collapsing floor. He was pinned. Fire raged through the train. He heard screams, moans and cries of people with severed limbs. The train had collided head-on with an eastbound gravel train. Wiggling out of his boot, Meagher was able to free himself. He staggered forward through hot smoke, tripping over a brakeman bleeding profusely.

Meagher jumped from his crumbled, steaming car. Outside, hunks of metal smoldered on wet grass, blood-splattered figures staggered about and wailed on the ground, an upside-down engine hissed with steam. The train had been shattered as if from an explosion. Meagher held a lifeless child who had a thick sliver of metal thrust through his head. He helped an old woman who bled from open wounds in both legs. A black porter cried for his life, two broken bones protruding from the skin of each leg. Meagher wiped foam from the man's mouth and offered a few words of encouragement. Another porter lay face-down in a pile of gravel, both legs torn off at the thigh. Looking away, Meagher caught sight of a thick-chested body, beheaded in the crash. A conductor shouted for help—a passenger was trapped in a car, bleeding to death. He and Meagher took turns sawing through the wreckage to cut the man out, a half hour of labor. The dead were thrown against an embankment, bodies atop other bodies, Irish and Germans with shattered bits of blankets and bindles and books meant to start a life. In all, forty-eight people were killed. "It is, undoubtedly, the worst accident by railroad collision that has occurred on this continent," the *New York Times* reported. For Meagher, though hailed as heroic by witnesses and the press, it was another dark portent. A bullet off Broadway should have killed him. Moving from the back of the train to the front had saved him. Why? He was running out of lives.

He found Elizabeth Townsend, or she found him. She was twenty-four, self-confident, bright, witty, with trellises of raven-black hair and the kind of smile that could prompt a grin from the grumpy—dimples, implying something more. She was everything the Irish in New York were not: different tribe, different religion, different financial circumstances. If Meagher had stunned his friends by marrying below his class in the penal colony, he drew gasps of another kind by romancing above his standing with a Fifth Avenue daughter of American royalty. By a consensus of those close to him, the love affair was doomed. He was Catholic, she Protestant. He was a Celt, she Anglo-Saxon. He was a convict, she the progeny of refined Yankee bloodlines. She knew nothing of Cromwell's cruelty or Brian Boru's bravery. He knew nothing of the Townsends of New York. To her, the Great Hunger was something that forced thousands of filthy wretches to wash up on Manhattan's shores and chase pigs down 57th Street. She could not tell a Gaelic word from a hairbrush. He was clueless about the rules of courtship for well-bred WASPs of New York. In one telling of the romance, Elizabeth had shown up at a Meagher speech and was instantly smitten by the charming exile. In another version, they met at a dinner party and could not take their eyes off each other. No matter the precise origin, by the end of 1854 the two were never apart, outcasts within their circles.

An Englishman of means, Elizabeth's great-grandfather had amassed a 23,000-acre tract of land straddling the colonies of New York and New Jersey in the mid-1700s. With this holding, he built an empire of iron, the furnaces going full bore to feed the ambitions of the Americans. He was best known for forging a chain, weighing in excess of 100 tons, that was strung across the Hudson River during the Revolutionary War to prevent British ships from sailing above West Point. The English held New York, but the Townsend metal chain kept them tied up at the mouth of the main water entrance to the interior. Thereafter, Sterling Iron Works was synonymous with the growth of the United States—its ships, it rails, its carriages, its carts, nuts and bolts. Elizabeth was the oldest of three daughters. She divided her time between the family estate of Southfield, New Jersey, and a sumptuous home on Fifth Avenue in New York, far enough from the dreadful clutter of Five Points.

Her father was no fan of Meagher or the Irish. He had brought up his girls to be among *their* kind. Daughter number two, Alice, had married a New York corporate lawyer and art collector, Samuel L. M. Barlow, a man very good at making money and making the right kind of friends. In short order, Barlow became fabulously wealthy. A Townsend was not involved in the politics of excess, whether abolition of slavery or liberation of the Irish. A Townsend was civic-minded, albeit without breaking a sweat. They were certainly not Know-Nothings, but sided with whatever politicians were less likely to imperil dynastic wealth. A Townsend could never be a Catholic; the family was a pillar of the Fifth Avenue Presbyterian Church. When Elizabeth brought her Irish lover home to the family residence at 129 Fifth Avenue, he encountered a stern-faced, 250-pound millionaire who would not suffer any silly poetry or penal colony tales. Mr. Townsend cared not a whit for what it was like to rot in Kilmainham Gaol or sleep within earshot of a scaffold being built to hang you. Well, at least they had wartime entanglements with the British Empire in common, yes? The iron chain across the Hudson? *That was Grandfather's business.* Should Elizabeth stay with *this man,* the New York papers reported, she would be disinherited.

On the second day of January 1855, Meagher decided to risk all. He was sure of very little about himself, except this: he wanted to spend his life with Elizabeth Townsend. And he wanted her to be the mother to his distant son. He knew her family could never accept him. But could she? During his low points, he tallied up the events of his life to date and found himself wanting—a man without success or standing, widowed, wanted as a fugitive by the world's mightiest power. As he said many a time, he had done nothing to leave his mark. He was famous for his noble failure in Ireland and his escape from a penal colony. Neither initiative had done anything to ease the plight of his countrymen.

Now he would not hold back; she must know about the doubts, the failures, the political passions, the need for someone to love and something to show for his life. He had been planning to move to California, where his fellow Young Ireland escapee Terence MacManus lived on a ranch near the little town of San Jose. But he was having a change of heart after meeting Elizabeth. Yes, he was sure of it now: she must know everything about him. He took pen in hand, writing in the winter chill of his room at the Metropolitan just before leaving on a months-long lecture tour.

He trembled. His instinct was to gush. "My dear, dear Miss Townsend," he began. Meeting her was like waking from a bad dream, he wrote, snapping him out of the purposeless life. She left him breathless. More surprising, she left him speechless. But these words were mush, the residual drag of the Stonyhurst schoolboy. Who was the Meagher who wanted the hand of a Townsend? He had confessed, days earlier, the words a man can be slow to say—*I love you.* And she had not slapped him, or walked away, or grimaced. She said she loved him back! He also sent her papers and newspaper clippings detailing his life. These sketches had not turned her from him.

> I can, therefore speak to you now more fearlessly and fully than I have hitherto done. The cowardice has fled. Heart, hand and tongue—all are free. The story can easily be told. The more easily, since, if I mistake not, you know most of it already. You know I was a "rebel"—and you know I am an "exile." You know I was married, and you know there has been left to me a little fellow who knows not what a mother would have been. Of other aspects of my life, you may not be aware. But . . . you know the worst, and you know the best.

That was the most important part. If Elizabeth should bind her life to his, those labels—*rebel, exile*—would be attached to her as well as him. For much of his life he was known simply as the son of another Thomas Meagher. He loved the American way of throwing off your past like last winter's coat. It was so easy to start anew, with a fiction of a life crafted by your own hand. But he would always be the outcast, his fate tied to Ireland's fate. This he finally understood. There was no getting away from it.

> The world knows what Ireland—the land of my birth and early home—has been. For years and years, a mere wreck upon the sea, she has had nothing but a long list of sorrows, ignominies, and martyrdom to contribute to the history of nations. Believing that such has been her fate through the culpable design of those who rule her, every generation has witnessed an effort made by her sons to redeem her sinking fortunes . . . In the last attempt of the kind in Ireland, it was my fate to be involved. The papers I sent you explain all. Through much idle flattery and exaggerated colouring, the fact and the truth of my short course in public life are clear enough, and that there is nothing in it—not a word, an act, a sentiment, from first to last—you would fear to own, or blush to own.

So, his past would be her past. Which meant the penal colony as well.

> Banished to an island in the South Pacific—sixteen thousand miles from home—compelled by the Government to move away into the very heart of the forest and there to stay my weary feet, left alone

with my memories, my thoughts, and the pale shadows that had once been my hopes, I grew sad and sick of life. In the darkest hour of that sick life, a solitary star shone upon me, making bright and beautiful the desolate waters of the mournful wild lake on the shore of which I lived in that wilderness. I met her who has left me the poor child, for whom as yet I have no home, and who knows not the warmth of a mother's breast . . . I had not been four months married when I saw she had to share the privations and indignities to which her husband himself was subject. A prisoner myself, I had led another from the altar to share with me an odious captivity. This I could not bear . . . We were three years married. Of those three years, but eight months we were together . . . It is a dream! . . . And I wake beside you to tell the dream.

He feared she would not love him back, that she was too good for him, or he not good enough for her. Better to commit all of this to paper: did she feel the same way?

I felt it would be a relief to me, even though my love was not returned, to let you know that I loved, and deeply loved you . . . But when I heard from you that "you could deeply love me," there passed through me a wild delight which made my pulse beat quick and my brain reel, a thousand suns to flash in the giddy air about me. Oh! I felt myself a generous, guileless, joyous, bounding, loving, hopeful boy again.

More gush, but *damn* it was how he felt. He couldn't bottle up the boy. He moved to confront the issue of money and social class. She may have thought, as many in New York did, that Meagher was a wealthy man, kept in high style by his father. Not so. And he wanted her to understand that her circle would shun them; life as Mrs. Thomas Francis Meagher would mean living with the insults, the cruelty, the whispers.

That there would be—that there will be—objections to our union I foresaw, and yet foresee. I had learned little of the world, if to these objections I had been blind. I saw them the moment I looked upon and loved you. In the bloom and pride, and the genial glorious dawn of womanhood, stationed in the highest social rank in a community of the wealthiest in the world—the eldest unmarried daughter of a family affluent in its circumstances, and by long descent and residence in the country rendered most noticeable and attractive—I was fully sensible that in claiming the honour to be your husband, I should have to meet no slight contributions and rebuke. For I have no fortune, at least nothing that I know of. I never asked my father a single question on the subject. I have fought my own way through the world and will fight it to the end. I am, as I have already told you, a homeless exile.

A Townsend would have to accept an Irishman without money or station, a man with a price on his head, a man without a country. Not to put too fine a point on it, but Meagher did just that. No secrets. He had given up a lot when he walked away from the life grooved for him in Waterford.

I am here alone. Family, old friends, the familiar interest which sustains, the honours which naturally attend on one in the land of his birth and boyhood—I parted from, to be true to my convictions, my conscience, my cause . . . Would to God I had a wound to show! But I have nothing to show. Nothing to give you. Nothing to promise you but a true heart and a willing hand. And that heart you shall have, with the fullest measure of its love, to the last beat it gives. And that hand, with all the strength and industry, and pride of manhood that is in it, you shall have.

As proof, he changed the course of his life. He'd planned to move to the West Coast, that frontier of gold. But after he met Elizabeth, he decided to stay in New York. Also, though it meant a career without the risk and drama that he'd tasted as an Irish revolutionary, he intended to become a lawyer, just like her brother-in-law Barlow. He would be a man that a Townsend could marry.

For some time past, I had been thinking of going to California and there permanently settling. But, from the moment I first saw you, this purpose began to waver. And now that I have the assurance of your love, now that I am to act and live and die for you, I shall remain here in the city of New York, and practice at the bar. To win distinction in this profession shall be my study and ambition—that so I may reflect honour on the noble girl, who in giving her hand and heart to one so humble and downcast, conferred upon him a dignity higher and more precious than even citizenship to which it has been my glory to aspire.

One last thing: he considered Elizabeth an equal. The salons of Dublin in the ferment of 1848—where he came to admire the views of Speranza and Eva as much as the political poetry of Thomas Davis—had been formative on the young man. In an age when women were expected to speak passively, to never question their husbands in the big decisions that chart a life, Meagher wanted a companion who was unafraid to ask him anything. If she were to be a co-owner of his past, she must have access to his doubts and his deepest thoughts.

> This brings me to the end of what I have, and had, to write. But I cannot close this letter without renewing the request I have already made — that you will never, never hesitate to question me concerning anything which interests you, painfully or otherwise, in my regard.
>
> Rest assured, I shall ever prove to you most truthful, frank and upright, and shall forever remain, as now, with fondest, deepest esteem and love, your devoted and betrothed, Thomas Francis Meagher.

They married on November 14, 1855, at the Madison Avenue residence of Archbishop John Hughes. "Dagger John" presided as well. The *New York Times* reported that Peter Townsend's reasons for disapproving of his new son-in-law "were of a serious nature, and based on some unpleasant antecedents" in the Irishman's life.

In defiance, Elizabeth took his name, his faith and his past, traveling on her own to Ireland to see Waterford, the boy and the elder Meagher, to take in the small world that had fostered her husband. The time was not yet right, the family felt, for the motherless child to move to New York and join the father he'd never seen. He was doing well with a doting grandfather. As promised, Thomas studied for the bar and passed; he tried to become a proper New York barrister, hanging out his shingle in an office near City Hall. Criminal law was his specialty, using the golden tongue to sway juries, the power of narrative being the best weapon of an attorney in court. As one newspaper had noted of Meagher's talents, "He has mastered the English language and bent all of its best powers to the purposes of his richest fancies." He became a citizen, not by marriage, but by statutory process that at the time allowed an immigrant to naturalize after five years. *To hell with the Know-Nothings.* As a new American, he used the First Amendment as a license to fly. And he wanted to see more of the world, and more of the expanding United States, as did Elizabeth. Less than five years after landing on these shores, America had changed Meagher. Now he looked for his chance to change it.

11

THE FEVER

The democracy turned ugly and violent, as the gauze of compromise that held together the largest slaveholding nation in the world started to tear. Americans would kill fellow Americans, it was now clear, over the fate of people with fewer rights than a horse. In Kansas, a mob led by a sheriff stormed into Lawrence and ransacked the river town where antislavery settlers had made a stand. They burned the Free State Hotel, broke apart two printing presses, barged through houses and businesses, smashing anything in their path. In retaliation, John Brown and his sons dragged proslavery settlers from their homes in the territory and hacked five of them to death, splitting their heads open as if they were melons. "I am now quite certain that the crimes of this guilty land will never be purged away but with Blood," Brown wrote not long before he was hanged for another violent outburst. In 1856, a congressman from South Carolina, Preston Brooks, attacked Senator Charles Sumner of Massachusetts with a walking stick in the chamber of the world's great deliberative body. He beat Sumner over the head until his cane snapped, until his victim staggered to the ground, skull fractured, nose split, blood running onto the marble floor. The senator never fully recovered. New canes were sent to the assailant congress-man, inscribed *Hit Him Again.* He became a hero in the South, along-side Senator David Atchison of Missouri, who had urged his constitu-ents to "kill every goddamn abolitionist in the district."

The next year, the Supreme Court attempted to settle things once and for all. Ruling 7–2 in the Dred Scott decision, the country's final judicial arbiter held that blacks, free or chained, could never be citizens.

Dating to colonial times, the nation had always looked at a Negro as property—"he was bought and sold, and treated as an ordinary article of merchandise," the court wrote. And what property it was: the total market value of slaves in the South at the time of the ruling was $3 billion, more than all the railroads, all the banks, any other American asset. To the founders, blacks were "beings of an inferior order, and altogether unfit to associate with the white race," explained Chief Justice Roger B. Taney in the written opinion, "so far inferior that they had no rights which the white man was bound to respect." The phrase "all men are created equal," in the Declaration of Independence, did not cover black people, said Taney. "It is too clear for dispute that the enslaved African race were not intended to be included." Regarding runaways, that history must be honored and upheld. The ruling fortified the South, with its vision to "carry slavery to the Pacific Ocean," as Senator Atchison had outlined. But it settled nothing. Northerners continued to help fugitives—"stealing our property," Georgia Senator Robert Toombs said. To harbor a slave from his master, said Toombs, was "a good and sufficient cause for war."

The decision moved Abraham Lincoln to make another run for public office. Ousted after one term in Congress, he was searching for some larger purpose in his life at the same time Thomas Meagher was floundering. Lincoln felt, as did Meagher, that he might have missed his chance. "Oh, how hard it is to die and leave one's country no better off than if one had never lived," Lincoln said. Self-educated, a reader whose tastes ranged from Shakespeare to self-improvement manuals, always tinkering with his speaking style, the praying mantis–limbed lawyer decided to take on the little senator who had authored the bill allowing slavery to expand, Stephen Douglas. "If the negro is a man, why then my ancient faith teaches me that all men are created equal, and that there can be no moral right in connection with one man making a slave of another," he said in one of their debates. Lincoln lost the Senate race of 1858, but became the moral voice of a new political party, the Republicans.

Meagher could not avoid the Great Question. Everywhere he went, speaking from a stage or in a saloon, he was asked about slavery. The Liberator, Daniel O'Connell, had been an abolitionist. "Irishmen and Irishwomen: treat the colored people as your equal, your brethren," O'Connell had said in a speech at Boston's Faneuil Hall. But Irish and blacks, having found much in common in their shared misery, now found much that ripped them apart. The competition for jobs at the bottom stiffened during the latest of the periodic panics that crashed the economy. Somebody was always willing to work cheaper on the docks, as a maid, a servant, a street cleaner, and that somebody became the hated face of his or her race. The Sixth Ward of New York, once home to Abyssinian Baptist churches, mixed marriages and nighttime entertainments where color was less important than a fiddler's tune, lost half its black population over the decade of the 1850s. In the newspaper caricatures, where the Irish had been drawn with tails, hirsute necks and exaggerated foreheads, African Americans were the monkeys now.

When Meagher and his wife traveled to the South, they were treated with the hospitality accorded visitors of standing and eloquence. In the parlors of stately old homes, slavery was dismissed as a Yankee obsession—*and they had it all wrong*. Writing after a tour of the region, Meagher was of two minds on the institution that threatened to shatter his adopted country. "It would be well if America could get rid of slavery," he said. "But we can't, in our time, and should therefore confine our efforts to alleviating the evils that accompany it."

During a reunion with Smith O'Brien in America, the two Irish rebels agreed on all the great issues of the day but one.

"How can you be an apologist for slavery in the South?" asked the elder conscience of Young Ireland.

"I am *not* in favor of slavery," Meagher replied. "I am devoted to the Union. The Union accepts slavery."

This was the Democratic Party position and that of its standard-bearer in the 1856 election, James Buchanan. By contrast, at their national convention that year, the Know-Nothings took up a platform in full support of slavery's expansion. The Southern delegates favored it, the Northerners less so. The Republicans were closest to abolition. They considered nominating Lincoln as a vice presidential candidate, before rejecting him, at their first national convention in 1856. Lincoln refused to pander to the nativists shopping for a political home. "I am not a Know-Nothing," he said. "That is certain. How can I be? How can anyone who abhors the oppression of Negroes be in favor of degrading classes of white people?" The Know-Nothings, organized behind the new American Party, ran Millard Fillmore, the former president. He stood for nothing, and was routed, finishing third.

Meagher built a forum for his opinions, the *Irish News,* in 1856. With his newspaper he was back in the arena. The *News* dedicated itself to the smudge-faced immigrants of the tenements, and beyond. Many of his readers were in and out of jail: the Irish accounted for less than 30 percent of New York City's population but 55 percent of all arrests in the second half of the decade. Meagher would give them a voice, he declared. It shamed him to see his countrymen wasting away in their squalid newcomer hives, susceptible to "drinking, debauchery and riotousness." After fleeing starvation across the Atlantic, they should not have to fester in the lethal slums of New York. Nor should they ever accept a drastic proposal floated by the Know-Nothings: to remove Irish children from their foul homes on the East Coast and assign them to non-Catholic families in the Midwest—an American version of the Penal Laws. But fresh air on fresh land *was* a good idea, Meagher felt. He urged the Irish to get out, to go west, to aspire and climb, to take advantage of the open country beyond New York.

"The tenement which the immigrant, in the vast majority of cases, is forced to resort to is by a thousand degrees less wholesome and affords less shelter than the rudest hut which could be thrown upon the prairie or within the forest." His paper was filled with such advice, as well as poetry, commentary, world news, odd items. It quickly gained a circulation in excess of 50,000, making it one of the top reads in New York. The *Irish News* carried things like a travel piece, "Three Months in Greece with William Smith O'Brien," and a long explanatory essay under the headline "Why Are Irishmen Democrats?" Without comment, Meagher also ran a few of John Mitchel's letters from the South. His old partner for freedom in Ireland had become a vigorous promoter of human bondage in America, even as the South fell further behind the rest of the world, backward and isolated.

With Elizabeth at his side, Meagher was sure of his step. The temper was contained, the drinking moderated, the speeches sharper. Almost a year after his marriage, he still could not believe his good luck. No longer "my dear, dear Miss Townsend." Now she was Libby—his Libby. He loved everything about her. The pride for his bride jumped off the page. "She is so intelligent, so cultivated, so generous, so gentle and un-affected," he wrote Smith O'Brien in 1856. He glowed in her presence and wanted to show her off. "I long, earnestly and fondly, to see Ireland and especially poor Waterford. The desire is all the more restless and intense owing from the fact of my having a very noble and very beauti-ful American wife . . . I would feel proud beyond measure to introduce her to my Irish friends. I would give anything if you could see her."

The Meaghers were frequently on the road. But when at home, they stayed at the Townsend house in New York, a place large enough to give them their privacy. Meagher was starting to understand what he could be in his new country. The Constitution was not only a gov-erning document, but a blueprint for how people of dissimilar back-grounds could live under a single flag. Religion, ethnicity (to a degree), economic standing—these were secondary concerns in the masterpiece of the Constitution, Meagher believed. The Old World's fatal flaw, en-forced in Ireland for centuries by England, was the establishment of a governing religion.

"I set my face against the alliance of Church and State—here and elsewhere—now and for all time," he said in San Francisco, further alarming his enemies in the Catholic Church's hierarchy. "I protest against it for Ireland, if Ireland so wills it. I protest against it for Rome, if Rome so wills it. Is this to be an infidel? . . . I am opposed to the exer-cise in political affairs of any and every clerical influence whatsoever."

He also praised his new country for the experiment of taking in people from all over the world. "Everywhere throughout this immense community, everywhere upon this prodigious territory, within which so many families, races, nationalities under a generous system of laws are indissolubly blended—everywhere an irrepressible vitality is evident."

The Irishman had found his American voice. In Dublin, the fine words had been in service of futility, tapping into an ancient vein of grievance. The United States was still forming, a fast-changing, fast-growing nation of thirty million people. An immigrant, barely five years from the penal colony, could influence its shape. Meagher's speeches continued to draw huge crowds—predominantly Irish on one occa-sion in New York, predominantly Jewish at another Manhattan venue. Even at the most convivial events he tried to keep alive the memory of the million who died in the Great Hunger. "There is a skeleton at this feast," he said at a Friends of St. Patrick banquet. "Some few may not behold it. But to me the shroud and the sealed lips and the cold hands and the beautiful head are visible . . . It is a festival of memory."

But he did not speak out on slavery. New York in the late 1850s was an ambiguous island in a rising sea of Northeast abolitionism. Yes, the influential publisher Horace Greeley expended barrels of printer's ink on behalf of ending the Peculiar Institution. And Henry Ward Beecher, the most popular preacher in the country, was tearing up the pulpit with fiery denunciations of legalized inhumanity, backing the sentiment of a sibling whose novel, *Uncle Tom's Cabin,* had become America's best-selling book of its time. Reverend Beecher's Plymouth Church was the top tourist destination in the city. But New York's mayor, an artful dandy named Fernando Wood, wanted no part of the do-gooders. In that sentiment, the Irish on the Lower East Side were with him, as was Tammany Hall. Wood was first elected in 1854, in part because the Sixth Ward had delivered several thousand votes from people who never existed. The mayor's real loyalty was to lining his pockets, and to the merchant class that had grown prosperous on the global cotton trade.

New York's animating cause was money, Wood said; the city would never risk its garment factories, its free port, its brokers who kept the South rolling, for liberation of the Negro. With forced labor, the American South provided three fourths of the world's cotton supply, yielding a stream of cash that flushed through the hands of his city's bankers. New York financial institutions even offered mortgages to plantation owners on their enslaved human machines in the field. Wood was manifestly corrupt: he was the first mayor to be physically yanked from City Hall and arrested. He survived the scandal, and after being out of office for several years, he won a second term in 1860, openly proclaiming his pro-Southern views. John Hughes, who had joined the Meaghers in marriage, was no abolitionist either. The archbishop made it clear that the Irish masses he presumed to speak for were not interested in a crusade that could bring thousands of free blacks north, to compete with Erin's unskilled workers in the basement of American opportunity.

Still, the Catholic cleric's declarations were soft-breeze diplomacy compared to the heat blast from John Mitchel. Slavery might have died a natural death, as Thomas Jefferson had predicted. But the technical great leap of Eli Whitney's cotton gin made the South all the more dependent on what it harvested with people in bondage, now on an industrial scale. Cotton became the chief U.S. export. Mills in New England and Olde England spun fine sheets and soft garments from raw material that had been picked by people whose backs bore the same mark of the lash as those of Irish convicts in Australia. Mitchel was blind to these parallels. "Those emigrants who have education, refined taste and means to buy Negroes had better come South for a living," he wrote from his home in Tennessee.

Mitchel started a proslavery paper out of Knoxville, baited the leading voices of the North and inflated the most radical voices in the South. The same muscular wordsmith who had backed the risky speeches of Thomas Meagher for a free Ireland, who saw nobility in the lowliest peasant dying of fever in the corner of a grass hut, now put his prose to work on behalf of white supremacy. "I am continuing to the best of my ability to 'save the South' from her enemies and oppressors and to break up the Union," he wrote a friend. "A great many people regard me as an incendiary and madman." He moved to Washington, there to be closer to his allies in the slaveholding cause. Just a few miles from Alexandria, Virginia, where people were kept in pens while waiting to be auctioned, Mitchel belittled those who called slavery a great evil. Blacks, he wrote, were far better off in chains in America than running free in Africa. When Smith O'Brien, on his tour of the United States in 1859, met with his former conspirator in Irish liberation, he was appalled at the change in Mitchel. The man he thought he knew so well, Smith O'Brien wrote, had become "a formidable monster."

Frederick Douglass could not understand this. During his trip to Ireland in 1845, then about the same age as most of the well-spoken rebels, Douglass had found a country of empty pantries that still opened its doors to him. "One of the most pleasing features of my visit thus far has been the total absence of all manifestations of prejudice against me on account of my color," he wrote. But in the late 1850s in America, he saw a hardening of Irish attitudes toward blacks. "Perhaps no class of our fellow citizens has carried this prejudice against color to a point more extreme and dangerous than have our Catholic Irish fellow citizens," he said. "And no people on the face of the earth have been more relentlessly persecuted and oppressed on account of race and religion than have these same Irish people. The Irish who, at home, readily sympathize with the oppressed everywhere, are instantly taught when they step upon our soil to hate and despise the Negro. They are taught that he eats the bread that belongs to them."

Questions of hatred and loyalty dogged the Irish in America, with Meagher in the middle of it. The immigrants were tenants, it was said, renting out a country as a staging ground to go after Britain. The critics weren't entirely wrong—a view affirmed by the defiance of Meagher's friend Michael Corcoran, the onetime constable for the Empire, now commander of the 69th Regiment of the New York State Militia. Since coming to America as a fugitive, Corcoran had sold oysters in the street, worked as a bookkeeper for a tavern and a clerk at the post office, and finally found his calling in the militia. By 1860, he was the commander of a unit full of Irish American volunteers, his reputation on the rise. But when asked to parade his soldiers in honor of the Prince of Wales, Colonel Corcoran balked. "I cannot in good conscience order out a regiment composed of Irish-born citizens to parade in honor of a sovereign under whose reign Ireland was made a desert and her sons forced into exile," Corcoran said. "In the Prince of Wales I recognize the representative of my country's oppressors." He was arrested, thrown in jail and ordered to face a court-martial.

His stand caused a national furor. Here was proof of the dual loyalties of the Irish fresh to America. As it was, they were thieves and scofflaws, violent and unruly, the nativists said. New terms—*paddy wagon, hooligan*—were coined for Ireland's lawbreaking outcasts. "Nearly seventy-five percent of our criminals and paupers are Irish," wrote *Harper's Weekly,* and "fully seventy-five percent of the crimes of violence committed among us are the work of Irishmen." Further, the Irish in America showed "an incapacity for self-government," the paper asserted. Now Colonel Corcoran's insubordination had proved that his people could not be trusted in military command and should be run out of the service. When it was revealed that Corcoran was a member of the Fenian Brotherhood, the Irish independence movement founded in 1858, it only added to the case against him and his people.

As influential voices called for Corcoran to be deported, Meagher rushed to his defense. The Irish were ready to shed blood against any enemy of the country that had taken them in, Meagher said. That should never be in doubt. Corcoran had done what a man of conscience must do, he argued. He had not refused a military order in time of battle. Rather, he simply did not have his men show up at a parade for a foreign royal. Were these men of Ireland to honor the Prince of Wales, he wrote, it would show that "her people are satisfied" being serfs of England. They could never forget the famine — *the skeleton at the feast*. These arguments did Meagher no good with the general public. In an election year, the most consequential in the young republic's history, with the country ready to break, a view of the Irish hardened in many parts of the land: they could not be counted on to hold firm against a renegade South, nor could they be trusted in the uniform of their adopted country.

Restless as always, Meagher sold his newspaper and left for Central America with Libby. He had been there before, in stopovers on the way to the American West Coast. He'd used those travels for writing assignments, climbing volcanoes, sailing across Lake Nicaragua, hacking through the jungle with Indian guides. This time, he and his wife were looking for fresh stimulation, lecture material, and to earn a healthy fee on behalf of a wealthy American who wanted to build a route to connect the seas, a dream of centuries. He also did diplomatic work on the side for the increasingly feckless President Buchanan, who had shown no stomach for holding the nation together. The Irishman and his New York wife were welcomed by the president of Costa Rica, and worked the survey and government circle for months. He thought he had a deal for a right-of-way in place, and hoped to return triumphant with a plan to build a rail route across the isthmus. But it fell through, snagged by doubters in Congress and obstructionists in Costa Rica.

Meagher despaired. Was he doomed to life as a serial dilettante? Many starts, nothing finished. He worried that he was an oratorical ornament who had lost his luster — yesterday's man, less than a decade after arriving in America. "I was then a dazzling novelty," he wrote one of the Meagher clubs that still invited him to speak. "A lock of my hair would have fetched consistently more than what most people would give now for a foot of the Trans-Atlantic submarine cable. But the most favorable novelties must fade."

The depression that found him whenever he was bereft of a cause returned. "I've ceased to be a participator in historic motions," he wrote

Smith O'Brien. "I've become an impassive spectator. Yet, a spark might re-light the fire, the materials of which have not been exhausted."

Abraham Lincoln had few friends in New York. Or so it would appear. Mayor Wood said he was unwelcome. So did half the newspapers. But Lincoln was determined to press his case against the great sickness infecting the country. From the Midwest, he took five trains over three days to reach Manhattan in the dead of winter, 1860. He arrived exhausted, his suit soiled, and checked into the Astor House. A change of venue was announced for his speech: because of advance interest, it was moved from Reverend Beecher's Plymouth Church to the basement hall of the Cooper Union, an institution dedicated to free education for the working class, regardless of color, then barely a year old. On the day of the speech, February 27, Lincoln stopped off at a studio on the corner of Bleecker Street and Broadway and had his portrait taken by Mathew Brady. He was fifty-one, beardless and sad-eyed, with a prominent mole on his right cheek, his facial features disproportionate to his gangly frame—a six-foot-four-inch paste-up of a man. He had learned to joke about his ugliness. Later, when an opponent called him two-faced, he said, "If I had two faces, do you think I'd be wearing this one?" In the evening, he took the stage in a room that was supposed to hold no more than 900 people; 1,500 showed up. Lincoln talked for an hour and then some, tearing apart the Dred Scott decision, trying to prove that the Constitution could never be used to expand slavery in the territories. He was cheered wildly. Four newspapers carried the full 7,000-word text of his remarks. One paper noted, "No man had ever made such an impression on his first appearance to a New York audience." The speech propelled him toward the presidency.

When the Democrats met in Charleston, South Carolina, to choose a candidate for the high office, they could not hold the Southern delegates together. Stephen Douglas, Lincoln's old political sparring opponent, was the nominee, but he had committed the unpardonable sin of allowing the territories to choose to be free or slave by popular vote. This, the slavery-or-nothing South could not tolerate; its delegates stormed out. For the general election, each faction of Democrats nominated a candidate: Douglas for the Northern wing; a vice president, John C. Breckinridge, for the Southern. Another party, a meld of Know-Nothings and aging Whigs, put forth a slaveholder, John Bell.

The Republicans, after three ballots, settled on the former one-term congressman, Lincoln, as their candidate. Honest Abe could speak and had a compelling personal story, raised from an earthen-floored cabin. He did not promise to abolish slavery. In Arkansas, Alabama, Mississippi, Texas, Tennessee, Florida, Georgia, Louisiana and North Carolina, Lincoln was not even on the ballot. He did not get a single vote from any of them. In Virginia, where his name was listed, he tallied 1,887 votes—a mere 1 percent. On election night, Lincoln won with just under 40 percent of the total. He got 1,865,908 votes, but the other candidates combined outpolled him by more than a million ballots. Lincoln carried every Northern state but New Jersey. He lost New York City by a sizable margin but took the state. The Irish voted Northern Democrat. They'd been warned of the consequences of a Republican victory. "If Lincoln is elected, you will have to compete with the labor of 4 million emancipated Negroes," wrote the *New York Tribune*.

The Meaghers returned home in January 1861 from a yearlong absence in Central America to find a nation they did not recognize—tense, fractured, cutthroat. By March 1, in the last days before Lincoln was sworn into office, more than half of the South had deserted the Union. South Carolina went out first, on December 20, 1860, followed by Mississippi, Florida, Alabama, Georgia, Louisiana, Texas—seven states in all, with slaves making up 47 percent of their population. Lincoln assumed the presidency on March 4, a cold day with a persistent wind lashing at the 10,000 people gathered near a Capitol dome bracketed by construction scaffolding. Chief Justice Taney, the former slaveholder who had written the Dred Scott decision, administered the oath. In his address, Lincoln tried to reassure the South: "I have no purpose, directly or indirectly, to interfere with the institution of slavery in the states where it exists. I believe I have no lawful right to do so, and I have no inclination to do so." He appealed to the runaway states to come home, bound by "the mystic chords of memory." He tried to play peacemaker, conciliator. "A husband and wife may be divorced," he said, "but the different parts of our country cannot do this."

The new Confederate nation soon removed all doubt about the reason for its existence. At the founding convention of the Confederate States of America, one of the first orders of business was to enshrine slavery in its constitution, in Article I. "No bill of attainder, ex post facto law, or law denying or impairing the right of property in negro slaves shall be passed." And if the legal footings of the rebel republic did not make the point clear enough, the Confederate leadership did. "African slavery as it exists in the United States," said President Jefferson Davis, "is a moral, a social and a political blessing." A committed white supremacist, Davis owned 137 people on his cotton plantation in Mississippi. The rebel vice president, Alexander H. Stephens, was even more explicit. "Our new government is founded upon exactly the opposite idea" of racial equality, he said. "Its cornerstone rests upon the great truth that the negro is not equal to the white man, that slavery is his natural and normal condition."

Meagher's New York looked to break away, not with the South but as an independent city republic, open for business. Mayor Wood would try to play both sides, but first he suggested that New York secede and declare itself a free city, loyal to neither. "With our aggrieved brethren of the slave states, we have friendly relations and a common sympathy," the mayor said at the start of 1861.

Meagher continued to respect the South's sovereign right to its institution, so long as it was the law of the land, but not to leave the Union. And if war came, how would the Irish respond? They had been forewarned about what a Lincoln presidency would mean to them—he was head of "a party that says a nigger is better than an Irishman," the *Albany Argus* cautioned. "We will not move an inch when you command us to march to a fratricidal war!" wrote the *Boston Pilot*.

Colonel Corcoran, who could rally his countrymen to one side or the other, was awaiting his court-martial, having endured the lash of Northern public sentiment for snubbing the Prince of Wales. The South exploited this opening: the Irish should not fight for those who hated them, Confederate leaders argued. They added a further disincentive: about 80,000 Irish immigrants lived in the breakaway states, the combustible John Mitchel among them. *These are your brothers, not the Yankees.* Meagher would not argue with this sentiment. The South had been gracious to Mr. and Mrs. Meagher in ways that Protestants of the North never had been. Was this rogue nation really an *enemy?* These thoughts simmered, all a moral muddle, until what happened on April 12 of that year made it clear to Meagher what he must do, and do without hesitation. He'd been called.

WAR

The man-made island of Fort Sumter was a smidge of American will in Charleston Harbor, surrounded by the guns of a renegade republic. By early April of 1861, the soldiers isolated in that brick-walled compound were facing starvation. The military, the government, even the currency of the United States no longer had any official standing in the seven states of the newborn Confederacy. Only four forts remained in the hands of the Union, and three of them were insignificant. Sumter meant something, with its masonry perimeter twelve feet thick in parts, its hollow-stomached officers a source of federal pride and its commander, Robert Anderson, a West Point instructor who had taught the general who now aimed his cannons at him how to use the big guns. Sumter stood for a nation cleaved but not yet bloodied. South Carolina refused to let food in or soldiers out, except under the white flag of surrender. The new president still thought war could be averted. "We must not be enemies," Lincoln pleaded in his first hour on the job. As a concession, he would send life supplies to the garrison of eighty-five or so men, and nothing more provocative.

But the time for words was over. War was a thrilling prospect. It excited the young, who knew nothing of its consequences, and the old, who drew blood by proxy. "Strike a blow!" one Southern politician urged the citizens of Charleston, barking from a balcony. They did not need the nudge, for many had already crossed a line; they were eager to kill their former countrymen. "There is nothing in all the dark caves of human passion so cruel and deadly as the hatred the South Caro-

linians profess for the Yankees," wrote a London *Times* correspondent
from Charleston. The harbor was lined with cannons, a lethal semi-
circle poised to "reduce the fort" at the call of President Jefferson Davis. Commanding one of those Confederate guns, with the 1st South
Carolina Artillery, was John C. Mitchel, the eldest son of the Irish polemicist. The boy stood ready to level the outpost of the nation that had
given his family refuge.

In New York, a man who had risked his life for John Mitchel in
Ireland tried to walk away from an argument with his father-in-law.
Thomas Meagher was a Democrat. He could never vote for Lincoln.
On this spring morning, Peter Townsend fumed about the former
Democrats agitating in the South. They were traitors, knaves, yahoos.
Meagher, never shying from debate, countered. Don't call them out-
laws, he said, "call them revolutionists." The voice that never went quiet
on behalf of landless and starving Irish tenants, and the pen that pulsed
with indignation against treatment of convicts in the penal colony of
Australia, had been missing in the great debate that broke up America.
Meagher and his father-in-law left their morning dispute at the table,
nothing resolved. It was yet another reason for the Townsend patriarch
—*Peter the Great,* as Meagher now called him—to wonder what his
oldest daughter saw in this Irishman. Meagher strolled over to Delmonico's for lunch. There, a few blocks from O'Gorman's law office, in
a restaurant with the city's largest wine cellar, Meagher joined a vari-
ant of the debate he had walked away from at the Townsend home.
The South, he argued, had done nothing to harm the North. Why go
to war?

The same message was being conveyed, in more extortionate terms,
to the American commander of Fort Sumter. The secessionist General P.G.T. Beauregard sent two men to the garrison in a rowboat. They
handed a note to Major Anderson: get out or get killed. A few rations
of dried pork, and very little water, were all that kept the men alive.
"Gentlemen," Anderson replied, "if you do not batter us to pieces we
shall be starved out in a few days." Darkness fell with no sign of retreat.
By midnight, much of Charleston was giddy. At 4:30 a.m. on April 12,
they got their war. The inaugural shot was a long, graceful arc of red
light, like the start of a fireworks show, illuminating the bay. At dawn
and throughout the day, the shells became a deadly shower. Fort Sum-

ter caught fire, though it was quickly put out. In town, people cheered from rooftops and in seats along the harbor, watching brother lob cannonballs against brother. For thirty-three hours the fort was hammered, more than 4,000 rounds. Before the weekend was over, Anderson surrendered. No one died from the rain of fire, but the garrison had nothing left—it was out of ammunition and out of food. The flag of the United States was lowered. Victory was declared in Charleston. The South had fired first. And one of those shots that had launched the bloodiest conflict in American history, it was reported in the *Charleston Mercury*, came at the hand of John C. Mitchel, "the worthy son of that patriot sire."

In New York, in Boston, in Chicago, in small towns and on farms where a majority of Americans lived, reaction was swift and visceral. The unimaginable had happened; it changed everything. People poured into the streets. Newspaper headlines screamed: the Union has been assaulted! Walt Whitman was walking down Broadway toward the Fulton Ferry just after midnight on April 13 when he heard the cry of newsboys, louder than ever before. He bought a broadsheet and joined a cluster of people reading telegraphed dispatches from South Carolina. Whitman felt himself swept away in "a volcanic upheaval." Having claimed a Union trophy, what would the South do next? March on Washington, was the great fear. With the capital exposed, Lincoln called for immediate help: the formation of a 75,000-man force from state militias to serve for ninety days. Surely, three months was all it would take to subjugate the South. The existing national army, all of it, was barely 16,000 soldiers, and many of those men were scattered on the far western frontier. Washington was defenseless.

Lincoln's plea was not a declaration of war—not technically. But his summons infuriated the slave states. Virginia, the mother of presidents, home to Washington, Jefferson, Madison and Monroe, was the next to secede, though the western half felt no sympathy with the tobacco masters in the east. It was followed by Arkansas, Tennessee and North Carolina. The border states with slave populations—Maryland, Missouri, Kentucky and Delaware—remained in the Union, for now. Chest out, fully committed to abandon its sovereign ties to the North, the full Confederacy now numbered eleven states, with a population of 5.5 million free, 3.5 million in bondage. As a new nation, it became the largest slaveholding country in the world, relieving the United States of the distinction.

In every town, neutrality was out of fashion. Meagher was with Irish friends in New York, who pressed him for guidance.

"What do you think of affairs now?"

"I don't know what to think," said Meagher. "I never saw such a change in public opinion. I feel like one carried away by a torrent." Would Irish America's best-known voice join the volunteers to defend the capital? Where, exactly, was his heart? Hadn't he expressed sympathy for the South?

"Damn them!" he snapped. "Damn them that didn't let that flag alone!"

"If you feel that way, perhaps you might think of coming with us," a member of New York's 69th suggested.

"I'll think of it."

He didn't think for long. When Fort Sumter was shelled, the head of the 69th New York State Militia, Michael Corcoran, was still facing court-martial for turning his back on the British royal heir. The charge of disloyalty was immediately dropped, and Corcoran sprang into action, offering the services of his Irish-born troops to the president. He said he would provide 1,000 men; 5,000 applied. Meagher joined his friend from the 1848 rebellion. The choice had been easy, with his wife Elizabeth concurring. And it should be easy for the Irish, Meagher said. The country that "had given us asylum and an honorable career" risked falling apart, he told the doubters among his former countrymen. "It is the duty of every freedom-loving citizen to prevent such a calamity at all hazards. Above all it is the duty of us Irish citizens who aspire to establish a similar form of government in our native land."

Jumping into the fray, he pumped up crowds with daily speeches, cajoled the comfortable among his influential friends, roused immigrants in the tenements. His rallying cry was consistent: rarely a mention of slavery or Lincoln, but a fight for America coupled with the promise of an eventual fight for Ireland, using a battle-seasoned force to sail across the Atlantic. Meagher decided to lead his own charge, establishing a unit of Irish Zouaves, named after the fast-striking elite of European soldiers, with their flowing pantaloons, billowy tops and tasseled fezzes. He took out an ad in the *Tribune*, in huge type:

YOUNG IRISHMEN TO ARMS!
TO ARMS YOUNG IRISHMEN!
IRISH ZOUAVES

One hundred young Irishmen—healthy, intelligent and active—
Wanted at once to form a Company under command of

THOMAS FRANCIS MEAGHER

Many in New York sneered at them. The Irish were criminals, drunks and quarrelsome—they couldn't organize a parade without fisticuffs, let alone become soldiers in a modern army. But in barely a day's time, Meagher was overwhelmed by volunteers. He was given the title of captain in the state militia, serving under Corcoran in the 69th. For this, the South could not forgive him, for many Confederates had hoped Meagher would join Mitchel in the rebel cause. "Never again shall the name Thomas Francis Meagher be united with any of our Southern institutions," wrote one Virginia paper. If anything, such slights only hastened the transition Meagher had to make in order to kill Virginians.

At age thirty-seven, Meagher was finally given the tools to do what the younger man in Ireland never got a chance to do. He drilled his men in Hibernian Hall, in city parks, on the streets. What did they know of fighting a war? Their muskets were musty and primitive, backfiring hand-me-downs, little better than the weapons used by farmers fighting the British in the American Revolution. They knew nothing of tactics, artillery logistics, treating the wounded. They could not march in a straight line, follow orders without dissent or sarcasm. They sang. They drank. They cursed. What carried them to battle was the zest to fight, the zest to belong to a country that had often mistreated them, the wish to prove their worth. A Whitman poem captured the mood:

> How you sprang! how you threw off the costumes of
> peace with indifferent hand;
> How your soft opera-music changed, and the drum and
> fife were heard in their stead.
> How you led to the war . . .

Barely a month after the assault on Fort Sumter, Meagher paraded his Zouaves through lower Manhattan, past St. Patrick's Cathedral on Mulberry Street, past Irish neighborhoods full of women waving flags from tenement windows, past the headquarters of the 69th on Prince Street. Meagher was at the front, his wife at his side, each on a horse. He scoffed at those who said a woman did not belong at the head of an army going off to war. The spring air was thick with pride and promise, with noble purpose and muscular words. No boy had yet had his shoulder blown open by a lead ball, no New Yorker had taken a bayonet to the face, no mother of seven had been left without a husband or a pension. Bagpipe music bounced along with Meagher's jaunty Zouaves. Priests blessed them. Children cheered them. They were the living link to the Wild Geese of the past, those Irish soldiers without a country fighting in Europe's conflicts, with a fierce reputation to uphold. The men left for Washington on a current of confidence.

In the first days after Lincoln's call to arms, the capital was empty and haunted. Neighbors sized up neighbors with suspicion. Sandbags were thrown in front of marble buildings. Food was hoarded. A handful of civilian volunteers patrolled outside the gates of the Executive Mansion. Across the river, the fires of Confederate camps burned at night. When would they strike? Meagher's Irishmen walked past the nearly abandoned Willard Hotel, the forsaken White House, and out to Georgetown College, where the 69th was bivouacked. For several weeks, instructors from West Point attempted to make soldiers of the street cleaners, bricklayers and pig farmers from Ireland by way of New York City. They tried to teach them how to load a muzzle and shoot, how to charge and when to fall back. To detractors, these men were motley, laughable, immigrant garbage—"gathered from the sewers of the cities, the degraded, beastly outsourcing of all the quarters of the world," as the *Raleigh Banner* wrote. On May 23, the Northern volunteers crossed the Potomac to the rebel state of Virginia and reclaimed Arlington Heights for the nation. They assembled a large, loud headquarters in the mud from May rains and named it for their commander: Camp Corcoran.

The Confederacy had just moved its capital from Montgomery, Alabama, to Richmond, Virginia—a hundred miles from the White

House. The city built along the upper braids of the James River was in full flower, with a leafy late spring on the high ground above water, while in the lowland, the massive Tredegar Iron Works geared up to produce the machines of war. Richmond was flooded with young men in mismatched uniforms, carrying their hunting rifles and pistols, their Bowie knives and the occasional sword of a distant relative. Among those soon to enlist in the militia would be another son of Young Ireland icon John Mitchel—James, in the 1st Virginia Infantry Company. Like his brother at Fort Sumter, he would kill for the slaveholding nation, in open treason of his adopted country. No Mitchel owned another man. What was there to die for? Home and hearth, of course, always a motivation. But something more was needed. Politicians urged poor whites to fight *against* equality; slavery would preserve their perch one rung from the bottom. "The only true aristocracy," said one Southern governor, is "the race of white men."

At Fort Corcoran, the Union Irish were put under the larger command of General Irvin McDowell, who had an army of 35,000 men and a diminishing allowance of time to use them. The ninety days of duty that these citizen soldiers had agreed to in the upheaval of April would soon be up. The cry from all quarters—in Gaelic, in Brooklynese, in the flatly drawn vowels of volunteers from the prairie states—was the same: "On to Richmond!" They would move first to Manassas Junction, about thirty-two miles away, and cut off key rail connections to the rebel capital. From there, the path would be clear all the way to the commode of Jefferson Davis. Quick and decisive. Joining McDowell was his old friend from West Point, William Tecumseh Sherman—bristle-bearded, red-haired, with no patience for Irish jollying. A tough man to like, Sherman wore a scowl and rarely made eye contact with the men from New York. He'd been in Louisiana, superintendent at the state military academy, when Southern states started to quit on the Union. As a grandson of a signer of the Declaration of Independence, it tore him up. "You people in the South don't know what you're doing," he told a Virginia friend. "This country will be drenched in blood, and God only knows how it will end."

Meagher knew something of war, but only of the chase—he of the hunted in 1848. But as he read poetry inside his tent at Fort Corcoran, as he paced the heights over the Potomac in the days lengthening up to the summer solstice, he felt ever more strongly that he was at the dawn of a two-part epic: one to save the democratic experiment of the United States, the other to liberate Ireland. *This* was what his life had led up to, though it had taken a curious route to get there. It was laughable to think that gaunt-faced men wallowing in the dirt of their first war could force the British Empire to give Ireland its independence. But Meagher had no such doubts. "If only one in ten of us come back when this war is over," he said, "the military experience gained by that one will be of more service in a fight for Ireland's freedom than would that of the entire ten as they are now." So, dual loyalties after all—and no hiding it now.

Sherman treated Meagher's men like farm animals, with a stench to go with them. They disgusted him, these excitable Micks, unfit for a grand army. Blacks were inferior to all whites, Sherman believed, but the Irish were just a notch above them. Look at their silly uniforms, a mishmash of blue and gray, and Meagher with his braided gold to go with his upgrade to a major. *What buffoonery.* The Irish played their fiddles at night, told drawn-out stories punctuated by laughter and prayed to a Roman Catholic God. At one point, a priest assigned to the 69th blessed a new cannon that was rolled into place. *A cannon!* And all the solemnity and ritual—the Irish could transform a flag-raising at Camp Corcoran into a High Mass. "No cohesion, no real discipline, no respect for authority," Sherman wrote.

Meagher expected the Irish to fight, he pronounced from a stump, "until the banner of the entire Union has been replaced on every fort and arsenal from which it has been improperly, illegally and nefariously torn down." To this, Sherman sniffed. Words were nothing, a great speaker of words even less. Sherman himself was talky in a twitchy way, without having much to say. Adding to his disgust toward the soldiers from the ratholes of New York, he heard many complaints about the ninety-day enlistment period's expiration date; some of these volunteers were ready to go home before they'd fired a shot, duty done. Meagher defended his immigrant troops, to little avail. He soon learned that the military was not a democracy. A man who'd never served a superior in any army, or for any government, was to do as he was told, without debate. No surprise, then, that Meagher developed a distinct distaste for his commander. William Tecumseh Sherman, he told a reporter, was "a rude and envenomed martinet."

Orders to move came on July 16, 1861. The men prepared to march and fight with three days of food and sixty rounds of ammunition. They broke camp in high spirits and with "an Irish cheer," in Meagher's words. They didn't get under way until noon, in the heat, and then sweating through their irregular uniforms, feet blistering in ill-fitting shoes, fifty pounds on their backs. Many of the soldiers strayed, falling away to pick berries or sit under shade trees for a spell. "For all my personal efforts, I could not prevent the men from straggling for water, blackberries or anything on the way they fancied," wrote Sherman. Meagher rode at the front of the 69th with his friend from 1848, Colonel Corcoran. One was tall, taciturn, long-faced, the other shorter, mustachioed, given to random observations framed in perfectly formed sentences. Often they laughed, happy to be going into battle. But more than that, they were happy to be together in a fight of real consequence. Arriving in a small village, Meagher was distracted by a two-story wood home, roses blooming in the front, a white picket fence all around. His mind drifted to domestic peace, sitting in a garden with a book and his wife with the dimpled smile.

The next day they ran into their first rebels, a scattering near Fairfax. These Confederates retreated before a shot could be fired. But the Irish lost a soldier to an accident, a loaded musket discharging when it fell from a wagon. The wounded man bled and cried in pain. The Irish commanders pleaded with Sherman to let them take him back to Washington for treatment. Sherman insisted the man with the open wound stay with his unit, dragged along in a rear ambulance.

On July 18, with the summer sun bearing down, the army arrived at Centreville, newly abandoned by the rebels. The town was a few miles from Bull Run, a frisky stream that skirted from amber-colored hills outside Manassas. Lincoln wanted a quick knockout: take the rail junction, then topple the capital. The big green flag of the 69th—a sunburst over a harp and a stirring Gaelic admonition, "They shall not retreat from the clash of spears," specially designed in New York—was planted in a field where the Irish bedded down after a meal of tea and chalky biscuits. Meagher poked his head in and out of tents, studied maps, went over details with Corcoran, checking on the badly wounded man who'd been hauled along with them.

Sunday, July 21, was the warmest day yet—hot and still, mosquitoes swarming, black flies biting. The clank of the Confederate Army, rebel horses and rebel soldiers, carried over the dead air of Virginia. From

Washington came congressmen with field glasses and women carrying picnic baskets stuffed with bread and wine, dressed in Sunday clothes. Again the call: "On to Richmond!" The mood was festive among the spectators settled on blankets with a view—war would be good entertainment, and a shame to miss.

The latest intelligence had it that the South had assembled 22,000 troops to defend its rail junction, led by General Beauregard, the man who had shelled the hungry men at Fort Sumter and launched the war. These Southerners were farm boys and fence menders, untrained, but confident of translating their rural skills into the execution of human beings. The other side would be no match. "You are green, it is true," Lincoln had told General McDowell, but equal to the enemy because "you are all green alike." Just hours before they would be ordered into organized butchery, Meagher and Corcoran's Irish were unsure of their role in the large assault of Union soldiers. Would they be at the front? Or in the rear? As a spear, or reserves? Could they kill on close contact, looking into the eyes of men who may have survived the Great Hunger like them, who came across the Atlantic to live, not to die at the hands of a fellow exile? At Sherman's call, speculation ended. It was time to move, time for volunteers to become warriors.

13

FIRST BLOOD

They broke for battle at 2:30 a.m., fumbling for something to eat, for muskets and powder, buck and ball. Sleep, if it came, had been shallow and turbulent. In the dark, they marched with stiff limbs toward Bull Run, where two armies the size of cities were massing to clash. At 5:30, cannons cracked open a day unlike any other in the short history of the republic. In the largest assemblage of soldiers yet on the North American continent, men of common language and heritage would try to slaughter each other until one side gave way. The Union army split, with a diversion crossing a bridge over the stream—a feint—and the bulk going north, fording Bull Run and then coming at the rebels from behind. The Irishmen under Colonel Sherman were held back, late to the fight. They heard weak screams of a charge, and louder screams of agony, and always the clap of cannonade in the near distance. For almost an hour, they sat by the creek, hearts skipping, sweat beading off their brows, listening to war—"shot and shell, and every sort of hellish missile swept and tore, whizzed and jarred, smashed and plunged through the trees all about," Meagher recalled. At midmorning, they splashed through the stream single-file and started to climb a low rise. "Everyone prepared for death," said Meagher.

Through white smoke, the men of the 69th crept close enough to see the fighting in flashes—a mashed face here, a broken gun there, an arm without a hand. It looked like a rebel retreat, scrawny men running uphill. In the heat of first combat, an Irish commander, Colonel James Haggerty, made his own charge without orders. He was a carpenter from County Donegal, Famine Irish like most of his men. Haggerty ran after retreating enemy soldiers, getting close enough to smell them. A rebel turned, aimed his musket at Haggerty and fired. The officer fell from his horse, a ball ripping open a gash in his chest. One minute he had been Meagher's chatty mate—"a constant play of humor and goodness." Now Haggerty was a quivering body on the field above Bull Run, his insides spilled onto his shirt. He died where he fell. A fellow Irishman from a Louisiana unit had killed him.

The Confederates regrouped above the stream, around a farmhouse owned by a widow, Judith Henry. The Union boys could sense it: the rebels were on the run and clustered for the kill. But one Southern brigade did not move, its forces commanded by General Thomas J. Jackson. He stood in the face of artillery and musket fire, said a rebel officer, "like a stone wall"—a name that Stonewall Jackson would carry from that point on. The fighting stalled at midday, allowing time for the South to move cannons into place around the widow's house. The lull did not last. The Northerners hammered the Henry compound, killing the widow as she cowered in an upstairs bedroom. The Confederates sent an equal amount of iron and shot back down the slope. To poke a head up and pause for a gulp of summer air was perilous.

In midafternoon, lying on grass slick with warm blood, an Irishman lost his ear. Through the smoke, men of the 69th had to dart one way or the other to dodge the bounce of heavy cannonballs. But the plum-sized iron balls that rained from overhead, after a lit-fuse shell exploded, were something else—a random shower. The soldier had looked uphill, into the whir of musket fire, when his ear was clipped clean by a shell fragment. He put his hand to the bloody opening in his head and screamed as he felt the loss.

The Union generals sent several waves up Henry's Hill, and each time they were repelled. Now it was the immigrants' turn. As the temperature climbed, the Irishmen stripped off their shirts and prepared to charge. Bare-chested, they formed a line behind their emerald flag, and with a loud cry ran toward the battery of Southerners. Tightly bunched, the men of the 69th dropped quickly. Legs were knocked out. Faces were torn open by fragments from canisters. Heads split. Every few minutes, a cannonball made a direct hit, decapitating a volunteer or cutting him clean in half. To shoot a man on the run is not an easy thing, not with a heavy musket that fired a single shot at a time. Teeth moved faster than trigger fingers, tearing open cartridges, the powder blackening lips. Compounding the problem was identification: some of the enemy buzzing around the house wore blue, some wore gray, some wore the clothes of a field hand. The Irish led one charge, with Meagher on a white horse, and were cut down. They tried a second time, even as other Union soldiers started to melt away in the wrong direction. This too was repelled. A third assault followed, and again was rolled back at high cost in blood.

Meagher tried to continue the fight, to push through to the house and break Confederate will. His men briefly crested the hill. "We felt quite elated," a soldier of the 69th told the *New York Times*. Then, out of the fields to the side, *out of nowhere,* a rush of fresh Southern soldiers charged forth. These reinforcements, thousands of them, had come from the Shenandoah Valley, where they were supposed to have been kept in place by another Union force. As tired, dehydrated and dispirited as the American soldiers were, the rebels new to battle were fully charged, letting loose a bloodcurdling yell. At the same time, showers of iron and grapeshot from cannons increased. Not a space between Union soldiers was free of lethal projectiles. Bodies covered the grass of the hill, the blood turning brown under the sun. "We beat their men," Meagher said. "Their batteries beat us. That is the story of the day."

Loss begot chaos. General McDowell's Union soldiers headed for safety, back across Bull Run—quick-stepping and then sprinting, a dash of fear. Already weakened by hunger and heat, many threw down their weapons and ran. Meagher was stunned at the sight of an army fleeing from a fight. To go to war requires the suspension of survival instincts. If the illusion cannot be sustained, base human fear takes over. Swept up in the stampede of retreat, the Irish stumbled back down toward the stream with the main army, protecting the rear. Their lips were cracked and parched, their legs heavy. Some were barefoot. Corcoran ordered his men to form into a square that could slow the enemy advance, and maybe start a counterattack. But his group was soon separated in the haze and surrounded by secessionists. Where was Corcoran? Meagher cried out for his friend from 1848. Word came that he was killed. No, wounded. Or captured. Command now fell to Meagher, whose cap had come off. He mounted his horse and waved the unfurled green banner of the 69th. "Look at that flag," he yelled. "Think of Ireland!" Would the harp, outlaw instrument in the days of the British Penal Laws, still have power in a New World clash?

Poised to spill Southern blood, the Irish captain tried to hold the line. Meagher was knocked from his mount and smashed into the ground. His horse had been pummeled, torn open by cannon shot, tossing him into a heap. His vision blurred, his hearing went to a white-noise monotone and then—nothing. He lay face-down, spread-eagled in reddish Virginia dust, unconscious, his body splattered in horse blood and scraps of the animal's flesh and hide. As waves of Federals fled, rebels chased them in high-spirited pursuit. Meagher would have been captured, or had a bayonet run through his rib cage, had not a lone soldier gone back to rescue him. Private Joseph P. McCoy, a student from a Jesuit college, grabbed Meagher and horse-collared him back toward the fleeing Union soldiers. The captain was placed in a wagon, which bounced along the uneven field. Minutes later, the horse pulling the carriage took a load of shot in its flank and reared up in agony. The animal fell, the wagon capsized, and Meagher was pitched into the stream. The splash shook him fully back to consciousness, but the sight all around him was a heave of loss and abandon. "Here it was that the panic took place," he recalled. "Up to this point, there was no fright, no alarm, no confusion." Caught in the break for safety was a New York congressman, Albert Ely, who had ventured down from the picnic grounds for a closer look at combat. A rebel soldier wanted to kill him. "You infernal son of a bitch! You came to see the fun, did you? God damn your dirty soul!"

Nearby, on the rise that the Union had failed to take, Jefferson Davis rode up to view the battlefield. He had come from Richmond on the train, traveling over the rail line that was supposed to be turned into a Union one-way to the Confederate White House. The fussy Davis arrived in time to hear Stonewall Jackson's boast on behalf of the slave-holding nation. "We have them whipped—they ran like dogs," Jackson told him. "Give me ten thousand men like them and I shall take Washington City tomorrow."

Lincoln's soldiers limped back to Camp Corcoran, collapsing into their tents at 3 a.m. The Union reported these casualties: 625 men killed, 950 wounded, 1,200 captured. Confederate losses were 400 killed, about 1,600 wounded. Thirty-eight Irishmen from the 69th died at Bull Run, another 59 were seriously hurt, and nearly 200 were missing. Corcoran was presumed dead or captured. And Meagher, some New York papers reported, had been killed. The Union had been humiliated.

That was true, to a point. The Irish had performed admirably, as even Sherman noted afterward in his official report. The "sewage from the city" won praise from both sides. The immigrants charged when others would not. They held firm and fired back when others threw down their weapons. They were among the last of the Union soldiers to retreat. Still, a British correspondent from the *Times* of London ridiculed Meagher, saying the fall from his horse was due to drunkenness, a story reprinted in the American press. There may have been a larger motive behind the misinformation: if Meagher was serious about raising an army to eventually liberate Ireland, better that he be stopped now. By contrast, the *New York Times* quoted an eyewitness who said, "Meagher was remarkable in his bare head, urging his men forward." A few days later, 29 officers in Meagher's unit wrote a letter to the New York papers praising Meagher's performance—"on the march, no one was more eager in battle; none more reckless of his life."

At camp, the deflated band made plans to return home. War was horrible and, it was now clear, would not be short. The day after the battle, Lincoln signed a bill authorizing the enlistment of 500,000 men for three years of duty—a professional army for the long haul. A second bill called for an additional half million men. Meagher was ready to follow Lincoln, but how? A citizen soldier for now, his tour of duty was up. He packed to go home to Elizabeth and an uncertain future. But William Tecumseh Sherman would have none of it. Eyes narrowed, hair unkempt, the colonel growled at Meagher.

"How can you go to New York?" he asked him, in the company of the unpaid men of the 69th. "I do not remember to have signed a leave for you."

Meagher said his ninety days had expired. He was a free man, not a professional officer in the regular army. So were the others.

"You are a soldier and must submit to orders until you are properly discharged." To make his point, Sherman moved closer, and spoke loud enough for every one of the soldiers to hear, no cloaking his West Point training with a veneer of civilian manners. "If you attempt to leave without orders, it will be mutiny, and I will shoot you like a dog." Meagher retreated to his tent. Sherman had shamed him before his friends; worse, he made it clear he had no respect for these men.

In the afternoon a gangly, black-suited visitor with a pallor of gloom came to visit the New York Irish—President Lincoln. "We thought we would come over and see the boys," he said. The unusual timbre of his voice, a bit high, caught the men by surprise. On Sunday, the blue-sky day of battle, Lincoln had gone for a ride in the country outside the capital, reasonably confident of victory. That evening, he read a tele-gram of startling news from his War Department: "The day is lost. Save Washington and the remnants of this army." Monday it rained, weather to match the mood of broken men in bandages and tattered clothes staggering through the streets.

"They come along in disorderly mobs," Whitman wrote, "queer-looking objects, strange eyes and faces, drench'd in the feet … Where are your banners and your bands of music?" Some supporters urged the president to give up the fight. "If it best for the country and mankind that we make peace with the rebels at once and on their terms, do not shrink even from that," Horace Greeley wrote Lincoln. But the Con-federates, despite Stonewall Jackson's boast, were in no shape after Bull Run to storm the White House. A much bigger Union Army stood guard on the banks of the Potomac. Lincoln's task was to gird a con-fused nation for a long war. In the days following the defeat, he wanted to see soldiers who would not run from battle. Sherman, despite his low regard for the Irish, knew what they were worth to him. "I have the Irish Sixty-Ninth New York, which will fight," he wrote the War De-partment.

Lincoln shook hands with the bedraggled Irishmen, offering encour-agement. Bull Run was just one battle, not the war. Next time would be better, and there was certainly a place in the vast new American force for the immigrants. More than a nod to ethnic tolerance, Lincoln needed the nearly two million Irish in the country to fight for a splin-tered nation. Northern factory owners, businessmen and Main Street merchants weren't about to give up their livelihoods to risk death in the South. The farmers, from whose ranks the American revolutionists had drawn some of their best marksmen, were seasonal soldiers—avail-able mainly in the winter, when fields were dormant but fighting was a logistical nightmare. The urban poor, the immigrants without trades, might have to form the backbone of the new Union Army. Whether they would die for this country was still an open question. To Lincoln's kind words, the Irish 69th gave a president they would never vote for a Gaelic cheer. He was moved, a crooked smile breaking the undertaker's face—"I confess I rather like it." Was there anything he could do for them? Be honest, he told the men. Meagher stepped forward. Since being thrown from his horse, and losing friends to combat, the shine of the orator was gone. He looked haggard, with lips tight, eyes clouded, a full half foot shorter than Lincoln.

"Mr. President, I have a cause of grievance."

"Yes."

"This morning I went to Colonel Sherman and he threatened to shoot me."

Lincoln tipped his head, puzzled. Unwilling to get in the middle of a spat between officers, he threw off a joke, with some truth to it. "If I were you," he said, "and he threatened to shoot, I would trust him." For one of the few times in his life, Meagher was speechless. Still, the 69th was mustered out of duty a few days later, free to return home, as the Irish captain had requested. Lincoln would remember Thomas Francis Meagher.

14

THE CALL, THE FALL

He could not forget Haggerty, his chest blown open, and Corcoran, gone to the fog of war, friends who'd followed him from Waterford to life's end in a Virginia field. War was not fit for poetry. Back in New York, he told Libby what he'd seen and what he'd heard: a horse shredded, a boy suddenly blind and crying for his mother, prayers and curses, one and the same. It was not glorious at all—"men I knew and loved, and they lie there in the rich sunshine discolored and cold in death." The rumors about Corcoran gave way to a letter in his hand from a cell in Richmond. He was held by the rebels, caught when he tried to defend the rear of the Union Army. After losing sight of his main unit, he and a dozen or so soldiers had holed up in a cabin, where the Confederates found them. More than a prisoner of a four-month-old war, Corcoran was a prize for the South: they offered to release him if he would publicly vow not to fight—a powerful disincentive to other Irish. He refused, and was eventually transferred to a damp, lightless cell in Charleston and put in solitary confinement. Should the North execute a single prisoner, it was announced, Michael Corcoran would be hanged.

Someone had to fill the void, to lead the Irish. No sooner had Meagher returned to New York than requests poured in for him to take up where Corcoran had left off. Orator, barrister, scholar, journalist, revolutionary, adventurer and part-time soldier he was, but a commanding military officer? His little Zouave unit of volunteers had put up a fight at Bull Run, yes, but they'd been routed along with the other New Yorkers. Still, there would be no sitting out this war for Meagher.

After a few days at home, he went back to Washington to look after the wounded from the 69th.

Young men who had run through an Irish vale as children, or played full-throated hurling matches with other lads, now lay on cots, their gangrenous limbs awaiting the surgeon's handsaw. It was stomach-turning, these boys with their disfigured bodies, but it spurred Meagher to give meaning to the loss. The War Department proposed to make him a captain in the regular army. Good pay, good post, perhaps mostly ceremonial, an Irish American on uniformed display. A better offer came from John C. Frémont—*the Pathfinder!*—onetime presidential candidate, now a major general in St. Louis, commander of the Department of the West. Meagher could be his aide-de-camp, as a colonel. Meagher turned down both requests. His fate was with the New York Irish. "I cannot find it in my heart to part from my tried and honored comrades," he wrote. He would "prefer the humblest position in their ranks to the highest I could hold with newer friends."

An idea was taking hold: why not outfit an all-Irish brigade? The 69th was Hibernian to the core, but not formally established as such. This new creation would be a distinct ethnic unit of at least four regiments, with its own flag, its own pipe and drum corps, its own priests and surgeons, its own poet laureate. The notion was floated in Boston, Philadelphia and New York, home to the largest concentrations of Irish laborers ripe for recruitment. The plan played to Meagher's heart, stirred by his reading of countrymen who had formed Gaelic units for the French and the Spanish in the past, the vaunted Wild Geese. It played also to his Irish insecurity, the chip holding down his shoulder. He would show William T. Sherman what it meant to lead men into battle, and yet bark out his orders with a brogue. But what would happen if the brigade was a bust? If the immigrants failed to fight, fell apart, deserted, turned on Meagher? If they only confirmed the low opinion held of them by the Know-Nothings? What if the Union lost? For what purpose, then, would Meagher have recruited people to risk death in a new country? To Meagher, the perils were outweighed by the draw: being part of something greater than any one Irishman or any one American.

For a man who fed off crowds, the gathering on August 29, 1861, at Jones's Wood in New York, was a feast. The patch of farmland overlooking the East River, 132 acres in what would be subdivided as 66th to 75th Streets, was a pleasure ground for New Yorkers fleeing their tenement traps. It had beer gardens, games of chance and strength, amusements and oddities, picnic tables. On this Sunday, it was transformed into the largest rally of Irish yet on the continent. The festival was ostensibly a benefit to help the widows and families of those killed at Bull Run—admission, 25 cents a person. But it became a recruitment drive for an Irish brigade that would be formed out of the New York 69th, with units from other parts of the Northeast. Meagher on Slievenamon Mountain in 1848 was a boy revolutionary under a summer sun, trying to raise soldiers from the starving. Now, at Jones's Wood, he once again put his voice to work for a fledgling army. The turnout was estimated at 60,000 by the *New York Times*. No gathering of that size and character "has ever occurred in this city," the paper reported. Meagher mounted a large stage at the front of grounds festooned with the flags of the harp, of the United States, of Ireland. The chatter stilled, the music and dancing stopped. It was the perfect match of man and masses, the *Times* noted. "Captain Thomas Francis Meagher understands the character of his countrymen better, perhaps, than any other man in this country. To great affluence of language he combines a quickness of imagery which, even to a duller race than the Irish, is delightful."

Life is but a shadow that passes over the earth, swiftly gone, Meagher began, not unlike those who fell in Virginia. Think of the men "sealing their oath of American citizenship with their blood—whose doorways are now hung with blackest mourning, and whose tables miss the industrious hands that once furnished them with bread." They perished for a nation that offered them refuge, "immigrants driven by devastating laws and practices from their native soil." This Civil War was a test for a people who'd been offered a second chance in a new land.

"What of the cause in which our countrymen fell that day? Was it urgent? Was it just? Was it sacred?" He let the words linger, the pause for effect, the long silence. Then he answered his own question. "Never was there a cause more urgent, more just, more sacred!" Through the big field came a ripple of applause and cheers. But also some jeers, some drunken catcalls, some cants of discontent. Who wanted to die for Abraham Lincoln? Or worse—slaves? Meagher powered forth, pressing the issue.

"Will the Irishmen of New York stand by this cause—resolutely, heartily, with inexorable fidelity, despite all the sacrifices it may cost, despite all the dangers into which it may compel them, despite the bereavements and abiding gloom it may bring?"

"We will! We will!" But again, more cackles from the Lincoln haters. Meagher sensed the doubt and was quick to improvise.

"I am a Democrat." To this, the biggest cheers yet. "For my part, I ask no Irishman to do that which I myself am not prepared to do. My heart, my arm, my life is pledged to the national cause. I care not to what party the Chief Magistrate of the Republic has belonged. I care not upon what plank or platform he may have been elected—"

"Hear, hear!"

"The platform disappears before the Constitution, under the oath he took on the steps of the Capitol, the day of his inauguration—"

"Hear, hear!"

"The party disappears in the presence of the nation . . ."

And then, a jab at the enemy of more than 500 years. "I should remind my countrymen that the English aristocracy—"

"Boooooo! Damn them!"

"—which is the dominant class in England, to which the navy, the church, the army almost exclusively belong. I should remind my countrymen that this aristocracy is arrayed against the government in Washington. And that it was dead against the Revolution . . . Every blow that clears the way for the stars and stripes deals to this English aristocracy a deadly mortification and discouragement." He could have carried on against Britain, punch lines against punching bag, all afternoon. But he closed, after speaking for an hour in the August heat, with a nudge to get people down to a recruiting office at 596 Broadway, above the Metropolitan Hotel.

"Let us who hail from Ireland stand to the last by the stars and stripes!"

Meagher would refine the case against the South over the following months, a traveling rally-igniter for the Union cause. He was also a fire hose, putting out flare-ups of opposition. His strongest argument for the Irish was linking the Confederacy to the hated oppressor England, as he had done in New York. The Great Hunger was never far from Gaelic memory—loved ones "driven from their own land, their huts pulled down or burned above their heads, turned out by the roadside or

into the ditches to die," as Meagher said at several stops. His case linking the English Crown and the American South was only part hyper-
bole. Great Britain had outlawed slavery more than a generation earlier.
But few nations benefited more from slave labor than England, with its
looms, mills and clothing factories running full bore to outfit and en-
rich the aristocracy that Meagher had chastised at Jones's Wood. The
textile industry was the dynamo of England's Industrial Revolution—
one in five Britons was connected to the trade—and almost 80 percent of the cotton for that industry came from the slaveholding South.
To keep the currency of cotton from crossing the Atlantic, the American navy set up a blockade of Southern ports. England was warned not
to interfere. At the same time, the South worked diplomatic channels,
seeking recognition of its sovereignty by the world's most powerful empire. All of that gave Meagher plenty to work with.

"It is a fact that after all her denunciations and horror of slavery,
England is for the South, where slavery is in full blast, and against the
North, where it has long been extinct," he thundered in Boston's Music
Hall one night in September 1861. "In spite of Shakespeare and Bacon,
England is no sentimentalist, no poet, and no philosopher," he said. It is
a nation where "cotton is more precious than political principle."

His case was buttressed when an American warship seized two
Confederate diplomats from a British vessel off Cuba in November.
The men were on their way to London in search of formal recogni-
tion of the breakaway nation. The Empire was outraged by the seizure.
"You may stand for this," Prime Minister Palmerston told his cabinet.
"But damned if I will!" He ordered troops to Canada, a menace on the
American border, and demanded an apology from Lincoln. A red-faced
England, bullying and saber-rattling, making demands of the United
States on behalf of the South: Meagher could scarcely have asked for
better material.

In Boston, in a hall so packed that 2,000 people had to be turned
away, in a state where the Know-Nothings had won political control a
few years earlier and disbanded Irish national guard militias, Meagher
hit all his high points. Almost ten years earlier, anticipating Meagher's
arrival after his escape from Tasmania, a paper in Boston had predicted
great things for the exile—as leader of the Irish masses in the New
World. He was in town now to build the largest army yet of Irish in
America. The nativists' day was done, he said; the immigrants' time was

at hand. "Here at this hour I proclaim in the center of that city where this insult was offered to the Irish soldier, Know-Nothingism is dead!"

He had to pause for several minutes to let the cascade of cheers subside. He praised the Irish laborers who built the railroads, who dug the canals and constructed the reservoirs, who cleaned the streets in their adopted country, who wiped the faces of the children of the wealthy. "This is the only nation where the Irish can reconstruct themselves and become a power . . . This, too, I know: that every Irishman this side of Mason and Dixon's line is with me. If there is one who is not, let him take the next Galway steamer and go home." He left Boston with commitments to fill two regiments in the Irish Brigade.

His Philadelphia pitch was so effective it alarmed Confederate spies in the city's midst. "He made a capital speech; I feared a telling one," an informant wrote Jefferson Davis. "I worked night and day to neutralize his speech . . . his marriage with a Yankee girl was an admirable argument against him."

That Yankee girl had thrown herself fully in with her husband's cause. She not only walked with him at the front of parades, but worked New York society behind the scenes and helped design one of the brigade flags. The fear of some Irish was that the marriage of a fiery Catholic Celt and Fifth Avenue Protestant would make Meagher more like a Townsend. The opposite was happening. It was an odd thing to see his "beautiful and gifted wife beside him," as one officer recalled, while he drilled new recruits at Fort Schuyler, at the southern tip of the Bronx. She was his shadow, and he hers, in the low-angled autumn light glinting off bayonets moving in formation, the waters of Long Island Sound in the near distance. Drums and bugles and bagpipes—a soundtrack for soldiers yet to see conflict.

Libby became so devoted to the Irish Brigade that one of the regiments was nicknamed "Mrs. Meagher's Own." When not at the fort, the couple worked on persuading immigrants to sign up in the headquarters of the Irish Brigade on Broadway. Young men with bruised knuckles and thin-soled shoes wandered in curious, unknowing of military matters, heads packed with half-truths about the "nigger-lover" Abraham Lincoln. In a room that was unfurnished but for a desk, a couple of chairs and a bench, the Meaghers tag-teamed strangers— soft-sell patriotism from her, high-minded appeals to Irish nationalism from him. Before long, he had nearly 3,000 men. "The name of Meagher," wrote one journalist who watched him in the months following Bull Run, "is now more than ever a word of talismanic power."

He came to know many of his soldiers well, their families, their home counties, their losses in the famine. As autumn dragged on and fresh warfare approached, Meagher made a vow of fidelity to his recruits. "I promise you I shall be with you in every scene of hardship, of privation, and of danger," he said in a speech at Fort Schuyler. "In the camp, on the march, in the battle, I shall be with you, close to you, true to you, heart and soul with you. With you in defeat, if such be the divine decree, and with you in death, if we have all to go down together."

In between heaping scorn on the South and trying to fill his Irishmen with a sense of national purpose, Meagher took a break to honor a close friend. Terence MacManus, the merchant who had abandoned his prosperous wool trade to take up revolution with Young Ireland, had died in California. Meagher took the loss hard. Both had been fated for hanging, drawing and quartering, both been condemned to a lifetime in Tasmania. Both found new life in America, though MacManus had kept a low profile. Meagher was ever grateful to MacManus for showing up at his wedding to the governess in the penal colony, when his other friends shunned him. As well, he remembered what a lift he got from the diversion of backgammon and fishing aboard the ship that took them to their exile, and how the escape of MacManus had spurred him to plot his own dash for freedom. At a large gathering in New York, prompted by the arrival there of MacManus's body, Meagher recalled a man of wealth, fully settled in Liverpool, who gave it all up to help his people across the Irish Sea. "Radiant, hearty, full of pluck and teeming with brain, and having a proud, dutiful, chivalrous thought for Ireland all the while."

During the short days of December 1861, the Irish practiced at being soldiers just outside Arlington, Virginia, at Camp California. They wore Union blue now, a jacket falling just below the waist, pants held up by suspenders and a big cape of heavy wool that served as overcoat and blanket. Their weaponry was old-century: Prussian smoothbore muskets, arms suited for the slow-marching masses of European cannon fodder. The fate of the Union had been placed in the hands of a little man with a big opinion of himself, General George B. McClellan. Well credentialed, from a wealthy family, McClellan had graduated near the top of his class at West Point, proved himself a brilliant logistician in the Mexican War and run a railroad in the private sector—all before his fortieth birthday. But he never mastered the military discipline of keeping his nonmilitary thoughts to himself. He despised abolitionists. "Help me dodge the nigger—we want nothing to do with him," he wrote one high-ranking political friend. "I am fighting to preserve the integrity of the Union."

McClellan did not think much of his commander in chief. Lincoln, he said, was "a well-meaning baboon," his inferior in class, breeding and intellect. McClellan's task was to make the Army of the Potomac, soon to be the largest fighting force on earth, into a war machine that could conquer. Everyone from the president on down played nice to McClellan. "I find myself in a new and strange position here," he wrote his wife from the capital. "By some strange operation of magic, I seem to have become the power of the land." After Lincoln named him general in chief of all Union forces, as well as the commander of the Army of the Potomac, it occurred to the president that he might have put too much on Mac's shoulder. The man some were now calling Young Napoleon shrugged. "I can do it all," he said.

Meagher liked McClellan, something in his swagger. As much as he despised the civilians above him, McClellan connected with the soldiers below him. And Mac treated the immigrants much better than Sherman ever did. The Irish Brigade was now outfitted with an artillery unit and several regiments. Meagher was the commander in all but title. Influential friends had pressed Lincoln to name him a general. His speeches, particularly at Jones's Wood, had impressed the president. Lincoln knew Meagher was a Democrat and had not voted for him—all the better for unity's sake. In some cases, Meagher stated the cause for the North better than Lincoln had yet done. His appeal also crossed the Atlantic, holding out the possibility that Meagher might recruit from the country he'd been prohibited from ever seeing again— though many in Ireland scorned him for siding with the Union. Lincoln would need every man he could get. "Let Thomas Francis Meagher be appointed a brigadier general," he told his War Department secretary. Still, there were concerns. Meagher was a fugitive, an outlaw, a man whose best weapons were words.

While Meagher waited for Congress to grant his commission, the Irish shivered through the winter in tents ripped by wind and sagged by snow. They slept on boards and boughs a few inches above the frozen ground, with heavy, foul-smelling wool blankets for warmth. Tents had a small stove for heat, the smoke vented by a pipe about the same diameter as Lincoln's top hat. A persistent problem was finding dry wood. The men built fires of soggy green pine logs and needles still holding frost. The smoke was so thick that tent flaps had to be opened at night, losing the heat. Outside, after much drilling and horse-trampling, the byways were a porridge of mud on warmer days. An officer walking from one row of tents to another got stuck in the Virginia mire; he sank so deep that he needed the help of a soldier to free him with a shovel. In the long lockup of winter, between incessant freezing rains and face-lashing blizzards, hundreds of horses died.

Meagher's appointment came through in February 1862. Among the top brass in the army he was dismissed as a "political general"—one of Lincoln's patronage plums, designed to bring an ethnic constituency to arms. No one expected him to be much of a warrior. But for the Irish, the new command lifted the gloom of winter camp. In celebration, soldiers lit an enormous bonfire, played music and honored Meagher with a dinner that stretched to the early hours. With a sense of style and vanity that dated to his upstaging of a Shakespeare play at Stonyhurst, Meagher was radiant in the costume of his latest role. He wore a uniform Libby had designed: a sash diagonally across the chest, a gold shoulder belt, a sword by his side, drooping to just above the ground. It was no small thing to have the patriot and revolutionary, a man still wanted by the British Empire for treason—*one of us!*—elevated to the highest ranks of the American military. In Meagher's time, the Irish had been starved, bundled off to the penal colony and forced to flee to dank tenements in strange cities. But here, less than a decade after the end of the Great Hunger, a few years after the Know-Nothings had tried to deprive them of standing in their new nation, the Irish were ascendant in a conflict to save a halved democracy.

When an Irish Brigade chaplain, Reverend William Corby, a college professor on loan from Notre Dame, met Meagher in the frigid muck of winter camp, he found a man whose uniform could barely contain him—"one of the finest looking officers in the whole army," he wrote. "General Meagher was more than an ordinary gentleman," the priest noted. "He possessed high-toned sentiments and manners, and the bearing of a prince. He had a superior intellect, a liberal education, was a fine classical writer, and a born orator. He was very witty." And when the brigade got instructions to move—responding to Lincoln's General War Order No. 1, to throw the huge expanse of men against the Confederate capital—the cleric saw another side of Meagher. It was while waiting to shed blood, certain that he would lose friends on his orders, that Meagher began to drink heavily again. As a brigadier general, he carried the hopes of the Irish in America on his gold-braided shoulders; the burden of grief was his as well. Though the prankster in him was finally tamed, he would do everything to find some joy at the margins of war.

"At times, his convivial spirit would lead him too far," said Father Corby. "But by no means must it be concluded from this that he was a drunkard ... Besides, he was polite and gentlemanly even while under the influence of liquor, never sinking to anything low or mean beyond indulging too freely in unguarded moments." He drank to elevate occasions, yes. But he also drank in the hours between bloodlettings, during numberless days of killing and dying, in moments when he felt weak and full of doubt.

SUMMER OF SLAUGHTER

B y late May of 1862, the Irish Brigade was close enough to Richmond to hear the groans of a city preparing for siege. The sound of church bells appealing to God and of cannons clearing their throats of shot and shell had a desperate ring. The Confederacy was in a panic. Born amid boasts of liberty, it now suspended the writ of habeas corpus and put Norfolk, Portsmouth and Richmond under martial law. The rebel government enacted the continent's first military draft, ordering all men from eighteen to thirty-five to join the fight against the United States. On a whisper or an anonymous note, people were thrown in jail for suspicion of Union sympathy. Shops closed. Barricades encircled the city. Women and children were sent away. The rebel nation's gold was packed for shipment. Prices spiked. Hoarding put sugar and butter out of reach for all but the well connected. The sale and production of alcohol was outlawed. To further the misery, torrents of rain fell throughout the spring, flooding streets and homes, sending rivers over their banks and washing away bridges.

After the humiliation of Bull Run, the Union had run up a string of victories. General Ulysses S. Grant captured key forts in Tennessee, and Federal ships conquered New Orleans, the biggest city in the South, giving them free rein of much of the Mississippi. In Virginia, the Union had amassed 105,000 troops to attack the slaveholding capital, against a much smaller force, though neither side knew precisely what the other had. Everything was in line for a knockout punch. But McClellan held back, setting up camp on the lawn of a house once owned by Martha Custis, wife of George Washington.

In the endless wait during a spring of fickle sunshine, General Meagher sought amusement for his boys and himself. He spent his days reading the *Dublin Citizen* (a month out of date), reciting the poems of martyred patriots, sharing whiskey with officers and infantrymen alike—all while Confederate cannons thundered in the near distance. "Heavy guns are opening their jaws every five or so minutes, right in front of us," he wrote his brother-in-law Sam Barlow. The Irish Brigade was "doing nothing more dangerous than cleaning muskets, mending jackets and stockings, grumbling and drilling, and doing it all to the music of artillery."

His men had steamed down the Potomac, through Chesapeake Bay, landing at the Virginia Peninsula. For many in the brigade, it was the longest journey they had made over water since crossing the Atlantic in coffin ships. After laying siege to Yorktown, the Union Army moved up the big finger of land, closing in on Richmond. Laborers before they put on uniforms, accustomed to using their hands as claws and their backs as levers, the Irish were put to work cutting and stripping timber for the corduroy of spongy roads heading north. Fueled by black coffee three times a day, they had worked their way up the Peninsula only to squat in the stew of wet earth within six miles of the Confederate capital. There, they waited on McClellan, as did the president.

"I think the time is near when you must either attack Richmond or else give up the job and come to the defense of Washington," Lincoln told his general in chief. Scouts in Union balloons, new to war in the Americas, had gone up in the air a few days earlier, giving the army a peek at more than 50,000 rebel soldiers south and east of Richmond.

But weeks more passed without orders. Clothes would not dry, and the much-hated ankle-high boots the soldiers wore—*brogans,* from the Gaelic—seemed glued to webbed feet. The soles were flimsy; going barefoot was a better option for many. The food was wretched and moldy. Dysentery was common. You could stare at a mess plate, a tin cup, a haversack full of teeth-dulling hardtack, and it stared back without mercy or enticement. Nor could you think about what was ahead. More than a year into the war, it was clear that when armies clashed, losses were enormous. The shock of Shiloh in April, where at least 20,000 men were killed or wounded on both sides, was hard to fathom. The sight of piles of bodies, headless and legless, mangled in gore, "would have cured anybody of war," one officer wrote. Shiloh, the surprise attack against Grant's soldiers on the Tennessee River, had produced a deadly marker: more people fell in that one battle than in all the wars in American history up to that point.

Time was spent cleaning smoothbores, the muskets that had been used by European armies since the seventeenth century. The guns were heavy—nine pounds without bayonet—hard to operate and inaccurate. When fired, a lead ball banged around the barrel and exited in the general direction of a target, an effective range of eighty yards, if lucky. After repeated action, the barrel heated up and could not be reloaded without risking explosion in the face of the shooter. Meagher preferred a shorter barrel, packed with buck and ball—.30-caliber pellets and a .69-caliber lead ball, which would spray out like the blast of a shotgun. This, and fixed bayonets. He left no doubt of the implication: the brigade intended to fight up close, in the faces of the enemy.

As a nod to the Irish love of horse racing, he decided to stage a steeplechase at Tyler's farm, their Virginia encampment. At the same time, he organized matches of Gaelic football, the ancient game once outlawed by the Penal Laws. The soldiers cut an oval in the wet grass and picked jockeys to ride their fastest horses. Uniforms were made of tablecloths. Bets were placed. Purses offered. Elemental grandstands were constructed. Top brass—Generals Israel B. Richardson and William French among them—arrived and took their seats. Meagher as maestro, with toasts and stories, egging on rivalries, was in high spirits. He loved a laugh; he was "overflowing with wit and humor of the raciest kind," one officer wrote.

If only Michael Corcoran could share the afternoon. Meagher's fellow exile was wasting away in a Confederate prison, ill with typhoid fever. One day a fire had broken out, filling the jail compound with smoke. Corcoran, on his back, ordered an escape—bedding tied together as rope to flee. Guards caught the brigade prisoners just as they landed on the ground.

Though he missed Corcoran, Meagher was boosted by the presence of another friend and veteran of Young Ireland's fruitless struggle, John J. Kavanagh. That he had lived to fight again, or lived at all, was a small miracle, for Kavanagh had been the one shot in the thigh during the sad Battle of Widow McCormack's Cabbage Patch of 1848. He bled profusely in the Tipperary garden; Smith O'Brien feared he would die then and there at the age of twenty. But here he was, an officer in the

Army of the Potomac by way of France and New York, watching Gaelic football with a fellow exile.

To music from the brigade's pipe and drum corps, the races got under way. The steeplechase was just that—fastest horse around a track blocked by hurdles, ditches and a water hazard. Horses that did not clear the obstructions fell and tripped other riders. The brigade chaplain from Notre Dame had never seen such a spectacle. "It was the invention of wild Irishmen," Father Corby observed, "who did not know what fear is." A race of mules ridden by drummer boys followed, winner getting $30. In another part of the grounds, thespian soldiers rehearsed lines for a play, then distributed hastily scrawled fliers for the evening's entertainment. Sport and theater—the Irish way of war.

In a moment's time, the merriment came to a halt. From leaden skies, a series of booms rattled the grandstands. This was close. In a bold move, the Confederacy had decided to rip a tear in the Union Army, which was on either side of Chickahominy River. Flowing eighty-seven miles from north of Richmond to the James River, the Chickahominy was usually little more than a creek without a plan. But the spring rains had engorged the river into a python of brown water. In parts, it was a mile wide. The water divided McClellan's men—Meagher in a large group on the north side of the river, and about 34,000 soldiers on the other side. The rebels attacked the southern wing on that Saturday, May 31. Their plan was to save Richmond by destroying the smaller half of McClellan's army.

Thirty minutes after the last Chickahominy steeple race, Meagher had his men marching toward the river, to cross and reinforce the battered Union flank. They took no blankets, tents or overcoats. "It was a cold and gloomy afternoon," he wrote. "The tremendous rain of the previous night had flooded the low grounds on both sides of the river to such a volume that only one bridge was found available for passage of the troops." Stragglers from the day's battle passed through them with grim news of bodies strewn just ahead. That one bridge meant to be the conveyance to the other side was tattered and sagging. While attempting to cross, men and mounts plunged into the river. Fording was the only reliable way. But then, horses were sucked into the muck, and the advance came to a dead halt. Soldiers who tried to move them sank up to their bellies. All the pushing and pulling could not get the big guns across the river. The artillery, and men to guard it, would have to stay on one side of the Chickahominy. Most of Meagher's men waded through the floodplain, snakes all around them, toward the sound of the guns. Just before midnight, in shin-deep mud littered with the dead and the near dead, Meagher's men came to a halt. The stench was awful, an open graveyard.

"Not a star was visible," Meagher wrote. "One vast cloud filled the sky, producing so dense a darkness you would have thought it was through a coal-pit in the bowels of the earth that we were marching. Here and there, you could catch the yellow glimmering—or at times the broad and sudden flashes—of the lanterns of the surgeons as they groped and stumbled over the field in search of the wounded. The saddest moans were heard on every side. A dull, heavy woeful murmur deepened the tramp of the regiments passing on through the darkness, over the slain and dying."

It was a good thing that the sky was so opaque, Meagher wrote. The shock of going from Gaelic games to a slurry of death was hard enough without having to see it in all its detail. They would try to get a few hours' sleep before the baptismal battle of the Irish unit. "The horrors of the battlefield were buried in the depths of that impenetrable night. The wearied men of the Brigade lay down to rest upon the drenched and torn ground ... hardly conscious of the ghastly companions who slept among them, bathed in blood."

They rose at 4 a.m. on Sunday, June 1. The dawn broke sunless and gravel gray. A putrid smell. Everything wet. Soggy biscuits for breakfast. No coffee. "We had been sleeping with the dead," Father Corby wrote. "We saw the ghastly appearance of their bodies which had been, as it were, our bedfellows." What had been a mud clump in front of Meagher as he rested during the night now was revealed to be a Confederate soldier from a Georgia brigade. His long hair, matted and dirt-encased, covered most of a face. White fingers clutched a broken musket. Meagher noticed a large splotch on the stiff's uniform. Next to him was the body of a horse, eyes gouged, cemented in a clot of clayish blood. The last of the darkness gave way to more graphic gore. Blankets in wet bundles wrapped around dead men with their eyes still open. Mangled muskets. Body parts and horse heads. The ground itself moved—not an illusion. Meagher came upon another Confederate, this one alive and dazed, leaning against a tree stump, his insides ripped, bleeding. In talking to him, Meagher learned two things: the rebel was from South Carolina, and he was an Irishman.

A soldier climbed a tree and shouted from a branch: he could see the church spires of Richmond. They were four miles from the capital of the Confederacy. Meagher's query of the dying man was interrupted by a burst of musket fire from the woods just to one side. Another round came from the opposite direction. The battle that had begun the day before on the outskirts of Richmond, between the Fair Oaks train station and the hamlet of Seven Pines, was reengaged.

"To their utter astonishment the enemy found us within pistol-range of them," Meagher wrote. "Nor were we less astonished at finding them, without any intimation or warning whatever, so close at hand." Before the Irish Brigade could assemble, a Union regiment went into the woods on the attack. Not long afterward, they scampered back, minus half the force. Another Federal unit charged the woods. Meagher could hear them, but not see them. In the midst of the back-and-forth attacks, General Edwin V. Sumner rode up to Meagher. Hatless and resolute, with an eagle's head of silver hair and a beard of the same tint, Bull Sumner at sixty-five was the oldest field commander of any Union Army corps. He'd fought against the Black Hawks and Mexicans, and still retained a lust for organized bloodletting. To make his voice heard in advance of an admonition, he removed his false teeth. His words for Meagher were short: he must not fail.

"I want to see how Irishmen fight," Sumner told him. "When you run, I'll run."

Meagher went up and down his line, cajoling, backslapping, reassuring, the orator's voice trimmed for war. They entered the fray on his command and quickly came under "a hurricane of bullets," in Meagher's words. There was nothing to do but scream louder and charge. With a Gaelic cry, the Irishmen ran toward incoming fire, unloading rounds into enemy bodies. Through mud and mire, through underbrush and downed timber, Meagher's men pressed against the rebels. "The Irish Brigade met them with fixed bayonets and a sweeping fire, hurling their lines before them," wrote Captain David P. Conyngham, who became an informal historian of the New York 69th. They never moved backward. The wounded in gray were not picked up along the way—a sign that Confederate will had been broken. Other regiments

General Meagher leading the Irish Brigade at the Battle of Fair Oaks, June 1, 1862. This Currier and Ives print helped make the brigade famous when the Union was starved for heroes and positive war news. COURTESY OF THE LIBRARY OF CONGRESS, LC-USZC4-1619

massed in the woods as well, flushing out the enemy. A small cabin was occupied by Union fighters, and served as a cover. Balls clanked off the roof and walls, the sound of a lethal hailstorm. Meagher saw the Notre Dame priest, with his black clerical garb and Mennonite beard, running astride the Irishmen, as much a part of the battle as the soldiers. The goal was a rail line near the river, leading directly to Richmond. By early afternoon, the Union owned the railroad. Other regiments reported a stalemate, but not the Irish.

"We've got them on the run," a sergeant from one of the New York regiments said. "Keep them running."

Now the Irish dashed past the sloughed-off weapons of the enemy, their wet coats and bedrolls. A soldier spotted a Confederate body, head and torso planted in mud, legs and feet sticking straight up, and made a mental note to return for the shoes of the corpse. The rebels ran as the Union men had run at Manassas. "Thousands of muskets were flung away—cartridge boxes, blankets, everything that ever so slightly checked or slacked the rabidity of that wild flight," Meagher wrote. When the firing ceased, the Union Army was intact. About 35,000 soldiers of the South fell back to defend Richmond behind entrenchments of timber and earth.

The Battle of Fair Oaks cost the Confederates 6,134 dead and wounded to the Union's 5,031. More than that—it failed to break the Northern army in two, and left it at the doorstep of the rebel capital. Now was the time to push. The crux of the war was here. "The city of Richmond was ours," Meagher wrote. McClellan hinted at what was ahead. "Soldiers of the Army of the Potomac," he said in an address issued a few days after the battle. "You are now face to face with the rebels, who are held at bay in front of their capital. The final and decisive battle is at hand." But Mac was full of doubt. Content to have his army united, to have repelled the largest charge of the rebels in the eastern theater of the war, McClellan decided to go no farther, for now.

In Meagher's official report, he recorded the loss of two officers and thirty-nine soldiers. McClellan personally complimented Meagher for how the Irish had performed in battle and asked him about the peculiar battle cry of his men. In the storm of musket fire, the soldiers of the brigade did not run. Meagher passed the compliment down to his mud-covered troops from the slums of eastern cities: the highest-ranking general in the Union Army had proclaimed that the immigrants could fight. They already knew that.

Privately, McClellan was seething. Though he outnumbered the enemy by almost two to one, he feared that they had thousands more in reserve. And what he had witnessed, a two-day battle taking more than 11,000 men, had weakened the Young Napoleon's appetite for carnage. "I am tired of the sickening sight of the battlefield, with its mangled corpses & poor suffering wounded!" McClellan wrote his wife. "Victory has no charms for me when purchased at such cost." On the other side, one casualty stood out: General Joseph E. Johnston, who led the Southern assault. He was hit twice, fell from his horse and was carried back to Richmond. The Confederate military would need new leadership. A day after the battle, as bone-rattled rebels stumbled back behind the barricades of Richmond, as the papers feared the fall of a nation barely a year into its existence, President Davis named a new man

to guide the South. He appointed Robert E. Lee, a gray-bearded gentleman of fifty-five, as commander of the renamed Army of Northern
Virginia. And, unlike McClellan, Lee preferred to attack.

For all of the first week of June they waited. For all of the second week
of June they waited. For all of the third week of June they waited. The
Irish were joined by a regiment of New England Yankees, the 29th
Massachusetts, on orders. The soldiers had the Union blue in common,
but little else. The Micks were clannish, the Bay Staters complained, a
tribe unto themselves; it was hard to understand what the hell they were
saying. In battle, they shouted out a name unknown to most American
soldiers—"To Fontenoy"—commemorating the French defeat of the
English in 1745, with considerable help of Erin's armed exiles. *Fontenoy?*
The brigade was "a class of Irish exquisites," one reporter wrote of the
culture clash, "good for a fight, card party or a hurdle jumping, but ex-
tremely too Quixotic for the sober requirement of Yankee warfare." As
a welcoming gesture, Meagher gave the 29th a green flag; it was furled
and packed away by an officer who was indignant at having to take orders from an Irish revolutionary. To break the tedium of June, the Irish
had picket duty, guarding the rear outside Richmond, rounding up the
occasional straggler and deserter. They could set their watches to the
chimes of the capital city's clocks, could overhear conversations of the
Southerners—drawled out bits of demoralized talk. At times, they were
fired upon and shelled. The pinpricks were annoying and fed the desire
for a full invasion. *Let's take Richmond,* the men told each other—get it
over with. What did McClellan want? "He never seizes his opportunities," Lincoln complained to his advisers. "That's where the trouble is."

The rains slackened. Roads hardened in the summer sun. The fighting stopped, but the dying continued. On a quiet day, Meagher visited
the field hospital, a laboratory of gore on the medical frontier. It was a
swamp of moaning and thirsty men crying for relief from the saline-
slop of blood in the mouth. He was overwhelmed by the damage that
industrial-age warfare could inflict on a body. Better to die quick than
to fester in agony. Severed legs, feet and arms piled up in corners, to
be carted away in wheelbarrows and then fed to pigs. Men lost their
eyes, their teeth, their noses, had their cheeks hollowed, their collar-
bones shattered, their fingers clipped off, their skulls cracked by fast-
flying lead balls and shell fragments. Infection was the biggest killer.

Wounds turned red in triage, white with pus, attracted maggots. Doctors with blood up to their elbows tried to carve out balls from muscles, a last measure before administering a dose of chloroform and taking to the saw.

And now this: in the heat of the first week of summer at their camp near the mush of the Chickahominy, thousands of soldiers came down with malaria. The shaking and chills, the spiked temperatures and profuse sweating, the vomiting, the intense headaches—it was as if the fever of the famine had followed the Irish to Virginia. The disease took hundreds of men. Funerals happened almost hourly, bodies buried to a band's mournful tune, guns emptied and reversed, placed over the graves. The commanders did everything in their power to keep the premises clean, but sick horses dropped and swelled at such a rate that the brigade could not keep up. At one point, the men burned the dead animals—more than 400—in a massive fire. To quell the malaria, the surgeon general of the army ordered each soldier to take a dose of quinine mixed with a small amount of whiskey every morning.

On June 25, the great battle that all had anticipated got under way. Except, a surprise: it was not McClellan moving to conquer Richmond, but the rebels on the offensive. Robert E. Lee would now try to drive the Northerners from the Virginia Peninsula, to destroy them with the largest Confederate attack of the year-old war. Lee had mapped a campaign to pummel troops north of the river, using Stonewall Jackson, who had come down from the Shenandoah, as his hammer, assisted by other divisions. Lee sent more than 50,000 men against a much smaller force that had been lazing through the month of June. Rising from the early summer stupor, General Fitz John Porter's 35,000 soldiers tried to block the gray-shirted masses. Staggered, they fell back to Gaines's Mill, took a position on a rise and threw together a wall of rocks and wood, allowing them to fight from the protected high ground. On June 27, Stonewall Jackson poured it on, confident as always that God was on the side of the slaveholders. "This affair must hang in suspense no more," said Jackson. "Sweep the field with the bayonet!" Brigades from Georgia, Texas, Alabama, North Carolina and a reckless unit out of Louisiana, the Tiger Rifles, rushed to overwhelm the Union men. Their pace forward was brisk, fifty, forty, twenty yards from Porter's line, closing fast. Now the rebels broke through, crushing skulls and piercing chests. Porter's men fell back, regrouping into another position. Not all stayed in place; hundreds of men scooted down the other side of the hill toward the Chickahominy, their backs to the enemy.

The Union command turned to Meagher's Irish: were they ready to fight again? It was an order posed as a question. In double time, the brigade hurried five miles to bolster Porter's battered forces. Once more the immigrants waded and dragged horses and caissons across the bloated river, and once more they steeled themselves for a close-range struggle to snuff other men's hearts. They were loaded with buck and ball, their bayonets fixed, Meagher on his horse with his sword unsheathed. The sight that greeted them on the other side of the river was pitiful: Union solders stumbling in retreat, crying out, "We've been cut to pieces."

Meagher's men made it up the hill, where most of Porter's soldiers had congregated, as the last of the light was bleeding from the sky, battle smoke holding a blush of sunset red. "Nothing more was seen or heard of the enemy through the night," Meagher wrote in his official report. What made him proudest was that he'd stemmed a Union collapse without firing a shot. The mere presence of fresh troops had forced a rebel withdrawal. A witness, Union Army Captain W. F. Lyons, remembered the scene at dusk: "Meagher's Brigade stood, panting and elated, between the army they had saved and the enemy they had vanquished." The first of the Seven Days Battles had cost Lee 8,500 men, to nearly 7,000 for Porter. Despite taking higher casualties than the North, Lee had shaken Union confidence. There would be no march on the Confederate capital. "We sleep in the field, and shall renew the contest in the morning," Lee reported by dispatch.

Before dawn the Union soldiers left the rise and crossed back over the Chickahominy, on McClellan's orders, a tide of wounded and combat-shattered men. The general said it wasn't a retreat but a repositioning. The soldiers knew otherwise. Instead of going one way, toward Richmond, the Army of the Potomac would go in another, to the James River. Tents, trunks, cots, wagons, much food and bedding—all were left behind in the big move. Field hospitals were collapsed, with many of the wounded still in place. Backpedaling soldiers passed black faces, in and out of hiding, in this largest slaveholding state in America. Officially, slaves were now classified as "contraband" if taken by the Union. But the North didn't want the burden.

Little Mac's retreat emboldened Lee, whose new plan was to cut off the Union supply lines and crush them before they could fall under the protection of gunboats in the James River. The nasty task of defending the rear, under incessant shelling and sniper fire, was given to the Irish. They were the last to cross the Chickahominy, and the last out of the month-old camp, burning caches of supplies as they went. In the mid-day heat, soldiers flung off their uniforms, got seared and dehydrated, and fell with sunstroke beside the road. For two days, marching be-hind cattle and a mobile hospital, the Irish had nothing to eat. They were under constant attack, scuffling and brawling their way forward. Both armies were hemorrhaging men to desertion and enemy capture. In haste, the bluecoats dug shallow, mass graves for their dead, sweep-ing some who were still breathing into the ground by accident. "Many not-yet dead were buried alive," Father Corby wrote, "as we have rea-son to know from some who revived enough to protest just as they were about to be placed in the pit."

At night, the skies unloaded a steady rain, making sleep impossible. On June 30, as the Union Army passed through the sludge of White Oak Swamp, heavy shelling signaled a fresh rebel assault: 20,000 Con-federates jumped the Federals. Exhausted, hungry, suffering from the heat, Meagher's men were held back until evening. At 6 p.m., they were ordered into combat. "Boys, you go in to save another day," said Gen-eral Sumner. They fought until nightfall, when guns from both sides ceased fire. The North used the cover of darkness to continue the re-treat, walking until well past midnight. There was enough moonlight for Meagher's men to catch glimpses of Confederates stripping the left-behind Union dead of their clothes and shoes.

Near the James River, McClellan's army now took up a position on Malvern Hill, 150 feet above the plain, cut by a pair of ravines on ei-ther side—a perch that would be hard to capture. Near the base of the hill, just as they were pulling mud-caked bedrolls over tired bodies, the Irish were roused by an attack from the Louisiana Tiger Rifles. No unit from the South was more feared than the Tigers, a regiment of thieves, wharf rats, convicts and roustabouts from New Orleans, the Southern equivalent of the Bowery Boys from Five Points. They were Irish, nom-inally Catholic and famine refugees—brothers in snarl and attitude, in culture and faith, in every way but for the fact that one side wore blue and the other gray. It had been a Tiger who killed Haggerty at Bull Run. Meagher's men had no time to grab muskets or fix bayonets. The brawl in the dark was all fists and knives, biting and head-butting, Irish on Irish. Spying a rebel officer on horseback who seemed to be taking in the fight for his amusement, a New Yorker grabbed him by the pant legs. "Come out of there, you spalpeen!" The word, born in Ireland, had only one meaning. He threw the officer to the ground, and later presented him as a prize prisoner. The fight ended with neither side claiming victory.

At dawn on July 1, Lee tried to take Malvern Hill. It was all that stood between his army and McClellan's new base on the James River, at Harrison's Landing. He had the momentum, he felt, having captured 6,000 Union soldiers during the bedraggled pullback. But he was losing his own men at an alarming rate, more than 15,000 since he took command. Lee ordered artillery to be hauled up nearby hills, giving him—he hoped—enough height and range to reach Malvern.

Meagher had not slept. After the skirmish with the Tigers, he was primed and jittery with adrenaline. He stayed up for the remainder of the night drinking black coffee with two generals: Richardson, who had been his guest at the horse races a long month ago, and Sumner, the old bull. He told his superiors that his men would fight again if they had to, but they were worn to the bone. For five days they had gone without food and had very little rest. Their faces were smudged with powder, dirt and blood. Every day had been a skirmish or a battle. Meagher had lost many friends. The generals told him they would try to hold the Irish out if they could. As Lee's shells, canisters of shot and ten-pound balls reached for Malvern Hill, Meagher's men killed a few stray sheep and built a big fire. They would feast on mutton while the last of the Seven Days Battles raged to one side of them. The Union, it was now clear, had the high-ground advantage: Lee would have to do more than lob lead uphill.

The Irish never got to taste the lamb. The brigade was needed on another side of Malvern Hill, where Lee had ordered a desperation infantry attack. Meagher donned his green plumed cap, mounted his horse, raised his sword and led four hungry regiments back into combat. It would be safer for him to remain on foot, less of a target, he was advised. Not a chance: Meagher would stay in the saddle and take the odds. He ordered his men to strip off their uniform tops, the better to kill in shirtsleeves or bare-chested. Meagher felt the sharp whistle of a ball passing within a quarter inch of his temple, shredding his cap. Another bullet grazed his hand. He led three charges, aided by artillery from above him. Again the muskets failed them, becoming overheated and useless. Meagher needed time for the weapons to cool before he could charge again. But high ground won the day. For the first time in the Civil War, more soldiers were killed by artillery fire than by gunshot. The rebel dead formed clumps on the ground, mounds of bodies cut down by bombardment. For every one Union soldier who fell on Malvern Hill, nearly three Confederates died.

When the guns quieted around 9 p.m., the hill was still in Union hands. "McClellan's army is saved," Captain Conyngham observed, "but that hillside is covered with the dead and dying of the Irish Brigade." He watched one man find the body of his brother, prop it up and try to speak to him. The soldier spent the night lying next to the lifeless sibling. In the morning, he built a coffin from boards of an old house nearby and lowered his brother into the ground. Lee had lost 20,000 men—almost one fourth of his army—in the Peninsula battles. Union casualties were more than half of that. But McClellan, in his timidity, had given the South new life: the slaveholding republic that had been his to take a month earlier had driven him away from Richmond. It was left to the Irish and all their fellow foot soldiers to wonder why they were now bivouacked on the James River, instead of parading down the wide main boulevard of Richmond.

Meagher grappled with the rationales of war, his conscience sometimes getting the better of him when his pride didn't. He showed Bull Sumner the bullet-riddled banner of his regiments. "This is a *holy* flag, General." But he wept at the price. The Irish Brigade had been cut down by nearly a third—the 69th alone had gone from 750 men to 295 in a week's time. His friend Kavanagh from Young Ireland was still alive, a small condolence. Lieutenant Temple Emmet, another man who had Erin's struggle in his veins, was sick with what appeared to be malaria. Meagher's closest aide, young Emmet lay on his back in the summer heat, hallucinating with fever. The boy was a grandnephew of Robert Emmet, whose words on the eve of his execution by the English in 1803 were known in all parts of the globe where the Irish had been scattered: "Let no man write my epitaph . . . When my country takes her place among the nations of the earth, then and not till then, let my epitaph be written."

In the ebb between episodes of butchery, Meagher fought his doubts. What had become of Captain John Donovan, last reported to have taken a bullet through the eye? All the good men he led into combat—O'Donoghoe, dead; Haggerty, who'd lost a brother at Bull Run, dead; Rafferty, a private, just turned seventeen, his jaw shattered, two bullets in the mouth, left behind in the rain, captured or killed. Captain Egan, badly wounded. Same for Lieutenants Carr, Burns and Maroney. And think of his countrymen on the other side, the Tigers of Louisiana. Why were Irish fighting Irish in the New World instead of turning guns as one against the Crown in Dublin? *Why, why, why?* Well, to show that they were worthy Americans. And indeed, a just-issued Currier and Ives lithograph of the Irish Brigade at Fair Oaks had made national heroes of Meagher and his immigrant warriors. That fame would do nothing for Ireland. The larger goal, as before, was to free their old country. *Just keep saying it, to yourself and your men. Never forget what the dying is for.* But in truth, how could these sickly and broken-boned boys force the British Empire to give up control of Ireland? Better to think of something else, to think of his wife, and how war sharpened the senses for love.

Meagher begged to go home. McClellan agreed to grant him a short leave of absence. But not for the purpose of seeing Libby. He would let him go to rustle up fresh recruits. "We want many more wild Irishmen," McClellan said later. Fine. But one more request: Meagher asked to take Temple Emmet, the patriot's descendant, with him to get medical attention. Permission granted. In the second week of July, they left for New York, on a mission to probe what was left of the Irish will to fight a war that had become theirs by blood.

REASONS TO LIVE AND DIE

With Libby, at her father's home in Manhattan, Meagher could be a husband again for a few New York nights, having and holding. Their lovemaking had yet to produce a child—perhaps it was not to be—but his proximity to sudden death had brought them closer. He could let down his general's armor, tell her of the bullets that whistled by him, of how the clear-eyed young who had paraded down Broadway behind a green flag had been left in a Chickahominy swamp—Irishmen in their prime, forever in that fetid hole. He could describe a lead ball going through Donovan's eye and exiting his ear, or Emmet shivering and sweating on the way home, the letters he had to write to parents of dead children who had decided to follow *him* to war. He could tell her because he told her everything, as he'd promised in 1855. No secrets. She said New York had changed, *if you haven't noticed.* The Copperheads, those venomous Democrats who wanted to negotiate an immediate settlement, were ascendant. Perhaps it was true what they said: Lincoln was not up to the task of repairing a national crackup. Maybe they were right that the North could never win, not so long as the South threw men like the Tiger Rifles at Federal forces.

In the slums of the Lower East Side, on the docks and in the pubs, the loudest voices came from those fired with suspicion and hate. The Irish were killing people they had no reason to kill, it was said, and dying for people who knew nothing of their struggles. The only reason to enlist in Lincoln's army was mercenary. Just outside the recruiting station, the papers made a big deal of men in top hats paying Irish laborers to join up, there and then. *Here, lad, here's $20 to sign for three years.*

The Union needed arms-bearing flesh. Who better than the Irish? If so, why not wait for a better price? A draft was coming, everybody knew it. In July, Congress had passed a militia law requiring each state to fill a quota of soldiers. You could see where this was going. Word on the street was that a couple hundred dollars would buy your way out of service, purchasing another man to take your place. This on top of a bounty from the state and federal governments of up to $160, and $13 a month in soldier's wages. For the Irish, it would be more profitable to sell yourself to a rich man, let him dodge conscription for a price, and collect all the incentive cash, than to give up a healthy body on the cheap.

Pillow talk stayed with husband and wife; such candor could not leave home. In public, Meagher was the doubtless face of the Irish Brigade, a sheen of honor and valor, armor back in place, fresh words rolled out again to serve the Union. On the evening of July 25, he made his way through a sweaty crowd packed into the armory of New York's 7th Regiment. His task was to fortify the case for a war that was not going well. The draft talk did not help. In Irish neighborhoods of East Coast cities, protests had broken out, some of the marchers carrying a bannered proclamation: "We won't fight to free the nigger."

Ten thousand people showed up to hear Meagher speak; half of them were turned away. The brigade had come in for a run of good press, even if the war had not, and Meagher was an idol. At Fair Oaks, at Gaines's Mill, at Malvern Hill—in each battle the reputation of Irish warriors and their eccentric flair was enhanced. The *New York Times* had praised "the noble sons of Erin who have so fearlessly thrown their lives into the breach to defend the land of the free from its traitorous assailants." The *New York Herald* wrote that "the brogue of every county from Down to Wexford fell upon the ear" after the Battle of Fair Oaks. "When anything absurd, forlorn or desperate was to be attempted, the Irish Brigade was called upon. But, ordinarily they were regarded as a party of mad fellows." McClellan had lionized them, as had the Confederate brass, grudgingly. General Sumner would not think of going to battle without them. Abraham Lincoln himself, meeting with Union generals at Harrison's Landing a week after Malvern Hill, was seen grasping the banner of the 69th. "God Bless the Irish flag," he said. So reported a Union officer. What's more, he said the president had kissed that green flag. No king of England, no prime minister, would ever do that. And yet this story could not be repeated tonight in New York; it would only stoke jeers that the immigrants were fighting Lincoln's war.

Before Meagher could speak, music set the mood. Several thousand voices rose to mouth the words of "The Exile of Erin," their song to a man and woman.

> *"Sad is my fate!" said the heart-broken stranger,*
> *"The wild deer and wolf to a covert can flee;*
> *But I have no refuge from famine and danger,*
> *A home and a country remain not to me . . ."*

Meagher was there to convince the mass of exiles that a home and a country were here for them now. Even if they were just warm bodies to throw at Southern bodies, musket holders and cannon loaders, still . . . something momentous, dare he say *historic,* was happening to the immigrants fighting another country's mortal conflict. The boys from Dublin and Drogheda, from thousands of villages beginning with the Gaelic word *Bally,* were becoming Americans, no different than boys from Indiana and New Hampshire. War made them belong. "It is a favorite thought of ours, contemplating the majesty and grandeur of the Republic, that the foundations upon which they rest have been cemented by the blood and brains of so many Celts from Ireland," a soldier in the brigade wrote his hometown newspaper. Meagher had seen the transformation. As further incentive, Lincoln had signed the Homestead Act, opening the West for settlement by people who could never fathom owning a large tract of land. Beginning January 1, 1863, for a $6 filing fee and a year's residency on the plot of ground, a veteran of two years in the Union Army could become lord and master of 160 acres—the size of an estate in Ireland!

The police ordered all windows opened in the stifling armory. When Meagher appeared, he was mobbed. The crowd would not let him move. In his general's uniform, gold on blue, he looked as if he'd sprung from an oil portrait in a castle, "like one of the old Irish princes from Medieval times," one spectator recalled. More music. "Garryowen," the song that accompanied the Irish Brigade in formation and announced their presence in battle, filled the hall. Despite its Anglicized name, the song was birthed outside Limerick as a drinking ballad. Like the best music to emerge from Gaelic cellars, it was part defiance against authority, part battle cry.

We'll beat the bailiffs out of fun,
We'll make the mayor and sheriffs run;
We are the boys no man dares dun . . .

From songs to cheers, from cheers to a chant as they called his name—*let the patriot speak.* Notable for his absence tonight was Archbishop John Hughes. Fourteen months earlier, he'd blessed the Irish Brigade in a Mass at St. Patrick's and a parade down Broadway. Seven years earlier, he'd opened his mansion to Thomas and Elizabeth at their wedding, sealing the Meagher vows. But Dagger John was not happy with the horrific number of Irish deaths. Surely the casualty rate was higher for them than for other Union troops. Even if not by design, it was too much sacrifice. And the latest rumors from Washington— a military draft on the way, yes, but worse than that, word that Lincoln might free the slaves—made a dyspeptic cleric clutch his stomach. He'd issued a declaration, embossed with the imprimatur of the archdiocese, aimed at Lincoln. It was read in parishes throughout New York. "We, Catholics and a vast majority of our troops in the field, have not the slightest idea of carrying on a war that costs so much blood and treasure just to justify a clique of abolitionists in the North."

So there it was from on high, without filter or equivocation: the Irish would not fight to liberate enslaved blacks. God himself may well have spoken. Line drawn. In his defiance, the archbishop had the support of the Irish American press. What Meagher did not know as he bounded to the stage on the night of July 25, what nobody in the armory could know, was that three days earlier Lincoln had drafted a proclamation that would eventually free four million people from their chains—at least on paper. The president showed an early version of an emancipation decree to his cabinet. Most of his aides were stirred. But a few cautious voices emerged, parsing the politics of something so consequential. Better to wait for a Union triumph on the battlefield, a knockout to cheer the North, and then let the slavery-freeing edict ride on the breeze of victory. On the other hand, what of England? This was the great diplomatic balancing act, its outcome equal in impact to any loss on a battlefield. Lincoln had returned those two Confederate diplomats seized from a British ship. "One war at a time," he said. But Britain appeared closer to recognizing the South than ever before. If Lincoln broke the manacles that held millions to their masters in the American

General Meagher in 1863. Hardened by war and facing criticism from fellow Irish, he continued to rally his countrymen to the Union cause despite suffering heavy losses. COURTESY OF THE HUNTINGTON LIBRARY, SAN MARINO, CA

South, the war would be—explicitly—about a great moral cause. This would force the issue. Would England recognize the largest, perhaps the last, of the Western nations to defend slavery? Surely not. For now, the president set aside his draft.

On stage, Meagher sweated through his dress blues. He had dreadful news to impart, the latest casualties. Everyone in the room knew someone on the list. Solemnity was not Meagher's strong suit, but he

proceeded. The regiments of the Irish Brigade were decimated, he explained, some of them barely functioning. He needed 2,000 men to
sign on for three years. To this, no applause, only a few insults from
hecklers.

"You're a fool!"

He unfolded a letter from Captain Donovan of the 69th, a prisoner
in Richmond, later exchanged, now recovering in a New York hospital. Lost one eye, he did. Told his captors that even with half his vision, he would fight them. And if he lost that other eye, he would fight
blind. With this, Meagher got a laugh and big cheers. *Damn right—
don't mess with a blind Irishman.* Donovan said that the rebels who in-
terrogated him in Richmond had little fear of Union soldiers—except
for the Irish. His captors told him if they knew of the brigade's precise
whereabouts during the Peninsula campaign, "they would have sent a
whole division to take it and General Meagher prisoners, and hang the
exiled traitor from the highest tree in Richmond." Another government
wanted to hang Thomas Francis Meagher. *Imagine that.*

The story produced a hearty rumble of claps. The Irish loved being
told they were fearless bastards, crazy and unpredictable. And Meagher
loved being called reckless, half mad, a life of improbable invulnerability riding along on a white horse—let 'em talk down south. After the
applause subsided, Meagher returned to the need for soldiers. He was
interrupted by a shout from the floor.

"Take the black Republicans!"

"What's that?"

"Why don't you make the black Republicans go?"

Red-faced, Meagher turned on the heckler who had used the deri-
sive term for a Lincoln supporter. "Any man who makes a remark like
that I denounce as a poltroon and coward."

The dissident was escorted out. Playing again to Gaelic pride, Meagher told a pair of anecdotes about his brigade's banner: General Sumner, almost begging, when he asked, "Where are my green flags?" And
the enemy: they knew about the North's Irish warriors throughout the
slave states. He quoted a Mississippi regimental leader, fear on his face
when Meagher's men charged: "Here's that damned green flag again."
That line nearly brought down the armory. Even the cops laughed.

But he still had to fill the empty ranks in Lincoln's army. Meagher
reached for his climax. "Come, my countrymen, fling yourselves with a

generous passion into the armed lines ... Come, my countrymen, one more effort, magnanimous and chivalrous, for a republic which to hundreds of thousands of you has been a shelter, a home ... Come, my countrymen, follow me to the James River."

In the end, the orator's words were not enough. By the close of Meagher's leave, only 250 new men had signed on for duty. "Filling up the exhausted ranks of the Irish Brigade," Meagher wrote in a blunt letter to President Lincoln on the last day of July, was, "to tell the truth, an uphill work." To reconstitute itself, Meagher's unit would need new soldiers from other parts of the North.

August delivered a fresh blow: the death of Temple Emmet from typhoid fever. Meagher was beside himself at the loss of a young man who had shadowed his every move in the Peninsula, his aide-de-camp. Having lobbied General McClellan to bring Emmet home, having taken personal responsibility for the lad, he thought he had saved him from the plagues of war. "I am grieved to the heart to hear of this," Meagher wrote a friend. "For I esteemed, trusted and loved him as a favorite brother." He said nothing of the cause for which Emmet had given his life.

In cornfields holding mid-September's tawny light, in orchards that rolled up from the Shenandoah Valley, in stubble on either side of Antietam Creek, an American pastoral presented itself to the Irish Brigade camped near Sharpsburg, Maryland. At the center of this tableau was a plain white church of the Dunker sect, whose members did not believe in war or ostentation, and so their house of worship was without a steeple. How sweet it would be to drift into a nap on the warm grass, to revel in the sunshine of the last days of summer, to gaze over these rumpled hills and see no fear in the land. It had taken the brigade a full month to get from Harrison's Landing outside Richmond to a farmland less than forty miles northwest of Washington. At the James River camp, the men had fattened up on fresh food and ample rations. Whiskey kegs were rolled out nightly, and cattle were slaughtered, the meat fast to the grill over Virginia hickory. They slept well, were given new uniforms and shoes. But then, when they shipped north and fell in line for a quickstep through Maryland, the food was swill, rest minimal, conditions harsh. For several days, breakfast and supper were the same fare—stale bread and a tin of sardines. They had walked in calcified clay, the horses kicking up dust so thick it obscured the sun. They bedded down on that same clay. Hair, beards, arms, legs, uniforms—everything was floured in reddish dust. Muskets had to be cleaned several times a day to keep them in firing order.

The soldiers were moved like set pieces within a set piece, seldom told of the master war game. Generals drew up schemes on maps and sent divisions to certain death. Then they reassembled them a few miles away and did it again. As a grunt, you could drop weapons and flee, and many did, but if caught you'd be shot. A man could make $30 for every stray he rounded up for execution. You could feign malaria or typhoid, but it would take an actor of rare skill to pull it off. You could shoot yourself, with a wound of convenience that might be a ticket to a hospital bed. More likely, the self-inflicted tear would kill you, given the high mortality rate in the primitive medical trenches. The best thing to do was to curse and follow orders. The odds of getting out of this thing alive were still better in a soldier's uniform than a deserter's rags. As for motivation, whatever Meagher had said at Jones's Woods or the 7th Regiment Armory was now vapor. Survival was the only reason to expose a face to a shower of musketry.

Among the Irish, as with many Union soldiers, desperation became contagious. The war's center had moved from the Southern capital to the Northern capital because Robert E. Lee had moved. The South had struck a large Union force in a second Battle of Bull Run and whipped them. That August, the South also advanced on Kentucky, a slave state with divided loyalties. Emboldened by the triumphs, Lee invaded the North for the first time, crossing the Potomac into Maryland on September 4, 1862. He would try to take ground under the American flag, then menace Washington, forcing Lincoln to the bargaining table. The riots in Northern cities, the open ridicule of the president and his outmaneuvered generals, had convinced the Confederacy that the time was ripe for a settlement. They would keep their slaves, call it a draw and go home. First, though, the South had to crush McClellan at Antietam Creek.

On September 13, 1862, Union soldiers discovered cigar leaves wrapped around the battle plan of the Confederacy—Lee's orders, an accidental gift to the North. Now McClellan knew that his counterpart's army was split, knew when and where they planned to strike, and knew that if he hit them quickly he could annihilate them. "Destroy

the rebel army," Lincoln told Young Napoleon. But once again Mc-
Clellan did nothing. After a few days' time, the advantage was lost. The
Southerners had reassembled, with upwards of 40,000 fighters around
Antietam, behind batteries on high ground and a rail fence protecting
a long sunken road in the center. They were dug in and perched above
their enemy—the ideal advantage for the kind of formation-leveling,
industrial butchery that this continental clash of brothers had become.
McClellan had about 65,000 men available; as usual, he saw only vul-
nerabilities and phantom divisions in gray. "If we should be so unfortunate as to meet with defeat," he said, "our country is at their mercy."

Under drizzling skies on the night of September 16, Confederate
guns pounded the Union periphery with canisters and lit-fuse explosives. By now, most of the Irish were veterans of the killing roulette;
they had calculated the chance of a cannonball decapitating a horse, or
being directly beneath a shell when it burst to a sunflower of hot fragments. Superstitions were trusted: if you wore your forage cap one way,
or didn't shave for three days, or directed your prayers to an obscure and
underworked saint, you might be spared. But more than 120 of the men
camped in the lilt of land where the rust-colored Antietam drained
into the Potomac were new recruits to Meagher's unit; they had no experience with savagery in the most lethal of American wars.

These boys looked for reassurance in the rheumy eyes of General
Meagher and the battle-worn face of Captain John Kavanagh. The recruits had been little children in a famine-flattened country when their
superiors took on the British Empire. If luck was the element that allowed the leaders of Young Ireland's stunted rebellion to live to early
middle age, the new soldiers could only hope that some of it would rub
off on them tomorrow.

At dawn the following day, the grand designs of both sides had come
down to this: Lee's army on one side of the creek, McClellan's on the
other—the Dunker church, a cornfield and a sunken wagon road between them. Whoever had the strongest stomach for catastrophic loss
would prevail. In first light, the Irish ate a hot breakfast a mile from
the creek, the mist slow to give up its cling to dewy fields, an opaque
morning. They chewed bacon and drained tin coffee cups to the sounds
of a battle already under way. Meagher had slept on the ground, and
his face looked puffy. The Union sent Fighting Joe Hooker, the general most tolerant of heavy casualties, forward to the cornfield, there

to meet Stonewall Jackson among others in clay-dusted gray. Hooker's men had a reputation for recklessness and heavy drinking equal to the Irish. As the fog thinned, the church of the pacifists glowed bone white in peekaboo sun. Callused from a summer of combat, the rebels raised the flag of the slaveholders' republic and pushed the Northerners back over trampled corn to the edge of the woods. A second Union general, Joseph Mansfield, was summoned to join the fray. As he tried to lead a charge, his horse buckled under musket fire. Scurrying for cover, the general was shot in the gut, a mortal wound. By then, 3,000 Union men had been cut down. The day had just begun.

At 9 a.m., Bull Sumner told the Irish it was their time to join the carnage. The old general removed his false teeth and called his men to battle. Some soldiers gulped mouthfuls of dried coffee and washed it down with water from the copper-colored creek—caffeine to supplement adrenaline. Before they could see the faces of the enemy, they felt the flesh-ripping power of bullets fired from long range. This was something new: minié balls from rifled muskets, named for the French captain who'd perfected the inch-long slug. A marksman could still fire only one shot at a time, but with a grooved barrel, the range and accuracy had increased fourfold. Snipers from a quarter mile out could pick off targets, particularly those on horseback, in officer's braids or carrying a flag. The advantage further shifted to defenders, who had rebuffed nearly 90 percent of infantry assaults through the war.

Meagher stuck with the elemental weapons that had served him well: close-range buck and ball, and razor-sharp bayonets. After fording the creek, holding their weapons and cartridge boxes aloft to make the crossing through waist-deep water, the Irish dropped to the ground and awaited orders. Over the next fifteen minutes, down near the cornfield, Sumner lost 2,000 men. Now a second Union general fell to gunfire: Joe Hooker was hit below the knees, his foot spraying blood like a loose hose. Meagher told his men to shed everything but their cartridge belts and rise for a charge. Ahead of them, 500 paces away on rolling ground, the rebels were entrenched behind a fence of rough-cut rails, safely bunkered in the Sunken Road. The graybacks could fire away with only their heads exposed.

Meagher mounted his white horse, his mustache and sash covered in dust, and moved forward.

"Raise the colors, boys!" he shouted, ordering his men to their feet.

The cost of war. Irish Brigade dead on the battlefield of Antietam, September 19, 1862, the bloodiest single day in American history. Lincoln was spurred to announce the Emancipation Proclamation after the battle. The brigade suffered horrific casualties at Antietam. COURTESY OF THE LIBRARY OF CONGRESS, LC-DIG-DS-05164

"Follow me!" The Notre Dame priest dashed in front of the brigade and shouted out a blanket absolution to an infantry on the run. At least these Irish Catholics would die with clean souls. To get to the rebel line, the soldiers first had to knock down the fence. Balls pinged off wood and splintered rails, tore away kneecaps and shattered skulls. A bullet in the head made a sound different from a bullet in a fence; it hit with a hard splat. At Bull Run, at Fair Oaks or Malvern Hill, men had fallen intermittently, a casualty for every half-dozen people in a row. Here they dropped as if in a shuffled deck, half the line cut down with every charge. Barely twenty minutes after Father Corby had conducted an act of group contrition, 500 of those men in the priest's wake had been hit.

With an opening in the fence, Meagher's plan was to fire two volleys, then lead a sprint of Irishmen with the knife-pointed ends of their weapons into the pit of the Sunken Road.

"*Faugh-a-Ballagh*" came the cry, echoing the poet's admonition that had first stirred the boy orator to action in Dublin. *Clear the way!*

But the way was not clear. The Irish gained only a few paces at a terrible cost. The bellowing, crying and whinnying of newly riderless horses drowned out feeble attempts at a Gaelic yell. One bearer of the emerald flag was shot down. Another picked up the banner and was also cut to the ground. The same happened to a third, a fourth, a fifth, until the flagpole itself was shattered. Men with brains spilling from their temples crumpled next to haystacks. During one volley, Captain Kavanagh took a blast of shell fragments in the face and fell dead just short of the Sunken Road. Meagher's best friend in the Irish Brigade, a man who'd helped organize the unit, was thirty-five years old and a father to seven children, with a wife of nearly eighteen years. His run from risk, dating to the Tipperary cabbage patch in 1848, had come to an end.

After three hours of fighting, Meagher's men made it to within thirty yards of the rebels.

"For Ireland!" they shouted.

"For Saint Patrick!"

Farther down the line of the road, other Union soldiers broke through and could now start pouring hot lead into the rebel trench. Graybacks who climbed over bodies and stumbled out met the fists and knives of Irish soldiers; the defenders were clubbed in the head, bayoneted in the back, strangled. Major General Israel Richardson, Meagher's guest at the steeplechase in May, as impetuous as the Irish, was hit by a shell fragment, a wound that would later kill him.

Meagher tossed off his hat and tried to finish the battle. Just then, his horse took a blast in the head, reared up in panic, a blood pattern sprayed on its white mane. Meagher was thrown to the ground—the fourth Union general to go down. Concussed by his fall, he couldn't tell up from down, light from dark. Two soldiers dragged him back among other wounded in the haystacks. The forage was not much of a refuge: soon the stacks caught fire in the rain of explosives, burning men alive.

The final clash at Antietam started in the early afternoon. The Union had lost more than 7,000 men by the time General Ambrose Burnside led fresh combatants across a stone bridge over the creek.

"Whose troops are those?" asked Lee, peering into the smoke with his field glass.

"They are flying the United States flag" came the answer.

The last of the set pieces played out as the numbers would dictate: a superior Union force driving an outnumbered Confederate Army backward, toward the town of Sharpsburg. Lee stiffened outside his entrenchments, saved by reinforcements from the west. The firing dropped off. By nightfall, both sides had seen enough. The lanterns of medics flickered over plowed fields covered with the dead and those who wished they were dead. Some bodies formed a gory frieze: Yank and rebel, each with a bayonet in the other's gut, united in death. Antietam Creek carried corpses of bloodied men who had snaked along the grass to get a drink of water, only to fall in and drown. Horses with just a pair of working legs dragged themselves forward, their rear limbs shattered. A merciful man shot them.

When darkness came at last, "the earth was absolutely hidden under acres of slain and dying," Meagher wrote his brother-in-law Sam Barlow.

If McClellan had steeled himself, he could have driven Lee into the Potomac, and perhaps won the war. But he feared that the general who'd mastered him at every turn had something hidden—more of those phantom reserves. Lee had no such thing, and soon, no hold on Union soil; the rebels retreated the following day back into Virginia. After more than twelve hours of fighting, only a few hundred yards had exchanged hands—here in a cornfield, there near the Sunken Road, known forever after as the Bloody Lane. The Dunker church stood, though perforated by grapeshot and musket balls. The bloodiest single day in American history had taken down 22,717 men, about 5,000 of them dead, the rest with smashed limbs, open wounds or burned flesh, others lost in fields that would grow corn and hay again, but whose main crop for generations would be despair.

Come, my countrymen, he'd pleaded in the armory two months earlier. And of those who responded, more than half the new recruits were gone. Kavanagh was dead. Lieutenant James Mackey, named by Meagher to replace Temple Emmet as his aide-de-camp, dead. Lieutenant Colonel James Kelly, shot in the face, dead. Same with Captain Felix Duffy, mowed down in front of his men. Captain Patrick Clooney, a fellow Waterford native, crippled by a bullet that shattered his knee, then shot in the heart and brain, dead. Several of the drummer boys— not even teenagers—killed by shell fragments. One lad died with shattered pieces of his instrument embedded inside him. All told, the Irish Brigade was sliced in half—540 casualties in a single day. In a letter to Libby, Meagher was blunt. "It was an awful battle," he told her. "The poor little Brigade was woefully cut up."

Come, my countrymen, to liberate Ireland at some future date, but not now, not with what was left after this slaughter. *Come, my countrymen,* a call of duty, honor and the like, words that could not seem more empty to families of those who'd answered the summons. They had come, all 540 of the dead, lost or dying, because Meagher's words could move men to sacrifice. But to what end? What was the point of claiming a victory when one side had lost 12,000 men and the other 11,000?

At the White House, Abraham Lincoln had no trouble finding meaning in the graveyard of Antietam. On September 22, five days after the battle, he assembled his cabinet and let them in on a secret. He told them he'd made a promise when the Southerners entered Northern territory: if Lee could be driven back across the Potomac, the president would make good on the idea he'd first floated to these advisers in July. "I said nothing to anyone. But I made the promise to myself . . . to my Maker. The rebel army is driven out now, and I am going to fulfill that promise." He then read them the preliminary Emancipation Proclamation. In a little over three months, at the first tick of the new year of 1863, "all persons held as slaves" within any state in rebellion against the United States "shall be then, thenceforth, and forever free; and the executive government of the United States, including the military and naval authorities thereof, will recognize and maintain the freedom of such persons, and will do no act or acts to suppress such persons, or any of them, in any efforts they make for their actual freedom."

The next day, Lincoln released this proclamation to the press. Democrats were outraged. McClellan was stunned. Leading Catholic clerics, Archbishop John Hughes among them, fumed. Jefferson Davis said Lincoln had broken his inaugural promise; the criticism, as Northerners noted, didn't mean much coming from a traitor. The clamor, often taking a violent form, would continue for decades. Still, from September 22 onward, there would be no doubt about why so many Americans had been killed at Antietam, no doubt about why men from either side of the Liffey River had answered Meagher's call to *Come, my countrymen*. It was not for Ireland, or for Saint Patrick, or even to *Faugh-a-Ballagh*, as many had shouted, their last words at the edge of the Sunken Road. The living could invoke those cries, and they would for the rest of their lives. They could cite the cause of holding together a nation that had sheltered them after a genocidal famine, and they would. But there was no getting around history's anchor: the men of the Irish Brigade had died to free the black slaves of America.

THE GREEN AND THE BLUES

Late November, snow already starting to swirl around the bare Virginia hardwoods. More than two months after Antietam, Meagher's men let their beards grow long and gnarly. They grubbed for turnips in cold fields and traded blankets for liquor. They dipped tin cups in vats of wretched coffee slicked from pork bits, and licked their blackened fingers for the grease. Meagher leaned on his tent pole one frigid night, his body wrapped in the flyleaf, staring into an immense bonfire a few feet downhill from his shelter. He was wobbly, strangely quiet. A soldier with the lowest rank in the army, William McCarter of the 116th Pennsylvania Infantry, tried to get his attention. Over the past two weeks the private and the general had developed a friendship fused by love of the written word. McCarter could barely speak; he had a debilitating stammer. But he could write—verse, prose, and he had the most extraordinary penmanship.

"Gen-Gen-General Muh, Muh, Muh Meagher?"

"Whaaaaa?"

The sound that emerged from the orator was guttural, almost incomprehensible. McCarter, as he confided to his diary, worshiped the Irishman who could speak at least five languages, recite an epic poem without missing a line, make roll call seem like an ode. "He had a voice that sounded like a lion," he wrote in one of his perfectly penned sentences, as if the words were standing at inspection. But now: who was this stumbling soul leaning against his tent pole? For a second time, the clerk called out to him. Meagher grunted, slurred something that sounded like nothing. The general reeked of whiskey, which he called "a smile," as in "Let's have a smile before dinner." Soldiers used a dozen other terms for the infantry's only real diversion—*busthead, knock-'em-stiff, dead shot* among them. In the worst year for the Army of the Potomac, liquor was medicinal and ubiquitous, for officers and infantrymen, Irish and native-born. The best general of the North, Ulysses S. Grant, was widely viewed as a drunk. He'd been forced to resign in 1854, his reputation in ruins. He got his second chance after volunteering in 1861, though his reliance on heavy drink had not diminished. "I can't spare him," Lincoln said. "He fights." And hearing yet again that Grant was overly fond of whiskey, the president asked what brand, and wondered if he should send a keg to each of his other commanders.

But even with all the high-octane spirits flowing through the depressed ranks of the Union Army, no one in the brigade had seen Thomas Francis Meagher like this—a standing man, blank-faced; the great conversationalist, mute; the wit of Bull Sumner's corps, staggered. "He was very drunk," McCarter wrote on November 13, 1862, "and looked strangely wild."

The private and the general had met after Antietam, as the war slowed, the skies darkened early and everyone smelled of smoke. The rebels had burned and shelled to a splinter pile much of the town of Harpers Ferry, on the Potomac, before hightailing it south. The Union Army moved in, a chipped centipede of cannons and canvas, horses and cattle, setting up camp on a rise just above the ruins. Would they spend the winter there? Or pursue the rebels? Who knew? Who cared? Nobody wanted to fight in the cold months.

For a few days in October, the high command allowed officers to bring their wives into their quarters at night. Some did not come; it was undignified to be so close to men at war. But Libby didn't hesitate. She rushed down from New York, nursed a boil on her husband's banged-up knee and tried to revive a flattened man. She made an impression on those who saw them together. The mud, the chill, the cluster of befouled and bloodied soldiers did not deter her. If anything, she wanted to see as much of the war as her husband had seen, if only to be closer to him. The chaplain, Corby, noticed that General Meagher had more cheer, was more graceful and solicitous, when around Libby. The Meaghers welcomed infantrymen into their tent for drinks and hot meals, card-playing and poetry. She got to know many of them well enough to grieve, later, when she read names on a casualty list. One bit of news cheered the couple: their friend Michael Corcoran had been released by the rebels in a prisoner exchange. He left the Confederate dungeon looking like a skeleton. Still, he was ready to go back at the South, and wasted no time organizing an Irish legion—Fenians, openly nationalistic. The God that had saved Michael Corcoran was the one that Meagher prayed to now.

A week, ten days of Indian summer passed, and Libby was forced to fly away, leaving the conjugal cot and buffalo robe cold inside the tent. Departure was hard, knowing how likely it was that they might never see each other again. Meagher went through his military motions, the days unmemorable, fog holding on to the lowlands a bit longer with every page turned in October. The routine broke when the Pennsylvania unit arrived, a fresh regiment for the devastated Irish Brigade. The soldiers of the 116th were city boys, mostly Irish but a number of Germans as well. Some of them were Protestants, not unlike Private McCarter. He was born in Derry, as the Irish still called their city in the north, had emigrated just after the famine. Belittled for his stammer, McCarter worked on his calligraphy every waking hour. His handwriting was a thing to behold; the letters looked as if stamped from a machine, but with enough of a bend or curve to humanize them. The soldiers of the 116th were not long out of their training by the time McCarter was a man in demand. A note home, crafted by the private with the magical pen, was a gift that would become an heirloom.

One of those handwritten masterpieces, a poem, had been passed along from a dying soldier to a living one, from an officer to Meagher. After poring over it, the general turned to a subordinate: *Find me the man who wrote this note.* A few weeks later, at the bivouac above Harpers Ferry, a slight, soft-shouldered young soldier with a weak chin was brought to Meagher's tent. He struggled to get his words out.

"Yuh, yuh . . . Y-y-you wahhhhted to, to see-see-see—"

"Be seated, Private." Meagher pointed to a stool inside his tent. Books, maps and a field glass covered a small table. McCarter was impressed by Meagher's bearing: mustache finely trimmed, buttons on the general's uniform polished. "He was a gentleman of no ordinary ability," he wrote in his diary. And when Meagher spoke, McCarter was transfixed. He heard Greek, Latin, French and Gaelic over the course of an hour, "the latter sounding like a mixture of all the others jumbled up together." Meagher sized up the kid from Pennsylvania, where the Know-Nothings had driven the Irish into hiding. He held a smile for a half minute without speaking, pulled up a stool close to him, fixed his eyes on the private.

"Well, you are from the Old Sod?"

"Yuh-yuh, yuh—yes! Yes, sir."

Meagher stood, walked to a table and riffled through some papers. He came back with a poem, "The Land of My Birth."

"Is that your handwriting?"

McCarter informed him that the poem indeed was his creation. A colonel who'd accompanied the private to Meagher's tent interrupted. He said his unit needed the boy for picket duty, and could they please be dismissed.

"Well, really, Colonel, that is all very good," said Meagher. "But he writes so well." Meagher could use him. He faced the private.

"Now, Mac," he said, all charm and informality. "You can go to your quarters and the colonel will instruct you this afternoon what to do."

At the same time, Lincoln and McClellan held a summit in a field tent. They despised each other and no longer tried to hide it. Why hadn't the commander chased Lee out of Maryland and into the river? What would it take for the general to finish something? He led the largest army in the world in 1862. What more did he want? Did McClellan expect victory to be wrapped in a ribbon? He bristled at the Emancipation Proclamation, *a real surprise, sir.* He may not have shared the anger of Jefferson Davis—"the most execrable measure recorded in the history of guilty man," the Confederate president said—but he didn't like it. Didn't like the timing. Didn't hold back from saying he didn't like it. Didn't like the sudden shift from waging war to keep the Union whole, to waging war to rid the country of slavery. He told his wife he "could not make up my mind to fight for such an accursed doctrine as that of a servile insurrection." But it didn't matter what McClellan thought: hereafter, the Army of the Potomac would be a force for liberation.

Lincoln's gamble with England had worked out brilliantly. The proclamation put the Empire on the defensive. Crowds gathered in the streets of London to cheer for the American president. As he'd hoped, the British could not recognize the Confederate States of America, because the C.S.A. stood for what the enlightened world now recognized as a relic of barbarism. "The triumph of the Confederacy would be a victory of the powers of evil," said John Stuart Mill, the English philosopher. A year earlier, Russia had freed its serfs. Support for the American South meant support for slavery, nothing more. The peripheral reasons for breaking up the Union—states' rights and defending a way of life—looked like a cloak for something civilized people would no longer tolerate. "Without slavery the rebellion could never have existed," Lincoln said; "without slavery it could not continue."

But the proclamation cost him political support at home. The Republicans were hit hard in the November midterm elections of 1862. Not only was the legality of the executive order questioned, but so was the mixed message it sent: slaves were free only in the rebel states, per Lincoln's interpretation of his wartime power. Still, with a clarity of mind and purpose that he'd lacked for two years, the president now tried to bring the country around. A month before the Emancipation Proclamation went into effect, he delivered a short message to Congress. "Fellow citizens, we cannot escape history," he said. "In giving freedom to the slave, we assure freedom to the free—honorable alike in what we give, and what we preserve. We shall nobly save, or meanly lose, the last, best hope of earth."

For Meagher, England's neutrality after the proclamation undercut one of his best arguments to the immigrant soldiers. They could no longer hold to the illusion that they were fighting two enemies—one in the New World, the other a tormentor through the centuries in the Old World. Some of the Fenians in the army still envisioned a future when hardened veterans of the Civil War would cross the Atlantic to liberate Ireland. Dreams born on weaker foundations had kept previous patriots going while they rotted in the Empire's prisons. But Meagher, if honest with himself, knew hatred of England could no longer be used to carry a tattered, bullet-riddled green flag up a hostile hill. He couldn't lie.

In the first week of November, Lincoln dismissed McClellan as commander of the Army of the Potomac. Now Meagher feared an uprising. His men loved fighting for Mac; with all his faults, he gave the Irish their due. After Antietam, in his official report McClellan wrote: "The Irish Brigade sustained their well-earned reputation, suffering terribly in officers and men, and strewing the ground with their enemies." When General McClellan's farewell address was read to the brigade, it was followed by much grumbling and open protest. They would go with him anywhere, the men said. Name the fight. Saying goodbye, the Irish lined up on either side of a road outside their camp, stiffened their posture, cannons in position. As the little general passed by to salutes, the big guns roared McClellan a sendoff—on his way to Washington, then to his home in New York, and eventually a challenge to Lincoln in the next presidential election. The soldiers, taking their cue from Meagher, felt empty and perplexed. Many of the immigrants cursed Lincoln openly, and turned to each other with a question: "What next?"

For some it was desertion—make a run before being ordered into another death sentence in tight formation. A few got away, hiding in the daytime, stumbling through the cold Confederate countryside at night. Most were caught just a few miles behind their lines. The Irish Brigade had to treat their own by army protocol: the sentence for those who tried to flee was execution. Father Corby witnessed one dispatching of a deserter. A dozen men lined up to face a blindfolded victim, standing above a pine coffin. A few soldiers were given guns with live ammunition, others were handed ones with blanks, so that no man would know who did the killing of an Irish brother. One volley was supposed to do the job, but sometimes a commander had to finish it. "Scenes like this jarred my nerves more than a battle," the priest wrote.

In mid-November, the Union soldiers broke camp. They marched with faces to the ground, stalled often in knee-deep mud, slowly south toward Richmond, about seventy miles away. Misery larded onto Meagher like layers of winter fat. When food rations ran short, he gave his men some of his own. When a bedroll was too wet for sleep, he brought soldiers into his general's tent, there to join others who had faced death by hypothermia. With each day's siphoning of the season's daylight, his drinking started earlier.

So now, on a late autumnal night, Meagher stared at the big bonfire, a glassy-eyed general supported by a tent pole. Private McCarter was petrified. He watched as his worst fear unfolded—a tumble forward. Meagher slipped from the tent and rolled down toward the big blaze. McCarter sprang to his rescue, using his weapon to stop the general just before he could fall into the flames.

"My God!" the private shouted. "He would have been roasted alive." McCarter dropped his musket and dragged the unconscious Meagher back to the tent. The stock of McCarter's weapon caught fire, and it went off, bringing a crowd of soldiers with guns at the ready. After a few hours on his back, Meagher came to—groggy and red-eyed, his lips dry with a powdery crust.

"You owe this man your life," a fellow officer said, pointing to the private with the stammer. The next morning, Meagher presented McCarter with a new musket. He said nothing of what had transpired the night before. "I never saw General Meagher intoxicated again," McCarter noted.

In the last days of November, the brigade finished its slog to the river and built a camp just upstream from Fredericksburg, Virginia. They were midway between Washington and Richmond, a geographic limbo to match the direction of the war. General Lee's army of 75,000 men was massed on the south side of the big, rat-colored Rappahannock— dug in for winter. The rebels were on high ground, as usual, and re- markably well fortified on a ridge behind a thick stone wall. Across the deep waters of the river, the new Federal base was close enough to the enemy that soldiers could watch the Southerners building their breast- works and putting heavy artillery in place all along the line of Marye's Heights. Clearly, any attack from below would be doomed.

"Don't trouble yourself," Father Corby assured a soldier passing on a rumor that the Irish Brigade would be thrown at the heights. "Your generals know better than that."

Perhaps some of them did. The new Union commander, General Ambrose Burnside, presented himself as a mass of fussed-over fa- cial hair running down the sides of his cheeks and curling up into his nostrils, bald on top. ("Sideburns" would be his legacy to the English language.) As Lincoln's new man, Burnside felt he had something to prove, and would not wait until the spring to do it. With an army of 110,000 men, he drew up plans to take Fredericksburg, then charge up the gentle slope to confront Lee behind that imposing rock wall. On his map, it drew out as a perfect success, set pieces again. First, though, pontoons had to be built and put in place for the Federals to cross the river.

Private McCarter was put on picket duty, which meant serving as kill-bait for rebels firing from the outskirts of Fredericksburg. For two weeks, as the Northerners waited for the pontoon pieces to arrive, the

Southerners shot at them. The Irish, unable to keep quiet, started to barter with their enemies across the Rappahannock.

"Hey, Johnny."

"Yeah, Yank."

"Any coffee today, Johnny?"

"Plenty. And tobacco too."

On November 28, Meagher summoned McCarter. The general explained to the private and an accompanying officer that the grunt now serving as target practice for rebel gunmen was the best penman in the Union Army. He'd never forgotten the poem.

"Here," said Meagher, opening a file to show off the attractive verse. "Here is some of his writing. Just look at it and see if you can beat it." The officer looked perplexed.

"Have some food," said Meagher, motioning to salted salmon, potatoes steaming in their skins, fresh biscuits and gravy, and a pitcher of cold water. "Help yourself." After some negotiation over the meal, Meagher finally got command of the calligrapher. McCarter became the general's secretary and ghostwriter, the man who finished his sentences in print.

"Now, Mac," he said a few days later, "I have a private matter of my own which I would like you to attend to at your convenience." For a brief moment, Meagher looked as if he were going to cry. McCarter never saw him more vulnerable—a man of war trying to hold back his innate sentimentality. The general opened a small tin box and produced several pages of his spiky handwriting and a blank book bound in leather.

"It is a poem of thirty-seven or thirty-eight verses, of my own composition . . . I wish it written in this book."

Meagher's plan was to give away his bound poem as a gift to a friend in Ireland, he explained. McCarter could not contain himself. "I was so completely overcome at this that I burst into tears," he recorded. A few days later, Meagher did something that nearly made the private weep again. He handed him what looked like a $5 bill.

"Now, Mac, here's a slight acknowledgment for your beautiful work." He urged the soldier to use the money to purchase goods sold by the black marketeers who swarmed over the Union Army, flies to the still-warm corpse. McCarter needed socks, suspenders, a handkerchief and a scarf. When he handed the currency to a field merchant, the man complained that he couldn't make change. Only then did McCarter realize Meagher had given him $50—a huge sum. The private rushed back to the general, insisting he'd made a mistake.

"I cuh, cuh, ca . . . can't keep it."

"To be in the army is to obey your superiors, Mac." Meagher arranged to have the money sent to McCarter's wife by special courier.

"Happy thought, my boy." He then gave McCarter $10 and told him to buy the clothes he needed. "Not another word, Mac."

Orders came on Wednesday, December 10, 1862, to prepare for the first big clash of armies in the east since Antietam. The Irish were told to pack three days of food rations and eighty rounds of ammunition—portending a drawn-out battle to the end. The camp was cacophonous with collapse and the quick slaughter of cattle for the soldiers' fuel. Private McCarter worked his pen at a feverish pace, writing official correspondence and doing favors for friends who begged him for last letters to loved ones. When he finished, about 9 p.m., Meagher offered him a glass of brandy and a cigar. The private walked outside, joining a cluster of soldiers around a fire on a brisk, cloudless night. Around midnight, he returned to the general's tent. Meagher was packing his books of poetry, history and philosophy, and his personal writings, into metal lockers. His limp was noticeable. A surgeon's attempt to lance the boil on his damaged knee had only made it worse. The private asked if he could help, but Meagher dismissed him. At 1 a.m., Meagher called him back inside. Now all of the general's possessions were in a neat stack in the corner. It struck McCarter that Meagher was preparing to die.

"Now, Mac, everything here is packed and ready to be put on board one of those wagons in the morning . . . I want you to remain in the rear, near my personal property, and on no account to go into action or to the front. Here is a duplicate key of my tin case. Keep it safe for me until the fight is over. If my fate is to fall, hand it over to General Hancock."

Meagher hobbled outside, mounted his white horse and rode off into the night. Within half an hour of his departure, Union guns started pounding the area around Fredericksburg. More than 8,000 projectiles rained down.

On Thursday, in the half-light of a metallic dawn, as Federal engineers tried to put pontoons in place for crossing the Rappahannock into Fredericksburg, they were being picked off by sharpshooters firing from the smoking hulk of the town. Once a thriving merchant and rail center of 5,000 people, nearly 25 percent of them slaves, Fredericksburg was empty now except for Southern snipers and a hapless refugee or two. Burnside sent squads across the river to hunt down the gunmen. After hours of house-to-house fighting, the nests were destroyed.

Meagher's men crossed on Friday with other Union brigades and went in search of protection. Now that their gunmen were gone, the Confederates started to bombard Fredericksburg from the ridge. Ceaseless shot and shell hissed at the thousands of Union men scrambling to find shelter in a house or building. One of those soldiers looking for cover was Private McCarter. He had disobeyed Meagher's orders; staying behind did not feel right. Before he left, he gave the general's key to another infantryman. A few residents—the old, the sick, some feeble slaves—had been unable to get out during the evacuation. McCarter saw an elderly black woman, shoeless, with three crying children clinging to her tattered dress. She stood at an intersection in the town, dazed and in shock. A minute later, she was hit by a Confederate shell and cut in two. The fragments killed the children as well.

General Burnside had insisted there be no fires at night, to conceal the troops. This was treated as a joke; surely the rebels knew that the town was now crawling with bluecoats. Snow fell in the evening, wet and heavy. The ground was saturated. As the Irishmen shivered, unable to get any rest in the dark hole of Fredericksburg, Meagher became livid. He waived the no-fire edict. His men dragged furniture from empty houses and built a few blazes on the cobblestone streets. It must have been a fine town in its day. Soldiers found barrels of flour in the rubble of an old mill. They mixed it with water and made gooey bread over the embers of charred table legs. Some of the flour was stuffed in small bags under blue uniforms, as insulation and protection. Meagher could not sleep.

On Saturday morning, December 13, under a haze of mist and artillery smoke, the general told his men to fall into place along a side street in Fredericksburg. Sprigs of green boxwood were distributed to each of the 1,200 members of the Irish Brigade, infantrymen and officers alike. Meagher ordered the soldiers to place the evergreen clips under their caps, and to make sure they were visible. He demonstrated with his own hatband. The general wanted the enemy to know whom they were fighting. They would not fall as nobodies in bloody heaps. They would die as Irishmen.

Walking down the line, he addressed each of the five regiments of the brigade. When he came to the New York unit that his wife had doted on, sending them sweets and new socks, he choked on his words. "Officers and soldiers of the Eighty-eighth Regiment: In a few moments you will engage the enemy in a most terrible battle, which will probably decide the fate of this glorious, great and good country—the home of your adoption." No mention of liberating Ireland. The fight was about this land, these people. He paused there, tears filling his eyes, stammering like Private McCarter, before he regained his composure. "This is my wife's own regiment, her own dear Eighty-eighth, she calls it. I know, I have confidence that with that dear woman's smile upon you ... this day you will strike a deadly blow to those wicked traitors who are now but a few hundred yards from you." Some of the soldiers started to cry.

"This ... this may be my last speech to you, but I will be with you when the battle is fiercest. And if I fall, I can say that I did my duty, and fell fighting in the most glorious of causes."

Next to the river, along the empty edge of Fredericksburg, they walked to certain death, away from town and up the rise to the rebel fortifications. They went past Caroline and Princess Anne Streets, then a left turn on George. Fitting—all these names from the English Crown. They crossed on planks over a small canal, the houses now at their backs. Ahead was an empty field, sloping upward, 400 yards or so. There was no protection, no place to hide or take cover, save a small home off to one side. At the top, along Marye's Heights, the stone wall ran along the length of the ridge. The graybacks stood four deep, and had 150 cannons in place to hurl lead balls, grapeshot and canister shot down on Union soldiers. One of the men behind the wall was a son of the Young Ireland revolutionary John Mitchel. Looking down at the field, James Mitchel was close enough to see the man who had been his father's blood brother in the uprising of 1848, an officer now barely able to walk.

The killing came too easily. For every one rebel who was hit behind the wall, almost three Union soldiers fell. The blues charged in waves, each more suicidal than the other. As deep as the Confederates were, they could spit nonstop fire down the hill. No pause for reloading; after one line exhaled a volley, another took its place. At this short range, canister shot was particularly lethal, spraying shards of metal from cannons that served as big shotguns. Unable to keep up with his line, Meagher fell back in search of a horse to mount. Captain Cavanagh took his place. Within minutes, a ball took his leg out. Private McCarter was hit in the calf with a shell fragment but kept moving upward, tripping over bodies. An order came to fix bayonets. The high end of the advance was about fifty paces from the wall — close enough for men to look into the mouths of smoking artillery guns. It was a marvel to the Confederates that the Irish kept coming and coming. "Your soldier's heart almost stood still as you watched those sons of Erin fearlessly rush to their deaths," said a rebel spectator, General George Pickett. McCarter raised his arms to fire one more time before the planned assault. He was hit square in the shoulder, a ball shattering parts of his arm and his collarbone. Blood trickled down his chest, into his pants, down his legs, a warm stream, into his shoes. Dizzy, the private fell to the ground. A friend dropped directly in front of him, dead when he hit the ground. McCarter closed his eyes and prayed. "Into thy hands, oh my God, I commit my soul and body."

Near town, Meagher found his horse and returned to the battle-field. As he galloped up the hill, he was passed by rollers of human carnage — his Irishmen, cut to pieces, among the thousands of other flesh-torn young men. Father Corby saw one soldier who'd been shot in the neck try to take a drink from his canteen; water poured out of the bullet hole. "The place into which Meagher's brigade was sent was simply a slaughter pen," the priest wrote in his diary. In two hours' time, after fourteen attempts to break through Marye's Heights, 3,000 Union troops had been mowed down. Soldiers begged Meagher to stay put — the butchery on that hill was murder, not warfare. Every officer in the 69th was hit. "We might as well have tried to take Hell," one captain said. Up beyond the wall of Marye's Heights, General Lee watched Stonewall Jackson and other commanders treat the Army of the Potomac like blades of grass before a scythe. "It is well that war is so terrible," Lee famously remarked to an aide. "Otherwise, we should grow too fond of it."

On the Union side, officers tried to dissuade Burnside from continuing with the attack. "It's a useless waste of life," said General Hooker, no faint heart to a fight. Burnside would not budge. The battle continued till the sun dropped below the fields in late afternoon, now with 8,000 casualties on the heights, and then sputtered into the dark, the rebels taking potshots at soldiers who tried to retrieve their wounded. Meagher knew before he had an official account, knew by the dead men he recognized on the ground, their blood-smudged sprigs of box-wood muddled onto their skulls: the Irish Brigade was shattered. He had lost half his men.

Meagher wept profusely, even as other officers tried to console him. He could not stop. A broken man, his tears fell in the mud.

No one associated with Marye's Heights tried to put a gloss of glory on it. "Oh! It was a terrible day," Captain William Nagle wrote his fa-ther. "Irish blood and bones cover that field today." An Irish Brigade historian, Henry Clay Heisler, summarized it this way: "It was not a battle—it was wholesale slaughter of human beings." The Union suf-fered nearly 13,000 dead and wounded, to a loss of about 5,000 for the Confederacy. Walt Whitman, doing newspaper duty in Fredericksburg, recorded a grim scene in his journal: "A heap of feet, legs, arms and hu-man fragments, cut, bloody, black and blue, swelled and sickening."

On Sunday, a cold rain fell. Humiliated in his one chance to shine, General Burnside gave the order to retreat. He would soon lose com-mand of the Army of the Potomac. Meagher was told a bit of incon-gruent news: the new green flags for the Irish Brigade had arrived from New York. Well, then, he said, *we must commemorate the occasion.* He rounded up food and whiskey, and invited officers to a little the-ater in Fredericksburg, its roof still intact, for a makeshift dinner. He called it a "Death Feast," an Irish wake in the midst of war. To those who didn't understand, Meagher explained: it was the Celtic way to honor the dead with some lightness of heart. The banquet got under way on Monday night. Toasts commenced as Confederate guns started in again on Fredericksburg, some of the heavy balls landing just out-side the theater. The new colors were presented. Songs were sung. Two tables in the center of the room were weighed down with food bought from black market merchants on the other side of the river. Meagher rose, grim-faced, eyes reddened and swollen.

"Generals, brother officers, and comrades of the Army of the Po-tomac: fill your glasses to the brim." He then toasted a man sitting next to him, General Alfred Sully, "who is not one of your 'political generals,' but a brave and accomplished soldier." The theater went still, an awkward silence broken only by artillery fire outside the door. Meagher was honoring a friend, but he was also talking about himself. A political general was the insulting term for those high-ranking officers who never had any formal military training, never went to West Point or fought in the Mexican War. General Burnside, the career military man responsible for the most incompetent, wasteful battle of the war, was considered a *real general.* And Meagher's appointment, it was said by many, was Lincoln's sop to the Irish—the most glaring example of a political general. But after he'd held the line of a panicky retreat by other regiments at Bull Run, after he'd saved a division outside Richmond, after he took the Sunken Road at Antietam and now had seen his most hardened men cut to flesh bits on the cold ground below Marye's Heights, after he'd been twice thrown from his horse in this war—the political general was due some respect.

One soldier put his hands together and clapped. Then another. And another, until the little theater was full of applause. During dinner, Meagher carried on, "in tones of almost unearthly eloquence," one witness noted, honoring the dead. It was a long list, and took up much of the remaining time of the banquet. Many of the fallen were still unburied, he said, their bloated bodies outside these doors on the slope.

In closing, Meagher drew attention to a dessert tray presented by a soldier waiter on a center table. A few minutes earlier, the man had been sent on a mission. Now the lid of the serving tray was lifted, revealing a cannonball that had bounced down a street outside the theater—dessert. Great gasps of horror filled the crowd. With that, Meagher left the room, ending a Death Feast for the bloodiest single day of the Irish Brigade.

18

A BRIGADE NO MORE

Before returning to Falmouth, just across the Rappahannock, Meagher and some of his soldiers went back to the killing fields. A temporary truce was arranged to allow the Union forces to retrieve corpses that had been left behind. Up Marye's Heights they walked again, the fields littered with severed limbs and unfinished letters to loved ones, clothing, cold muskets and cannonballs. Meagher was slow and gimpy-legged, helped by his men. They turned over face-mashed bodies, looking for a green boxwood sprig under the cap. They found their lifeless flag-bearer, a sergeant, leaning against a tree, the brigade banner wrapped around him and riddled with bullets. Near the stone wall, they discovered what was left of Major William Horgan of the New York 88th—Mrs. Meagher's Own. Horgan was thirty years old, an original member of the Irish Brigade. He'd been in every battle with Meagher since the start. The major had been cut down just twenty-five paces short of the wall. No Union officer made it closer. The body was carried through the blood-smeared field, through Fredericksburg, across the river and then to winter camp. Meagher made sure Bill Horgan was embalmed for transport. He had plans.

A new year, bringing with it the liberation of the Confederacy's slaves, could not shove aside quickly enough the worst year for American forces. Lincoln was distraught. He'd been pressed by Democrats to delay the Emancipation Proclamation; the country was not ready to break the chains of four million blacks—it was a desperate move by a desperate president, they claimed. Look at the recent midterm elections: opponents of abolition had routed Republicans. On military matters, the president was in another kind of ditch. After the disaster of Fredericksburg, the most lopsided battle of the war, he was besieged by officers urging him to sack Ambrose Burnside. The hirsute-faced general was incompetent, his subordinates said, or worse—a mass murderer, sending wave after wave up Marye's Heights.

The White House, its drapes closed and Mary Todd Lincoln in mourner's black, had been like the waiting room of a funeral parlor for almost a year. The first family had lost a son, eleven-year-old Willie, to typhoid fever, most likely from contaminated water coming into the Executive Mansion from a nearby canal. "The poor boy," Lincoln said. "He is too good for this earth." The commander in chief tried to keep up his routine, but many days he would closet himself in his office and weep at the loss of his child. Mary fell into an even deeper depression, had visions at night of the dead boy, her favorite child, and cried in hysterics, months after he was gone. At one point Lincoln took her to a window and pointed to an insane asylum across the way. She needed to be strong, he said, or she might have to change residences. "If there is a place worse than Hell," Lincoln told a friend, "I am in it."

There was such a place: the Union camp at Falmouth, Virginia. Desertion was never higher: 1,800 soldiers went missing after Fredericksburg, many of them using the chaos of battle to slip away, one in four soldiers now AWOL. Meagher could barely walk, but his agony was a minor annoyance in an army of pain. "I am quite safe with the exception of a bruised knee," he telegraphed Libby, anxious to counter stories in the papers that he'd been killed. "I am remaining for the present with what is left of my noble brigade. But should I get the necessary permission, I will return to you as soon as my wounded are cared for."

What was left of that noble brigade was in no condition to fight. They were shattered, had not been paid for months, were sick with dysentery, colds and fevers. Meagher counted barely 500 men to call his own. And now a wet winter, rain turning to snow and vice versa. "Such a sight as the Army now presents never was seen before," wrote Captain Elliot Pierce to a friend. "We are stuck in Mud. Bivouacked in Mud. Sleep in Mud. Eat in Mud. Drink in Mud. If we do move we shall move in Mud. I am sitting in Mud as I write." The food was maggot-infested, the uniforms tattered and damp. Anything that could burn had been stripped and chopped and put to flame. Every fog-en-snarled tent had an empty cot or two—holes where there had been life a few days before. "All of us were sad," Father Corby wrote, "very sad."

Meagher's books and writings had not been touched. Since the battle, Private McCarter had been missing. The general sent out queries looking for the boy with the master penmanship, keeper of his written thoughts. The brigade surgeon, Dr. Laurence Reynolds, took a look at Meagher's leg and ordered him to a field hospital or home. The knee oozed pus; infection, in this war, could be more lethal than loaded shell. "He is suffering from a furunculous abscess of the left knee, which quite disables him," the doctor wrote. "It is further my opinion that an absence of 20 days is absolutely necessary to prevent loss of life or permanent disability." Granted a medical leave, Meagher set off for New York, traveling with the embalmed body of Major Horgan.

On Christmas Eve, 1862, at the Broadway headquarters of the Irish Brigade, Meagher stayed up late writing letters to families of the deceased. Libby urged him to come home, to be festive for a few hours. For too long, sorrow had shadowed their marriage. Horgan lay in a casket next to Meagher's desk, his body full of lead balls, his facial features improved by a mortician's magic. For three nights and two days, the officer's corpse was on display. It was, to say the least, not an inducement to further recruitment. But Meagher didn't need the shaking heads, the hushed signs of the cross, the mutterings of "shame, shame," to understand how things had changed among his people. The Irish had turned against the Union cause. From the press and the pulpits, from the laborer in the Tammany hiring hall to the widow in church, he heard a dirge. "The Irish spirit for the war is dead!" cried the *Boston Pilot*, voice of the Bay State's Celts. "Absolutely dead."

New Year's Eve arrived with some suspense regarding Lincoln's intentions. Awaiting word, blacks in New York City staged a jubilee to count down the final hours of Confederate slavery. A crowd that was one third white filled Shiloh Presbyterian Church, at the corner of Prince and Marion, to capacity. At 10 p.m., a preacher asked the congregants to imagine what would have happened if slaves had been freed immediately after Fort Sumter was fired on. The war would now be over, he said, to a clap of amens. No one was more loyal to the United States, he said, than the descendants of those brought to these shores in chains. Another speaker attacked clerics who had used their religion to defend slavery. An ex-slave spoke of growing up in North Carolina—"a most excellent place to get out of," he said, to laughter. A few minutes after midnight, a dispatch was read from Washington: the Emancipation Proclamation had been issued. It was "the greatest event in our nation's history," said Frederick Douglass. Thunderous cheers for Abraham Lincoln erupted in the Shiloh pews, tears and some fainting and breathless asides, then more huzzahs for the Union Army, in which blacks would now be able to serve, and then a hymn from the choir, beginning, "Blow ye trumpets, blow, the year of jubilee has come."

In another church, two weeks later, the Irish held a Grand Requiem Mass for the fallen of Fredericksburg. St. Patrick's Cathedral on Mulberry Street was draped in black and packed with widows, many refusing to meet the gaze of Thomas Meagher, who sat in the front row with Libby. In the center aisle was a single coffin, representing those buried in hastily dug graves along the Rappahannock. The choir sang Mozart's Requiem, the music rising to the top of the eighty-five-foot-high vault, morning light streaming through stained glass that the Know-Nothings had once tried to smash. Baskets were passed for families without fathers, and Dagger John Hughes sent the souls off to an eternal Irish repose. Afterward, officers of the Irish Brigade retired to Delmonico's for lunch. Meagher gave a few short remarks, but there was no spark in him; he was visibly aged and made sluggish by war's physical toll. "We have but two wants today—one for the dead, the other for the living," he said. He was supposed to be recruiting, but on this day could not bring himself to corral another man with his words, only a cryptic thought: "War for me has no attraction, beyond those developments it gives for hearts and minds."

After weeks of rest, he returned to the front. But first a detour to Washington, for a meeting with the president on Lincoln's fifty-fourth birthday, February 12, 1863. Lincoln looked gaunt, sunken-cheeked, his clothes loose and oversized. He moved about in a strangely soundless manner, as if he were there in spirit and not in corporal form. Meagher had gone to Washington to beg for the Irish Brigade's life. The unit needed time to recover and rebound, and only then could he hope to fill its ranks with new soldiers. The general's reputation had preceded him: his bravery in battle, first to the front, last to retreat, certainly—but also the drinking. As well, the odd tale of the Death Feast, with the cannonball at dessert, had circulated among the high command. Meagher did not try to explain the inexplicable life of an Irishman at war. He spoke only of trying to save his creation. Lincoln listened without word. Meagher made a pitch for promotions of his officers: good men, Colonels Robert Nugent and Patrick Kelly, had been passed over despite stellar performances in combat, while men who'd done less fighting in other brigades had been elevated. Lincoln unfolded the large, sticks-in-winter fingers of his, walked across the room and shook Meagher's hand. No sooner had the general left than the president wrote a letter to the War Department: "General Meagher, now with me, says the Irish Brigade has had no promotions," and that "they had fairly earned them."

Not far from the White House, Private McCarter had taken a turn for the worse in a crowded ward for the wounded at Eckington Hospital. After he had committed his soul to the afterlife at Marye's Heights, the boy remained conscious, bleeding on the ground, consumed by thirst. "I would have given $1,000 for a cup of cold water," he wrote. In the evening, under cover of darkness, McCarter was dragged down the hill by his comrades and helped across the river. At Falmouth, the medical corps set up forty tents to hack away at the wounded—a "village of butcher shops," McCarter called it, with pyramids of severed limbs outside every tent. When McCarter was brought in for his turn at medical attention, a doctor told him, "You must have that arm taken off."

"Nix," said McCarter, without a hint of his stammer.

From Fredericksburg, the wounded were taken by rail to a river port, and then by steamer to Alexandria, and off to the hospital outside Washington. Through January, McCarter's upper arm festered, turning the color of rotten fruit. By February, it did not even resemble a human appendage: the flesh and some muscle had fallen away, and what was left ballooned out of proportion—"two times its natural size, assuming a most sickening and revolting appearance." Crammed into a large room with fifty other wounded men, McCarter was on track to an early grave. The ward surgeon, Dr. Edling, arrived with a sheaf of papers. He was unusually solicitous this morning, McCarter noticed, taking personal interest in his condition. After the doctor left, an extravagant meal arrived: roast beef, potatoes, bread, mince pie and a glass of bitter ale. They were fattening him up for the kill, the private thought. The next day, a nurse brought him a fresh gown and told him he was wanted in the office of the head surgeon. Three doctors greeted

McCarter warmly. The wound, a mush of broken bone fragments and a bullet, was unveiled and studied. McCarter asked if they were now going to saw his arm off.

"Oh, no, I hope that won't be necessary," said Dr. Edling. "We have brought you up here to place you in more comfortable and quiet quarters. You shall receive our best attention."

Taken aback, McCarter wondered what had happened to change his fortune. The doctor produced a lengthy handwritten note in a spiky penmanship that was vaguely familiar to the private. "A letter . . . from a friend of yours, who wants you to be well cared for. He is a friend of my own, too." The doctor showed McCarter the note, but covered the signature at the end. The wounded young man now recognized Thomas Meagher's scrawl, the letters unable to keep up with the mind that committed them to paper.

"How . . . how di-di — did he nuh, nuh, know I wah — was here?"

The doctor kept his secret, pressed his fingers to his lips, smiled. Private McCarter never found out how General Meagher got wind of his whereabouts. And he never heard from him again. In March, McCarter was released to a hospital in his home state of Pennsylvania, his right arm still attached at the shoulder, though largely useless except when he formed his fingers around a pen to cautiously craft the most exquisite calligraphy a certain lover of longhand had ever seen.

Ambrose Burnside was out, Fighting Joe Hooker was in. The mood lifted considerably at Falmouth when another major general took over command of the Army of the Potomac. Hooker outfitted his men in new uniforms and brought in wagonloads of fresh food from a supply line that seemed to stretch the length of the Rappahannock. Clean latrines were dug, cabins and tents sanitized. Brick ovens produced hot bread every other day. Robert E. Lee was still across the river, about three miles downstream, camped beyond Marye's Heights. Hooker was eager to take a whack at the rebels, but he couldn't go anywhere until the ground firmed up in early spring.

When Meagher returned to camp after nearly a two-month absence, his men were so happy to see him they serenaded him. He spent his first weeks writing copious correspondence to the War Department, occasionally dropping Abe Lincoln's name, trying to get a leave for the original three regiments he'd recruited from New York. "The Brigade has ceased to be a brigade," he wrote Edwin M. Stanton, the secretary of war. Days went by without a reply. Worse than a rejection, the high command ignored him—punishment, perhaps, for the Death Feast.

Those close to him saw that Meagher was at sea in his life. He had rallied his fellow exiles to this fight, and so carried the weight of his words. But he did not move men to die just because it was his great gift. He believed that hope for the Irish in America would never be realized if the nation remained torn in two. And he understood that his brigade, in this new year, was a force for ensuring that humans would never again be owned by other humans in the United States. As for freeing Ireland, well . . . *someday, lads, someday.* These convictions, hardened by the losses of Horgan and Haggerty, of Kavanagh and Clooney and dozens of others whose young faces came to him at night when he tried to sleep with a gut full of whiskey, had cost him standing within the fractious diaspora of Irish America. No longer was the press friendly. "We did not cause this war," wrote the *Boston Pilot.* "But vast numbers of our people have perished in it." The commentary ranged from cynical to hostile—as if it were up to Meagher to lead the Irish out of a war as he had led them into it.

He never lost the talent, or the nerve, to take the ordinary and try to make it memorable. Stuck in winter mud, stuck without a way forward, stuck by the shunning silence from the War Department, Meagher concocted a St. Patrick's Day festival that the Army of the Potomac would never forget. For the second time in this war, he put his men to work laying out a track for a steeplechase. He bargained for champagne and whiskey with the sutlers who trailed the Union supply line. A chapel of boughs and pine posts was assembled, and there on the morning of March 17, Father Corby commenced the saint's holiday with Mass, cannons firing in place of church bells ringing. For a day and a night, the forlorn Falmouth camp was thick with brogue, blarney and bluster, and everybody wanted a part of it. Mostly it was a festival of sports: horse and mule racing, and foot racing by the swiftest of soldiers, contests to chase down a greased pig, contests of strength, all with cash prizes. More than 10,000 showed up, including the highest-ranking generals of the army—Joe Hooker, prominently. Meagher, the master of ceremonies, dressed in a white beaver-skin hat, green scarf and blue swallowtails, launched the races with a warning.

"Stand from under," he said. "If that stage gives way, you will be crushed by four tons of major generals." This got him a big laugh, even from the four tons. Long wooden tables groaned with thirty-five hams, a side of roasted ox, fire-baked pigs stuffed with turkeys. And for the officers: ten gallons of rum, eight cases of champagne and punch spiked with twenty-two gallons of whiskey. Meagher's face had gotten fleshy and worn in this winter of dread. But just as he had made merry music with his clarinet at Stonyhurst while under suspension, as he had grinned his way through readings of verse while awaiting execution at his cell in Clonmel, as he had "laughed till the woods rang around" in a shepherd's hut reunion in Tasmania, Meagher always found a way to find scraps of joy in a cellar of despair. He needed those moments, needed to mark them in memory in order to call on them later in melancholy, to keep himself from giving up.

His last battle with the brigade got under way in late April 1863. It was Joe Hooker's turn to move the set pieces, and he designed a flanking move on General Lee's left. The diminished Irish unit crossed the Rappahannock on April 30 and camped at the hamlet of Chancellorsville. Hooker had nearly twice the number of men as Lee's Confederates, but only half the nerve. He struck first, and withered quickly as the rebels did not fold and the Union men got bogged down in a tangle of brush called the Wilderness. Lee sent Stonewall Jackson around back, to encircle the attackers from their rear. He cut the Army of the Potomac to pieces. When the Irish were sent to the front, they ran into fleeing Federals. Their orders were changed from charging to holding the line of retreating soldiers at bayonet point. The losses were horrific. Captain John Lynch exploded in front of his men when he was hit by an artillery shell. Directing troop traffic, Meagher took a few steps one way. A minute later, the ground where he had stood was cratered by another shell.

After three days of battle, Hooker straggled back across the river. He had lost about 18,000 men — dead, wounded, captured or missing — to 13,000 for the South. Among the casualties was the best general of the Civil War. As Jackson was galloping out of the brush, a Confederate commander mistook his troops for Federals. "Pour it into them, boys!" shouted Major John Barry. Jackson had always believed that a righteous God had directed the general in battles on behalf of the slaveholders. If so, the providential design at the end was a cruel twist: shot by his own men, Stonewall Jackson died eight days later.

Meagher was finished. Five days after the battle ended, in a letter to Major General John Hancock, he tendered his resignation as commander of "what was once known as the Irish Brigade." There were no diplomatic niceties in this resignation note, no pander in the prose. Meagher was angry and indignant. He went through the casualties in the major battles, reminded the general of how his men had been sacrificed at Marye's Heights and yet fought again last week. And when he'd begged for relief, a break for his men to recover, it was "never even acknowledged." This "ungenerous and inconsiderate treatment of a gallant remnant of a brigade that had never once failed to do its duty" left him deeply depressed, he wrote. Still, he remained faithful to the Union cause, and offered to serve in any other capacity but one: he could no longer send Irishmen to their deaths.

The resignation was accepted on May 14. Meagher assembled his immigrant soldiers around him for a farewell to arms. He told of his life to date, how remarkable it was for a man who'd seen so much of the underside of history to be breathing spring air in 1863. On three continents, at every turn, someone had tried to take from him the things he loved about his native land. What he held dear, he told his men, was the locket the Irish carried when so far from home—memory, self-tailored to joy. He could summon happy faces going back to Waterford, the schoolmates at Clongowes Wood and cellmates at Kilmainham, and every kid he'd talked into leaving a tenement in Five Points to become an American soldier. Then he said goodbye, shaking hands and offering personal words to each member of the Irish Brigade.

New York was a steam bath on July 13, 1863, the street stones hot to the touch, the brick walls of tenements reflecting back a merciless sun. It had been this way for some time. Outside a four-story building at 677 Third Avenue, a crowd waited for fresh results of the first military draft in the United States. They smelled of sweat and liquor, and swore like a wretched choir. The Union, its fighting ranks badly depleted, was doing what the South had already done—forcing men to go to war. Congress had passed a conscription act in March. Now came the lottery, names spinning in a hand-cranked drum, then picked by a blindfolded clerk.

When read and published, there were Kiernans and Kellys, McGees and O'Briens. Already, no city had given more bodies to the Union cause than New York. The fevered men clutching broken cobblestones and iron pipes outside the draft office shared the same surnames. They had poured out of the tenements, had come with knives and clubs to go with bricks and rocks.

The draft law, as long rumored, had allowed an exemption for the rich: for $300 you could buy your way out of service to the United States. Either that or come up with a substitute. Cold cash or a live man—that's what it took to dodge a war that would claim more lives than any other American conflict. For many of the poor Irish cursing in the humidity on July 13, the price of freedom was equal to a year's wages. For the well-off, it was a trifling. One of the New Yorkers who had hired a substitute to fill his place in the army was a philanthropist and active Republican—Theodore Roosevelt Sr. The decision haunted his son Teddy; the guilt would roll over into another generation of family warriors trying to make up for the missed call to duty. Newly freed blacks were not eligible for the draft, for they were not citizens. They could enlist, and many did. Or they could straggle along behind Union supply lines.

An hour before noon, a pistol shot was fired outside that Third Avenue location of the draft lottery. No one was sure where it originated. But it became a starter's signal for the worst riot in American history. The mob pushed past police officers, broke windows with stones and clubs, and charged into the office. The lottery drum was smashed, the room set afire. Outside, telegraph lines were cut, and the rails of street cars were torn apart with crowbars. The cops who had tried to hold back the fisted crowd ran for their lives. One who stood his ground was the police superintendent, John Kennedy.

"That's Kennedy!" came shouts of recognition. "Get him!" He was knocked to the ground and beaten senseless. When Kennedy tried to stagger away, he was mauled again and dragged to a puddle. His face was smashed into the mud, and he nearly drowned. A tailor's shop nearby was ransacked, the Irish proprietor beaten to a pulp. A colonel in the Union Army, Henry O'Brien, was lashed and pummeled until he died. The Irish, at least those in uniform or owning a business, would not be spared the wrath of other Irish.

A handful of troops who'd been convalescing from wounds of Fredericksburg arrived to try to keep the peace. They were overwhelmed, losing their weapons, many knifed in the face or back. With stolen muskets, the mob went on a rampage through the center of Manhattan, setting fire to stores and breaking down the doors of townhouses. They shot at police officers and Union soldiers. A black man, William Jones, was grabbed as he walked toward a fruit vendor's store. He was stabbed, beaten, a noose coiled around his neck, and he was strung from a lamppost. They burned him as he died. Now frenzied, blood on their hands, the mob moved to the Colored Orphan Asylum, on Fifth Avenue at 43rd Street. The rioters took the children's bedding and clothing, then torched the orphanage. They cheered as walls collapsed and the roof crumbled. When fire crews arrived, they were stoned, and their hoses cut. Some of the firemen dropped their axes and joined the rioters. The 200 orphans who lived at the asylum were rushed out a back entrance, narrowly escaping death in the firetrap that had been their shelter. Nighttime brought more New Yorkers to a swelling river of rage, itinerant laborers joining Irish from the slums. They moved outward and uptown, toward homes of the rich, breaking in and looting, smashing chandeliers and fine china, setting fire to tapestries on walls and upholstered couches in sitting rooms. By the end of the day, much of New York was aflame, the city defenseless and lawless. Surely, many residents felt, this was a plot from the South.

The Confederate role, if any, was indirect. Earlier that month, the three-day Battle of Gettysburg ended with a loss for the South. But repelling Lee from Pennsylvania came at an unfathomable cost for the Union, almost 23,000 casualties. Throughout July, the names of the dead soldiers were published in New York papers—Irish names disproportionately, just like the draft. Meagher's brigade was well known, but it was a fragment of his countrymen who fought overall. At Gettysburg, a remnant faction of the brigade, led by Colonel Patrick Kelly of County Galway, lost 200 of the 500 or so men still fighting under a green flag. In the days leading up to the riot, race-baiting Democrats fanned ethnic flames, and anti-Lincoln politicians worked up class rage.

The question of three years earlier—would the Irish fight?—had now become: whose side are they on? Some Irish voices, Thomas Meagher's still among them, urged their countrymen not to listen to the demagogues trolling the tenements. Just weeks before the first names in the draft were called, Meagher had given a brisk defense of the president and the Union cause at a public lunch in New York, where he was awarded the Kearney Cross for valor. Most of those who heard him speak sat on their hands. He was in Washington the day the riots erupted, seeking a fresh commission to serve Lincoln.

The next day, a Tuesday, no black person in New York was safe. Burning the docks where African Americans labored, lynching dark-skinned men caught in the crush, the mob moved without any design save the unpredictable direction of rage. They attacked symbols of wealth: Brooks Brothers, the clothing store, was plundered. They attacked symbols of authority: the mayor's residence was pelted with stones. And they attacked voices of emancipation: Horace Greeley was a target. The editor of the *New York Times,* Henry Richmond, manned a Gatling gun outside his building near City Hall. The mayor sent a desperate telegram to Washington, pleading for Union troops to save the city—it was in a "state of insurrection." The secretary of war dispatched five regiments to Manhattan; they arrived on Wednesday and camped at Gramercy Park. In the midst of open savagery, Democratic politicians looked the other way, as did some clerics.

"You will no doubt be hard on us rioters tomorrow morning," a man wrote the *New York Times* on the second day of anarchy, "but that 300-dollar law has made us nobodies, vagabonds, and cast-outs of a society, for whom nobody cares when we must go to war and be shot down. We are the poor rabble, and the rich rabble is our enemy by this law ... Why don't they let the nigger kill the slave-driving race and take possession of the South?"

A more refined mind, that of the novelist Herman Melville, tried to understand what had brought his city to ruin. At night, listening to the sounds of shattered glass and gunfire, the writer sketched a few lines of verse. "All civil charms like a dream dissolve ..."

On the third day, the mobs moved on to armories, including one that housed the 69th, and stole away with guns and ammunition. They attacked the Broadway headquarters of the Irish Brigade, where Major Horgan had lain in state on Christmas Eve seven months earlier. Protestant charities were burned, as were the homes of prominent Republicans. A Federal gunboat steamed to New York and anchored at the foot of Wall Street. On the fourth and final day, nearly 6,000 soldiers fought house to house, tenement to tenement on the Lower East Side, artillery to go with musketry. By week's end, following the announcement that the draft had been temporarily suspended in New York, the city looked as if it had been shelled by Lee's army. Officials put the death toll at 105, though it was later found to be closer to 500.

All of it was sickening to Meagher. Had the rioters known where to find him, he might have been killed by his own people, he said—"torn limb from limb if they caught hold of me." Failing to grab Meagher, the mob marched on the house of his top lieutenant in the Irish Brigade, Colonel Robert Nugent, wounded at Fredericksburg by a bullet to the stomach. They sacked his house, cursing him as a "nigger-lover," and raised cheers for Jefferson Davis. In the colonel's den, enraged men slashed a portrait of Meagher. The face of the general, the man who had been hailed a decade earlier as the Irish American savior—"a chief to unite and guide them"—was cut and trampled and burned in the bonfire of hatred in Nugent's home.

A SECOND BANISHMENT

In just four days' time, the reputation of the Irish in America, a standing that Meagher's Brigade had built at the cost of much loss of life, was in tatters. The papers decried the "murderous Paddies" and "Celtic beasts" who became the ethnic face of the New York draft riots. Cartoonist Thomas Nast drew the immigrant poor as simians again in *Harper's Weekly*, gutting stores for liquor, clubbing policemen, stringing up blacks. "I am sorry to find that England is right about the lower class of Irish," wrote George Templeton Strong, the influential New York lawyer and diarist, a pillar of the city's Episcopalian elite. "They are brutal, base, cruel cowards." Further, he saw them as subhuman, as he recorded in his private notes — "creatures that crawl and eat dirt and poison every community they infest." He wanted them gone from the country. "For myself, personally, I would like to see war made on Irish scum." There was talk among the powerful in Northern political circles of reviving the Know-Nothing Party. With class and religious passions stirred, Archbishop Hughes defended the mobs. But Meagher could not. He saw nihilism and numb-hearted violence for what it was. He had found the love of his life and a second cause to kill and die for in this city. And he would not rest his voice, at the age of forty, as New York smoldered.

Meagher had gone to war as an agnostic on slavery, something he shrugged off. "It cannot be changed," he'd said. Now he was evangelical in his opposition to it, as he tried to find a larger meaning for the deaths of so many of his young countrymen he'd led to battle. The rubble in the streets had barely cleared when Meagher rushed to show a side of the Irish at odds with the thugs who nearly brought down the city. He put his voice and pen to work in defense of Abraham Lincoln and against slavery. To the *Irishman* in Dublin, he explained what was at stake in a country holding nearly half as many Irish as those who never left. Make no mistake, he told his readers in the old country: the great American conflict was a fight against "the Slave Lords, the kings and princes of the cotton fields and rice swamps." He recalled how difficult it was as a Young Ireland revolutionary to praise the United States, the enlightened democracy that had thrown off the British Empire, while trying to ignore that country's slavery—"the cancerous disease, the glaring disgrace of this great nation and a violent contradiction of the principles on which it was established." He regretted not speaking out earlier, regretted the excuses, regretted looking the other way. And one more confession: the brig that brought him to New York in his long escape from Tasmania in 1852 had returned a runaway slave from South America to Georgia a year before. Same ship—one a passage to freedom, the other a voyage back to bondage. He remembered the saintly Smith O'Brien shaming him with a question: "How was it I could bring myself to be an apologist of the slavery existing in the South?"

How indeed. Ambition was the simple answer. Meagher never shied from the role so many of the Irish wanted him to play as their leader in America. His fellow exiles were Democrats—foes of abolition—and so was he, by his earlier silence. And even though he was still a Democrat, with an election barely a year away that could toss Lincoln from office, he would not betray his commander in chief. But going public with a new burst of feisty opinions came at great cost to Meagher's standing. He was castigated in the Irish American press, called a fool, a Lincoln lover, a "negrophiliac," among the printable epithets. So be it. He was done with all that. He wanted no more quarreling with defenders of slavery, or with those who would refight the fights of the Old Sod—scabs of history that had prevented a unified Ireland from going forward. "As for the great bulk of the Irishmen in this country, I frankly confess to an utter disregard, if not a thorough contempt of what they think or say of me." He could scarcely say which was worse, the riots or the apologists for that mayhem. "To their own discredit and degradation, they have suffered themselves to be bamboozled into being obstinate herds."

This was from a private letter, sent to a brigade officer in the Union Army. But when it was later published in the *New York Times* and other outlets, the target put on Meagher by the Irish was as big as the one the Know-Nothings had placed on him. Meagher became a pariah among his people—at least those who wielded a pen. A decade earlier, the *Irish American* had proclaimed, "All honor to Thomas Francis Meagher." Now that paper viewed him with "contempt" and shed no tears for his "fall from the high position he once held in the esteem and affection of his countrymen."

He visited Lincoln in late November 1863. The president had been in bed for much of the prior two weeks. He had looked ghostly, people noticed, when he rose to speak the 272 words of the Gettysburg Address on November 19. On the train ride back to Washington, he felt feverish and weak. Headaches and back pain plagued him over the next few days; his temperature spiked and a scarlet rash appeared on parts of his body. His doctors diagnosed the illness as a form of smallpox. On the twenty-sixth, the day he met Meagher and a fellow Irish officer, one of Lincoln's personal secretaries wrote, "The President is quite unwell." Meagher, a general without soldiers, meant enough to Lincoln that he was the only guest the sick president consented to see over the course of several days. He had tried, like Meagher, to slough off the hatred that came his way in the first year of liberation for slaves. "Abraham Africanus," his opponents called him—a dictator, a king, a tyrant. The two men discussed a future role for Meagher in a war with no visible end. Lincoln would try to find something for him. His commander in the west, Ulysses S. Grant, had taken Vicksburg in Mississippi that year as part of the largest amphibious operation conducted by an American force. He had shown the kind of steel that Lincoln was looking for in a general in chief. Maybe Grant had a position for him.

While pursuing another run with the Union Army, Meagher did not forget about Ireland. The heavy losses of the brigade had torn him up. His belief, unshakable through a half-dozen major battles, that he was a warrior with two destinies, had never left him. But by mid-1863, it was hard to see how an army of Irish veterans in America could defeat the British Empire. He could stew and drink and find like-minded lost Irish souls to commiserate with. Or he could revive the fight in his heart. So, at the very time the *Irish American* and other papers were attacking Meagher, he was negotiating to become a member of the Fenian Brotherhood, the Irish nationalist group whose members were well represented among the ranks of police officers and military members throughout North America. When the Fenians were founded a few years earlier, Meagher had resisted joining, mindful that a political career in the United States would require him to reach beyond the Irish masses in Boston and New York. Four years later, after the deaths of so many of his countrymen, after being pilloried by Catholic clerics and press bullies who claimed to represent the exiles, Meagher had lost his hesitation. Free of caring about the fickle winds of public opinion, he took the oath. "I, Thomas Francis Meagher, solemnly pledge my sacred word of honor as a truthful and honest man that I will labor with earnest zeal for the liberation of Ireland from the yoke of England and for the establishment of a free and independent government on Irish soil."

A fellow Fenian, Michael Corcoran, hosted Meagher a few weeks after the Lincoln visit—the two best-known Irishmen in America, together again. Freed in a prisoner exchange in 1862, Corcoran had founded the Irish Legion—separate from Meagher's brigade—and had stung the rebels in a series of smaller battles in Virginia. Like Meagher, he was a brigadier general. The two friends made plans to celebrate Christmas with their wives near a winter camp at Fairfax Court House. Corcoran had been complaining of headaches. His doctors said he had never fully recovered from the privation he suffered at the hands of his Confederate captors. On the morning of December 22, 1863, the two officers rode off to the train station, Meagher on his way to New York to pick up Libby and Corcoran's wife and escort them to Virginia for the holidays. Riding back to camp, Corcoran fell from his horse and tumbled into a ditch. His went into convulsions, his face bruised and red. He died hours later, most likely from a burst blood vessel in his head—a stroke. A County Sligo man, he had survived the Great Hunger, a threatened court-martial after he snubbed the Prince of Wales in New York, the Battle of Bull Run, dark months in a Confederate cell and fresh battles in the South. Michael Corcoran was thirty-six at his death. Meagher was inconsolable; he felt as if he'd lost a sibling.

"There, in that very room which I had occupied for several days as his guest . . . he lay cold and white in death, with the hands which were once so warm in their grasp, and so lavish in their gifts crossed upon his breast," Meagher wrote. The body was sent to New York, arriving on

Christmas Day. He lay in state in the Governor's Room at City Hall, flags flown at half-mast throughout the city.

The last Civil War orders of General Meagher arrived in September of 1864. He was sent west to Tennessee, to help guard the tail end of a very long and oft-severed Union supply line stretching from Nashville to Atlanta. Rebel fighters, hungry and hiding, no longer marching in crisp formation to brigade-leveling deaths, were trying to bleed the artery that pumped food and fresh men into a Union assault to end the war. At the front of that line, making plans to march to the sea and choke the South, was Major General William Tecumseh Sherman. He shelled Atlanta, killing civilians who had stayed behind, tearing up railroad tracks, raiding farms for field provisions. "War is cruelty and you cannot refine it," Sherman wrote to Atlanta's mayor. He hit the slaveholders everywhere—in their homes, their plantations, their public buildings. The Union now had a million men in uniform, and more on the way. The South was out of money, out of food, out of troops to counter the steamroller making its way toward Richmond. The leaders of the Confederacy considered a last-ditch plan to force thousands of slaves into fighting on behalf of their masters—prompting a dissonance that political minds shaped by white supremacy could not countenance. "The day you make soldiers of them is the beginning of the end of the revolution," said Howell Cobb, a Georgia politician and former speaker of the House of Representatives and a rebel general. "If slaves will make good soldiers, our whole theory of slavery is wrong." For the North, they made excellent soldiers: 180,000 blacks served in the Union Army.

Surrender terms were offered to the breakaway nation, not yet four years old. Jefferson Davis, his billy goat tuft of chin hair flapping in rage, rejected calls for peace. He was as haughty and uncompromising as ever. His army executed black soldiers they'd captured, troops that were now fighting some of the very men who had enslaved them. "You may 'emancipate' every negro in the Confederacy, but we will be free," the Confederate president declared, even "if we have to see every Southern plantation sacked, and every Southern city in flames." The flames came soon enough. Pounded by Sherman, the rebels abandoned Atlanta on September 1, burning everything of military use.

Meagher had never forgiven Sherman for how he treated the Irish at Bull Run. And Sherman could not let go of Meagher's description of him, which had found its way into print—the "envenomed martinet." In the three years since the first big battle of the war, Meagher had lost his brigade. But Sherman had lost his mind. The cinnamon-haired officer fell into an unshakable depression in the fall of 1861. Unable to see beyond a fog of despondency, he was temporarily relieved of his command. Newspaper headlines proclaimed what Sherman himself had feared: the general was "insane." He talked to the floor, mouth motoring, sputtering gibberish. He repeated certain refrains—of woe, of doubt, of anger—over and over and over. His fingers tapped ceaselessly on desktops, his eyes darted back and forth, and his bewhiskered chin was in a constant twitch. He couldn't sleep, and ate very little. "I am up all night," he wrote his wife. "I find myself riding a whirlwind unable to guide a storm." During a convalescence at home in St. Louis, he took to books and long walks, his mind uncoupled from war. At the start of a new year, 1862, the darkness passed. He revived his career under General Grant.

"He stood by me when I was crazy," Sherman said of Grant. "And I stood by him when he was drunk."

Meagher kept his distance from his old nemesis. While Sherman marched toward Savannah in the fall of 1864, torching fields and farmhouses along the way, Meagher took to the stage in Nashville, orating for the president's reelection, speaking to the state legislature. The army let him campaign for the commander in chief and take other speaking engagements when he wasn't in the field. In public he was still the man who made music with his spoken words. In private he was lonely, vulnerable, and had premonitions of death. "Do come," he wrote Captain W. F. Lyons, a longtime acquaintance, "and bring any true friend (or two) of mine along with you you can find. It may be the last time (God only knows) that you shall see me." Another blow was the loss of William Smith O'Brien, the gentleman of Young Ireland. He'd been traveling in Wales when he collapsed, dead at the age of sixty. His coffin was mobbed on the streets of Dublin, en route to the family home near Limerick. Three of the seven rebels shipped to Tasmania—the merchant Terence MacManus, the law clerk Patrick O'Donoghue and the member of Parliament William Smith O'Brien—had now died.

. . .

Both Meagher and Sherman, in their own ways, helped Lincoln become the first president to win a second term in more than thirty years. The Democrats had nominated McClellan, Lincoln's former military right arm. The Little Napoleon's party ran on a peace platform: the Union should call a truce and negotiate terms to end the war. But Sherman's autumn triumphs in Georgia made that platform look like a retreat, just as the tide was finally turning for the North. McClellan's backers also played to race fears. A covert campaign spread word that Lincoln wanted blacks and Irish to breed and blend, creating a degraded race at the bottom. "Miscegenation"—a fright line boldfaced in thousands of pamphlets circulated in Hibernian havens—was his secret plan.

Meagher would not abandon the president who had never abandoned him. He liked McClellan personally, but he told the Irish who would still listen to him, the Irish who filled the ranks of nearly every Union infantry division, that it was in their best interest to stick with Abraham Lincoln. In November, McClellan was crushed, losing every state but three. More than 75 percent of Union soldiers voted for Lincoln. But the president lost New York City, getting just 33 percent of the vote.

In the war's final six months, Meagher was sustained by poetry and drink. Verse he could still use to draw a crowd and a cheer. One of his fans, the Reverend George W. Pepper, had last heard Meagher speak at his sentencing to death in Clonmel in 1848. At the time, the English press said Meagher's words—"the history of Ireland explains this crime, and justifies it"—would last no longer than his life, then scheduled to end at the age of twenty-five. "Fools!" wrote Pepper. "They might as well attempt to crush the Andes or the Rocky Mountains." A Protestant from the north of Ireland, the chaplain idolized Meagher for the gift of his speech. Men like him came along but once every other generation, he believed. On stage, facing a roomful of strangers, "Meagher was an athlete." When he heard of Meagher's plan to devote an evening to poetry, the chaplain went to General Sherman to ask for a short leave. Sherman muttered a caustic aside, lumping Meagher in with the New York Irish who had rioted and shown sympathy for the South.

Not true. After ex-slaves—paid less than other Northern soldiers, mistreated, fighting for a nation that would not let most of them vote or hold office—had fought and died for the Union, Meagher came out publicly for full rights to "our black comrades on the battlefield." He defended them as he had defended starving Irish peasants grabbing pitchforks to stare down British artillery. "By their desperate fidelity to the fortunes of the nation, in many a fierce tempest of the war . . . they repaid in torrents of generous blood the proscription and wicked bondage in which, under the Stars and Stripes, they have been for generations held," Meagher said. "The black heroes of the Union Army have not only entitled themselves to liberty, but to citizenship." In that sentiment, he was well ahead of much of the country.

He was starting to build a case, born in his lowest moments after Fredericksburg, that the Irish had sacrificed their lives for the cause of a nation that must live up to the egalitarian promise of its founding. Meagher saw it now with the clarity in which he had seen the need for Irish rule at the height of the Great Hunger. He was out on a far limb, a minority voice among the exiles in America. Freeing the slaves was one thing. But full citizens? Fellow Democrats wondered what had gotten into Meagher—feuding with the Irish, and now killing any chances of political opportunity within his party. He was dismissed as a lost soul.

On a cold Tennessee night, Meagher packed a hall with people wary of war and the language of violence. They came to Nashville to hear him talk about Chaucer and Shakespeare, Lord Byron and an old favorite of his from Dublin, someone only a few people in the audience would recognize—Speranza, the mother of ten-year-old Oscar Wilde. War was temporary, he reminded them, the worst thing that humans can do to each other. But the images constructed by the poets were immortal, our "better angels," as another man of words, Lincoln, had said. The audience swooned. Women waved handkerchiefs and men stood and shouted "Bravo!" Pepper returned to his post in Georgia with the loft of Meagher's love of poetry in his head.

The drink increased with his final duty. Meagher had command of a passel of men who'd been wounded, misplaced or disciplined—the soldiers who didn't fit. They called themselves the convalescents, their lives dimmed and damaged in battle. As one of them, Meagher was a perfect man to lead. But though they were bandaged and battered, they were expected to fight. An army of convalescents didn't sound like anything that would strike fear in the heart of Johnny Reb. So they were renamed the Provisional Army of Tennessee, more than 10,000 strong—the military equivalent of a mutt. No one expected Meagher's wounded warriors to do anything more than put up a show of limping bluecoats to keep a desperate cadre of graybacks from attacking the railroad between Chattanooga and Knoxville. The South was down to a few last hopes; one was to bleed Sherman's rear.

As Meagher had molded immigrants from Five Points into some of the best fighters in the Union Army, he made this provisional army into a formidable force. Strategizing and skirmishing by day, and drinking heavily by night, Meagher surprised the generals who'd written him off. Over three months, Meagher's convalescents did what was asked of them: the rebels were rebuffed, allowing the Northerners to march freely to the sea. On December 22, Sherman telegraphed Lincoln: "I beg to present to you, as a Christmas gift, the city of Savannah."

For his role, Meagher won high praise from his commanding officer. "Your splendid success . . . and the harmony and good order maintained by your men throughout the district have given me much satisfaction," wrote General James B. Steedman. "The officers of the entire command" were proud of him. Well, not the *entire* command. Sherman withheld any praise for the Irish general. He ordered Meagher to pack up the best of his convalescents and travel by river to Pittsburgh, then overland to meet the bulk of the Union force as it advanced north through the Carolinas.

Out of harm's way, with idle days on the railroad, the provisional army lived up to the earlier low expectations. They partied, they drank, they disobeyed orders, they left without leave, they slept late, they harassed locals at train stops. Meagher, never much of a disciplinarian, was blamed. By the time they arrived in Pittsburgh, in January of 1865, the 6,500 remaining convalescents were more trouble than help. Conflicting orders dispersed them to different places. Many deserted. Meagher went ahead to a hotel in Baltimore and a likely liaison with Libby. "The whole command is but a mob of men in uniform," one general complained to Sherman. That was it. The Union brass had seen enough of the Irish general. Meagher was mustered out of the army in March.

He returned to New York in time for St. Patrick's Day. No doubt he would appeal again to Lincoln, and expect a fair hearing. While in Tennessee, he'd been thinking about a new life—starting from scratch in the far West. He'd always liked California. And what he'd seen in between was an alluring swath of open country. Lincoln should be favorably inclined to offer the general an appointment in one of the territories, as a reward for all he'd lost in political capital among the Irish by campaigning for a Republican. But it would never be.

Sherman ripped a path through South Carolina, no apologies for pyres and plunder in the Palmetto State. Many in Sherman's army wanted revenge. South Carolinians were traitors—the silky-voiced politicians, the crisp-collared officers manning big guns, the wives who egged their men on, and the slave masters in whose cause all the killing had been done. Sherman's men showed little restraint.

Richmond was abandoned on April 2, 1865, Jefferson Davis and his war cabinet fleeing town on one of the last operating rail lines. In retreat, his soldiers burned bridges and factories, fires spreading to a larger conflagration that left the city in ruins. Mobs ran through Richmond, elegant no more, setting flame to Confederate currency, axing open barrels of liquor from the cellars of Virginia aristocrats. By dawn, the capital of the Confederacy looked like a garbage dump, smoke curling from piles of rubble. Lincoln went to Richmond with his twelve-year-old son, Tad, sat in the very seat of the rebel president, the American flag overhead. "Thank God I have lived to see this," he said. In the streets of the conquered city, he was mobbed by blacks savoring their first days out of bondage. "You are free—free as air," said Lincoln. "You can cast off the name of slave and trample upon it."

The military had now completed its part, after Lincoln had mastered the political realm. In January, the president had cajoled reluctant Democrats to join Republicans in Congress to pass the Thirteenth Amendment, outlawing slavery in every part of the United States. At war's end, he was fifty-six years old, but it was striking how much the great conflict had broken him physically. Scuffed by time, he was both wizened and made wise by the Civil War. "I sometimes think I am the tiredest man on earth," he said. Lincoln lived just a few more days. On April 14—Good Friday—the president was shot by an actor and Confederate sympathizer, John Wilkes Booth, who had seethed about "nigger citizenship" while hatching a plot to kill the Great Emancipator. With a bullet in his bleeding skull, Lincoln died on the morning of April 15. Whitman grieved in verse:

O Captain! my Captain! our fearful trip is done,
The ship has weather'd every rack, the prize we sought is won ...
My Captain does not answer, his lips are pale and still,
My father does not feel my arm, he has no pulse nor will.

Meagher assembled some of his ex-officers at the Astor House in New York to mourn the commander in chief who'd once kissed the flag of the Irish Brigade. He drew up plans to travel to Washington to be part of the honor guard as Lincoln's body lay in state. And he made sure that the emerald flag that had been knocked down at the Sunken Road and wrapped around the body of the last color-bearer in the slaughter at Marye's Heights would be displayed under the Capitol dome, near the dead president. The orator offered a few words about what Lincoln meant to him and to the Irish—"eloquent" remarks, as the *New York Times* reported, without further elaboration.

Robert E. Lee, his Army of Northern Virginia shredded, surrendered to General Grant on April 9, at Appomattox Court House, to generous terms. Rebel officers were allowed to keep their sidearms, and soldiers to walk away with their horses, mules and muskets. Several members of the Irish Brigade stood by, just outside the room where Lee put an end to the short, violent life of the Confederate States of America.

Not far away, John Mitchel scrambled through the ruins of Richmond in search of safe haven, having given up two of his sons to what many in the South would later call the Lost Cause. One of the Mitchel boys died at Gettysburg, another at Fort Sumter. A third was wounded at Marye's Heights, behind the rock wall. Mitchel was arrested and sent to Fort Monroe, on the southern tip of the Virginia Peninsula. During the war the moated compound had been a refuge for runaway slaves— Freedom's Fortress, it was called. Now it was a warehouse for traitors, Jefferson Davis and John Mitchel its two best-known occupants.

All of the awful tallies were not yet in, but scholars would eventually determine that more than 700,000 people died in the war. When the wounded, the sick, the lost, the captured, the missing and never found were added to the toll, the human cost of the fight over America's original sin was at least 1.5 million people. Nearly 140,000 men of Irish birth fought for the Union, a third of them from New York City.

Only two other units suffered greater battlefield losses than the Irish Brigade—a casualty rate of more than 50 percent.

Early summer 1865. New York was clogged with Irishmen newly out of uniform, officers devoid of command, free blacks trying to find a place in a nation where the broken pieces were not easy to fit together. The brigade was long disbanded. Some of the soldiers had joined the Fenians, who were plotting to strike across the border at British North America. Father Corby was back at Notre Dame, soon to be named president of the school in South Bend. Meagher's friend Captain Lyons found him at the place he now called home in Manhattan, his brother-in-law's brownstone on East 23rd Street. The house was bursting with riches and books, said to be the largest private library in America. Meagher leaned against a fireplace mantel, a letter and small photograph in one hand. Lyons couldn't tell if he'd been crying when he came upon him; his eyes were clouded. That would not surprise him. He knew that the toll of the past two years—losing the brigade, losing Corcoran, Kavanagh, Emmet and countless others, losing his name among influential Irish Americans, losing Lincoln—had taken much of the life out a man who had seemed irrepressible.

He was gazing at a picture of the son he had never seen, eleven years old—Thomas Bennett Meagher. The boy had his father's good looks, and judging by the letter, some of his skill with words. Now Lyons drew close enough to tell that Meagher was not crying. "He was laughing at the pleasant and loving things the lad had written, and handed me the letter with a proud allusion to the manliness of its style," he said.

Meagher thrust the image of his son at his friend, an absentee father's pride bursting. He wanted the boy to know something of the legacy of memory that he would inherit—it wasn't all *skeletons at the feast*. The youngest Meagher would soon be burdened with a sizable number of centuries to keep alive in narrative form. Family stories. Tipperary struggles during the Penal Era. New life in Newfoundland, and a merchant renaissance along the River Suir. Defiance in one of England's best schools, and finding a voice in the revolutionary salons of Dublin. The great horror of the Great Hunger. An uprising of poets that never had a chance. Bravery in a cell while waiting to be hanged. A stirring of the senses in Tasmania, the dead mother of this boy. And love a second time in New York, a woman who could still be mother to another Thomas Meagher. America's promise, and America's crime.

The boy had surely read in the Irish press his father's explanation of what the immigrant soldiers meant to every son and daughter of Erin. "Thank God!" Meagher wrote, in words reprinted across the tormented island, "that disgrace" of slavery is no more, "averted from our race by the splendid conflict of the thousands of Irish soldiers who have been the life, the heart, the soul of the Federal armies."

He expected to see young Thomas soon, to be a proper father yet, in this coming turn in a life he himself found so improbable as to not try to recount it in a single sitting with new friends. First he needed to make some money. The West was opening quickly; fortunes were being made overnight in the goldfields and towns sprouting from the sageland. It could be a last chance, or a first chance. "I leave this evening for the far west, for one of the richest of our new territories," he wrote his son and his father on July 17, 1865. "I entertain the liveliest hopes that this enterprise will prove a profitable one to me, and that it will enable me to pay you a visit in France next summer." Thomas and Libby would close out their New York life, their military life, their eastern life. The wilds of Montana Territory called. Meagher was forty-one years old when he lit out for the sunset side of the continent.

NEW IRELAND

S o, off to the new land, far from gaslit interiors and dinners at Delmonico's, far from graveyard eulogies for young men, far from the familiar. Meagher went first to Minnesota, talking his way into a job with a professional emigrant, James L. Fisk, whose trade was guiding pilgrims from the flatland to the promised land. Meagher had heard Fisk speak in New York, where he sketched a picture of a big sky country so full of gold dust you had to shake it from your hair after lying on the ground. Afterward, with the war still on, with friends in the press now enemies, with the jabbing questions of the father-in-law, Peter the Great, about their future, he and Libby had taken the first steps toward a fresh chance in a faraway place. They would start from scratch, unknown, unfettered. Meagher would find a place to build a life. His wife would follow. The permanent home that had long eluded them would be theirs at last in the Rocky Mountains.

Something much larger than any one couple was envisioned for the unturned ground that touched the clouds in the West. Eastern cities were not healthy places for the immigrant masses. The New York riots showed just how toxic the tenements had become. Meagher himself had urged the Irish to leave the thin-walled, smoke-filled, low-ceilinged hovels of urban America for the open-aired promise of the high country. But how? A transcontinental move was not cheap. Gold was a lure, of course—a lure and a gamble. All you needed was a pan, a pick, a strong back to sift yellowy flakes from the gravel of a streambed. So went the pitch. Big strikes in little gulches had drawn deserters from both armies to Montana—$50 million in gold in three years' time!—and prompted thousands of men in California to leave for the snowbound north. The Homestead Act, which went into effect on the same day as the Emancipation Proclamation, was a greater attractor. You didn't have to be a citizen, you could just *intend* to become one, to lay claim to 160 acres. Free land: the two most powerful words in the nineteenth-century American West. Single women, former slaves, immigrants—all qualified. Yet a poor family living in the filth of Five Points, a neighborhood still said to have the highest murder rate of any slum in the world, could find enough reasons to stay put. At least Tammany Hall could guarantee meal money for turning a shovel in the city. The Irish were not loners or mountain men, had little experience as ranchers, sodbusters or prospectors. They cherished community, clan gatherings, rituals attached to place. Montana Territory was the end of the earth—a big blank spot on a map.

But what if a swath of that big blank spot was set aside as a lasting home for the exiles of Erin? A refuge, a colony, or something in between, still under the American flag but free of English Protestant domination? The Mormons had their Zion at the Great Salt Lake, a theocracy with its own militia and a radical sexual philosophy that allowed old men to marry teenage girls by the dozen. Free blacks were establishing towns on the Kansas frontier, and beyond. Free-love advocates were drawing up communes for islands in Puget Sound. The social frontier followed the geographic frontier. From Dublin, the American consul, William West, floated an idea in the final months of the Civil War. The plan put Meagher at the center, though he'd yet to be informed.

"It has long since occurred to me, that in complement for his valuable services, and those of the Irish soldiers generally, it would be fitting acknowledgment on the part of our Government, to select some desirable portion of our territories and call it New Ireland, of which no doubt General Meagher would in due time be elected Governor," the consul wrote Secretary of State William H. Seward.

New Ireland? Why not? There was a New England. A New Jersey. A New York. A New South Wales in Australia. A Newfoundland in a long-known land. Certainly, there were Little Irelands in the cramped underbellies of nearly every American city of standing. But no place where the Irish diaspora, now footloose after the war, could plant its stories and religion, where people could become something more than laborers, servants or embittered ex-soldiers scarred by Confederate grapeshot. Seward never acted on the suggestion. And there's no evidence Meagher was told of the grand design for the wayward son of Waterford—the part that had long been prophesied for him. But he was thinking along the very same lines. He was also hoping to stake his claim to some of that gold in the Montana dust, or get a piece of raw ground that could be turned for city-building and a quick profit—the two routes to overnight wealth in the West.

While in Minnesota, Meagher got word that his status as a western-bound traveler had been greatly elevated. By telegram, he was informed that President Andrew Johnson, the Democrat named to Lincoln's national unity ticket in 1864, had appointed Meagher the Secretary of Montana—the second-highest office in the territory. As one of the primary architects assigned to organize the foundations of government and civilization in a rawboned land, Meagher would be fortune-seeking as well as nation-building. He had asked for such a thing while the war was still on. He'd sent a note to a high-ranking friend at the White House—"Let me have Idaho." That was the original name of a territory stretching from the Dakotas in the east to Washington in the west, from the Canadian border in the north to most of present-day Wyoming.

Meagher didn't get Idaho. But he got the new Montana Territory, barely a year old, 143,776 square miles. At the time, there were more people living on the Lower East Side of Manhattan than the entire non-Indian population of Montana, about 15,000. And nearly all those had arrived in the past four years. Meagher's imagination churned. He sensed a second Great Migration, time for the Irish to move again, en masse. Just as they'd taken one big heave-ho across the Atlantic, they could take another leap over the ocean of prairie grass to Montana. He'd been thinking about this for months, but in his diminished state, he kept these musings to himself. Now, with a small measure of his confidence restored, he shared some expansive thoughts. "An Irish laborer, with his wife and children hived into a badly plastered den in the back part of a tenement house in New York . . . is very little better off than he was at home," he wrote a friend. Meagher pictured that Irish laborer with some dignity, "with his own hearthstone under his unshackled foot." In Minnesota, speaking to the Immigration Society, he expanded on this notion. As he'd summoned his countrymen to war against the slaveholding South, he urged them to pick up and build something from nothing in the West.

But getting from Manhattan to Montana Territory was much harder than crossing the Atlantic in a coffin ship—much costlier too. A family looking to claim a quarter square mile of land could follow a straight line west, more than 2,200 miles. Of course, nobody traveled in a straight line. You floated down a river, or steam-paddled up one. You hugged a valley floor by rail, stage or wagon, rode on the back of a horse until a trail lost its way in summer snow, and then cautiously stepped down a corkscrew of rocky turns overlooking straight drops to sure death. In the high desert you picked up a stage again, or a fresh horse, now nearly 3,000 miles into it, and all the while wondered what you were thinking.

Meagher went down the Mississippi to St. Louis—the Father of Waters, all of it, under one flag again. From there, he chugged up the Missouri, to Atchison, Kansas, named for the flame-throwing slave enthusiast. By stagecoach, he traveled over the grasslands to Denver, arriving in the mile-high boomtown in late August of 1865. His movements were heralded, via telegraph and horse travel, in the first newspaper to pop up in the year-old territory, the *Montana Post*. "This illustrious Irishman," the paper's editor informed his readers in September, would be bringing to the wide-open country a "persuasive elegance that held spellbound both Celt and Saxon." But the concept of New Ireland could not expect a hearing in the pages of the *Post*. The editor, Thomas J. Dimsdale, was an Englishman. Oxford-educated, short, sickly and humorless, with a waxed mustache and badger-like tight-set eyes, Dimsdale was also a strong supporter of a secret society that ran Montana Territory without formal recognition or adherence to the Constitution. He praised the general for doing much to improve the reputation of his dreadful people. "He has made the name of an Irishman respected wherever the story of the deeds of the heroic Irish Brigade is told." With the pandering out of the way, Dimsdale put the incoming secretary on notice, three weeks before his arrival. He expressed hope that Meagher, though a revolutionary at home against the Crown, was now a good Irishman: someone who might "rein in the hearts" of bad Irishmen.

The English editor had reason to fear the Celtic tide in the West. Members of the Fenian Brotherhood, their military skills hardened in the war, were making plans to invade Canada. They intended to seize a few forts and hold them as leverage to get concessions from Britain. Canada would be the hostage; a free Ireland was the ransom. The plan was crazy, preposterous and ill formed—yet somewhat plausible. Canada was lightly guarded. The British Empire's forces were elsewhere, trying to hold down natives in India, in Burma and Canton, in Africa and the Middle East, ensuring the stamp of Her Majesty on a quarter of the earth's land, from the Falkland Islands off the Patagonian coast to the Malayan states in the South China Sea. After the Civil War, the Fenians were flush with fresh members—Irishmen from all ranks. They were unafraid of England; indeed, primed for a fight with the Empire. The plan to invade the north was not a well-kept secret. It was publicized in the papers, aired out in meetings, heralded in a popular song:

> We are the Fenian Brotherhood, skilled in the arts of war,
> And we're going to fight for Ireland, the land we adore.
> Many battles we have won, along with the boys in blue,
> And we'll go and capture Canada, for we've nothing else to do.

Meagher had joined the Brotherhood a year earlier. He'd taken the oath—to "labor with earnest zeal for the liberation of Ireland from the yoke of England." And he'd recruited untold numbers of Irishmen to fight for the Union with an endgame of freeing the country of their birth. But he was also a representative of the U.S. government. If it wasn't technically treasonous to advocate war against British territory on the American border, it was certainly less than diplomatic. In public, Meagher underplayed his Fenian sympathies.

From Denver, he crossed the Front and the Wasatch Ranges of the Rocky Mountains, descending into the valley of the Great Salt Lake. Irish miners in the Mormon stronghold greeted General Meagher as a Hibernian hero, there to release them from the theocratic hold of Brigham Young. His business was in another territory, north over the Bitterroots. By coach on the overland express, Meagher set out for the last 475 miles of his journey, crossing the Snake River, up over the Continental Divide at Monida Pass, and down, through mountains upon mountains, to icy waters that drained to the Pacific. All told, he had passed through the homelands of the Omaha and the Pawnee, the Sioux and the Arapaho, the Ute and the Shoshone, the Cheyenne and the Crow, the Nez Perce and the Blackfeet. They had stitched their languages, their customs, their rituals, their religions, their livelihoods to the big blank spot on the map. But Meagher knew little of the natives, save for what he heard around the campfires of panicky pilgrims.

Downslope from the divide, still more than 6,000 feet above sea level, Meagher entered a world unlike anything he'd seen on any of the three continents he'd lived. No place in Ireland held summits of snow in late summer. No creature in Tasmania was the size of a grizzly, *Ursus arctos horribilis,* 700 pounds of beady-eyed bear. No mountain in the East was as high as the no-name peaks bracketing the territory, a horizon of jack-o'-lantern–smile granite and slate, a vertical world larger than many European countries. But where were the valleys and sun-kissed lakes, the places to grow potatoes and apples and wheat, to raise pigs and cattle, to build cities? Meagher was not alone in his disorientation upon entering Montana Territory. Wondrous, yes—in the late light of summer, a painting worthy of Albert Bierstadt's brush. But did snow really fall every month of the year?

"Rained, snowed and hailed all day," wrote one new arrival, James P. Miller, in his diary on June 16, 1865, a few days before the calendar proclaimed summer. "Horrible weather and very cold." And then in the first week of September, just days before Meagher's arrival, Miller told of trying to get to the town, Virginia City, that had just been designated the new territorial capital. "Up half past six. Snow three feet deep and still snowing." And still summer.

Well, what fell from the sky never bothered an Irishman. What mattered was underground, or barely beneath the surface. Surely it would not take much to get rich in this place. "I'm resolved not to turn my back on the Rocky Mountains until I have the means to whip my carriage and four through the New York Central Park and sail my own yacht, with the Green Flag at the Mitzen-peak, within three miles of the Irish coast," he wrote a friend. *Three miles of the Irish coast.* As a wanted man, he could get no closer. And in the meantime, you lived well off the fat of the new land, yes?

"Dear Parents: Nothing is sure here but what one has in his hands." So began a letter home from Cornelius Hedges to his family in the Midwest. "I have seen about enough of the mountains as I desire without I get some good pay for it. It is a hard life at best, full of self-denial & hardship. Living is very high, without any luxuries. We hardly ever see any fruit—vegetables are scarce ... Everyone expects to make a fortune any minute. Life is full of danger here. We have lots of men who are ready to murder for a few dollars. Only yesterday a man was shot not half a mile from town in open daylight and robbed of all his money ... I wish I could have some apples and cider once in a while. I dreamed the other night of eating apples."

He wrote these words from Virginia City, ten days before Meagher's arrival.

The end of the coach line was Bannack, a mining camp that already had the shamed appearance of a played-out burg, barely two years after it sprang to life in southwestern Montana. Government, such as it was, was moving to Virginia City. The buildings in Bannack were shingled shacks with unpainted fronts, the main street a dust-choked byway smelling of horseshit. Not a tree in sight. What pines that once stood had been burned for fuel or spliced into framing timber. Across a brackish little waterway, Grasshopper Creek, slouched a huddle of tents and leaky sheds, home to Confederate deserters. Meagher was met by the governor, Sidney Edgerton. He was dressed for travel and packed to go, with his family. A radical Republican, with a long face whiskered to an arrowhead below his chin, Edgerton looked like a Gothic preacher with a toothache. He'd been governor for a little more than a year, and before that, the territorial judge. When Meagher asked a few perfunctory questions, he discovered that this "richest territory" had its own way of dispatching people on the wrong side of right-thinking citizens.

The sheriff, for example. What of him? That would be the *late* sheriff, a Mr. Henry Plummer. *Late?* Considerably so. He'd been hanged. Oh. Was there a trial? No. A specific charge? Not really. But as one of the early leaders of these upstanding gentlemen had written in his diary, Edgerton could "recognize a bad man when he saw one." Wait—they'd killed the lawfully appointed sheriff without a trial or due process? *He had it coming.* How so? Plummer was handsome, well spoken, with a cloudy past. He'd killed a few men in California, and here in Bannack City he dispatched a prospector who lusted for his young bride—killed him in self-defense, in a saloon, in front of dozens of witnesses. After the victim fell, with a gunshot in the gut, he blurted out, "You won't shoot me when I'm down." Plummer replied, "No. Get up." Then he shot him in the chest and head. For this, he was applauded and, months later, elevated to sheriff of Bannack City by a grateful citizenry. But in the year since that shooting, the right-thinking townsfolk had soured on Plummer. They decided to take the law into their own hands. First they strung up two people in Alder Gulch, where Virginia City was forming around a cleft in Montana's bristled hide. And then, in January of 1864, they went after Sheriff Plummer.

The vigilantes suspected Plummer was stealing from coaches carrying gold dust. They had no hard evidence of this. Just rumors. People said things. Also, he'd deputized men known to be outlaws. But none of this was presented before a jury, or subject to a trial, or even explained to Sheriff Plummer before his neck was snapped. After forming the Vigilance Committee, two dozen men swore out an oath: "We the undersigned uniting ourselves in a party for the laudable purpos of arresting thievs & murderers & recovering stollen property do pledge ourselves upon our sacred honor each to all others & solemnly swear that we will reveal no secrets, violate no laws of right & never desert each other or our standard of justice so help us God as our witness our hand & seal this 23rd of December 1863."

The "laws of right" weren't written down. Right was what the Vigilance Committee, meeting in secret, judged to be right. Their ranks included a banker, a storekeeper, a few merchants, at least one lawyer and assorted pioneers, but no speller, apparently. The committee had formed after one man had been hanged without legal trial—sent to his ignoble grave with the authoritative words, "Men, do your duty." Sheriff Plummer was the third victim. On a day when the temperature dropped to thirty below zero, Plummer was dragged from a cabin, bound and marched to an execution site. Wilbur Sanders, an attorney, the leading voice of the Vigilance Committee, joined the abductors at the moment of the killing. Stone-faced, he addressed the sheriff. "It is useless for you to beg for your life," he said. "You are to be hanged. You cannot feel harder about it than I do, but I cannot help it if I could." Plummer still begged. Just a year or so earlier, he'd opened his home and his town to Sanders and Edgerton, given them Thanksgiving dinner. What were the charges? He had the right to a trial. At the gallows, the rope was tied around Plummer's neck and pulled tight. The doomed man asked for a good drop.

Killing the sheriff seemed to whet the appetite of the vigilantes for more summary executions. A few hours later, they decided to murder

José Pizanthia, called "the Greaser." His crime? He was a Mexican, un-likable, with a temper and no friends and bad intentions. Everyone said so. When the righteous mob tried to break into Pizanthia's little cabin, he fought back in self-defense, firing at the home invaders. Two men were wounded. The commotion attracted a bigger crowd; they went to the house of Sidney Edgerton to fetch a small howitzer. With the big gun, the men blew open the Mexican's shack. Storming inside, they found Pizanthia on the floor and filled him with bullets. His body was dragged across the ground outside and strung up for all to see. But they weren't done yet. People were invited to take shots at the dangling corpse, while others burned his house down. Another suggestion fol-lowed. "A proposition to burn the Mexican was received with a shout of exultation," wrote an early chronicler of the vigilantes. When the fire was stoked to a high blaze, Pizanthia's body was thrown atop it and charred to a crisp. By the end of that month, twenty people had been killed after being targeted by the Vigilance Committee.

Meagher knew nothing of these citizen-sanctioned murders. He had only just arrived in the territory. But here, *meet one of the good men.* Governor Edgerton introduced him to his nephew, Wilbur Sanders — the same Wilbur Sanders who was the guiding voice and moral author-ity behind the wave of hangings, burnings and assorted homicides com-mitted under the cover of do-it-yourself justice. He'd been the nominal prosecutor, and it was he who commanded, "Men, do your duty." San-ders, like his uncle, was a radical Republican—favoring revenge and repression against the conquered Confederacy, taking a much harsher view than Lincoln had. He expected that the new territorial secretary would be a political fellow traveler; after all, Meagher had broken with his party and his fellow Irish to support the former president. Montana was full of Democrats, Sanders explained. They were all "rebels and traitors," as he called them, "unfit to exercise the right of self-govern-ment." And given that Meagher had made headlines a few months ear-lier by supporting the one thing that many Democrats feared most — granting ex-slaves full citizenship and the right to vote — Meagher was urged to keep his distance from the opposition. That is, if he wanted to govern effectively.

Govern? Yes, Edgerton had more news, more jarring: he would be leaving on the very stage that had brought Meagher into town. He was taking his family east, away to school for his daughter. Did President

Johnson know about this? Was the leave authorized? No. Edgerton was fleeing the territory without permission. And fleeing in haste. But for how long? Would he be returning? He offered no assurances. And one more thing: finances. There were none. No money from the federal government, yet, for building roads. No money for erecting public buildings. No money for raising a militia or bargaining with the Indians. And no money for salaries, Meagher's included. With that, Edgerton handed Meagher a sheaf of official documents, wished him the best of luck and disappeared. He would not return for twenty-five years. Meagher, then, would be governor of Montana Territory, an Irish fugitive overseeing an area twice as large as England. Acting Governor Thomas Francis Meagher, as of, oh ... *now*.

With the formal papers of the territory packed into his saddlebag, Meagher rode to the new capital of Virginia City, seventy-five miles to the east. Over eleven hours, he crossed Rattlesnake Creek, trotted over khaki-colored foothills and fields, then went on to Stinkingwater River, named for the sulfuric hot springs that bubbled up at its edge. Anyone settling in New Ireland would have to get used to brown shock, as the summer sun bleached green from the land. When the skies weren't threatening snow, the temperature could climb to a hundred degrees. Down Stinkingwater, he angled toward Alder Gulch and Virginia City. There he was met with another shock, this one unrelated to color. The gulch no longer had any alder trees; it was cluttered with garbage, toilet pits, soiled bits of clothing and blankets, ramshackle sheds and broken picks. The ground had been clawed open, as if by a village of vision-impaired prairie dogs, and never resealed. The "city" was thrown together on high ground, 5,761 feet above sea level, like dice on an uneven table that tilted down toward the gulch. A drunk could roll, unassisted, from the center of the main street to the gulch. Many did. Flies buzzed around manure piles. Rats scurried under the planks of boardwalks, the main reason that a cat was a prized commodity, a single animal selling for $100. Buildings were in various stages of rising and falling, some painted, most not. A saloon owner had recently burned his bar down to get at the gold dust that had filtered through the floorboards.

After a year of relative quiet, the vigilantes had issued another spree of death sentences in the days leading up to Meagher's arrival, even though a new federal judge, Hezekiah Hosmer, had tried to dissuade them. "Let us inflict no more midnight executions," the judge scolded the settlers, after reassuring them that all prior extrajudicial killings would be forgiven. But establishing the rule of law in a lawless territory was much harder than proclaiming it. The mayor of Virginia City, Paris Pfouts, the man who'd laid out the town, was also president of the Vigilance Committee. On September 15, an unfortunate traveler named Jack Howard was hanged, with a sign pinned to his body: "Robber." On September 18, Tommy Cooke was strung from a tree in Helena, to the north. "Pickpocket" was the label placed on his body. *Pickpocket!* Not even England hanged a pickpocket. And on September 27, the day before Meagher rode into town, a pair of men were executed in Virginia City. James Miller noted the ghastly scene in his diary:

"Two men found hanging in the air this morning up the gulch a little bit with a card on their backs on which were the words 'Hung by the Vigilance Committee for being road agents.'"

The executions were approvingly recorded in the pages of Thomas Dimsdale's *Montana Post*. He would soon be serializing a history of the vigilantes, painting them not as murderers or lawbreakers, but as heroes. To those who objected to a secretive clutch of men deciding who could live and who could die in a territory under the flag of a constitutional republic, Dimsdale explained that the vigilantes were justified "even if the sun of every morning should rise upon the morbid picture of a malefactor dangling in the air."

The editor welcomed Meagher to Virginia City, the prickly and fastidious Englishman trying to co-opt the Irish revolutionary. *Just don't make any waves.* As for home, Meagher would eventually settle into a log cabin, about 500 square feet of pine patched with mud and clay, slightly off plumb, dark inside but for a few small windows, a block from the main street—the governor's mansion, formerly a butcher shop. Most of the animal blood and viscera had been scrubbed from the floor and walls. But before Libby arrived in the spring, he would have to do something about the mice.

When word spread that the new man in charge of the territory had hitched his horse to a Virginia City post, Irish miners, laborers and servants popped out of the gold diggings and dingy kitchens to greet the orator. His fame had grown since the surrender of the Confederacy, even as his soul sagged. The Irish Brigade, it was said on both sides of the conflict, had been one of the best fighting units in the war. In a

Meagher's cabin in Virginia City, Montana, which he and his wife jestingly called the "gubernatorial mansion." Meagher intended to find his fortune in the territory but was drawn into another cause, against the vigilante forces who opposed him there. COURTESY OF THE AUTHOR

long interview, Robert E. Lee singled out the Irish warriors and gave particular praise to General Meagher. Lee recalled the slaughter of immigrants trying to overtake the rebel line behind the rock wall above Fredericksburg. The Confederates mowed them down, and yet they kept coming, Lee marveled. "Never were men so brave," he said. "Their brilliant and hopeless assaults upon our lines excited the hearty applause of my officers and soldiers, and General Hill exclaimed, 'There are those damned green flags again.'" *Hearty applause?* Meagher had a different set of emotional memories of Fredericksburg, not of high-minded military gallantry. Still, his name was starting to be burnished into legend.

To Meagher's surprise, there were Fenians in this tumbledown town tucked in a crease of the mighty Rockies. Dozens of them, and very open about hatred of their country's oppressor. Also, the Irish of the territory counted among their ranks a world-class boxer, Hugh O'Neil. Earlier in the year, he was in the ring for the biggest cultural event in the territory, taking on an oversized saloon owner. A promoter charged $10 a seat to watch the brawl; it drew people from hundreds of miles around. Twice, O'Neil knocked his opponent down. Still, after 185 rounds, the referee called it a draw. Fenians and prizefighters—the foundations of New Ireland. They organized a welcome party. In a torchlight parade punctuated by songs in defiance of England and love of the old country, the Fenians walked from one end of Alder Gulch to the other, finishing with a grand assembly in town. They carried banners that marked the year of the Young Ireland uprising. The general was touched. He gave them a taste of his oratorical skills—rusty after months out of the public eye—and pledged to govern in a fair way. The editor, Dimsdale, frowned on the Fenians in his midst, questioning their patriotism and telling his readers that the rebellion of 1848 was, in fact, a miserable failure.

As the days grew shorter, Virginia City became ever more claustrophobic. It was crowded with gossip and intrigue, grim-faced gamblers trying to fool prospectors in all-night games of three-card monte and walls holding the smell of stale cigar smoke. The town could not have been more isolated, pinned in by mountains and weather, without a telegraph connection or regular stagecoach. Earlier in the year, in the desolation of late winter, Virginia City had run out of food. A mob stormed a dry goods store and made off with sacks of flour, gunfire at their rear. Fending off loneliness and fears that he had removed himself from anyplace that mattered, Meagher threw himself into governing. With his goose quill pen in perpetual motion, he fired off letters and orders on stationery stamped "Executive Office, Montana Territory." He made plans for public schools free of religious bias, angering Dimsdale, who doubled as the superintendent of education, and had insisted that the King James Bible be part of a child's curriculum. Dutifully at first, and then less frequently, Meagher consulted with the right-thinking citizens. A cultural crack grew to a chasm. The most prominent vigilantes and Republican leaders were also Freemasons. Their leader, Wilbur Sanders, was the Right Worshipful Grand Master of Virginia City's Masonic Lodge. The Masons and vigilantes were coconspirators in a raft of executions. The Masons had taken a sacred oath. "We knew each other by outward signs and met each other as brothers," wrote a founder of Montana's Freemasons. Their stated goal was "the protection, improvement and purification of our little society." In practice, that translated to meetings that were boiler room hot with anti-Catholic and anti-immigrant rhetorical steam.

In Montana, the biggest question of the day was whether to convene a territorial legislature. The acting governor was urged by Sanders not to call a session or a convention that might lead to statehood, because it would be dominated by Democrats. At first Meagher agreed with the right-thinkers. Then he changed his mind, which infuriated them. He further aggravated the territorial elite by taking a strong position against granting monopolies to a handful of businessmen (including vigilantes) for steamboat navigation and ownership of wagon trails. Roads and riverways belonged to all the people, Meagher insisted.

Viewed with suspicion when he arrived, Meagher was, by midfall, an enemy of the secretive syndicate that had been running Montana by terror. They started a smear campaign, planting rumors of the acting governor as a besotted whoremonger. "On his arrival in Virginia City he became intoxicated and remained so for a number of days in his room polluting his bed and person in the most indecent and disgusting manner," one Republican attorney, William Chumaserro, claimed in letter to an influential U.S. senator. The Irishman, he wrote, "is beastly and filthy in the extreme," exhibiting all "the natural proclivities of the people from whom he sprang." Neutral observers saw a different Thomas Meagher—a drinker, yes, but a bon vivant and man of words who brought a dollop of elegance to a debauched town. In this latest chance to make a mark and build a life, Meagher's love of argument and a good fight was revived. But Chumaserro's opinion counted: he was the brother-in-law of Wilbur Sanders. In no time, Meagher's enemies wore him down.

Nature restored him. The sky overhead, especially at night, was an antidote to the indoor assaults on his character. Through the fall, stands of aspen trees glowed during weeks of balmy days. There was frost on the ground in the morning, the air cutting and crisp, but the afternoons warmed to shirt-sleeve weather. The land itself beckoned possibility, with views from the territorial capital that stretched to the Ruby Range in one direction, the summits of the Madison in the other. On long rides to inspect the province under his authority, Meagher reveled in the hurried rituals of the natural world at the curtain-time of the year—rivers snap-happy with fat trout, herds of elk gorging on stiff grass, nimble-limbed pronghorn springing over fields, an osprey alighting on the bundled branches of a nest. Falling asleep at night as winter approached, wrapped in animal fur, Meagher could stare up at jolting flashes of fluorescent green—the aurora borealis. "Nothing delights me so much as being on horseback," he wrote.

In late November, Meagher and a party of five set out to visit Jesuit missions, en route to Fort Benton on the Missouri. They followed the Madison north, camping one night not far from where three rivers formed the big artery that would feed into the Father of Waters. In fresh-hatched Helena, Meagher was amused by the tent town of shacks and groggeries that were staked to Last Chance Gulch. "Every collection of log huts is called a city in this ambitious country," he wrote, recounting the journey in a long letter to Father De Smet, the much-traveled Jesuit of the West. As he rode north of Helena, the sky darkened and the temperature plunged. Meagher was exuberant, in constant patter even as snow started to fall. At dusk, the travelers found the log home of Paul Vermet, a former trapper. He threw together a stew of mountain sheep meat and brewed up pots of coffee. The wind raged, throwing snow against the cabin walls. The drama outside stirred Meagher's need for interior drama. Their host had a tattered book of Shakespeare. Lucky man, Meagher pronounced himself. He bundled up in his bison robe, with a saddle for a pillow, and read *The Tempest* deep into the night. Montana was starting to grow on him.

"It is a perfectly beautiful and delightful country, singularly rich and singularly grand," he wrote his friend George Pepper, the Irish Protestant minister from Ulster, now living in Ohio. "We have too great a preponderance of Yankee blood out here. I want to see a strong infusion of the rich, red, generous royal Celtic blood to counteract the acidity and poverty of the other." In the West a man could start clean, and find his self-respect in a patch of ground to call his own. "Come out to Montana—take up and fence in your one hundred and sixty acres, under the Homestead Act, in one of our wonderfully fertile, abundantly-watered, and well-timbered valleys . . . You will feel yourself a new man, and an American citizen in full." The last sentence was as much a self-description as a recruitment pitch.

More wonders lay ahead. Near the end of the Fort Benton journey, Meagher's party spent three days waiting out a snowstorm under the big tent of Father Xavier Kuppens, a tall, charismatic Belgian Jesuit who'd been working with the Blackfeet. The priest cooked up dinners of prairie hen and rabbit, his coffee laced with eau de vie. From the Indians, the priest had heard about a place with towering geysers, steep, gold-plated canyons and white crystalized formations that looked like wedding cakes the size of buildings—Yellowstone. He then saw it with his own eyes. Nothing in Europe could compare. "I spoke to [Meagher] about the wonders of Yellowstone," the priest recalled. "His interest was greatly aroused by my recital." The acting governor was eager to see such a thing. If true, he told Father Kuppens, he would do everything in his power to ensure that this American spectacle of fire and steam would become a park.

While Meagher was in the saddle, the vigilantes issued a new round of death sentences, as if no governing authority existed. They would occasionally refer to "the Acting One"—and laugh. It didn't matter what his title was; they had no use for him. The decision to kill a citizen was made in secret; the execution was not. The vigilantes asphyxiated their victims in the light of day, and left them hanging well past the point of rigor mortis. On October 3, Con Kirby was strung up in Helena, from the branch of a big pine called the Hanging Tree, at the corner of what would become Blake and Highland Streets. The same month, three men—nameless all—were hanged in Prickly Pear Gulch, to the north. The following month, another three men were roped to Helena's Hanging Tree. Some died by strangulation, a painful slow choking, others by a neck-snap. As 1865 came to a close, the executioners had murdered thirty-seven people in barely two years' time—"the deadliest campaign of vigilante killing in American history," the author Frederick Allen later concluded.

In November, a fight led to a fatality inside a saloon in Helena—gamblers taking on other gamblers. Guns, knives and fists were bared. One cardplayer pointed a gun at another, James B. Daniels, and was stabbed to death. The vigilantes seized Daniels and turned him over to a Republican judge. The jury, at first divided, ultimately brought a conviction equal to manslaughter. For this, Daniels was sentenced to three years in a frigid territorial penitentiary. His defenders said the penalty was too harsh—Daniels, they insisted, had acted in self-defense against a card cheat who drew a gun. Thirty-two citizens of Helena, including some of the men on the jury, petitioned the governor to pardon Dan-

*James Daniels, hanged by vigilantes from the Hanging Tree in Helena, Montana.
Not long after Meagher granted Daniels a reprieve, the vigilantes seized him.
March 1, 1866.* COURTESY OF THE MONTANA HISTORICAL SOCIETY

iels. Meagher did not have that power—only the president did, he felt.
But he could grant a reprieve from the sentence while Daniels sought a
presidential pardon.

The convict Tom Meagher knew what it was like to stare at the
world from inside a cage, to feel unjustly punished, to be on the wrong
side of authority. Under sentence in Tasmania, he'd lived among outlaws. His own father-in-law there—Bennie's dad—had been banished
for robbing a stage. Many of his fellow convicts in the penal colony
were guilty beyond doubt. But a great many were not. And one of his
earliest memories was of Waterford's old wooden bridge where Fran-

cis Hearn was hanged by the British. After looking at the evidence, Meagher ordered Daniels released. As well, Daniels was Irish. Ethnicity hadn't mattered, in Meagher's view, during the New York riots. The mobs who burned Manhattan were violent criminals who should be brought to justice, as Meagher condemned them. But Montana was a place where the Irish could start anew without being looked on as second-class people.

The vigilantes were infuriated. The Acting One had dared to cross them, and done so without showing the least respect. Already Meagher had angered the custodians of Montana law by siding with Democrats — on keeping the king's Bible out of public schools, convening a legislature, insisting on publicly owned roads and riverways. He was proudly and loudly Irish and Catholic, an affront to the Masonic Order, Protestants and nativists. He feared no man in the territory. And he mocked those who disliked the immigrants who answered the call to New Ireland. "Let the marrowless bigot carp and deprecate," he said in one Montana speech. "Let the hungry Puritan with his nasal music importune the God of Blue Laws to save the Yankee from the witchcraft of St. Patrick's daughters and devilry of St. Patrick's sons . . . The Irish people in America will not, and can not, forget the land of their birth, their sufferings, their dearest memories and proudest hopes."

Still, he had kept his distance from the organized killers. Now, on the dirt streets of Virginia City, when the vigilante prosecutor passed Meagher, he said nothing to the governor. Wilbur Sanders used his glare as a wordless warning, eyes that were normally vacant lighting on a target. To him, Meagher was already past tense. "He is dead beyond all hope of resurrection," Sanders wrote to a friend. The Irishman shrugged it off. In a life of inexhaustible political pugilism, he'd fought the British Empire, the Know-Nothings and the Confederate States of America. A handful of self-appointed moral wardens in the vastness of the Rocky Mountain West did not make him cower. Who was Wilbur Sanders, anyway? "The most vicious of my enemies," Meagher wrote to the White House, addressing the complaints of the right-thinking citizens, "an unrelenting and unscrupulous extremist."

But Sanders was an extremist with a long reach. When James Daniels returned to Helena the day Meagher let him out of jail, he was a free man awaiting a pardon. By 9 p.m. on the evening of his arrival, he was seized by the vigilantes. An hour later, Daniels was hanging from

Helena's most notorious tree—his windpipe throttled, his boots, pants and coat on, and Meagher's reprieve in his back pocket. Even some of the pioneers of frontier justice were horrified at the suddenness of the killing. The Vigilance Committee "committed an irreparable error in the execution of this man," wrote Nathaniel Langford. And Langford was a founding member of that committee. Still, his was a rare voice of dissent. The strangulation of Daniels was delivered with a blunt message to the governor. Witnesses reported seeing a note pinned to the dead man's chest: "The Acting One is next."

THE REMAINS OF A LIFE

From atop the treeless bluffs overlooking the big river, they could see them coming: high-decked, clangorous ships churning upstream to dock at the world's innermost port. At the end of the marine highway to the West, at Fort Benton, the steam-wheelers spit out people, bearded and armed, their skin the color of the cliffs above the Missouri River. The prospectors hired wagons to take them farther into buffalo country or bought ponies to gallop south to the goldfields. They scraped and clawed at land stroked by water, and then moved on to scrape and claw again. They were in such a hurry. The Blackfeet, so named because of the dark markings on the bottom of their moccasins, called themselves Niitsitapi—the Original People. Their words had skipped along this river and their chants had disappeared into night skies long before anyone introduced a god on a cross or a gun that could fire a twelve-pound ball. When they had this part of the high, rumpled northern Rockies to themselves, they chased bison herds over drop-offs or cornered them in cul-de-sacs where the short grass ran into basalt walls. And when the bison herds thinned, and then didn't appear at all, the Original People went hungry and became desperate and started to kill the new people. During a dark, cold spell known as the Starvation Winter, Blackfeet died in great numbers. At their weakest point, they were told to give up their language, their religion and their land. It was a federal crime, subject to jail or fine, to worship in the old way, an affront to speak the tongue of their grandparents. What had they done to deserve this? They had refused to stop being Niitsitapi.

Thomas Meagher was recalling his own people's years of starvation, his own fight against occupiers intent on emasculating a nation, out-lawing a religion, banning a language, during his first journey to see the natives of Montana Territory. After descending by horseback on the bank along the great falls of the Missouri—a series of thundering cataracts that brought to a halt all upriver travel—he was a day's ride from Fort Benton. This late in the year, in the flats, the river was no longer tawny and swollen, but clear and shallow, ice forming in pools along the shore. The land was the golden brown of a Tipperary spud, dusted by snow along the north-facing ridgelines, the cottonwoods bare in the canyons. Shunned by the ruling clique in Virginia City, the governor fell in again with a handful of well-read Jesuit priests. In them he found a world of acceptance and civility that he could not find in the capital. Around a campfire, he was back at Clongowes Wood, remembering much of his Latin, at Stonyhurst without the risk of get-ting his hand whacked by a disciplinarian in a clerical collar. The Jesu-its, many of them from Europe, loved the stories of his life, which he would stretch over several winter nights. And Meagher loved telling them. "The springtime of my youth was renewed," Meagher said, in re-calling "the days of brightest happiness."

The American authorities of church and state regarded the longtime inhabitants of the territory with disgust. "The general condition of In-dians of the Blackfeet nation, taken in light of civilization, is degrading in the extreme," wrote Gad E. Upson, the government's Indian agent. As the go-between of the native and American worlds, Upson was pre-sumed to have some sympathy for the tribes, but he could not hide his hatred. In a similar vein, an early Catholic missionary wrote, "The In-dian, as everyone knows, is a wild human being, bred in moral and ma-terial barbarism." Meagher, with his keen ear for history's echoes, might have heard in such talk the British Crown during the Great Hunger.

Among the Jesuits were a few men who showed more tolerance of the tribes, trying to learn their language and something of their ways—all in service of converting them to Roman Catholic Christianity. The Indians put up with the spiritual condescension, with the missions ris-ing on the buffalo grounds, in the hope of finding a powerful antidote to the plagues besetting their people. They wanted Big Medicine from the black robes. The native population had crashed. White ailments—cholera, smallpox, measles—to which the Indians had no immunity, took out young and old in mortal sweeps. To the north were the Blackfeet and three related tribes, feared by Lewis and Clark, feared by their enemies the Nez Perce and the Shoshone. Disease had taken much of the fight out of them. To the southeast were the Crow, more docile, trembling at the advance of their traditional Indian foes from the east. Looming over all were the mighty Oglala Sioux, led by Red Cloud, the most brilliant Indian tactician of the nineteenth century. He had proclaimed 1866 the year to rid Montana of whites. His plan was to close the door to immigration by making the main wagon trail into the territory a war zone.

At Fort Benton, more than 7,000 natives massed for a treaty session, led by Gad Upson with the Jesuits as interpreters. Meagher was an observer. He learned quickly how homelands were broken up by the government. The Blackfeet and the Piegan were expected to relinquish all land south of the Missouri and Teton Rivers and east of the Milk River—the heart of some of the most bountiful bison country—to occupy a rectangle to the northwest, hard up against what would become Glacier National Park. In return, the bands would get an annuity of $5,000, and each chief would be paid $500 for twenty years. Many of the payments would be in farm implements. The Blackfeet, horsemen and hunters for generations, were expected to become ranchers and wheat growers. Some of the chieftains signed, others did not. As governor at the treaty session, Meagher was offered gifts of buffalo robes by the tribal leaders; he turned them down. "You are poor and need to keep your property," he told them. "Keep it for yourselves and your children."

Meagher was astonished that a nation could be diminished so cheaply. "The original owners of this vast domain," he noted later in a speech in Virginia City, had given up everything for "a comparatively small reservation." But he did not object—not publicly. No sooner had the treaty papers with tribal X's on the signature lines been folded into the pocket of the Indian-hating Indian agent Upson than some of the Blackfeet realized they'd been taken, and attacked a few white stragglers around Fort Benton.

The Sioux refused to take the treaty bait. Like the Comanche in the southern plains, they used torture as a deterrent. They honed their skills on fellow Indians, cutting off noses and ears, fingers and toes, lopping penises from bodies and stuffing them into the mouths of victims. With enemy tribes, the goal was to deny them passage to the afterlife in any-

thing but a mangled body, leaving them incapable of enjoying the plea-
sures of heaven. With whites, the aim was to plant fear, and occasional
cottonwood stakes, in the hearts of interlopers. Throughout the second
half of 1865 and into 1866, the Sioux attacked cavalrymen, wagon trains
and miners on their way to Virginia City. With more than 2,000 warriors, Red Cloud moved freely throughout large parts of Montana and
Wyoming Territories. He disdained the trinkets, blankets and money
promised by the Americans — *wakpamni*, the bribes designed to get natives to give up their land, as well as *miniwakan*, the water that makes
men crazy. By early 1866, he'd been so successful that the government
closed most of the Bozeman Trail, which cut north from the Oregon
Trail and could save 400 miles, or almost six weeks, of a journey to the
goldfields of Montana.

The attacks sent the population of whites into a panic. They appealed to Meagher for help, and he turned to the federal government.
If Meagher wanted soldiers in Montana to defend against Indians, he
was told that he would have to go through the man in charge of the upper West, the commander of the Department of the Missouri — William T. Sherman. The general's opinion of the native population in the
territories was little better than his opinion of Georgians during his
march to the sea, or the Irish who'd fought for him at Bull Run. "We
are not going to let a few thieving, ragged Indians check and stop progress," Sherman wrote to the War Department. Still, a grudge was a
grudge — *envenomed martinet* — and the general refused Meagher's request. Nor would he grant him the respect of his title; he addressed him
as "secretary," though Meagher had been the sole governor of the territory for half a year.

Meagher called the legislature into session on March 5, 1866. The House
of Representatives assembled on the second floor of a saloon; the upper body met in a billiard hall. Snow buried Virginia City, but Meagher
warmed the politicians, most of them Democrats who'd been elected
under the previous governor. He said the territory should be governed
free of ethnic or religious taint. Those who fought for the Confederacy
were as welcome as those who had tried to kill them. Radical Republicans could find common cause with Copperhead Democrats. He re-
iterated his position on public schools: they should not teach religion.
The lesson of Great Britain — forcing the Crown's faith on the peo-

ple of Ireland—had never left him. And when Dimsdale, the British-born editor of the *Montana Post*, attacked Meagher for this stance, the governor fired him from his position as school superintendent. Later that year, the first public school in Montana opened in Virginia City—without the king of England's Bible.

He kept the frontier lawmakers furiously legislating. He also kept them fed and lubricated. His saloon bill, "for food and wet goods," was $434 over 38 days, a sum that paid for 74 meals, 19 bottles of wine, 12 pitchers of beer and 43 cigars. And when the legislature tried to pay Meagher $2,500 in salary, he turned it down, even as his remaining personal assets were running perilously low. "I do not wish to have a single dollar voted me out of territorial funds," he said. "The federal government ought to provide for its officers." The governor in motion was his own force of nature—equal parts nudge, threat and silky-voiced eloquence. In the Ireland of his birth, he could not have served in Parliament without denouncing his faith. In Tasmania, the prisoner could only write by pen name from the underground, helping the ex-convicts of the penal colony force the Crown to grant them self-government. But under the big sky of Montana, he was the executive branch, with a veto threat to back his powers of persuasion. By the close of the session, Meagher sent the citizen legislators back to their gold diggings and homestead shacks, but not until they'd passed sixty-four bills.

"Everything is delightful to me," Meagher wrote Secretary of State William Seward, "with the exception of those ill-bred bigots . . . who vent their vexation against me in vulgar and infamous detraction."

Those well-placed enemies steamed and plotted. Meagher had unleashed a citizen government of populist Democrats, and the mechanics of that rough-edged democracy sent the vigilantes into fits. At the same time, they continued with their executions. In February, two men were strung up in the community of East Gallatin. The next month, just as the legislature convened, another man was hanged in Helena, and a fourth victim was strangled by rope in Deer Lodge, bringing the total number of vigilante killings to forty-six. If there was a pattern to the death sentences, it was noted that most of the victims were Democrats and laborers. A store owner who shot and killed his business partner was given a pass. Wilbur Sanders, the self-proclaimed vigilante prosecutor, Republican leader and aspiring congressional delegate, could barely contain his rage at the Acting One for the crime of acting as governor. In a letter to a supporter about what to do with Meagher, he wrote, "We must put a quietus on the doings of this pretender." The word could mean only one thing.

Meagher exuded invincibility. Could the vigilantes of Montana seriously hope to do to him what the British Empire, the governor of Tasmania's penal colony and the Confederate generals could not? A wanted man? Take a number.

All of Virginia City, or those who could get in, packed into the People's Theatre on St. Patrick's Day, 1866, to hear the orator in a mile-high performance. He did not seem like someone afraid of the noose. "Sixteen years ago I spent the 17th of March in the forest of Tasmania," he told the spellbound audience. "It was a very beautiful island, which her gracious majesty of Great Britain enabled me to visit, having placed a sloop of war at my disposal for that delightful purpose." Laughter. Meagher turned serious, his voice almost a whisper. He closed his eyes to show himself in a dream state, then opened them, slowing his words to let the audience in on a secret. He was a homeless exile, he explained, as he had told Libby when asking for her hand, a man cast about on three continents. One thing had sustained him through the despair of the open sea aboard the *Swift,* through the smothering of life in the penal colony, through the butchery of friends at Marye's Heights. One thing: he had figured out a way to summon Ireland—in color and sound, scent and texture. No idle reminiscence, this was a trick, born of internal discipline, he had practiced in the first weeks of his banishment, then mastered during his bleakest hours in Tasmania.

"The wild birds, flashing and whirling over the waters, were my only companions," he said of Lake Sorell. "But I peopled the lonely scene with friends who were far away, and made it teem with memories and visions of the land of my birth. That lake became the lake of Killarney. An island in the center of the lake was changed to Innisfallen, the ruined cloister of the monks ... the round towers ... the castles ..." He asked his audience to transport themselves from snowbound Montana to the spring green of Ireland. "Every foreign Irishman goes home on St. Patrick's Day ... Why ... every one of you are at home with me today. There's not a one of you in Montana. There's not one of you has seen the Rocky Mountains this morning. The Rocky Mountains are gone for the day, and won't be back till midnight." Laughter here, for reprieve from the siege of a six-month winter. But even if Ireland were not beautiful, even if it were a desert, it would be mustered forth to rouse the soul of those who believed in the cause of forgotten people. "We should love it, be jealous of it, be proud of it, and cling to it all the more devotedly on account of the deprivations with which it has been stricken."

From passing on his trick of a memory mate in bad times, to the high-passion zone of any Irish immigrant, Meagher moved, strolling across the small stage. He faced men with scarred hands and women who scrubbed plank floors in Virginia City, people who'd been derided as *harps*. "Give me the peasantry, the reviled, scorned, ignored peasantry of Ireland! Their wretched cabins have been the holy shrines in which the traditions and hopes of Ireland have been treasured and transmitted. Never, never let the Irish heart give up the hope of seeing, on Irish soil, the fatal destinies of centuries reversed, and a restored nation, wisely instructed and ennobled in the school of sorrow planted there." The roar inside the theater lasted for several minutes, Meagher unable to continue. When he picked up again, he turned on those who thought that Irish and American could never be one and the same. He was talking to the Know-Nothings, to the vigilantes, to Peter Townsend.

"There are some vicious bigots, men of small brains and smaller hearts, men of more gall than blood, who even here assert that love of Ireland, devotion to her cause, active sympathy with the protracted contest for her redemption, revoke an unequivocal allegiance to the United States." The boos rang out—*not here!* He called for calm, the better for the crowd to hear his answer, the vow of the immigrant doubted, his citizenship sealed in blood. "Let the woods and swamps of the deadly Chickahominy, the slopes of Malvern Hill, the waters of Antietam, the defiant heights of Fredericksburg, the thickets of the Wilderness—a thousand fields now billowed with Irish graves, declare that love for Ireland blends in ecstasy with loyalty to America."

But such loyalty was not unquestioning. Yes, the United States was a wonderful country, a refuge for those who would have died of starvation at home. But there were too many in this new nation who were empty of love for something greater. "It is the soulless American who has no heart, who has no thought beyond putting a mighty dollar out at mighty interest, who has no zest for any other book than his soulless ledger."

When he uttered these words, Meagher himself was broke. He had turned down a salary from the territorial legislature, hoping that the federal government would eventually pay him what he was owed. But they hadn't. Traveling to the West in search of a fortune, he found only new battles to fight, variants of his persistent lifelong struggle to grant dignity to those without it. No matter. In his mind, the bigots were doomed. The soulless rich more so. He closed on a hopeful note. Any other way would have been out of character. Ireland and the United States, "hand in hand, down the great road of time," would always be on the side of "the freedomless, the beggared, and the crushed."

His ardor for the old country did not escape notice outside the drafty interiors of Virginia City. In Waterford, the press proclaimed Meagher the head of a large Irish nationalist movement in the American West. *He was back!* This time, as leader of the immigrant masses on the far frontier, poised to strike the Empire in its territory up north. "His plans are said to divide the Fenian Army into two immense bodies and with one to invade Canada." But the English knew better: they had infiltrated the Fenian ranks in Dublin, suspending habeas corpus yet again, and did not find their old foe from Young Ireland to be among the leaders of the biggest threat to British rule since 1848. Still, the Crown had good reason to keep track of the fugitive Thomas Meagher.

While Meagher did his fighting with words, the Fenians took to battle. They struck Canada in the late spring of 1866, sending a thousand Irish Americans across the Niagara River at Buffalo into Ontario. The invading force — Civil War veterans, itinerant laborers, new immigrants — fought a company of the Queen's Own Rifles and seized Fort Erie on June 1. The plan was to hit key locations in New Brunswick, Quebec, Ontario and Manitoba at the same time, but the attack was poorly coordinated and executed. At Fort Erie, the Irish were led by John O'Neill, a former captain in the U.S. Cavalry. They were prepared to fight English troops for control of the Union Jack's redoubt. Instead, they skirmished with a Canadian militia, 840 volunteers. By the third day, with their supply lines cut by an American naval ship, the Fenians retreated back across the river to the United States. They were promptly arrested, the invasion of Canada a bust.

Libby arrived on June 5, 1866, after sixty-five days on a steamboat up the Missouri from St. Louis to Fort Benton, about 2,600 river miles.

Husband and wife had been apart for nearly a year. He had lost some of the snap in his life, complaining of stomach ailments and trouble sleeping. The pain of a serious skin burn from a campfire was ever present. She had put on weight during the long weeks of sedentary travel, but her physical beauty, at the age of thirty-five, could still impress. "She is a fine looking woman ... with the blackest eyes and queenliest presence and prettiest face I've seen in the mountains," wrote the territory's Episcopal bishop, Daniel Tuttle. The cleric was struck by her mind as well; the acting first lady of Montana was clever, smart, quick in conversation, he noted. Meagher was overjoyed to be back in the arms of "my dear Lib." She had to love her pioneer husband after he escorted her to the governor's residence: their new home was the leaky log cabin in a town that could collapse in a sneeze. Tiny, mouse-infested and primitive the shack may have been, but with two Meaghers now occupying the crude cabin, it became a parlor—the "gubernatorial mansion," they dubbed it. A picture was commissioned of the executive residence, for laughs and posterity. They hosted poetry readings and nights of backgammon and claret, the educated talk moving outside on summer evenings when light glowed in the mountains till a few hours short of midnight. Also, to the alarm of the Masonic Temple, the Meaghers buttressed the Catholic community, lobbying the church to send a bishop to tend to the growing ranks of immigrant faithful.

The Meaghers fought as well. Money was now a serious problem. Libby's father had always provided a residence in New York for the couple, but little else. Another Townsend daughter, Alice, who had become wealthy by her marriage to Samuel Barlow, was part of one of the richest couples in the United States. Barlow kept a finger dipped in banks, railroads, war contracts and presidential politics. Meagher had nothing. His earnings were from speaking, and he had done precious little of that—for pay—since becoming a warrior and politician. Montana's motto was bottom line, *Oro y Plata*. Meagher had neither gold nor silver. He still intended to invest in a mine, or some land, but he never found the time. Tangling with the vigilantes and trying to get the new territory on its feet had consumed him. What he wanted most, he said, was to be a man who brought honor to his people. The Irish Brigade, the soldiers sacrificed, his own near-death experiences facing Confederate musketry, should have been enough. But he still had to prove himself. "It is my ambition," he wrote a friend, "to be the representative and champion of the Irish race in the wild great mountains." New Ireland, though, was slow to fill.

His enemy Sanders had been put in his place, or so it seemed: he was roundly defeated in an election that year for territorial delegate to Congress. The rebuff to Montana's leading Republican was seen as an endorsement of Meagher by the voters. Unable to govern legitimately, the Vigilance Committee that Sanders had guided killed another round of men by secret edicts in mid-1866. Leander Johnson was hanged in Deer Lodge, accused of "a want of appreciation of the law," no small irony. J. L. Goones was strung up in German Gulch. A man named Frenchy Couchet was hanged in Helena a few days after Libby's arrival, with a note, "robber and perjurer," pinned to his body.

At the same time, Sanders also plotted to bring a new governor to Virginia City. Montana Republicans leaned on leaders of their party in Washington to appoint someone who fell in line with the Freemasons and other upstanding people in the territory. A proper replacement was promised by the fall.

Throughout the summer and into October of 1866, Meagher set out to introduce Libby to those "wild great mountains," while also gathering material for an assignment from *Harper's Weekly*. If he was afraid, he didn't show it. He'd killed for the Union. He'd promised to kill for Ireland. He would kill to defend himself. "Every day intensifies my hatred of the Radicals," he wrote Barlow. "Here in Montana, they have ever since my arrival, been violently endeavoring to do, on a smaller scale, what in the states they have virtually succeeded in doing—that is, disorganizing and paralyzing the government because they could not control it."

The Meaghers crossed over the Continental Divide, went west into the drainage of the Blackfoot River, to the Clark Fork—clear-running streams a few days removed from snowmelt, rushing to join the Columbia, which empties more water into the Pacific than any river in the Western Hemisphere. At sunset, occasional storms passed through; more often was a show of alpenglow along the ridges that lined up like sentinels. North from Hell Gate Village, renamed Missoula that year, the Meaghers traveled through the Flathead Valley, gazing on the big lake of the same name. He found Jesuits again, at the Mission of St. Ignatius, lonely black robes working in the shadow of the imposing wall of the Mission Range. Wandering among those peaks, Meagher named a waterfall for the love of his life.

But the closing of the season of light, with snow flying again on the journey back to Virginia City and ice forming in the creekbeds, brought fresh intrigue, and no checks from the government. Now Meagher was desperate, more than $2,500 in debt. He turned to a friend, Cornelius O'Keeffe, for a loan of $1,000. What he had in collateral was his way with words. Meagher would file his *Harper's* piece under O'Keeffe's byline, a great ego boost for a man trying to make his name in the territory. Meagher didn't want to grovel. "I want to return to Virginia City a proud and independent Irish gentleman—having no one insult or even give me the cold shoulder because I owe a miserable little bill of 50 or 100 dollars," he wrote O'Keeffe. "I want my countrymen to place me up and beyond the sneers of these 'blackguards' who are ever ready to run down an Irishman."

Back in the capital, the town was abuzz over the arrival of a well-regarded gentleman: the new governor, Green Clay Smith. He was from Kentucky. A member of Congress. A Protestant—evangelical Christian. And a teetotaler who dreamed of a day when all of the United States would be dry. He was everything Meagher was not, and everything the right-thinking people of the territory could hope for. Around Governor Smith, Meagher was himself—chatty, solicitous, funny, dropping an allusion to Ovid here and a quote from Thomas Jefferson there. The new man was charmed. As it turned out, they had several things in common. Smith had been a general in the Union Army; like Meagher, he had led men to death against the slaveholding republic. They shared a love of certain authors, a habit of summoning a line of verse to good effect and a governing philosophy. Several times, they stayed up past 1 a.m. talking about history. In short order, the Irish Catholic tippler and the nondrinking evangelical were fast friends. "Green Clay Smith is in complete accord with me," Meagher confided to Barlow. "He is a genial, bright-hearted, high-minded fellow." But Smith had no sooner arrived than he decided to leave, just like the first governor. He promised to be back in half a year. Leave he did, barely three months after arriving, giving full power back to Meagher, who resumed his title of the Acting One.

His enemies hit him twice, first with great force, and then less so.

In early 1867, Wilbur Sanders traveled to Washington on a mission to cripple his Montana rival. The midterm elections of 1866 had given Republicans more power than they ever had in Congress. In the House, they held 174 of 224 seats. At the same time, they started impeachment proceedings against the unloved president, Democrat Andrew Johnson. Doors in the capital opened for Sanders. *This Meagher fellow,* the great Irish general, the Acting One, was a fraud, Sanders claimed—and had to be shut down. In response, Congress passed a sweeping measure: it nullified the legislative session of Montana. All laws and acts passed in the 1866 assembly were held to be null and void—"an extraordinary and unprecedented action," as the western historian Gary Forney called it. Back in Montana, in case Meagher didn't get the message about power in the territory, vigilantes issued another death warrant. They hanged a man—his last name, Rosenbaum, tagged to his body—for reasons unexplained. No arrest. No trial. No due process. No last words. In the fall, Rosenbaum had been whipped and told that he was banished from Montana. But he refused to move out of the territory, and paid for it with his life.

Meagher had been given a similar message. Riding from Virginia City to Helena, he was stopped by a posse of vigilantes. Did he not understand the note attached to the dangling corpse of James Daniels? Leave Montana, they told the Irishman—*leave.* Afterward, a crude drawing was dropped off at the governor's cabin. It pictured a body hanging from a tree, and a noose around a name: "General Meagher."

22

RIVER WITHOUT END

Summer 1867. The Missouri held fresh snowmelt still; it was fat and full of swagger. Riding all day with a small party traveling north to Fort Benton, Meagher was sick, unable to keep his food down, his stomach convulsive. The clop of horses raised swarms of grasshoppers and drew biting flies and blood-sucking mosquitoes. Days were cloudless, hot and slow, the sky white with heat in the afternoon torpor. He'd left his wife in Helena, promising to return in about two weeks. When they were together, his pain passed, and they could laugh and make love and pretend that life in New Ireland was working. He missed old Ireland. He wanted to see what his son was like. He'd written to his father a week ago, inquiring about young Thomas and Waterford. Yes, he could summon the land of his birth and people it, using his great mental trick. But he missed the touch. He wanted to dip his toe in the Suir, to sit with Duffy and Speranza, to sing a rebel song in Kilkenny, to climb Misery Mountain and look down on the home of three living generations of Meaghers. He'd been away almost twenty years, had lived nearly half his life as an exile. In late afternoon, his ass chapped from the saddle, his back sore, his face sunburned, his stomach snarling, he looked around at the flat-topped mesas, treeless and brown, gazed up at that infinity of sky, and wondered how he got there, so far from home.

And what would his father think of him now? Judged by accumulated wealth, not much. In a note to the territorial auditor, Meagher begged for the pay denied him over nearly two years as governor. "I am utterly—utterly—out of funds." It was humiliating to admit, even harder to commit to paper. He could not ask his father for help; he was well past that. The elder Meagher never understood his rebel son, *acting* on principle instead of just pretending to act, as most people did. Young Meagher believed in luck and lost causes. The old man followed the rules, even if the rules kept Ireland in bondage: member of Parliament, mayor of his hometown, living well in a family manor stuffed with inherited riches from the merchant life. The rules rewarded him, to a point. If he could see the creaky assemblage of logs in Virginia City that the onetime Prince of Waterford called home, he would be appalled.

Meagher's mission this last week of June was joyless: go to Fort Benton to pick up a cache of arms for use against the native inhabitants. After much resistance, General Sherman had agreed to send weapons for defense of the territory. This, after Red Cloud's warriors had whipped the army in December of 1866. They had lured Captain William Fetterman out of his post at Fort Phil Kearny, in northern Wyoming, and directly into an ambush. Eighty men were killed, their eyes gouged, heads scalped, bodies mutilated for good effect—one of the few times an Indian army had annihilated the Americans. Fetterman had served under Sherman in Georgia. The general swore revenge. "We must act with vindictive earnestness against the Sioux, even to their extermination—men, women and children," he wrote.

With Red Cloud's victory, the rest of the Bozeman Trail was closed to all travel, choking the route of pioneers who insisted on going to Montana the short way. The forts along the trail would soon be abandoned. For one final time, the bison grounds belonged to the Sioux, the last big swath of Indian country completely in the hands of native people. But John Bozeman—an ambitious hulk of a frontiersman, founder of the town and the shortcut named for him—would have none of it. In April, Bozeman and several white men ventured out along the off-limits trail, astride the Yellowstone River. There, he was killed by Indians, or so it was reported—a sensational murder that put the territory on edge. Somehow, Bozeman's business rival who was with him at the time, Thomas Cover, escaped. And it was he who blamed the killing on the Blackfeet, though he may have had a hand in the death himself. A call for war against the natives—Blackfeet, Sioux, Arapaho, Northern

Cheyenne—went up in Virginia City. "It is high time that the sickly sentimentalism about humane treatment and conciliatory measures should be consigned to novel writers," wrote the *Montana Post*. "If the Indians continue their barbarities, wipe them out."

Meagher organized a militia and galloped off in a dust swirl to fight the tribes. But his heart wasn't in it. He ventured east, into the nerve-racked Gallatin Valley, and found no hostiles. On a swing to the north and west, he was supposed to kill Indians of any tribe. The Jesuits urged him to show some mercy, to not fire a shot unless he was fired upon. Red Cloud was the Indian Meagher of the Sword, said one of the priests. He honored their request. A reporter noted that Meagher didn't have to fight. "He will quiet the Indians by talking their heads off." At summer's dawn, the militia had disbanded without bloodshed.

By the time he dismounted at the Sun River junction with the Missouri, in late June, Meagher had been on a horse, in one form of service to Montana or another, for almost two months. He could go no farther, he said. Whatever it was that ailed him—a serious intestinal disease, dysentery, typhus—he felt terrible. For six days he didn't move, coiled in the predawn cold around the last embers of a fire, sweating through the blistering sun by day. He'd decided he was done with politics in the Rocky Mountains. The governor, Green Clay Smith, would be back any day. "On his arrival, I shall be free—and right glad," Meagher wrote Barlow, "for I am downright sick of serving the government in a civil capacity." The Democrats had urged him to run for territorial delegate to the U.S. Senate—his for the asking, given the majority political sentiment of Montana. He turned them down. "I'm not rich enough, yet, to support the grand responsibilities of that position," he wrote his brother-in-law. Barlow was in on the joke. At this point, he knew that the great Irish general was a pauper.

On July 1, Meagher roused himself for a final push to Fort Benton, at the bony footings of the mountains in the north. Several steamships were at anchor. The town was jumping with gamblers, prospectors, washed-up slaveholders, missionaries, Indian killers, liquor merchants, prostitutes, soldiers, mercenaries for various causes, Meagher haters and Meagher lovers. The general was instantly recognized as he hobbled down a boardwalk fronting the Missouri. Every other establishment was a saloon or an inducement to vice. A woman named Madame

Mustache ran the Jungle, a place for a man to get a quick poke and a pop of corn whiskey, while Lily's Squaw Dance, in a false-fronted shack next to the euphemistically named Board of Trade, catered to similar clientele. Men who recognized Meagher pointed at him, staring. They turned away, muttering what sounded to the governor like a threat— *There he goes.*

Sweating and exhausted, Meagher went to the home of the merchant I. G. Baker, an adobe cabin that doubled as a store—two rooms under a sod roof. Bad news greeted him: his back pay, which was supposed to have been forwarded to Baker's residence, had not arrived, nor had Sherman's shipment of guns. The weapons were stuck downriver, another hundred miles or so. Meagher tried to hold down lunch with Baker inside the cooling refuge of his home, the finest in Fort Benton, with its whitewashed, three-foot-thick walls and timbered, rough-hewn beams overhead. The merchant offered Meagher blackberry wine as a palliative.

At midday, a well-dressed man with a pointed beard poked his head in the door, acting on a rumor that had rumbled through the river port. "General Meagher?"

It was Wilbur Sanders. The vigilante leader had just returned from his trip to the nation's capital, having thrown out the work of the legislative session Meagher had labored so hard on. And here was the governor himself, still defiant, still conducting official business, not "dead beyond all hope of recognition," but unbowed. Sanders was solicitous, seeking to join Meagher and Baker. Men of political disagreement could still share a meal, yes? Surely Meagher was ready to give up this New Ireland *nonsense* and the promotion of Catholic immigrants to the territory. And what was with his animus toward the Freemasons? Meagher had called them pimps and bigots in a speech; they were Know-Nothings in cowboy hats. *See here:* as the recently elevated grand master of the Masonic Temple in all of Montana, Sanders could assure his rival that the defenders of pureblood Americanism were only getting stronger on the frontier. Resistance was futile. The established order would prevail.

Meagher had to be surprised to bump into the man he'd called "the most vicious of my enemies" in this upriver outpost. Pure coincidence? Perhaps. The governor waved off his rival, retreating to the back room of Baker's house to read the paper, work on official business and answer some correspondence.

In a weakened hand, Meagher wrote Richard O'Gorman in New York. They'd been schoolboys together at Clongowes Wood, rebels during Young Ireland's rise in the face of the Great Hunger and fellow Manhattan lawyers. Meagher sketched a plan to travel with Libby to Europe, do some speaking about his Civil War experiences and see if there was a back door into Ireland. He wanted to look into the eyes of the son he had never met. He could count on friends in high places: some of the leading figures from the 1848 uprising were now pillars of society, a few members of Parliament among them. Speranza was more influential than ever; her house in Dublin was one of the liveliest parlors in Europe. But Meagher was conflicted. He and Libby were mostly happy. Montana could still be home for his people. He was not done yet with the dream of New Ireland.

The pilot of the *G. A. Thompson*, tied up on the riverfront outside Baker's store, interrupted him. Johnny Doran was electrified at the chance to meet the Irish American patriot. Also, he had guided the stern-wheeler that brought Libby to Fort Benton a year earlier. Meagher was grateful to the riverman for bringing his wife safely back to him. And how was the missus? Very well, Meagher said. He was just dashing off a note to her now. The brutal two-week ride to Fort Benton was his last official mission; he'd be home with Lib soon, and free of public service. Doran invited Meagher to dine with him in the comfort of his riverboat and spend the night in a guest room. Meagher explained that he wasn't well. Doran insisted. They had many things to talk about. For one, British authorities were supposedly on their way to Fort Benton, if not already there, to look into reports of another Fenian plot against the Empire. An Irish American cavalry soldier—said to be a Fenian—had killed a British army captain a few days earlier aboard one of the Missouri River steamboats. Shot in the head. The victim was a nobleman of some rank, and wealthy. For another, Doran had a decent library on his ship. With that, Meagher perked up. Fresh literature, as always, was a bigger draw than fresh food.

In the evening, belted kingfishers swooped for trout over the wide, swift expanse of the Missouri, gliding just above the waterline. As the heat broke, the river fell under the shadow of high, beveled cliffs on one side. White-tailed deer foraged in the shallows, and pelicans scanned the surface for the dimples of rising fish. Tree limbs, broken-off logs and other bits of flotsam rushed by. Across the way and downstream, exposed tiers of the ages were burnished in the last sunlight on the high mesas. Over a light meal, Meagher and Johnny Doran talked of Ireland and the navigational tricks of the upper Missouri, of Gaelic poets and death on Marye's Heights. As sick as Meagher was, he could still tell a story, still bring a stranger to tears of outrage or laughter, even an audience of one.

But he was not himself. The charm was forced. He was preoccupied, sensing that mortal danger was at hand. Of all the ports in all the world, Meagher found himself in one at 2,700 feet above sea level, where the enemies of his life—the Crown, the dregs of the Confederacy, vigilantes—lurked nearby. Ah, but not just enemies. Friends as well. Irishmen. Fenians at the American fort, in uniform. Johnny Doran. After their dinner, they crossed the gangplank back to town for a leisurely stroll over cigars along Front Street. Again Meagher noticed the stares and murmurs of men who looked away when he tried to meet their gaze.

"Johnny, they threaten my life in that town."

As the last light melted at dusk, the two men retreated back to the steamship. The pilot tried to reassure Meagher. He had a pair of pistols he could lend him for the night. And, even more comfort, a riveting book, as promised: *The Collegians*, a thriller set in rural Ireland, written by Gerald Griffin. The author had died young, but his novel enjoyed a long life in all parts of the English-speaking world. Johnny Doran escorted Meagher to the stateroom, on the port side—open to the river on the upper deck. Meagher insisted that Doran stay with him for a time. But Doran had some business to attend to. He left him with the novel that took Meagher, in his last hour, back to his homeland.

About 10 p.m., a crewman on the lower deck of the *G. A. Thompson* heard a cry and a splash. The night was windless with a strong moon; sound carried across the open surface of the river. He said he heard gasps, a gurgling sound—the desperate noise of struggle.

"Man overboard!"

Johnny Doran knew immediately that it was Meagher, the only occupant of the guest stateroom. He considered jumping in, and then not, "for it would be almost certain death." He ordered lights cast on the river, threw out boards attached to ropes. Doran ran to the shore and raced downstream, calling out. The final sounds he heard were "two agonizing cries from the man, the first one very short, the last prolonged." The pilot waded hip-deep into the river, holding the ship's paddlewheel as a tether. Small boats were launched. But they found not a trace of Thomas Meagher.

It fell to Wilbur Sanders to announce the death and shape the story that would be told for generations to come. Poor fellow, *our acting governor*, had gone to an early grave. Meagher was the most brilliant conversationalist he'd ever met, said Sanders. And the sudden death of one so full of life. *Such a pity*. A suicide, he implied. Sanders said he had shared warm words with the Irishman that day, an afternoon "delightfully spent." At night, as Sanders told the story, he saw the governor again, on Front Street, and this time "it was apparent he was deranged . . . loudly demanding a revolver to defend himself." Why, he could not imagine. The vigilante leader, the man Meagher most despised in Montana, escorted his enemy to his stateroom and all but tucked him in. So he said. But Johnny Doran, who actually did put Meagher to bed, said nothing of that sort happened. It was just Doran and Meagher. This would not come out until later. Sanders then went back to town, in his telling, and about thirty minutes later heard the shocking news that the governor had drowned. During that same half hour, Sanders or a hired killer could have crept into Meagher's room. It was not heavily guarded. Sanders claimed that a witness told him Meagher had jumped into the water in his nightclothes. Jumped. On his own. Sanders sent these details out with the evening post, leaving at 11 p.m. for Helena.

They searched into the morning. Searched all day and the following one, up and down the banks of the Missouri, dragging the river. Governor Smith, now back in the territory, immediately authorized a $1,000 reward for the recovery of the body. He praised the general as a gentleman and a friend, recalling their late-night talks. In Virginia City and Helena, people crowded into assembly halls to mourn the best-known Irish American in the country. Nobody believed the Sanders version of the disappearance. Suicide? Though he quarreled with the high clergy, Meagher was a Catholic by culture and faith. He would never kill himself. Nor did they believe that he'd tripped over a coil of rope on deck, as others said, falling to his death. Even if he did fall, Meagher was a strong swimmer. All his life he'd been around water. He grew up on the River Suir, went to his first Jesuit school along the Liffey, endured his banishment on the shores of Lake Sorell, escaped from the penal colony in the treacherous swells of Bass Strait, led soldiers through the rain-swollen hold of the Chickahominy. In Tasmania, he had offered to swim to his rescue boat, had his pirate friends not offered to take him. No, the Missouri currents, strong though they were, could not alone take Meagher to his grave. Even when sick, he was robust, with an oaken barrel of an upper body, a stubborn bastard.

More likely he was assassinated, these friends of Meagher believed. Citizens of Helena packed into the same theater where, a few months earlier, Meagher had given a stirring lecture on the Irish Brigade. They put together a fund to find the killer; it grew to ten times what the governor was offering. They passed a resolution, reprinted in papers throughout the nation: "That in his death, our country has lost a true patriot, a friend of universal liberty, a sympathizer with the oppressed of all nations, a foe to tyranny . . ."

The governor ordered thirty days of official mourning. Now Meagher's enemies were among the most effusive in praise. No more talk of a drunk, whoremonger or tyrant. "There was nothing in his faults to extinguish the fire of great virtues," wrote one Republican leader who had battled Meagher in the territory. The Irishman was "a ripe scholar," said the *Montana Post*, which had slandered him at every turn, "courteous, amiable and hospitable."

Throughout the East—in Meagher clubs, Meagher bands and Meagher militia units, in New York and Boston and Philadelphia, wherever lived the men who'd been soldiers in the Irish Brigade—there was disbelief. What they knew of the Waterford rebel, some of it legend, much of it factual, was that he had lapped the globe on a wave of immortality. The ancient gods of his homeland always had his back. The man was never quiet, never still, never slow, never far from history's front edge. The idea of his death, now, at age forty-three, by an "accident" that was no match for the life lived—this was preposterous. The *Irish American*, a hagiographer at first, then an opponent, and now again on Meagher's side, published a commemorative poem among its many tributes:

And is the patriot, Meagher, dead?
Who in his youthful glory, rose,
A champion of his race, and led
His country 'gainst her foes . . .

His childhood friend Richard O'Gorman, recipient of what may have been Meagher's last letter, was aghast at the loss. At the Cooper Union in New York, where Abraham Lincoln had given the speech that made him a national figure, where Red Cloud would make a plea for independence of the Sioux Nation, a huge crowd converged on a hot night in August to remember Meagher's life. Earlier that day, a Requiem Mass was held at St. Francis Xavier Church. Veterans of the Irish Brigade lined either side of a portrait of their leader, each man wearing a sprig of green boxwood in his lapel.

"He is gone," O'Gorman said in his eulogy. "The pitiless Missouri, hurrying fast to sea, has enwrapped him in a watery shroud and dug him a lonely grave beneath its turgid waters." The hall was bedecked with flags of the brigade, the United States and the tricolor that Meagher had designed for the country of his birth. O'Gorman told the story of an outsized life, the basic profile familiar to most, the details not. A boy of wealth and standing had risked it all for Ireland. The famine made him a revolutionary. The voice made him famous— "a trumpet blast to rouse the whole island." In the docket at Clonmel came a speech that would long outlive him: "I know this crime entails the penalty of death; but the history of Ireland explains this crime, and justifies it." Then, shackled and forced off to the end of the world, the loneliness, the escape, finding his way in New York. Always, Meagher was propelled by a desire to put a dent in history.

"His was a mind that needed the inspiration of great purpose," said O'Gorman. "To see the great game of life played by other hands, and to stand by inactive, and only watch . . . was to die a living death." That great purpose came with the Civil War. The mortal conflict against the slaveholders was not his fight, nor that of the Irish. But he made it his, and theirs. In doing so, they became Americans.

"Aye! Be proud of the Irish Brigade! Be proud of him who led it . . . Three thousand men were in the Brigade when it went to war; five hundred were all that left it." And was the general not flawed in ways large and small? Without doubt. "His faults lie gently upon him. For he had faults, as all of us have." O'Gorman closed with a final aspiration for his mate through nearly four decades.

"Would that his grave were on some Irish hillside, with the green turf above him."

The widow Elizabeth Meagher left the territory in late summer, never sure what had happened to her husband, never to leave letters or diaries behind for glimpses into her heart. His death ended a life adventure for her. She was the only person who could keep up with him. She had rescued him in his lowest moments, had said yes to the uncertain destiny he was always following, had curbed his excesses when he was full of self-pity or vanity. They never had a child together. But she adopted Ireland's struggle, now orphaned in this raw and violent place. Libby departed by steamboat from Fort Benton, down the river that would become his grave. His body was never found.

Wilbur Sanders could be reasonably sure that, in a few months, Meagher would be forgotten, and, in a few years, he might be a footnote, his words never to inhabit the beautiful high territory that had been his last home. As Sanders would have it, the story of the end of Thomas Francis Meagher, the story that took hold, was tragic and fitting and uncomplicated. But that story has not stood up in the nearly century and a half that has passed since his death.

23

INQUEST FOR IRELAND

O n the Fourth of July, 1905, one of the largest crowds in Montana assembled in front of the capitol in Helena to unveil a statue. A procession, led by a band, marched from Last Chance Gulch to the government grounds, where it was greeted by women in white dresses and bonnets, men in crisp suits and hundreds of miners who had contributed their earnings for this memorial. The idea had the backing of Marcus Daly, the copper magnate from Butte and then the most powerful Irish American capitalist in the United States. When deep veins of the metal used in wiring in every town were found just below the surface near the Continental Divide, Butte was transformed into an industrial hive, known as "the richest hill on earth." Daly recruited Irish immigrants to his mines and paid them well. They came in droves, the sons and daughters of people who had survived the Great Hunger. It was a hard town, hazardous and dirty, winter-cold for half a year. But the Irish flourished there, establishing literary societies and patriotic clubs, opera houses and theaters, schools and churches, raising large families in two-story houses. In the Rocky Mountains, their stories found a home. At one point, more Gaelic was spoken in Daly's mines than anywhere on this side of the Atlantic. New Ireland, when it finally came to the American West, was Butte, Montana.

Elizabeth Meagher had sent her regrets: "I am there in spirit," she wrote by telegraph from her home in Rye, Westchester County, north of New York City. She had returned to Montana but once, in the summer of 1887, to visit Yellowstone National Park. She was informed, as later scholars would discover, that her husband's suggestion that the

area be explored and considered as a preserve of some sort had contributed in a small way to the formation of what would become the
world's first national park. Cut out of her father's inheritance by her
marriage to Meagher, she lived modestly in a small cottage, subsisting
on a Civil War widow's pension of $50 a month. She never remarried,
never stopped stoking the memory of the Irishman whose life became
hers.

At the noon hour, silence fell over the capitol grounds in Helena.
The Declaration of Independence was read, every miner's head nod-
ding at the fistful of fighting words aimed at England. A still moment
followed. On command, solemn-faced men removed the large American flag that had been wrapped around an imposing object. The crowd
gasped: there stood a bronze equestrian statue mounted on a massive
block of granite. It was Thomas Francis Meagher, forever young, forever defiant, facing the distant Big Belt Mountains and the waters of
the Missouri. Chiseled on the side were excerpts from the 1846 speech
he gave in Dublin at the age of twenty-two—his attempt to rouse the
starving to resistance.

A few blocks away, Wilbur Sanders was huddled inside his three-
story manse, close enough to hear the music and cheers that went up
during the dedication of Meagher's life. He was dying, and probably
knew that he might not live to see summer's end. For almost forty
years, Sanders had been determined to have the last word. He had co-
founded the Montana Historical Society, serving as its president for a
quarter century. In that position, he guided the accepted narrative of
how the land under the big sky was settled by righteous pioneers. The
version of Montana's early days that children would learn would come
from the vigilante Wilbur Sanders. In *A History of Montana,* the author wrote that the killers Sanders had unleashed were a force for good,
the summary executions necessary, the hangings all justified, for they
"had the support of every decent, law-abiding citizen of the community." The writer was Helen Sanders, daughter-in-law of Wilbur, who
presumably had an easy job of sourcing. The Freemasons worked with
the vigilantes, in secret, to assure this order, she explained. And if they
got a few things wrong, if an innocent man was strangled to death or
a family banished without cause, if the Constitution was trampled on,
so be it. "The planting of civilization, like all experiments, is subject to

The equestrian statue of Meagher at the Montana state capitol in Helena, erected in 1905. Words from his most defiant speech in Ireland are etched into the stone's pedestal. COURTESY OF THE AUTHOR

many mutations, miscarriages and much mistaken toil," Wilbur Sanders had said in a Pioneer Day address in 1903.

In the burnished twilight of his final years, Sanders had added a few details to his story of what happened to Thomas Meagher. On the day of his disappearance, he recalled, the Irishman was his talkative self.

"General Meagher seemed at his best in a conversational way," Sanders said. "But he resolutely and undeviatingly declined that form of hospitality with which Fort Benton then abounded"—that is, he didn't drink, gamble or buy himself a whore, a backhanded compliment at best. He next saw the general at sunset. And by then he was a different man—not drunk, but mad. Sanders had no idea why Meagher felt so defensive, "loudly demanding a revolver to defend himself against the citizens of Fort Benton, who in his disturbed mental condition he declared were hostile to him." Sanders claimed again that he helped escort Meagher to his stateroom "on the starboard side of the boat." He saw him change to nightclothes and put to bed. "We did not apprehend there would be further trouble." And it was Sanders who broke the awful news to the general's wife, implying that Meagher had killed himself. "It seemed my duty to tell her the sad story." All of this came from a man who had insisted, barely a year before his death, that "we must put a quietus" on Thomas Meagher.

Among those who had been with Meagher on that last day, no one backed the Sanders story. "He has been charged by the ungenerous with suicide, but with no grounds of possibility," said I. G. Baker, the merchant who welcomed Meagher into his house on July 1, 1867. He spoke, years later, to an army officer who was compiling a history of Fort Benton. Logic alone reinforced Baker's conclusion. For what man of words would leave the world without a final word? What man readying to close out his final day would write his best friend on that day to outline ambitious plans for the future, a speaking tour of Europe, a family reunion, meeting a son for the first time? What suicidal husband would send a note of routine details and love to his wife? And what taker of his own life would cry for help in the grip of the river that carried him away?

Meagher did not kill himself—that seems clear. But this leaves another explanation that some of those closest to him could never believe: that he died in a tipsy tumble from the deck of the *G. A. Thompson*. It's easy to blame it all on a drunken fall, as if that were the only fatal destiny for an Irishman who lived large. But that version also conflicts with witness accounts. The merchant Baker said Meagher drank only the medicinal pouring of blackberry wine he'd given him for his stomach troubles in the afternoon. "I am prepared to state that he was stone, cold sober," Baker said in 1901. Doran, the river pilot, said the same thing.

In his eulogy, Richard O'Gorman had told of an ordinary ending for a most extraordinary man: Meagher tripped and fell. Drink was not involved. Perhaps it was a coiled rope that snagged him. Or the deck railings had been damaged earlier, as had been reported. But these versions do not explain Meagher's lack of an apparent struggle to save himself. If he fell on his own, sober or intoxicated, and shouted for help, he was conscious enough to make for the shore, or stay afloat long enough to land on one of the many small islands and sandbars just downstream. The Missouri currents at Fort Benton were strong, but white water they were not. A decent swimmer could make some progress moving to shallow depths, and Meagher was more than a decent swimmer.

A few of Sanders's other recollections give credence, inadvertently, to the assassination theory: Meagher fearing for his life, calling for a gun to defend himself, and suspicion of those skulking around the Bloodiest Block in the West. Why would Meagher, a man whose unerring sense of survival had never failed him through a lifetime of peril, "loudly demand a revolver" if he had not seen killers in the shadows? And the notion that Sanders, fresh from the trip to Washington, where he had manipulated the undoing of all of the legislative work of his archenemy, would join Meagher solely for convivial conversation seems a fabrication at best. Also, Sanders got at least one significant detail wrong: he said he put Meagher to bed on the starboard side of the steamship, facing town. This claim was at odds with all eyewitnesses. If Meagher had fallen from the starboard side, he would have been only a few feet from shore, an easy swim.

How could Sanders be so wrong about the side of the boat where Meagher was put to bed? One explanation emerged a few years later. On May 29, 1913, a newspaper in Missoula printed the startling confession of a man calling himself Frank Diamond. An aging convict, sick and facing death, Diamond told the paper he'd been paid $8,000 by the vigilantes to murder Meagher on the night of July 1, 1867. The blood money was an enormous sum in the day. Diamond said he pushed the governor into the river, then slipped away in the commotion of "Man overboard!" Here was the break the Irish had been waiting for, justification for a half century of suspicion. Did Sanders not know the whereabouts of Meagher's guest room because it was Diamond—bankrolled by the vigilantes—who had been to Meagher's room in his final minutes? And did Sanders concoct a story about Meagher committing suicide to divert any suspicion from his own role in a murder plot? The answers awaited a formal inquiry. But within a few days of the convict's story appearing, Diamond's health recovered. Facing prosecution for a homicide case with no statute of limitations, he recanted the confession, saying he must have been hallucinating.

Finally, Sanders appears to have lied about breaking the news of Meagher's death to the widow. A Catholic priest, not the vigilante leader, notified Libby of her loss, according to several Montana newspapers.

As for motive: Sanders desperately wanted to be the territorial representative to Congress. Meagher stood in the way, and Sanders probably knew nothing of Meagher's last-minute intention to get out of politics. Statehood was on the way eventually, meaning a pair of Senate seats would open up. Had he run, a Democrat from a place where Republicans were a feeble minority, Meagher would have crushed Sanders. He was the best-known man in Montana, and judging by the crowds that turned out for his speeches, the lines snaking down dust-choked wagon roads outside halls that he warmed with his words and his wit, he was revered. Sanders, after being rejected by voters five times in various runs for office, was finally named a U.S. senator in 1890, by Republicans in the Montana legislature. His seat was disputed from the start. He served one term and was ousted in a reelection bid.

Sanders was never forced to explain the many contradictions in his telling of Meagher's final night. By the time the Frank Diamond story broke, it was too late for a prosecutor to formally question Sanders. The vigilante leader had died in 1905—three days after the statue of Thomas Meagher was unveiled in Helena. From that week onward, no governor, legislator, lobbyist or citizen could walk up the steps of the Montana capitol without passing the imposing sculpture of the Irish revolutionary.

Nor could some of them ever forget the mystery surrounding Meagher's death. And so, on June 9, 2012, at the courthouse of the hollowed-out little town of Virginia City, a coroner's inquest was staged as a play, using all the available evidence. Paul Wylie, an attorney, author

and Montana historian, felt the need to close a circle, since no original inquest had ever been done. He assembled a real judge, lawyers and
medical professionals to examine Meagher's last night. Witnesses were
called. Evidence was presented. Closing arguments were made. At the
conclusion, a jury of six was asked to render a verdict. They found that
the governor's death was a homicide, and Wilbur Sanders was the cul-
prit. If true, it meant that Thomas Meagher had lost his life for standing up to people who committed murder in the name of authority.

More than a half century after Meagher was cast in bronze against the
Rocky Mountains, President John F. Kennedy arrived in Ireland to pay
homage to the land of his ancestors. One of them, Patrick Kennedy, a
laborer, had left New Ross, County Wexford, in the worst year of the
famine, the same time that Meagher was sentenced to death by hanging—1848. Like Meagher, Patrick would never see his father again, nor
his brother and sister. When the great-grandson of that exiled Kennedy touched down in 1963, he was greeted as royalty, the Last Prince
of Ireland—"like a rainbow coming off a plane," as one historian wrote
of his arrival on June 26. Kennedy was the first American president to
visit Ireland during his term in office. He was feted at a parade through
the streets of Dublin, riding past statues of the rebel William Smith
O'Brien and the liberator Daniel O'Connell, showered in shredded bus
tickets, used for lack of ticker tape. In New Ross, he ate salmon sand-
wiches with a cousin, and joked that he might be working at the local
factory had Patrick not left for Boston.

"It took 115 years to make this trip," said Kennedy. He was traveling
with a few precious remnants of Thomas Meagher's life, and was mull-
ing a speech that included a section about the general. He wanted to
explain why the words and deeds of an Irishman long dead still mattered.

The rebels of 1848 had done well. The prison sentences, the harassment,
the banishments by the British Empire, had only delayed the careers of
a generation of brilliant Irish. Richard O'Gorman, Meagher's eulogist,
a fugitive, became one of New York's most prominent legal authorities
and a superior court judge. Another Clongowes Wood school friend,
Patrick J. Smyth, was elected to the House of Commons on an Irish

home rule ticket, serving three terms. For his work on behalf of democratic movements worldwide, he was made a Chevalier of the Légion d'Honneur in France.

Kevin O'Doherty, the doctor whose presence was a palliative for Meagher's loneliness, sharing grog and laughs on a bridge touching both of their prison districts in Tasmania, moved to Paris and married his lover, Eva the poet. After being pardoned, he was allowed to return to Dublin, where he became a fellow at the Royal College of Surgeons and set up a practice. But degraded Ireland did not suit him. He and Eva moved to Australia, where he pioneered medical societies, set up hospitals and schools. The couple had eight children.

Charles Gavan Duffy, the editor who was overjoyed by the "thrilling music" of Meagher's voice in 1846 and counseled the lad through the days of the uprising, lived to become a bewigged and honored figure on two continents. He also was elected to the House of Commons, representing New Ross, using his voice in London the same way he used his pen in Dublin—advocating Irish independence. Disgusted at British intransigence, he moved to Australia in 1856. He rose to become the premier of Victoria and the speaker of the Legislative Assembly—a popular and dashing figure among the large population of Irish whose families had been taken to the penal colony in chains. Sir Charles Gavan Duffy was knighted in 1873 by the very monarch, Queen Victoria, who had jailed him in his youth. His book *Four Years of Irish History* stands as the definitive account of the uprising of poets and orators.

The man who had betrayed the Young Ireland leaders, John Donnellan Balfe, spent his remaining years in Tasmania, auctioning his principles to the highest bidder. Denounced at a public dinner not long after Meagher had unmasked him, he was jailed in 1852 for attacking one of his accusers. Balfe was arrested again 1863, for assault. After being elected to the legislature in 1868, Balfe was censured for selling his vote—"a more nefarious transaction cannot be instanced in the miserable annals of parliamentary corruption," one newspaper noted.

John Mitchel, the most gifted writer and most flawed human among the Young Ireland leaders, was released from Fort Monroe in 1865 after spending four and a half months as a prisoner of the United States. A proud racist, he was "a traitor to humanity," in the words of Frederick Douglass. For a brief time after his release, Mitchel was editor of the *New York Daily News*. He moved to Paris, and then was allowed back into Ireland. In 1875 he was elected to Parliament, from Tipperary, even though British authorities said his status as a convicted felon disqualified him. It didn't matter: Mitchel said he would never serve in the British House of Commons. In 1914, his grandson, John P. Mitchel, was elected mayor of New York City at the age of thirty-four.

As for the Meaghers, the elder Thomas Francis always stood by the son whose temperament could not have been more different from his own. While the boy was imprisoned, he had paid his legal fees and was a regular visitor. Though he seldom showed it, his "affection for his son is extreme," his hometown newspaper reported during the days that Thomas awaited execution. The Meagher patriarch lived well into his eighties, dying in 1874. Elizabeth Meagher grew close to the son that her late husband never saw, Thomas Bennett Meagher. On her suggestion, the boy moved to the United States, living with her for a time in New York. He bore an uncanny resemblance to his father. He enrolled at West Point but, showing another family trait, was kicked out of the military academy for multiple demerits. Libby died in 1906, at the age of seventy-five. Young Thomas wandered, moving west, then to the Philippines, where he died in 1909. His son, Thomas Francis Meagher III, lived a quiet life in California, dying in 1943. He is buried in the lovely Napa Valley town of St. Helena.

Two days after landing in Dublin, President Kennedy addressed the parliament of an independent Irish republic—the centerpiece of his visit. It had taken two more rebellions, in 1867, led by the Fenians, and the 1916 Easter Rising, led by a linguist with a love of Gaelic, for the little island to finally break free of the 800-year hold of England.

Meagher's words had been resurrected by leaders of the fight in 1916. His speeches were reprinted, passed around in underground posts, muscled into service before blood was shed. When the rebels took over key government buildings, they read a proclamation in the streets of Dublin: "We declare the rights of the people of Ireland to the ownership of Ireland"—an echo of Meagher's rallying slogan, "Ireland for the Irish." The proclamation was signed by seven men. Within days, those men were captured and imprisoned at Kilmainham Gaol, where Meagher had awaited his execution; a picture of him and Smith O'Brien, shadowed by guards, was still in the archives. One by one, on select days in May, the seven leaders of the Easter Rising were dragged into a graveled courtyard of the jail and shot to death. The last man to be executed, James Connolly, was unable to stand because of wounds to his legs. The killings outraged the Irish in America, the Irish in Europe, the Irish in Australia and millions of others. The executions were followed by an outright war for independence against the exhausted rulers of the British Empire. This conflict ended in 1922 with the establishment of the Irish Free State, consisting of 26 of the island's 32 counties; the 6 in the northeast opted to stay with England. The terms were contentious, and civil war followed, families killing families from the same counties, the same villages where they lived. That fratricide ended in 1923. With the establishment of the Republic of Ireland in 1949, the nation formally severed all ties to the British monarchy and the Commonwealth, and bound itself to a constitution that guaranteed freedom of worship. Gaelic was recognized as the national language, along with English.

Kennedy recalled some of this history, Ireland's misery and Ireland's triumphs, in his speech before the parliament. When he ran for president, many in his own country doubted whether an Irish Catholic could serve a nation of many creeds. In Texas during the campaign, Kennedy minced no words before an audience of Protestant ministers. "I believe in an America where the separation of church and state is absolute," he said, a nation "where no religious body seeks to impose its will directly or indirectly upon the general populace or the public acts of its officials." It sounded remarkably similar to the speech that Meagher, a man of faith, had given in San Francisco, praising the design of a constitution that kept the state out of the affairs of the soul—a reaction to Britain forcing the church of a hated monarchy on the people of Ireland for centuries.

At the time his great-grandfather fled, the Atlantic was "a bowl of bitter tears," Kennedy told his Irish audience, quoting James Joyce. Many tears followed. From 1851 to 1921, nearly 3.8 million people left Ireland for the United States. He noted that Benjamin Franklin had sent leaflets to Irish freedom fighters, that Daniel O'Connell was inspired by George Washington and that the emancipator Abraham Lincoln was influenced by the rebel Robert Emmet. Kennedy's longest anecdote was the story of General Meagher and his Irish Brigade. He recounted the bloodbath at Fredericksburg, a band of 1,200 men going to battle with a pinch of green in their caps, only 280 surviving. And after telling about the immigrants of the New York 69th, Kennedy displayed a present he had brought from the United States—one of the flags from Meagher's Irishmen.

What was it, Kennedy asked, that got so many families through centuries of subjugation, through starvation, through mass eviction, through exile, through Know-Nothing persecutions, epics of tragedy broken only by temporary periods of joy? What was it that made people like Thomas Meagher never lose faith? The "quality of the Irish," the president concluded, is "the remarkable combination of hope, confidence and imagination." In a short few months, Kennedy would be gone, killed by an assassin in Dallas. He left words on that early summer day in Dublin that the Irish recall today—praise for "one of the youngest of nations, and the oldest of civilizations."

The Civil War flag that the president gave to the people of Ireland joined other mementos of Meagher's life in the land of his birth. The lad's clarinet, silenced as an act of schoolboy civil disobedience at Stonyhurst, then used to entertain his cellmates awaiting death at the prison in Clonmel, was put on display in Waterford. Around town, bright banners proclaim, "Birthplace of the Irish Tricolour, First Raised Here by Thomas Francis Meagher in 1848." A large equestrian statue, a match for the one in Montana, was erected in 2004, just off the River Suir at the entrance to the city. This Meagher is tall in the saddle, next to the 1,100-year-old Viking round tower that still holds a cannonball from Cromwell's rampage. A few doors away, a plaque adorns the house of Meagher's birth, now a hotel, with these words: "With my country, I leave my memory." In 2015, the new Waterford Bridge over the river, the longest single-span crossing in Ireland, was named for the favorite son of the nation's oldest city. Across the Atlantic, in the same year, the artist Ron Tunison was commissioned to create a bronze portrait of Meagher. The general's visage will be placed next to the grave of his widow in the country that took him in, at Brooklyn's Green-Wood Cemetery.

It is the living, of course, who need these markers of the dead in order to make sense of their place in this world—more than eighty million people with some Irish blood, most of them no longer looking for a country to call home. For them, memory is not an unwelcome burden but the raw material of stories that will always be passed on, in song, verse or tale, the great survival skill of the Irish.

ACKNOWLEDGMENTS

Tracking a ghost from the Victorian Age across three continents is not the easiest of pursuits. But I've been helped by the keepers of Erin's history among the global Irish diaspora. My roll call of gratitude starts in the home country, where the National Library of Ireland is a fine-functioning storehouse of letters, diaries, photographs, charts and paintings of the nation's past. They made me feel like a Dubliner with a library card. In Waterford, the house where Meagher grew up—now the Granville Hotel—was welcoming, as were the custodians of family artifacts at the Georgian-era Bishop's Palace, an excellent museum. And I was happy to have a professional excuse to visit another part of County Waterford, where my family—on my mother's side—hails from.

Across the Atlantic, the Great Hunger Museum at Quinnipiac University—and its related institute, run by the tireless Christine Kinealy—is a bountiful source of art, letters and assorted firsthand accounts of Ireland's worst tragedy. Dr. Kinealy, whose famine scholarship has broken fresh ground on several fronts, also gave me guidance on Young Ireland and was enthusiastic about this project. Thanks also to Boston's John F. Kennedy Library and Museum for help on the president's family roots and details of his visit to Ireland in 1963. In Manhattan, I'm grateful to the New York Public Library for giving a westerner access to its vast vaults, to the city's Tenement Museum for bringing some of the grittier aspects of the immigrant experience to life, and to the American Irish Historical Society for letting me into its rich interior space on Fifth Avenue. May their doors always be open to citizen scholars. And a tip of the cap to McSorley's, New York's oldest Irish pub. Meagher himself drank there.

In Washington, D.C., the Library of Congress, as usual, proved its worth as the nation's archival mother lode—for photographs, letters and Civil War battle details.

Many kudos to the National Park Service, perennially underfunded if not underappreciated, for ensuring that the Civil War battlefields where Meagher fought—at Fredericksburg, Antietam and Bull Run—are the kinds of solemn and moving experiences that they were for me. And in Richmond, Virginia, the National Battlefield Park was quite helpful.

For the penal colony section, I'm grateful to Professor Stefan Petrow, at the University of Tasmania, for sharing some of his work with me, particularly on the spy John Balfe. Thanks also to the Allport Library and Museum of Fine Arts and the Tasmania Archive and Heritage Office for allowing me to use pictures from their collection. And thanks to the writer Kip Greenthal, a fellow Pacific northwesterner, who shared with me some of her original observations on Tasmania, after a visit, and for a literary supplement that helped when I was trying to find the right tone for this book.

I couldn't have put together the Civil War section, or the part on Montana, without the Huntington Library in San Marino, California. Particularly helpful were the custodians of history at the Munger Research Center there. The Huntington gardens, by the way, are a great diversion from the claustrophobia of indoor research. The Montana Historical Society, in Helena, was most useful in all things related to Acting Governor Meagher. Also, my gratitude to them for documents on the vigilantes. Thanks to Fort Benton, on the Missouri, and Virginia City, the onetime territorial capital, for keeping their stories alive in the streets, in museums, on guided walks and other places of living history. And to Butte, where my great-grandfather lived and died in the glory days of New Ireland—a proud, resilient town. In the Big Sky State, I'm most grateful to Paul Wylie of Bozeman for reaching out to a fellow author. This lawyer/scholar/writer/historian was kind enough to send along a video of the 2012 inquest into the death of Meagher, which he masterfully put together.

The crew at Houghton Mifflin Harcourt was first rate in all the sometimes sausage-making aspects of building a book. Andrea Schulz, the editor in chief when we started this journey (she's now at Viking in a similar role) was a loyal and creative editor—two descriptions that do not always pair with that job title. I'm immensely grateful to her for the collaboration we shared. A surfeit of thanks to Deanne Urmy for bringing out the best in this manuscript, handled with style and intelligence; to publisher Bruce Nichols for keeping the wind at our backs as deadlines loomed; to Larry Cooper for the expert weir of his manuscript editing, filtering out the bad, refining the good; and to the tireless efforts of Carla Gray, Lori Glazer and Megan Wilson—who build bridges for authors to the real world. None of these working relationships would have been possible without the matchmaking skills of my agent and friend Carol Mann.

I owe a debt to those in my circle of early readers and critics, who risked friendship and family slights in service of this epic story. Starting with my wife, Joni Balter, I take a bow to you, and to our kids, Sophie and Casey—now old enough to set their father straight and have it stick. Thanks to Sam Howe Verhovek, who deserves status as an honorary Irishman, and to Tim Golden, whose extraordinary talents in the craft of editing are just starting to blossom.

Finally, my thanks to the late Giovanni Costigan, an Irish-history professor at the University of Washington in Seattle, for his passionate love of the poetry and spirit of a people who were so long under an oppressor's thumb. He lit a fire of pride in many lapsed Irish Americans, myself included.

SOURCE NOTES

INTRODUCTION: LAST DAY — JULY 1, 1867

Most details of the last day of Thomas Francis Meagher (TFM) come from the account of John T. Doran, pilot of the *G. A. Thompson,* who gave a narrative of that day in a letter written on December 16, 1868, to Captain W. F. Lyons, as recorded in Lyons's book *Brigadier General Thomas Francis Meagher,* published by D & J Sadlier & Co., 1869. This includes the quotes "Johnny, they threaten my life in that town" and "There he goes."

Description of Fort Benton, the Missouri River and surrounding area, hours of sunlight and history, from two visits by the author to Fort Benton, Montana.

British authorities looking for Meagher in Fort Benton, from *Fort Benton: World's Innermost Port* by Joel Overholser, Falcon Publishing Co., 1987.

Meagher still a fugitive, from story on Meagher in the *Missoulian,* July 4, 2010.

Vigilantes, from "Montana Vigilantes and the Origin of the 3-7-77," *Montana: The Magazine of Western History,* Spring 2001, and *Montana's Righteous Hangmen: The Vigilantes in Action* by Lew L. Callaway, University of Oklahoma Press, 1997.

Meagher low on money, from a letter, TFM to the territorial auditor, July 15, 1867, on file at Montana Historical Society, Helena.

His net worth on the last day, from the estate, probate court files, Madison County Courthouse, Virginia City, Montana.

His disparagement of moneymaking Americans, from *Lectures of Gov. Thomas Francis Meagher in Montana,* Bruce & Wright Printers, 1867.

TFM and wife never happier, from Doran, as cited in Lyons, *Brigadier General Thomas Francis Meagher.* His love of Libby, and her last days, from "Mrs. Thomas Francis Meagher's Sad Departure from Fort Benton in Sept. 1867" by Ken Robson, *Fort Benton River Press,* August 3, 2005.

Meagher's vanishing "the greatest of Montana mysteries," in view of the *Missoulian,* July 4, 2010.

CHAPTER I: UNDER THE BOOTHEEL

Quote of Chancellor Bowes, from *A History of Modern Ireland* by Giovanni Costigan, Pegasus, 1969.

Saint Patrick traveling with his own brewer, from *Irish America*, April/May 2014.

Penal Laws, reprinted with modern interpretation, from the University of Minnesota Law School, http://library.law.umn.edu/irishlaw/intro.html.

Outlawing the harp, from *A History of Irish Music* by William Grattan Flood, first published 1905. Dodo Press edition, 2008, used here. And *The Irish Harp* by Joan Rimmer, Clo Mercier Publisher, 1977.

Importance of the harp to Irish culture, from *The Melodic Tradition of Ireland* by James R. Cowdery, Kent State University Press, 1990.

Elizabeth and the Irish, from *Elizabeth I* by Anne Somerset, Anchor Books, 2003.

Meagher family history, from "Genealogy, Geography and Social Mobility: The Family Background of Thomas Francis Meagher" by John Mannion, in *Thomas Francis Meagher: The Making of an Irish American*, Irish Academic Press, 2005.

Papal letter, "Laudabiliter," from "Pope Adrian's Bull *Laudabiliter*" by Eleanor Hull, in *A History of Ireland*, Volume 1, Appendix 1, National Library of Ireland, http://www.libraryireland.com/HullHistory/Appendix1a.php.

English pope, from *Adrian IV, the English Pope* by Brenda Bolton and Anne Duggan, Ashgate Press, 2003, with additional information from Costigan, *A History of Modern Ireland*.

Statutes of Kilkenny, from National Library of Ireland, http://www.library ireland.com/HullHistory/StatuteKilkenny2.php.

Henry VIII and Anglican Church, from *Making Ireland British* by Nicholas P. Canny, Oxford University Press, 2001.

The Pale, from *Ireland and Her People* by Thomas W. H. Fitzgerald, Fitzgerald Book Co., 1911.

Trinity, from Costigan, *A History of Modern Ireland*, and the Trinity College website, https://www.tcd.ie/.

Plantation of Ireland, from Costigan, *A History of Modern Ireland*.

Plantation and starvation, from Rutgers University Center for the Study of Genocide and Human Rights, http://www.ncas.rutgers.edu/cghr.

Plantation of Ulster, from *The Plantation of Ulster* by P. Robinson, Ulster Historical Foundation, 2000.

Men thrown overboard, and ordinance, as quoted in *Ireland* by Gustave de Beaumont, originally published in 1839, Harvard University Press edition, 2006.

Cromwell, from Rutgers Center, cited above.

Cromwell officer quote on the Burren, from author visit to Burren National Park.

Cromwell and Drogheda, from "Cromwell and the Drogheda Massacre," www.bbc.co.uk/education.

40,000 deported as slaves, from Rutgers Center, cited above.

Beaumont quote, from his book *Ireland*.

Penal Laws, in their entirety, a project of the University of Minnesota Law School, www.law.umn.edu/irishlaw/subjectlist.html.

Potato, from *The Great Hunger: Ireland, 1845–1849* by Cecil Woodham-Smith, Hamish Hamilton, 1962.

Debunking Sir Walter Raleigh potato origin, from "The Introduction of the Potato into Ireland" by William McNeill, *Journal of Modern History,* September 1949.

Half the families lived in windowless huts, from Woodham-Smith, *The Great Hunger.*

Newfoundland history, from *Newfoundland in the North Atlantic World* by Peter Neary, McGill–Queen's University Press, 1997.

Earliest hurling game in North America, from *Irish America,* February/March 2014.

Meagher's childhood and descriptions of Waterford, from author visit to TFM's home in Waterford, with special thanks to guides at Reginald's Tower and the keepers of Meagher family possessions at Bishop's Palace Museum.

Hanging victim from the Waterford Bridge, from author visit.

Clongowes, including tuition, from *Decies: The Journal of the Waterford Archaeological and Historical Society* 59 (2003).

Clongowes, Meagher's complaint about nothing of Irish history, from *Memoirs of General Thomas Francis Meagher* by Michael Cavanagh, Messenger Press, 1892. Hereafter referred to as *Memoirs.*

Young Meagher's essay on "happy old age," from "A Curious Relic of Thomas Francis Meagher," *Irish Monthly* 14 (1886).

CHAPTER 2: THE BECOMING

Date of TFM's arrival at Stonyhurst, and length of the journey in the mid-nineteenth century, from the Stonyhurst website, http://www.stonyhurst.ac.uk/.

Stonyhurst descriptions, from *Centenary Record: Stonyhurst College, Its Life Beyond the Seas* by Reverend John Gerard, S.J., Marcus Ward and Co., 1894.

More on Stonyhurst, from "Thomas Francis Meagher: His Stonyhurst Years" by David Knight, *Decies* 59, (2003).

Catholic relief in Great Britain, from *Encyclopaedia Britannica,* www.britannica.com.

TFM expelled from Clongowes, from "Pen and Sword: Thomas Francis Meagher and Clongowes College" by James Durney, in County Kildare history journal, www.kildare.ie/library/ehistory/2012/06.

Learning to drink at Clongowes, from *Meagher of the Sword: His Narrative of Events in Ireland in July 1848, Personal Reminiscences of Waterford, Galway and His Schooldays,* edited by Arthur Griffith, M. H. Gill & Son, 1916.

Clarinet and Waterloo story, from an interview TFM gave to the *Hobart Times* (Tasmania), December 7, 1852.

Scope of the British Empire, from *Empire: The Rise and Demise of the British World Order and the Lessons for Global Power* by Niall Ferguson, Basic Books, 2004.

Britain's peak, from *Columbia History of World,* Harper and Row, 1972.

King Lear episode, from *Memoirs.*

Daniel O'Connell, from Costigan, *A History of Modern Ireland.*

TFM's return home, from his "narrative" in Griffith, *Meagher of the Sword.*

Quotes upon arrival in Waterford, ibid.

Waterford population and eligible voters, from *Memoirs.*

"Flaunting and fashionable," ibid.

O'Connell's arrest, feud with Peel, from "Thomas Francis Meagher: Reluctant Revolutionary," in *Thomas Francis Meagher: The Making of an Irish Revolutionary.*

Larger garrison in Ireland than in India, from Woodham-Smith, *The Great Hunger.*

CHAPTER 3: POETRY IN ACTION

Davis, from *Thomas Davis of Ireland: A Biographical Study* by Helen F. Mulvey, Catholic University of America, 2003.

Davis first quote, from his essay "The Library of Ireland," cited in ibid.

Smith O'Brien speech, from *Memoirs.*

Duffy recollections on first meeting TFM, from *Four Years of Irish History, 1845–1849* by Sir Charles Gavan Duffy, Cassell, Petter, Galpin & Co., 1883.

Death of Davis, ibid., and from *Memoirs.*

Jane Elgee (Speranza) disguised as a man, from Duffy, *Four Years of Irish History.*

Speranza quotes on TFM, and poetry in general, from *Mother of Oscar: The life of Jane Francesca Wilde* by Joy Melville, Allison and Busby, 1999.

One acre could feed a family, from author visit to Ireland's Great Hunger Museum, Quinnipiac University, Hamden, Connecticut.

Types of potatoes grown, from St. Mary's Famine History Museum, www.faminemuseum.com.

What will happen to Ireland, question on first notice of potato failure, from Woodham-Smith, *The Great Hunger.*

Lord Mounteagle "alarming" report, ibid.

Frederick Douglass, from "The Black O'Connell" by Christine Kinealy, *Irish America,* October/November 2013, and from "Frederick Douglass's Irish Liberty" by Tom Chaffin, *New York Times,* February 2, 2011.

Prime Minister Peel ousted, from *The Great Shame: The Triumph of the Irish in the English-Speaking World* by Thomas Keneally, Anchor Books, 2000.

Peel "cordially detested" the Irish, from Woodham-Smith, *The Great Hunger.*

Meagher witnessed ships leaving under armed transport, from *Memoirs*.

Death of Thomas Davis, from Duffy, *Four Years of Irish History*.

Meagher speech on Davis, from *The Life and Times of Thomas Francis Meagher* by P. J. Smyth, The Irishman Office, 1867.

Arthur Griffith quote, from the book he edited, *Meagher of the Sword*.

Davis quote, ibid.

Conversation between Meagher and O'Connell, at his home, from an undated letter by TFM on file at Montana Historical Society.

Father Mathew quote, from *Paddy's Lament* by Thomas Gallagher, Harcourt, Brace and Co., 1982.

Alexis de Tocqueville quote, ibid.

Mitchel on famine, and Brits, from *The Last Conquest of Ireland (Perhaps)* by John Mitchel, University College Dublin Press, 2005, first published in 1858.

Meagher "savagery" quote, from *Memoirs*.

Speranza poem, from Melville, *Mother of Oscar*.

O'Doherty writing on hunger scenes he witnessed, cited in *Heart of Exile* by Patsy Adam-Smith, Nelson Publishers, 1986.

Riot in Cork, from the *Cork Examiner*, September 30, 1846.

Deaths at Skibbereen workhouse, from Woodham-Smith, *The Great Hunger*.

Quaker relief, and Routh taking issue with Trevelyan, ibid.

1846 crop biggest ever, from Duffy, *Four Years of Irish History*.

Landlord quote, "what the devil," as reported in the *Freeman's Journal*, July 1846.

Poem on hunger, from the *Nation*, November 8, 1846.

Trevelyan on famine being God's will, from letter of Charles Edward Trevelyan to Lord Mounteagle, October 9, 1846. Thanks to the National Library of Ireland, which has a copy on file, author visit. "Do not encourage," from Woodham-Smith, *The Great Hunger*.

Brits wouldn't keep mortality count, from author interview with Dr. Christine Kinealy, professor of Irish Studies at Quinnipiac University and founding director of Ireland's Great Hunger Institute.

Mitchel quote on "surplus" and Skibbereen, from Mitchel, *The Last Conquest*.

Mitchel meets Meagher, from Smyth, *The Life and Times of Thomas Francis Meagher*.

Mitchel quotes on first meeting Meagher, from Lyons, *Brigadier General Thomas Francis Meagher*.

Duffy arrested, from Duffy, *Four Years of Irish History*.

Meagher's sword speech, from *Memoirs*.

Reaction to speech, from Duffy, *Four Years of Irish History*.

CHAPTER 4: PITCHFORK PADDIES

Conditions in workhouses, and notations, from copies seen by author on visit to Ireland's Great Hunger Museum at Quinnipiac University.

Protestant soup kitchen and "soupers," from *Irish Miscellany* by Dermot McEvoy, Skyhorse Publishing, 2015.

Soyer's recipe for soup, and *Lancet*, from Gallagher, *Paddy's Lament*.

Soup kitchen picture, from the *Illustrated London News*, April 17, 1847.

Prime Minister Russell closing of soup kitchens, and "cannot feed the people," from author interview with Professor Christine Kinealy.

"Hardly been decent," from Woodham-Smith, *The Great Hunger*.

Speranza poem, from *Memoirs*.

Coercion law, crime to be outside, from preface to Griffith, *Meagher of the Sword*.

Doctor stopped by curfew, as quoted in *Memoirs*.

Speranza's feelings on love, from Melville, *Mother of Oscar*.

TFM's home in Waterford, from *Memoirs*. Not voting for his father, from Griffith, *Meagher of the Sword*.

Speech on "burning black field," ibid.

Death rate of 5,000 a day, from the *Nation,* quoted in Duffy, *Four Years of Irish History*.

Bennett quote on famine, from "Transactions of the Central Relief Committee of the Society of Friends," March 16, 1847, National Library of Ireland, http://www.historyireland.com/18th-19th-century-history/the-widows-mite-private-relief-during-the-great-famine/.

Speech on exports, January 13, 1847, from Griffith, *Meagher of the Sword*.

Song based on ban of shamrock, from *Irish America,* April/May 2014.

Clarendon letters to Russell, May 1847, from Woodham-Smith, *The Great Hunger*.

Death of 400,000, from Christine Kinealy, cited in interview in *Irish America,* June/July 2012.

Death of O'Connell, from *Liberator: The Life and Death of Daniel O'Connell* by Patrick Geoghegan, Gill and Macmillan, 2010.

Meagher, others attacked, TFM nearly stabbed, from Griffith, *Meagher of the Sword*.

Information on Balfe the spy, from "Irish Plots with a Tassie Twist" by Leon O'Donnell, in the *Mercury* (Tasmania), www.mercurynie.com/au/print_museum/editors.htm, and from *Australian Dictionary of Biography,* Volume 3, Spring 1969.

Meagher letter to Duffy, dated fall of 1847, in Duffy, *Four Years of Irish History*.

Emigration figures, from Woodham-Smith, *The Great Hunger,* and from *Emigrants and Exiles: Ireland and the Irish Exodus to North America* by Kerby A. Miller, Oxford University Press, 1985.

Orphan girls sent to Australia, Trevelyan comment, from "Lost Children? Irish Famine Orphans in Australia" by Trevor McClaughlin, *History Ireland,* Winter 2000.

Storming of Tipperary, Donegal, etc., from Duffy, *Four Years of Irish History*.

TFM speech in early 1848, "be bold," from Griffith, *Meagher of the Sword.*

Letter to Smith O'Brien, "fix at once the fate of Ireland," from *Memoirs.*

Revolts in France, Sicily, from *The Greater Journey: Americans in Paris* by David McCullough, Simon & Schuster, 2011.

O'Brien and Meagher speeches at Music Hall, March 15, from Duffy, *Four Years of Irish History.*

Balfe the spy, from "John Donnellan Balfe and 1848: A Note on a Confederate Informer" by Takashi Koseki, *Saothar* 23 (1998).

Thomas warned by his father in London, from TFM's account of the uprising in the *Waterford Chronicle,* February 15, 1851.

Experience in France, and Brits intervening, from Duffy, *Four Years of Irish History.*

Beggar in Paris comment, "all drunks," from *Memoirs.*

Advance of British warships, from Woodham Smith, *The Great Hunger.*

Speranza at Music Hall, from *Memoirs.* The witness was Michael Cavanagh.

Flag quote, ibid.

Lone Catholic on Meagher's jury, and the quote, ibid.

Mitchel trial, etc., and journal, from *Jail Journal* by John Mitchel, University Press of Ireland, 1982.

Meagher's reaction to Mitchel sentencing, from *Memoirs.*

Meagher at home, details of the conversation with his father, from Griffith, *Meagher of the Sword.*

Arrest of Meagher at home, and the near riot, from *Memoirs.*

TFM at Slievenamon, speech from *Memoirs.*

Last days of TFM in Waterford, from "A Personal Narrative of 1848," in Griffith, *Meagher of the Sword.*

CHAPTER 5: THE MEANEST BEGGAR IN THE WORLD

Moving in the shadows, reaction to suspension of habeas corpus, quotes to Smyth, all from TFM's "A Personal Narrative," in Griffith, *Meagher of the Sword.*

Young Ireland last days, from *The Young Ireland Rebellion in Limerick* by Laurence Fenton, Mercier Press, 2010.

TFM's movements, from his account in *Memoirs.*

"What a hurry we were in," from Griffith, *Meagher of the Sword.*

Smith O'Brien at Ballingarry, from eyewitnesses, cited in Duffy, *Four Years of Irish History.*

Speranza quote, from Melville, *Mother of Oscar.*

Speranza, *"Jacta Alea Est,"* from the *Nation,* July 29, 1848.

Smith O'Brien betrayed by Balfe, cited in Duffy, *Four Years of Irish History.*

Rock of Cashel description, from author visit to the site. (Well worth it!)

Meagher's last days on the run, including negotiations, and arrest, from a narrative in the *Freeman's Journal,* November 14, 1848. Another account, which backs this one, is "The Final Days of Meagher's Irish Uprising" by William Nolan, in *Thomas Francis Meagher: The Making of an Irish American,* edited by John M. Hearne and Rory T. Cornish, Irish Academic Press, 2006.

Rotten potatoes, from Michael Doheny's unpublished memoir, on file at the National Library of Ireland.

Kilmainham Gaol details, from author visit and private tour of the prison in Dublin. Additional details from *A History of Kilmainham Gaol,* published by Ireland's Office of Public Works, 1995.

Visit of Meagher's father, working on a deal, from "The Social Origins and Family Connections of Thomas Francis Meagher" by J. Mannion, *Decies* 59 (2003).

Meagher on regrets, from *Memoirs.*

Smith O'Brien comments at trial, and order of trials, ibid.

Meagher at trial, ibid.

Speranza visits, from Melville, *Mother of Oscar.*

Meagher trial, sergeant's testimony, from Griffith, *Meagher of the Sword.*

Speranza came to see him, from Melville, *Mother of Oscar.*

Meagher on Saturday night of verdict, from the *Nation,* no date, reprinted in Griffith, *Meagher of the Sword.*

TFM letter to Waterford friend, November 9, 1848, at the National Library of Ireland.

Speranza and Duffy, from Melville, *Mother of Oscar.*

Speranza and Oscar Wilde, etc., from "Speranza, the Hope of the Irish Nation" by Christine Kinealy, paper presented in 2008, later revised and published in the Oscholars Library, www.oscholars.com/TO/Appendix/Library/Speranza1.htm.

Global pressure to pardon prisoners, from *William Smith O'Brien and His Irish Revolutionary Companions in Penal Exile* by Blanche M. Touhill, University of Missouri Press, 1981.

Smyth visit, observations, from Smyth, *The Life and Times of Thomas Francis Meagher.*

Description of Meagher in jail, from an undated piece in the *Dublin Nation,* quoted in Lyons, *Brigadier General Thomas Francis Meagher.*

Plot to rescue them, ibid. Lyons claims that he was a participant in the ill-fated rescue.

Commutation, from Duffy, *Four Years of Irish History,* and from *Memoirs.*

Letter to Dillon, undated except year, 1848, courtesy National Library of Ireland.

Sentence commuted, from *Memoirs.*

Last letter, ibid.

John Lennon family, from *Tune In: The Beatles, All These Years,* Volume 1, by Mark Lewisohn, Crown Archetype, 2013.

Final farewell, Smith O'Brien crying, off Waterford, from *Memoirs.*

CHAPTER 6: ISLAND OF THE DAMNED

Description of the journey to Tasmania, from Smith O'Brien's letters and MacManus's journal, both quoted in various issues of the *Nation*, but primarily from TFM, "Narrative of the Penal Voyage to Tasmania," a long letter to Duffy written in February 1850 and reprinted in serial form in the *Nation*.

Mitchel quote "brave men," from Mitchel, *The Last Conquest.*

Meagher poem, from *Young Ireland in Exile* by Reverend J. H. Cullen, Talbot Press, 1928.

Homesick, daydreaming, from TFM, "Recollections of Waterford," in Griffith, *Meagher of the Sword.*

Figures on emigration. The numbers vary, but this one—1.8 million to North America—is from a scholar on exiles, Kerby A. Miller. All emigration figures used here are from his book *Emigrants and Exiles.*

17,000 died in the crossing, from Woodham-Smith, *The Great Hunger.*

African slave death rate, from the Trans-Atlantic Slave Trade Database, http://www.slavevoyages.org/tast/index.faces.

"The smallest nail," etc., from Miller, *Emigrants and Exiles.*

Number of Irish slaves sent to Barbados, from *To Hell or Barbados: The Ethnic Cleansing of Ireland* by Sean O'Callaghan, Brandon, 2000.

Mitchel quote, "the sun never sets," from Mitchel, *Jail Journal.*

Cape Town, plans to go ashore quashed, from Smith O'Brien journal, 1849, cited in Touhill, *William Smith O'Brien.*

First fleet, and quote by Robert Hughes, from his book *Fatal Shore: The Epic of Australia's Founding*, Alfred A. Knopf, 1986.

Bad reputation of Van Diemen's Land, and quote from Lake Sorell, ibid.

Between hell and earth quote, from *The Irish in Australia* by James Francis Hogan, Robertson & Co., 1888.

Earl Grey and Denison, ticket-of-leave and gentlemanly oblivion, from an Irish website devoted to the history of all exiles and emigrants, http://www.from-ireland.net/.

TFM descriptions of the island, from "Narrative of the Penal Voyage to Tasmania," letter to Duffy, later published in the *Nation.*

TFM descriptions of Campbell Town and Ross, ibid.

TFM quote on Ireland, "I am with her still," from Cullen, *Young Ireland in Exile.*

TFM depressed, no future, letter to O'Brien, December 16, 1849, from William Smith O'Brien Papers, National Library of Ireland.

Meagher, recounting the depth of his depression and how he had changed, letter to O'Doherty, January 2, 1851, from Cullen, *Young Ireland in Exile.*

"My books, my pen and my horse," letter from TFM to Smith O'Brien, May 11, 1850, William Smith O'Brien Papers, National Library of Ireland.

Meagher's willful delusions, from speech Meagher gave on St. Patrick's Day, 1866, in Virginia City, Montana. Reprinted in *Lectures of Gov. Thomas Francis Meagher in Montana.*

Mitchel's fate at sea, from *Jail Journal*.

Smith O'Brien, failing health, from *To Solitude Consigned: The Tasmanian Journal of William Smith O'Brien*, Crossy Press, 1955.

Smith O'Brien quote, ibid.

Meeting at the bridge, from Griffith, *Meagher of the Sword*.

O'Donoghue on vices, from letter to his wife, printed in the *Nation*, April 27, 1850. His sexual romp, Martin to O'Doherty letters, National Library of Ireland.

Meeting on the bridge, from *The Irish Exiles in Australia* by Thomas J. Kiernan, Clonmore and Reynold, 1954.

Smith O'Brien and the teenage girl, from Keneally, *The Great Shame*.

New Yorkers help, from the *New York Tribune*, October 12, 1850.

Millard Fillmore appeals to Brits and says prisoners welcome in U.S., from "Men of Honour? The Escape of the Young Irelanders from Van Diemen's Land" by Stefan Petrow, *Journal of Australian Colonial History* 7 (2005). Professor Petrow was most kind in sending me his scholarship on the Young Irelanders down under.

Smith O'Brien's escape, from a story in the *Limerick Chronicle*, undated except 1850, and a reprinting of the transcript of a court hearing on the escape that first ran in a Hobart paper, the *Irish Exile*. Additional details from Cullen, *Young Ireland in Exile*.

Smith O'Brien letter on depression, and Governor Denison's feelings after the thwarted escape, from Adam-Smith, *Heart of Exile*.

CHAPTER 7: THE TRAITOR OF TASMANIA

Balfe, from *Judas in Tasmania* by Stefan Petrow, Crossing Press, 1995.

Meagher, typical day at Lake Sorell, and his life without purpose, from an undated letter (though several references indicate that it's early 1851) to Colman O'Loghlen, quoted in Adam-Smith, *Heart of Exile*.

Meagher Sr. scolding son on Smith O'Brien escape, from Touhill, *William Smith O'Brien*.

Meagher meeting Dr. Hall and Catherine, the dialogue, from *The Life and Times of Thomas Francis Meagher* by Reg. A. Watson, Anglo-Saxon-Keltic Society, 1988.

Mitchel, first diary entry on hearing news of being sent to Van Diemen's Land, February 13, 1850, *Jail Journal*.

Mitchel's description of the place, March 8, 1850, ibid.

Mitchel's description of the population, April 30, 1850, ibid.

Reunion, from Mitchel diary entry, April 15, 1850, ibid.

Mitchel's description of flora and fauna being foreign, July 30, 1851, ibid.

TFM leading "The Bells of Shandon," from Cullen, *Young Ireland in Exile*.

Harsh sentence of the three, and O'Doherty warning TFM, ibid.

Balfe ghostwriting, and his job as deputy comptroller, from *Australian Dictionary of Biography*, Volume 3 (1969).

Balfe's secret uncovered, from undated letter from O'Donoghue to Meagher, Montana Historical Society.

Meagher outs Balfe in a series of letters. Fascinating. This has been overlooked by many scholars of Young Ireland. I found the evidence in three sources: the quote from Meagher in his role as Virginius is from the *Launceston Examiner* (Tasmania), December 7, 1864, recounting the whole affair; in Touhill's *William Smith O'Brien;* and in a book published in 1885, a memoir by a Tasmanian newspaper editor, Henry Button, *Flotsam and Jetsam,* in which Button says he was "personally aware" that TFM was Virginius, http://archive.org/stream/flotsamjetsamflooobuttiala/flotsamjetsamflooobuttiala_djvu.txt.

Duffy starting to piece it together, from O'Donnell, "Irish Plots with a Tassie Twist."

Meagher quote on Balfe and Tara Hill, from Petrow, *Judas in Tasmania.*

TFM and Bennie, from Kiernan, *The Irish Exiles in Australia.*

Smith O'Brien journal disapproval, from his journal, National Library of Ireland.

Martin disapproves, from Watson, *The Life and Times of Thomas Francis Meagher.*

TFM pushes ahead, acknowledges disapproval, from undated letter to O'Doherty, Thomas F. Madigan Papers, New York Public Library.

Meagher on his happy bride, from letter to O'Doherty, August 15, 1851, ibid.

Mitchel description of a sunburnt Meagher, from Cullen, *Young Ireland in Exile.*

Mrs. Mitchel observations on the young married couple, from letter, July 21, 1855. Letters of Mrs. John Mitchel, 1851–1855, New York Public Library.

Meagher starting to chafe at life at Lake Sorell, from letter to Duffy, undated but from 1851, Montana Historical Society.

TFM quotes on being useless, letter, August 15, 1851, from him to Mrs. Connell, from a University of Tasmania website devoted to the rebels, www.utas.edu.au/young-irelanders/their-story/.

Meagher writing against Balfe, ibid.

Denison warning about the perils of democracy, from *A History of Tasmania, from Its Discovery in 1642 to the Present Time* by James Fenton, Geo. Robertson and Co., 1884.

Denison warning Earl Grey of Irish stirring up trouble, from his correspondence, cited in Touhill, *William Smith O'Brien.*

Irish winning over the island, etc., from Petrow, "Men of Honour?"

MacManus escape, from Touhill, *William Smith O'Brien.*

Meagher longing to live under a flag he could love and serve, letter, May 21, 1851, to a neighbor, Dease, as quoted by Petrow, "Men of Honour?"

Meagher escape plan, re Bennie, from his note to Elizabeth Townsend, telling her the story of his life, January 2, 1855, Montana Historical Society.

Meagher description of giving up parole, from *Memoirs.*

Further details of Meagher escape, formal note, reprinted in the *New York Times,* June 7, 1852.

Order to arrest Meagher, one Irishman refused, from Jenny Mitchel letter, February 22, 1852, New York Public Library.

CHAPTER 8: FLIGHT

Meagher's escape. His own account, backed by witnesses, from a letter he sent to the *New York Times,* written on June 5, 1852, and published on June 7.

"I am O'Meagher," from a contemporaneous account, *South Australian Register,* March 8, 1852, republishing a story from the *Launceston Chronicle* (Tasmania).

Meagher's account of the ten days he spent on Waterhouse Island, from "Six Weeks in the South Pacific," his story of the escape, printed serially in the *Irish News,* April 9, April 14 and May 21, 1859.

Papers rooting for Meagher, quoted in the *Nation,* May 22, 1852.

Escape stories of other convicts, from "On the Run—Daring Convict Escapes," an exhibit of the state library of New South Wales, Australia. http://www.sl.nsw.gov.au/events/exhibitions/2006/ontherun/docs/ontherun_guide.pdf.

The end of transportation, from Fenton, *A History of Tasmania.*

CHAPTER 9: HOME AND AWAY

The day Meagher landed, from *New York Times,* May 29, 1852.

Population, from Census of the State of New York, 1855.

Chant of "hot corn" girls, from *The City in Slang: New York Life and Popular Speech* by Irving W. Allen, Oxford University Press, 1993.

Price of a room and brewery description, from "The Dens of Death," *New York Daily Tribune,* June 13, 1850.

Five Points, Dickens's description and tourists "slumming," from "Gangs of New York: Fact vs. Fiction" by Ted Chamberlain, *National Geographic News,* March 24, 2003, news.nationalgeographic.com.

Five Points, more details, no grass or trees, from *American Metropolis: A History of New York City* by George J. Lankevich, NYU Press, 1998.

Depiction of New York in 1852, including population figures and ethnic groups, from *The New York Irish,* edited by Ronald H. Bayor and Timothy J. Meagher, Johns Hopkins University Press, 1996.

The brewery, and New York politics in 1852, from *New York City Mayors* by Ralph J. Caliendo, Exlibris Corp., 2010.

Highest death rate, ibid.

Immigrants came from more than 20,000 villages, from *Machine Made: Tammany Hall and the Creation of Modern American Politics* by Terry Golway, Liveright, 2013.

Volume of manure swept into East River, and "pigs and Patricks" together, from *Taming Manhattan: Environmental Battles in the Antebellum City* by Catherine McNeur, Harvard University Press, 2014.

Anticipation of great things for Meagher, from the *Boston Pilot*, quoted in Keneally, *The Great Shame.*

Greeting O'Gorman and Dillon, from *Memoirs.*

More on how TFM met old friends at law office, from *Thomas Francis Meagher: A Memoir in Four Parts* by Gerald R. Lalor, handwritten ms. Thanks to the American Irish Historical Society, New York, for allowing me to thumb through it.

New York under British during the Revolutionary War, from Lankevich, *American Metropolis.*

Cavanagh greets TFM, and the reception of the 69th, from *Memoirs.*

Reaction to Meagher in America, from the *New York Times,* May 29, 1852, and the *Irish American,* June 19, 1851.

Quotes from the *Nation,* reprinted in *Memoirs.*

Brooklyn Common Council resolution, from the *New York Times,* June 28, 1852.

Speech at the Astor House, from *Memoirs.*

Smith O'Brien reaction, from letter, March 15, 1851, Letters of William Smith O'Brien, National Library of Ireland.

Loss of baby, from *Memoirs.*

Burial of baby, from http://www.tasmaniangeographic.com/iris-exiles-thomas-o-meagher.

Meagher and Smyth, Fourth of July, from *Memoirs.*

Meagher oath and intention to become a citizen, ibid.

The Know-Nothings and riots, from "Nativist Riots of 1844" by Zachary M. Schrag, in *Encyclopedia of Greater Philadelphia,* Rutgers University Press, 2013.

Peak of Know-Nothing membership, from Golway, *Machine Made.*

Father De Smet's letters on the Know-Nothings: two letters, August 2, 1854, and November 28, 1854, from *Life, Letters and Travels of Father Pierre-Jean De Smet,* Harper, 1905.

Know-Nothing song about Meagher, from *Eccentric Nation: Irish Performance in Nineteenth-Century New York City* by Stephen Albert Rohs, Fairleigh Dickinson University Press, 2009.

Speech at Metropolitan Hall, huddling with President Pierce, from *Memoirs.*

TFM family visit, including Bennie, dates and details, ibid.

"It is said they do not suit," from Adam-Smith, *Heart of Exile.*

Death of Catherine Meagher, dates, from *Memoirs.*

O'Donoghue's drunken fight at TFM's birthday party, from the *New York Herald,* August 6, 1853.

Details of escape and death of O'Donoghue, from Touhill, *William Smith O'Brien.*

Details of Mitchel escape, and his comments on Van Diemen's Land, from his *Jail Journal,* and ibid.

Mitchel's arrival in New York, from Touhill, *William Smith O'Brien.*

Mitchel showing anti-black and anti-Semitic feelings, from Duffy, *Four Years of Irish History.*

Jenny Mitchel letter on slaves, from her correspondence, April 20, 1854, on file at New York Public Library.

Mitchel letter on "healthy negroes," from *John Mitchel: Irish Nationalist, Southern Secessionist* by Bryan P. McGovern, University of Tennessee Press, 2009.

The pardon, from Touhill, *William Smith O'Brien.*

Meagher's sadness at never seeing Ireland, "homeless exile," from letter to Elizabeth Townsend, January 2, 1855, Montana Historical Society.

CHAPTER 10: IDENTITY

Meagher's drinking, from personal observations by James Stephens, "Diary of an Irish Patriot," numerous dates, courtesy New York Public Library.

Father's declaration of being a teetotaler, from the *Waterford Chronicle,* July 14, 1847.

Electoral power of Know-Nothings, from Golway, *Machine Made.*

1855 letter from Abraham Lincoln to Joshua Speed on Know-Nothings, from "The Other Emancipation Proclamation" by Adam Goodheart, in the *New York Times: Disunion: Modern Historians Revisit and Reconsider the Civil War,* Black Dog & Leventhal Publishers, 2013. Hereafter referred to as *Disunion.*

Letter to O'Brien on church, from Hearne and Cornish, *Thomas Francis Meagher: The Making of an Irish American.*

Attacks on Meagher, from the *Freeman's Journal,* July 5, 1854.

The fight, all the details, between TFM and McMaster, from the *New York Times,* July 19, 1854.

Meagher humbled, and on "time to be let down," from letter to W. E. Robinson, undated but 1855, courtesy New-York Historical Society.

Train wreck, details of TFM's heroism, from a witnesses quoted in the *New York Times,* November 2, 1854.

Meagher falls in love, from *Memoirs.*

Townsend family background, from obituary of Peter Townsend, *New York Sun,* September 27, 1885.

Disinherit, from the *New York Times,* November 16, 1854.

Meagher's letter to Elizabeth telling all, January 2, 1855, on file at the Montana Historical Society. Here also is his description of himself as a "homeless exile."

TFM oratorical powers, from the *Sacramento Daily Union,* January 27, 1854.

Marriage date and minor details, from the *New York Times,* November 15, 1855.

CHAPTER II: THE FEVER

Kansas battles, from *Bleeding Kansas, Bleeding Missouri,* edited by Jonathan Earle and Diane Mutti Burke, University of Kansas Press, 2013.

Lawrence, Kansas, details, descriptions, etc., from author visit to Lawrence and the hotel that was burned.

Senator Sumner beating, from "The Crimes Against Sumner" by William Gienapp, *Civil War History,* September 1979.

Dred Scott quotes of Chief Justice Taney, from the *Scott v. Sandford* decision.

Value of cotton, productivity, from author visit to exhibit at the American Civil War Museum at Tredegar, Richmond, Virginia.

Senator Tombs quote, from "Moses' Last Exodus" by Adam Goodheart, in *Disunion.*

Lincoln adrift, decides to run for Senate, quotes, from *Abraham Lincoln: A Life* by Michael Burlingame, Johns Hopkins University Press, 2008.

Decline in black population of Five Points, from Bayor and Meagher, *The New York Irish.*

O'Connell quote on slavery in Boston, from *The Harp and the Eagle: Irish-American Volunteers in the Union Army* by Susannah J. Ural, NYU Press, 2006.

Meagher position on slavery, from the *Irish News,* reprinted in the *New York Daily Tribune,* August 27, 1856.

Meagher and Smith O'Brien exchange views on slavery, from *Letters on Our National Struggle* by Thomas Francis Meagher, public domain reprint, letter to the editor of the *Dublin Citizen,* September 26, 1863, wherein he recounts the exchange.

Lincoln quote on Know-Nothings, from an 1856 speech, quoted in *The Civil War: A Narrative,* Volume 1: *Fort Sumter to Perryville* by Shelby Foote, Random House, 1958.

Description of *Irish News,* from author perusal of a year's issues, beginning in 1856. Courtesy American Irish Historical Society, New York.

Proposal to ship Irish children to Protestant families, from Golway, *Machine Made.*

Thomas Jefferson quote, from author visit to the Jefferson Memorial, Washington, D.C.

Letter from Mitchel on slavery, August 8, 1857, from McGovern, *John Mitchel: Irish Nationalist, Southern Secessionist.*

Meagher advice to tenement Irish, from the *Irish News,* July 5, 1856.

Mitchel letter from Tennessee, undated, from Adam-Smith, *Heart of Exile.*

Meagher on his wife, from letter to Smith O'Brien, August 8, 1856, from the Correspondence of William Smith O'Brien, National Library of Ireland.

Meagher on separation of church and state, and vitality of American diversity, from a speech given in San Francisco, January 24, 1854, reprinted in Lyons, *Brigadier General Thomas Francis Meagher.*

Meagher speech on "festival of memory," from the *New York Times,* March 18, 1855.

Lincoln at the Cooper Union, from the National Park Service website, www .nps.gov/liho/historyculture/cooperunionaddress.htm.

Fernando Wood, from Lankevich, *American Metropolis.*

Mitchel a "formidable monster," from Adam-Smith, *Heart of Exile.*

Frederick Douglass on no prejudice in Ireland, from Kinealy, "The Black O'Connell."

Douglas on hardened attitudes, from "Frederick Douglass in Ireland," in the *Irish Echo,* February 16, 2001.

Michael Corcoran, from "Colorful and Gallant: General Michael Corcoran" by John J. Concannon, from his monograph written for the unveiling of a new gravestone for Corcoran in 1990.

Meagher comments on Corcoran, from *Harper's Weekly,* October 20, 1860, and from Ural, *The Harp and the Eagle.*

Meagher letter on being yesterday's novelty, from a letter in September 1858 to a Meagher club, as quoted in "Thomas Francis Meagher and John Mitchel" by Joseph Jude Rzeppa, M.A. thesis, Texas Christian University, 2007.

Meagher to Smith O'Brien, "I've become a spectator," letter, August 15, 1859, William Smith O'Brien Papers, National Library of Ireland.

Lincoln in New York, speech, from National Park Service transcript. Details of the speech may be found on the Cooper Union website, www.cooper.edu .about/history.

Presidential election outcome of 1860. I relied on the American Presidency Project, which has good state-by-state numbers: http://www.presidency.ucsb .edu/showelection.php?year=1860.

Slavery in the Confederate States Constitution, http://avalon.law.yale .edu/19th_century/csa_csa.asp.

Quote from Davis, number of slaves owned by him, from *Embattled Rebel: Jefferson Davis as Commander in Chief* by James M. McPherson, Penguin, 2014.

Davis and liberty cap, http://www.aoc.gov/blog/liberty-cap-art-us-capitol.

Quote from Confederate vice president on slavery, from Foote, *The Civil War,* Volume 1.

"Nigger better than an Irishman," from the *Albany Argus,* September 7, 1860, quoted in *Battle Cry of Freedom: The Civil War Era* by James M. McPherson, Oxford University Press, 1988.

CHAPTER 12: WAR

Fort Sumter on the eve of war, from National Park Service handbook at Fort Sumter National Monument, Department of the Interior, 1984, and author visit.

Strike a blow, from McPherson, *Battle Cry of Freedom.*

Quote from London *Times,* ibid.

Mitchel fired one of the first shots, from the *Charleston Mercury,* April 13, 1861.

Whitman's reaction, from "How Manhattan Drum-Taps Led" by Tom Chaffin, in *Disunion.*

Meagher making up his mind what to do, the conversation, from *Memoirs.*

Meagher's ad, reprinted in ibid.

Southern newspaper critical of Meagher, from the *Staunton* (Virginia) *Spectator,* May 14, 1861.

"Beauty and booty," from a flier on display at Manassas National Battlefield Park, Virginia, author visit.

Meagher and formation of Irish Zouaves, from the *New York Times,* May 17, 1861.

Sherman quote, from Foote, *The Civil War,* Volume 1.

Sherman background, from *Fierce Patriot* by Robert L. O'Connell, Random House, 2014.

Sherman on "no cohesion," from *Memoirs of William T. Sherman,* Penguin Classics, 2000.

Soldiers "gathered from the sewers," from the *Raleigh Banner,* as quoted in Foote, *The Civil War,* Volume 1.

Lincoln in camp, Meagher view of Sherman, blessing of a cannon, all from *Memoirs.*

March from Fort Corcoran to Bull Run, from *The Irish Brigade in the Civil War* by Joseph G. Bilby, Da Capo Press, 1995, and from *The Last Days of the 69th in Virginia* by Thomas Francis Meagher, quoted in *Memoirs.*

CHAPTER 13: FIRST BLOOD

The details of the battle are taken, in the early part, from *Memoirs of William T. Sherman,* public domain publication and http://www.gutenberg.org/files/4361/4361-h/4361-h.htm.

Haggerty's death, ibid.

Haggerty's life, from "Irish in the American Civil War," www.irishamericancivilwar.com.

Meagher's description of Haggerty is from a funeral oration TFM gave in New York, August 1861, cited in *Memoirs.*

Battle details, from Meagher, *The Last Days of the 69th in Virginia,* cited in his *Memoirs.*

More details of battle, from "Report of Captain James Kelly, 69th," Civil War Official Records, Series 1, Volume 2.

Description of the battle site, from author visit to Manassas National Battlefield Park, Virginia.

Quotes on battle, from the *New York Times,* July 26, 1861.

Meagher knocked from his horse, rescued, from *Memoirs,* and from Bilby, *The Irish Brigade in the Civil War.*

Corcoran missing, forms rear guard, from his letter, July 24, 1861, reprinted in *Memoirs.*

Stonewall Jackson quote, "We have them whipped," from the official story at the National Park Service battlefield site, author visit.

Congressman Ely captured, from "Civil War Trust: Spectators Witnesses to History at Manassas," www.civilwar.org.

Quote from rebel soldier after capturing Ely, from *Fighting for the Confederacy: The Personal Recollections of Edward Porter Alexander,* University of North Carolina Press, 1989.

Praising Meagher as heroic, from the *New York Times,* July 26, 1861.

Officers praising Meagher, reprinted in *Memoirs.*

Whitman describing bedraggled Union soldiers, from *The Greatest Brigade* by Thomas J. Craughwell, Crestline, 2012, quoting from the *Brooklyn Standard.*

Horace Greeley, quoted in Foote, *The Civil War,* Volume 1.

Meagher confronts Sherman, Lincoln reaction, from *Memoirs of William T. Sherman.*

CHAPTER 14: THE CALL, THE FALL

Details of Michael Corcoran's capture, from his letter, July 24, 1861, reprinted in *Memoirs.*

Corcoran's ordeal in prison, threatened with hanging, from "Irish Identity— Michael Corcoran," www.irishidentiy.com/geese/stories/corcoran.htm.

Meagher turns down two offers, including one by Frémont, from TFM's letter of August 5, 1861, reprinted in *Memoirs.*

Idea for an Irish brigade, from the *New York Times,* August 26, 1861.

Speech at Jones's Wood, reprinted in *Memoirs.* Reporting about the event and transcript of the speech, from the *New York Times,* August 30, 1861.

Cotton statistics, from McPherson, *Battle Cry of Freedom.*

Meagher speech in Boston's Music Hall, from the *New York Times,* September 24, 1861, and excerpts reprinted in Lyons, *Brigadier General Thomas Francis Meagher,* although Lyons has an incorrect date for the speech.

Yankee girl, quoted in *Thomas Francis Meagher: Irish Rebel, American Yankee, Montana Pioneer* by Gary R. Forney, Exlibris, 2004.

"a word of talismanic power," from the *Irish-American,* quoted in Bilby, *The Irish Brigade in the Civil War.*

Meagher promise to never leave, at Fort Schuyler, from the *New York Times,* October 14, 1861.

Meagher, three cheers for Mitchel, from *Memoirs.*

McClellan quotes, from McPherson, *Battle Cry of Freedom.*

Largest army on earth, McClellan attitude toward Lincoln, from *Lincoln and*

McClellan: The Troubled Partnership Between a President and His General by John C. Waugh, Palgrave Macmillan, 2010.

Camp life, from *Memoirs of Chaplain Life* by Very Rev. William Corby, La Monte, O'Donnell & Co., 1893.

Meagher appointment as general, and his uniform, from Bilby, *The Irish Brigade in the Civil War.*

Meagher's drinking, his highs and lows, ibid., and from Corby, *Memoirs of Chaplain Life.*

CHAPTER 15: SUMMER OF SLAUGHTER

Union position, from Bilby, *The Irish Brigade in the Civil War,* and McPherson, *Battle Cry of Freedom.*

Quote on Meagher's love of racy humor, from *The Irish Brigade and Its Campaigns* by Capt. D. P. Conyngham, Cameron and Ferguson, 1866.

Arrival of Kavanagh, from *Memoirs.*

Cannon fire while they waited, from TFM letter to Samuel L. M. Barlow, April 24, 1862, courtesy Huntington Library, San Marino, California.

Background on Kavanagh and details of steeplechase and weapons, from *Memoirs.*

Called to battle, from Lyons, *Brigadier General Thomas Francis Meagher,* with Meagher's description of the march and battle.

Crawling through the mud, sleeping with dead, finding soldiers in morning, all from Meagher's own account in *Memoirs.*

General Sumner, "How Irishmen fight," from *Memoirs.*

Description of initial fighting, from Conyngham, *The Irish Brigade and Its Campaigns.*

McClellan compliments the Irish, from *Memoirs.*

McClellan, to his wife, privately seething, from *The Longest Night: A Military History of the Civil War* by David J. Eicher, Simon & Schuster, 2002.

Irish Brigade casualties, from Report of Brigadier General Thomas Francis Meagher, June 4, 1862, in Official Records.

Lincoln fuming about McClellan, from Waugh, *Lincoln and McClellan.*

Medical scene, implements, surgery, what Meagher saw, from Corby, *Memoirs of Chaplain Life.*

Malaria, horses burned, hundreds died, ibid.

Culture clash, Yankees join Irish, and quote, from www.historynet.com/the-irish-brigade-fought-in-americas-civil-war.htm.

First day of Seven Days Battles, from TFM's official report, cited above.

Larger strategy, Robert E. Lee quote, from Foote, *The Civil War,* Volume 1.

Irish at Gaines's Mill, reinforcing Porter, from story in the *New York Times,* June 30, 1862.

Captain Lyons's assessment, from Lyons, *Brigadier General Thomas Fran-*

cis Meagher. Also, Meagher repeatedly said the Battle of Gaines's Mill was the high-water mark of the Irish Brigade.

Union dead stripped of clothes, and Union wounded buried alive, from eyewitness account of Father Corby, *Memoirs of Chaplain Life.*

Battle with Louisiana Tigers, from *Memoirs,* and general information on that brigade, from "The Terrifying Tigers" by Terry L. Jones, in *Disunion.*

Irish brigade at Malvern Hill, other details, from Report of Brigadier General Thomas Francis Meagher, Series 1, Volume 11.

Additional brigade details, mutton, summoned to battle, from Lyons, *Brigadier General Thomas Francis Meagher.*

"Not war—murder," D. H. Hill quoted in McPherson, *Battle Cry of Freedom.*

Union and Confederate total casualties in Virginia. Figures vary; I used the *New York Times,* taking into account contemporary scholarship in *Disunion.*

Brigade casualties, from TFM official report, quoted in the *New York Times,* July 26, 1862.

First time more people killed by artillery, from McPherson, *Battle Cry of Freedom.*

McClellan, "We want many more Irishmen," from *The Civil War Papers of George B. McClellan,* edited by Stephen W. Sears, Da Capo Press, 1992.

CHAPTER 16: REASONS TO LIVE AND DIE

Meagher at home, from *Memoirs.*

Toffs paying $20 to recruits, ibid.

Protests against draft, including words on the banner, quoted in McPherson, *Battle Cry of Freedom.*

Meagher speech at 7th Regiment Armory, from the *New York Times,* July 26, 1862.

Lincoln, "God bless the Irish flag," from Bilby, *The Irish Brigade in the Civil War.*

Meagher quote on "equal to him in his allegiance," from "The Fighting Irish Brigade," the *New York Times,* December 12, 2012, later collected in *Disunion.*

Archbishop Hughes declaration on abolition, from Foote, *The Civil War,* Volume 1.

Soldier writes home on how sacrifice made them American, from an unsigned letter that ran in the *Irish American,* October 5, 1862.

Quotes from Meagher's speech at the armory come from a transcript that ran in the *New York Times,* July 26, 1862, except for the reading of Donovan's letter and the description of the Irish prince, which comes from Conyngham, *The Irish Brigade and Its Campaigns.*

Meagher letter to Lincoln, July 30, 1862, quoted in Forney, *Thomas Francis Meagher.*

Death of Emmet, and Meagher's reaction in a letter, from the *New York Herald,* August 11, 1862.

Lee's master plan, from Foote, *The Civil War,* Volume 1.

Ate well at Richmond, ate poorly on march north, and the dust, all from Corby, *Memoirs of Chaplain Life.*

Battle plan at Antietam, from Foote, *The Civil War,* Volume 1.

Irish at Antietam, from Meagher's report, September 30, 1862, in Official Records.

Father Corby administering blanket absolution, and within twenty minutes half shot down, from Corby, *Memoirs of Chaplain Life.*

Death of John Kavanagh, from the *New York Times,* September 25, 1862.

Additional details of Antietam, and description of the area, from author visit to Antietam National Battlefield, Sharpsburg, Maryland.

Number and timing of all casualties in the battle, and quotes from Lincoln and McClellan before the battle, from the National Park Service, http://www .nps.gov/anti/historyculture/upload/Battle%20history.pdf.

Details of deaths, by bayonet, drowning, etc., from witness, Conyngham, *The Irish Brigade and Its Campaigns.*

Meagher on "acres of slain and dying," letter to Samuel L. M. Barlow, October 1, 1862, from Samuel L. M. Barlow Collection, Huntington Library.

Irish casualties, Meagher's account, from Report of Brigadier General Thomas Francis Meagher, September 18, 1862, in Official Records.

Meagher letter to Libby, October 1, 1862, quoted in Keneally, *The Great Shame.*

CHAPTER 17: THE GREEN AND THE BLUES

Men cold and stealing turnips, from Conyngham, *The Irish Brigade and Its Campaigns.*

Opening scene, TFM drunk, and drinking in general, from *My Life in the Irish Brigade: The Civil War Memoirs of Private William McCarter,* Savas Publishing Co., 1996. This is a great and much-overlooked firsthand account of the war, edited by Kevin E. O'Brien from McCarter's unpublished ms.

Grant viewed as a drunk, and Lincoln's response, from Foote, *The Civil War,* Volume 1.

Lincoln's message to Congress on slaves, December 1, 1862, from *The Collected Works of Abraham Lincoln,* edited by Roy P. Basler et al., Rutgers University Press, 1953.

McClellan loses command of Army of the Potomac, and letter to his wife on his feelings about fighting to end slavery, from McPherson, *Battle Cry of Freedom.*

McClellan praising the Irish Brigade after Antietam, from Report of General George B. McClellan, September 17, 1862, in Official Records.

McClellan's farewell to Irish Brigade, from McCarter, *My Life in the Irish Brigade,* and *Memoirs.*

Deserter's execution, from Corby, *Memoirs of Chaplain Life.*

Bartering along the river, from Conyngham, *The Irish Brigade and Its Campaigns.*

Meagher's gift, from McCarter, *My Life in the Irish Brigade.*

Artillery pounding Fredericksburg, other details leading up to battle, from "The Battle of Fredericksburg" by Wilson A. Green, a National Park Service historian's account, from author visit to the Fredericksburg and Spotsylvania National Military Park.

Population of Fredericksburg, description of town and field, from author visit.

Troops at night in Fredericksburg, the fires and the battle itself, from Meagher, Official Report, Series 1, Volume 21. Meagher said the men didn't have a fire. But Corby and the National Park Service's history say otherwise, mentioning the town plundered and furniture burned.

Meagher and green sprigs, his speech, from *Memoirs.*

Lee's comment, from the National Park Service battlefield, author visit.

Pickett's comment, from Bilby, *The Irish Brigade in the Civil War.*

McCarter wounded, and his prayer, from McCarter, *My Life in the Irish Brigade.*

Wounded soldier, water coming out neck, from Corby, *Memoirs of Chaplain Life.*

Nagle on Irish blood–covered field, from Bilby, *The Irish Brigade in the Civil War.*

Slaughter pen, from Corby, *Memoirs of Chaplain Life.*

Whitman, on the bloody scene, from *Disunion.*

Meagher weeping uncontrollably after the battle, from *Fredericksburg! Fredericksburg!* by George C. Rable, University of North Carolina Press, 2002.

The Death Feast, including Meagher quotes, from *Memoirs.*

More on Death Feast, reported in Conyngham, *The Irish Brigade and Its Campaigns,* with matching details.

CHAPTER 18: A BRIGADE NO MORE

Looking for Hogan's body, Meagher's account, from *Memoirs.*

Background about Hogan, from the *New York Times,* December 28, 1862.

Horrible conditions of winter camp, letter from Captain Elliot C. Pierce to Mary Baker, January 22, 1863, courtesy Massachusetts Historical Society.

Number of AWOL, from *The Civil War* by Geoffrey C. Ward, Ric Burns and Ken Burns, Alfred A. Knopf, 1990.

Medical report of Dr. Laurence Reynolds on Meagher, reprinted in Lyons, *Brigadier General Thomas Francis Meagher.*

Boston Pilot on Irish spirit for war is dead, from *A City So Grand: The Rise of an American Metropolis, Boston, 1850–1900* by Stephen Puleo, Beacon Press, 2010.

Lincoln family reaction to death of son, from "Civil War 150: Ripples of War," *Washington Post,* October 7, 2011.

New Year's Eve jubilee of blacks, from the *New York Times,* January 1, 1863.

Grand Requiem Mass, http://irishamericancivilwar.com/2013/01/19/the-dead-of-the-irish-brigade-the-music-and-message-16th-january-1863/.

Meagher meeting with Lincoln at White House, and Lincoln's letter, from Basler et al., *The Collected Works of Abraham Lincoln.*

McCarter details in hospital, from his book, *My Life in the Irish Brigade.*

Meagher back at camp, writing letters to War Department, from *Memoirs.*

Details of St. Patrick's Day feast, from Corby, *Memoirs of Chaplain Life,* and ibid.

Battle of Chancellorsville, from Bilby, *The Irish Brigade in the Civil War.*

More Chancellorsville, Meagher letter to Lyons, reprinted in Lyons, *Brigadier General Thomas Francis Meagher.*

Death of Jackson, from *Rebel Yell: The Violence, Passion and Redemption of Stonewall Jackson* by S. C. Gwynne, Scribner, 2014.

Meagher's letter of resignation, May 8, 1863, reprinted in the *New York Times,* May 14, 1863.

Meagher's farewell speech, reprinted in *Memoirs.*

Draft riot, how it started, from the *Washington Post*'s 150th anniversary retrospective, April 29, 2013.

Draft riots, blacks targeted, from *In the Shadow of Slavery: African Americans in New York City, 1626–1863* by Leslie M. Harris, Historical Studies of Urban America, 2002.

Draft riots, details, stores targeted, individuals hanged, from the *New York Times,* July 14–19, 1863.

Draft riots, mayor's plea, troops arrive, from the *New York Times,* July 16, 1863.

Letter from a rioter, published in the *New York Times,* July 15, 1863.

Melville poem, from the *New York Times*'s 150th anniversary retrospective, July 14, 2013.

Sacking Nugent's home, slashing Meagher's portrait, from Bayor and Meagher, *The New York Irish.*

Meagher praise by mayor, from *Memoirs.*

Meagher, commenting on rioters and his belief they would have killed him, from *Thomas Francis Meagher and the Irish Brigade in the Civil War* by Daniel Callaghan, McFarland & Co., 2006.

CHAPTER 19: A SECOND BANISHMENT

Thomas Nast depictions, from *Harper's Weekly,* August 1, 1863.

Comments of George Templeton Strong, from *The Diary of George Templeton Strong,* University of Washington Press, 1988.

Meagher to Smyth, views on slavery, one letter of September 5, 1863, and another of September 26, 1863, from Meagher, *Letters on Our National Struggle.*

Meagher's disgust at fellow Irish, published in the *New York Times,* October 9, 1864, from a private letter written October 7, 1863. Reaction from the *Irish American,* November 12, 1864.

Lincoln visit, as reported in *The Irish General* by Paul R. Wylie, University of Oklahoma Press, 2007.

Lincoln's illness, smallpox diagnosis, from "Abraham Lincoln's Gettysburg Illness," *Journal of Medical Biography* 15 (2007).

Meagher takes Fenian oath, from *Memoirs.* Note: There is a dispute over whether Meagher was ever a Fenian, but as Bilby points out in his history of the brigade, one of the founders of the Brotherhood, John O'Mahoney, claimed late in life that he had initiated Meagher into the organization in the summer of 1863, which matches the time given in *Memoirs.*

Fenian oath, from *Memoirs.*

Michael Corcoran's death, ibid.

Meagher's comments after Corcoran's death, from "The Irish in the American Civil War," http://irishamericancivilwar.com/2013/12/22/our-orphan-children -will-not-soon-forget-him-the-death-of-general-michael-corcoran/.

Sherman quote, war is war, from *Memoirs of William T. Sherman.*

Jefferson Davis quote, from McPherson, *Battle Cry of Freedom.*

Confederates executing captured black soldiers, from Gallagher, *Fighting for the Confederacy.*

Jefferson Davis attitude at end of war, from McPherson, *Embattled Rebel.*

Sherman's insanity, from "Sherman's Demons" by Michael Fellman, in *Disunion.*

Meagher "do come visit" letter to W. F. Lyons, September 22, 1864, cited in Lyons, *Brigadier General Thomas Francis Meagher.*

Blacks and Irish, from McPherson, *Battle Cry of Freedom.*

Pepper recalling Meagher the orator, from "Personal Recollections of General Thomas Francis Meagher," *Donahoe's Magazine* 41 (1899).

Meagher's night of poetry, ibid.

Praise from General Steedman for Meagher's new assignment, from *Memoirs.*

Meagher's movements by rail with the provisionals, summarized in the *New York Times,* January 24, 1865.

Howell Cobb biographical details, from *New Georgia Encyclopedia,* http://www.georgiaencyclopedia.org/articles/government-politics/howell -cobb-1815-1868, and the quote about making soldiers of slaves, from McPherson, *Battle Cry of Freedom.*

Lincoln in Richmond, from a 150th anniversary story in the *Washington Post,* March 29, 2015.

Members of Irish Brigade at Lee's surrender, from Bilby, *The Irish Brigade in the Civil War.*

Meagher at the Astor House, and plans for honor guard, from the *New York Times,* April 23, 1865.

War casualty numbers: The long-accepted figure was 620,000 total deaths. But new research, accepted by many Civil War scholars, has placed the figure at well above 700,000, and perhaps as many as 800,000, as reported in the *New York Times,* April 2, 2012.

Number of Irish who served the Union, from Bayor and Meagher, *The New York Irish.*

Irish Brigade's high casualty rate, from "The Fighting Irish Brigade," in *Disunion.*

Meagher and the letter from his son, as recounted by the witness Lyons, in his *Brigadier General Thomas Francis Meagher.*

Meagher quote in letter to son, July 17, 1865, courtesy National Library of Ireland.

CHAPTER 20: NEW IRELAND

Five Points highest murder rate of any slum in the world, from the *New York Times,* August 22, 2009.

New Ireland suggestion of American consul to Seward, from Keneally, *The Great Shame.*

Meagher's thoughts on colony, and getting out of tenements, from his essays in his newspaper, the *Irish News,* and from *Indians and Whites in the Northwest, 1831–1891,* by L. B. Paladino, S.J., Wickersham Publishing, 1922.

Meagher speech to the Immigration Society, from the *Irish American,* August 19, 1865.

Meagher's travels, and words of praise and warning from editor, from the *Montana Post,* September 9, 1865.

Population of Montana, 1865, from *Territorial Politics and Government in Montana, 1864–1889* by Clark C. Spence, University of Illinois Press, 1975.

Fenian plans, from *The Fenians: Irish Rebellion in the North Atlantic World* by Patrick Steward and Bryan P. McGovern, University of Tennessee Press, 2013.

Meagher "whip my carriage," quoted in *Thomas Francis Meagher: An Irish Revolutionary in America* by Robert G. Athearn, University of Colorado Press, 1949.

Diary of James P. Miller, June 16 and September 9, 1865, from www.virginia city.com.

Diary of Cornelius Hedges, September 13, 1865, courtesy Montana Historical Society.

"Recognize a bad man when he saw one," quoted in *A Decent, Orderly Lynching: The Montana Vigilantes* by Frederick Allen, University of Oklahoma Press, 2004.

Vigilante pledge, courtesy Montana Historical Society.

The vigilante killings, from Plummer to the end of the month, from Allen, *A Decent, Orderly Lynching.*

"Burn the Mexican," account of Pyzanthia's death, as recorded by Thomas Dimsdale, the vigilante chronicler, quoted in *A History of Montana, 1739–1885*, edited by M. A. Leeson, Warner, Beers & Co., 1885.

No money for the territory, from *Montana, the Land and the People* by Robert George Raymer, Lewis Publishing Co., 1930.

Descriptions of Virginia City, from author visit to town and pictures from the era.

More executions, from Miller's diary, September 26, 1865, Montana Historical Society.

Judge Hosmer, and Dimsdale's defense of vigilantes, quoted in Allen, *A Decent, Orderly Lynching*.

General Lee's postwar praise of Meagher, from an interview conducted by George Pepper, as reprinted in his book *Under Three Flags, or The Story of My Life*, Curts and Jennings, 1899.

Fenians greet Meagher, from the *Montana Post*, October 7, 1865, and from the *New York Times*, November 11, 1865.

Meagher lecture on Emmet, from Forney, *Thomas Francis Meagher*.

Prizefighter in Virginia City, note on building plaque, from author visit.

Freemasons, from Leeson, *A History of Montana*.

Meagher's position against monopolies, from Spence, *Territorial Politics*.

Chumaserro on Meagher the whoremonger, letter, March 12, 1866, courtesy Montana Historical Society.

Trip to trapper's ranch, reading Shakespeare, etc., from a long letter Meagher wrote to Father De Smet, December 15, 1865, reprinted in the *Irish Monthly*, September 1902.

Letter from Meagher to Pepper on settling in Montana, December 17, 1865, reprinted in *Donahoe's Magazine* 41 (1899).

Meagher and Father Kuppens on Yellowstone, from *Yellowstone National Park: Its Exploration and Establishment* by Aubrey L. Haines, Department of the Interior, 1974. Interesting note: Meagher is credited, and not just here, with being one of the first American authorities to talk up the idea of what would eventually become, in 1872, the world's first national park.

Hanging Tree, from author visit and tour of execution sites in Helena, Montana.

Vigilante spree, Daniels case, the pardon and Sanders's threat — "dead beyond all hope" — all from Allen, *A Decent, Orderly Lynching*.

Daniels hanged with Meagher's reprieve in pocket, from "Montana Vigilantes," *Montana, the Magazine of Western History*, Spring 2001.

Deadliest campaign of vigilante executions in American history, from Allen, *A Decent, Orderly Lynching*.

TFM letter to Secretary of State Seward, February 20, 1866, about Sanders, from Spence, *Territorial Politics*.

"Carp and deprecate," quoted in *Beyond the American Pale: The Irish in the West, 1845–1910* by David M. Emmons, University of Oklahoma Press, 2012.

Second thoughts on death of Daniels, from *Vigilante Days and Ways* by Nathaniel P. Langford, University of Montana Press, 1957.

Note in Daniels's pocket threatening Meagher as next victim: There are various accounts of the note. Mine is taken from three sources: a modern newspaper story reassessing the era, "Thomas Meagher Was a Man of Many Lives," the *Missoulian*, July 4, 2010; a book, *Bloody Bozeman*, by an authority on Montana in the 1860s, Dorothy M. Johnson, Mountain Press Publishing, 1983; and another history, *The Calamity Paper: Western Myths and Cold Cases* by Dale L. Walker, Tom Doherty Associates, 2004.

CHAPTER 21: THE REMAINS OF A LIFE

History of the Blackfeet, from *The North American Indian* by Edward S. Curtis, Taschen, 2005.

The quotes from TFM to Father De Smet, from a letter, December 15, 1866, reprinted in the *Irish Monthly*, September 1902.

Indian agent's disgust, from *Montana 1864* by Ken Egan Jr., Riverbend Publishing, 2014.

Meagher turns down offer of buffalo robes, from "Account of the Drowning of General Thomas Francis Meagher," *Contributions to the Historical Society of Montana* 8 (1917).

Sioux war, Red Cloud, from *The Heart of Everything That Is* by Bob Drury and Tom Clavin, Simon & Schuster, 2013.

Sherman's view of Indians, ibid.

Sherman note to Meagher, February 16, 1866, Montana Territorial Papers, Montana Historical Society.

Legislative session, from Spence, *Territorial Politics.*

Firing Dimsdale, from "The Death of Thomas Francis Meagher Revisited" by Angela Faye Thompson, M.A. thesis, University of Montana, 1998.

Meagher's bar bill, from "Thomas Francis Meagher's Bar Bill" by Elliott West, *Decies* 59 (2003).

Meagher turns down $2,500 salary, from a formal note signed by Meagher, March 19, 1866, courtesy Montana Historical Society.

Meagher letter to Seward, "everything is delightful," from Spence, *Territorial Politics.*

Pattern to vigilante-led deaths, from Emmons, *Beyond the American Pale.*

Store owner given a pass, from *Alder Gulch and Virginia City, Montana* by Larry Barsness, Hastings House Publishers, 1962.

"put a quietus on the doings of this pretender," letter from Wilbur Sanders to James Fergus, February 14, 1866, courtesy Montana Historical Society.

Meagher's St. Patrick Day speech, from *Lectures of Gov. Thomas Francis Meagher in Montana.*

Fenian invasion of Canada, from Steward and McGovern, *The Fenians.*

Report of Meagher as head of Fenian army, from the *Waterford News*, January 21, 1866.

Cleric's impression of Elizabeth Meagher, from *Missionary to the Mountain West* by Daniel Tuttle, University of Utah Press, 1987.

Meagher's ambition, "champion of the Irish race," from letter to O'Keeffe, September 26, 1866, courtesy Montana Historical Society.

Latest vigilante killings, from Allen, *A Decent, Orderly Lynching.*

Naming waterfall after Elizabeth Townsend, from TFM letter to Barlow, June 15, 1867, courtesy Huntington Library.

Letter to O'Keeffe asking for money, September 26, 1866, Montana Historical Society. The plan to give O'Keeffe the byline is explained in a later letter to Barlow, ibid.

Fast friends with Governor Smith, from letter to Barlow, October 26, 1866, courtesy Huntington Library.

Congress throws out legislative session, from "Wilbur Fisk Sanders" by Gary Forney, *Montana Pioneer*, February 2014.

Meagher stopped and threatened, and letter sent to him with hangman's drawing, as reported in the *Montana Post*, August 18, 1866.

CHAPTER 22: RIVER WITHOUT END

Meagher's desire to go home, from letter to O'Gorman on the day of his death, cited by O'Gorman in his eulogy in New York, from *Memoirs.*

Meagher out of funds, from letter to J. H. Ming, territorial auditor, July 1, 1867, courtesy Montana Historical Society.

Sherman quote on Sioux, from Drury and Clavin, *The Heart of Everything That Is.*

Wipe out Indians, from *Montana Post*, January 26, 1867.

Death of Bozeman: It has long been reported that he was killed by Blackfeet, but new scholarship points to several white suspects, including his business partner. From the *Bozeman Chronicle*, October 3, 2014.

Meagher organizes militia and goes off to fight in Gallatin Valley, from *Montana Post*, May 18, 1867.

Meagher's heart not in fighting, and his restraint, from "Thomas Francis Meagher, Montana Pioneer" by Father Francis X. Kuppens, *Mid-America, an Historical Review* 14, No. 2 (October 1931). Also, Lieutenant James H. Bradley noted the restraint in his journal, published by the *Historical Society of Montana* 2 (1896).

Description of I. G. Baker house, where Meagher had his last meal, from author visit to the house in Fort Benton, Montana, where it still stands, in good condition.

Sanders arrives in Fort Benton the same day, from an account Sanders gave, later in life, of Meagher's last day, reported in detail in the *Butte Miner*, June 10, 1913.

Further details of Meagher letter to O'Gorman, mentioned in O'Gorman's eulogy, from *Lectures of Gov. Thomas Francis Meagher in Montana.*

Meagher letter to Pepper, January 20, 1866, in *Donahoe's Magazine* 41 (1899).

Details of last day and death, as reported by pilot John T. Doran, in a letter reprinted by Lyons in *Brigadier General Thomas Francis Meagher.*

Sanders's detailed account of TFM death and his reaction to it, from Raymer, *Montana, the Land and the People.*

Governor Clay orders thirty days of mourning and reward to find body, from *Lectures of Thomas Francis Meagher in Montana.*

Enemies now complementary, ibid.

Praising TFM, from *Montana Post,* July 6, 1867.

Tribute poem, from the *Irish American,* July 20, 1867.

A fund to find the killer, $10,000, from Forney, *Thomas Francis Meagher.*

O'Gorman eulogy, reprinted in *Lectures of Thomas Francis Meagher in Montana.*

CHAPTER 23: INQUEST FOR IRELAND

Unveiling of statue, from the *Helena Independent,* July 5, 1905.

Meagher's influence in the creation of Yellowstone Park, from Haines, *Yellowstone National Park.*

"No grounds" for suicide, from "Account of the Drowning of Gen. Thomas Francis Meagher," based on the ms. of James Bradley, published in *Contributions to the Historical Society of Montana* 8 (1917).

Accepted account of Montana history, from *A History of Montana* by Helen Fitzgerald Sanders, Lewis Publishing, 1913.

Wilbur Sanders, Pioneer Day quote, and his role in historical society, from *Contributions to the Historical Society of Montana* 4 (1903).

Sanders's version of Meagher's death, from the *Butte Miner,* June 10, 1913.

Frank Diamond confession, from the *Missoula Sentinel,* May 29, 1913.

Kennedy ancestry, from the John F. Kennedy Library, http://www.jfklibrary .org/JFK/JFK-in-History/John-F-Kennedy-and-Ireland.aspx.

JFK "like a rainbow," from *JFK in Ireland* by Ryan Tubridy, Collins Publishers, 2011.

Easter Rebellion prisoners, from *A History of Kilmainham Gaol* by Pat Cooke, OPW Publishing, 2006, and from author visit to the prison in Dublin.

O'Doherty's life, from *Australian Dictionary of Biography,* Volume 5 (1974).

Balfe's life, from Petrow, *Judas in Tasmania.*

Mitchel's life, from McGovern, *John Mitchel: Irish Nationalist, Southern Secessionist.*

Meagher inspiration to the rebels of 1916, from Griffith's introduction to *Meagher of the Sword.*

TFM's father's "affection for his son is extreme," from the *Waterford Chronicle,* November 1, 1848.

Death of Mrs. TFM, from the *Montana Daily Record,* July 6, 1906.

Death of Thomas Bennett Meagher, from his obituary, cited in the *Journal of the California Genealogical Society* 3, No. 2.

Meagher's descendants, from Meagher papers, Montana Historical Society, including a letter from the widow of Thomas Francis Meagher III.

Total number of Irish immigrants to 1924, from Miller, *Emigrants and Exiles.*

Kennedy's speech, from the John F. Kennedy Library, http://www.jfklibrary .org/Asset-Viewer/lPAi7jx2soi7kePPdJnUXA.aspx.

Waterford details, statue, banners, etc., from author visit to Waterford.

New bridge named for TFM, from the *Irish Examiner,* January 19, 2015.

Modern inquest in Montana, from author interview with Paul Wylie, who staged the inquest. Wylie also made available a DVD of the event, *Coroner's Inquest into the Death of Thomas Francis Meagher.*

Artist commissioned to create Meagher sculpture at Green-Wood Cemetery, from *Irish America,* February/March 2013.

INDEX

Page numbers in italics refer to illustrations.